Interdisciplinary Studies in Human Rights

Volume 6

Human rights are one of the normative cornerstones of contemporary international law and global governance. Due to the complexities of actual or potential violations of human rights and in light of current crises, new and interdisciplinary research is urgently needed. The series Interdisciplinary Studies in Human Rights recognizes the growing importance and necessity of interdisciplinary research in human rights. The series consists of monographs and collected volumes addressing human rights research from different disciplinary and interdisciplinary perspectives, including but not limited to philosophy, law, political science, education, and medical ethics. Its goal is to explore new and contested questions such as the extraterritorial application of human rights and their relevance for non-state actors, as well as the philosophical and theoretical foundations of human rights. The series also addresses policy questions of current interest including the human rights of migrants and refugees, LGBTI rights, and bioethics, as well as business and human rights.

The series editors are Members of the Centre for Human Rights Erlangen-Nürnberg (CHREN), an interdisciplinary research center at Friedrich-Alexander-University Erlangen-Nürnberg. The Advisory Board brings together human rights scholars from a wide range of academic disciplines and regional backgrounds. The series welcomes suggestions for publications of academic research falling into the series subject matter.

More information about this series at http://www.springer.com/series/15339

Miriam Saage-Maaß • Peer Zumbansen •
Michael Bader • Palvasha Shahab
Editors

Transnational Legal Activism in Global Value Chains

The Ali Enterprises Factory Fire and the Struggle for Justice

Springer

Editors
Miriam Saage-Maaß
European Center for Constitutional and Human Rights
Berlin, Germany

Peer Zumbansen
Faculty of Law
McGill University
Montreal, QC, Canada

Michael Bader
European Center for Constitutional and Human Rights
Berlin, Germany

Palvasha Shahab
Rasheed Razvi Centre for Constitutional and Human Rights
Karachi, Pakistan

ISSN 2509-2960 ISSN 2509-2979 (electronic)
Interdisciplinary Studies in Human Rights
ISBN 978-3-030-73834-1 ISBN 978-3-030-73835-8 (eBook)
https://doi.org/10.1007/978-3-030-73835-8

This Springer imprint is published by the registered company Springer Nature Switzerland AG.
The registered company address is: Gewerbestrasse 11, 6330 Cham, Switzerland

This book is dedicated to those who lost their lives in the Ali Enterprises factory fire on 11 September 2012:
Muhammad Adil, Muhammad Azif, Inayatullah, Zaitoon, Hameedullah, Shahzad Jerome, Aneel Jerome, Hafizullah, Muhhamad Muzamil, Irshad Khan, Abdul Shakoor, Muhammad Latif, Jaffar Hussain, Muhammad Imran, Hamid, Arslan, Shahbaz Ahmed, Anil Khan, Muhammad Noor Alam, Muhammad Kalimuddin Ansari, Muhammad Azeem, Muhammad Jameel, Muhammad Amir, Hayat Hussain, Muhammad Nadeem, Muhammad Ejaz, Shafquat Mehmood, Deedar Ahmed, Muhammad Asghar, Abid Ali, Muhammad Hussain, Aamir Ghulam, Junaid Malik, Muhammad Rafaquat Ali, Shamsuddin Ahmed, Qaiser Noman, Muhammad Raheel, Amna Bibi, Muhammad Jabbar Khan, Muhammad Shahabuddin, Rafiq Ahmed, Shoaib, Sajid-ur-Rehman, Noshad Ali Shah, Ayaz Ali Shah, Nasreen Naz, Mujahid Hussain, Attaullah Nabeel, Pervez, Ghulam Sarwar, Ahsan Jawed, Amanat Ali, Muhammad Owais, Pervez Ghulam, Farhan,

Saeed Muhammad, Muhammad Ayaz, Muhammad Kamran, Muhammad Shoaib, Irfan Ali, Kamal-ud-din, Muhammad Atif, Nasreen, Perveen, Saima Ghani, Shah Alam Hussain, Aamir Aftab, Muhammad Arman, Shahid, Ruqayya Perveen, Muhammad Farhan, Muhammad Hanif, Muhammad Dilawar, Ghulam Rasool, Abid Ali, Waqas, Muhammad Ahsan, Raees Ahmed, Muhammad Ashfaq, Shazad Junaid, Shah Nawaz, Shabbir Ahmed, Jahangir, Gohar Ali, Irshad Ali, Muhammad Shan, Tajuddin, Muhammad Mehmood, Saba, Zahid Akthar, Ikhlaq Kiran, Muhammad Sohail, Rizwan Ahmed, Muhammad Faizan, Asim Ahmed, Sjida, Muhammad Alam, Jaffar Alam, Salma Bibi, Danish, Shamim Akthar, Muhammad Faisal Shah, Mujahid Ali Khan, Muhammad Hafeez-ur-Rehman, Muhammad Iqbal, Qamar-uz-Zaman, Ashfaq, Zeeshan Ahmed, Syed Muhammad Iqbal, Habib Khan, Muhammad Waseem, Imran Khan, Sameer Ahmed, Tanveer, Muhammad Naeem, Muhammad Jahanzeb, Allah Nawaz, Muhammad Shahid, Wahid, Syed Masood-ul-Hassan Rizvi, Muhammad Siddique, Alyan Ali Hamza, Muhammad Anwar Hussain, Abdul Qayyum Aziz, Muhammad Jawed, Muhammad Iqbal Qadri, Furqan Alam, Muhammad Saleem Ahmed, Shoaib, Khalil Ahmed, Muhammad Mustafa, Allah Rakha, Muhammad Kamran, Zahid Hussain, Abbas Ali, Muhammad Waseem, Farzana Begum, Syed Wali Hussain Mazhar, Zaqar-un-nisa, Muhammad Shabaz, Abdul Majeed, Abdul Rauf, Allauddin, Naim-ud-din, Nadir Hussain, Rashida Bibi, Nasar Ali, Tanveer Ahmed Siddiqui, Muhammad Israr,

Muhammad Abdullah, Muhammad Nadeem, Farhan, Syed Sarfaraz Hussain, Muhammad Afzal, Adil Ahmed, Muhammad Haris Khan, Sajid Ali Haider, Muhammad Aamir, Zareena Begum, Tehmeena, Zohra Khatoon, Muhammad Adeel, Sajid Ali, Israr Ahmed, Faisal, Muhammad Ali Hussain, Muhammad Farooq, Ziaul Haq, Muhammad Waqas, Muhammad Shabaz, Saijid Hussain, Zeeshan Ahmed, Kalam Khan, Syeda Zoya, Muhammad Aamir, Muhammad Kashif, Muslim, Muhammad Akram, Muhammad Hashim, Hasnain, Muhammad Kamran, Shabaz, Muhammad Imran, Amman, Muhammad Essa, Mushtaque Ahmed, Muhammad Fayyaz, Muhammad Ejaz, Muhammad Kamran, Nazim-ud-din, Muhammad Ishaque, Mahrab Khan, Muhammad Akram, Sanawar, Muhammad Farhan, Muhammad Fasihuddin, Shamsher Ali, Hammad Ali, Muhammad Zubair, Waqas Ahmed, Syed Ejaz Ali, Huma, Sana, Naeem Ahmed, Muhammad Nadeem, Ikhlaq Hussain, Kamaluddin, Muhammad Jamshed Chughai, Attar, Muhammad Nazeer, Ejaz Ahmed, Elahi Bux, Sameena Jawed, Muhammad Jawed, Usman Ali, Sajid, Zeeshan Serwar, Athar Ali, Muhammad Azeem, Nabi Hussain, Faisal Rehman, Muhammad Saeed, Muhammad Rizwan, Muhammad Khan, Muhammad Basit, Nabi Hussain, Muhammad Badar Iqbal, Muhammad Shamim, Akthar Siddiqui, Allah Rakho, Muhammad Saud, Faraz, Muhammad Hanif, Rahmat Ali, Muhammad Akmal, Ghulam Husnain, Muhammad Majid, Riaz Ahmed, Muhammad Danish Jamil Faridi, Obaidullah, Muhammad Sohail, Rubab Azmat, Saba, Sumaira, Saeed, Syed Mehmood

Shah, Rafiqan Bibi, Adil Khan, Asif Aziz, Waqar Ahmed, Muhammad Wasim, Muhammad Tufail, Muhammad Jawed Khan, Sharjeel Ahmed, Shafiq-ul-Islam, and Abdul Hafeez.

Preface

The fire at the Ali Enterprises textile factory on 11 September 2012 in Karachi, Sindh, is the deadliest industrial disaster recorded in Pakistan's history since the country's independence in 1947.[1] At least 255 workers lost their lives in the flames and 55 more were severely injured. The high number of deaths was due to the widespread neglect of basic fire safety measures in the factory building: windows were barred and emergency exits closed; fire alarms and fire extinguishers were absent; and workers were not trained on what to do in emergency situations. The immediate responses from both government agencies and companies largely sought to shift responsibility for the high death toll from one actor to the other. Still, the horror of the incident was so undeniable that different branches of the Pakistani state came under pressure to quickly provide some form of immediate financial relief. The same was true for the only known international buyer sourcing from the Ali Enterprises factory, the German retailer KiK Textilien and Non-Food GmbH (KiK). Given the inadequate and haphazard responses to the fire by the Pakistani state as well as the owners of the factory and the international brand KiK, resistance started forming among families of the deceased and survivors under the roof of the National Trade Union Federation (NTUF), with the objective of attaching responsibility to all actors who contributed to the tragedy. What began as a loose assembly of grieving families and survivors transformed over the year and a half following the fire into the Ali Enterprises Factory Fire Affectees Association (AEFFAA).

As an immediate response to the disaster, and in collaboration with NTUF and the Pakistan Institute of Labour Education and Research (PILER), Pakistani lawyer Faisal Siddiqi and his team filed public interest litigation cases before the High Court of Sindh, namely two constitutional petitions against the Pakistani government agencies responsible for labour inspections, building and fire safety, and social security. Siddiqi and his team also assisted the court on behalf of the victims' families in the criminal proceedings against the Ali Enterprises factory owners and

[1]The incident is known and referred to as Ali Enterprises Factory Fire or Baldia Factory Fire.

managers. The public interest litigation at the High Court of Sindh resulted in the identification of all the victims through an arduous year-long process that eventually led to the formation of a Judicial Commission for the disbursement of the initial compensation and relief offered by the provincial and federal bodies of the Pakistani state.

A few months after the fire, workers' rights activists and organisers also shifted their focus to the European companies KiK and RINA. In December 2012, PILER negotiated an agreement with KiK for US$1 million in immediate relief funds and the commitment to engage in long-term compensation negotiations. When these negotiations between KiK, the AEFFAA, PILER, and NTUF stalled in 2013 and 2014, the European Center for Constitutional and Human Rights (ECCHR) on behalf of the AEFFAA initiated civil litigation against KiK in Germany, claiming damages for pain and suffering on behalf of four Pakistani plaintiffs. When the transnational lawsuit against KiK was filed in March 2015 and the District Court of Dortmund (Landgericht Dortmund) accepted the legal standing of the four Pakistani plaintiffs in August 2016, KiK agreed to a further unprecedented payment of US $5.15 million the very next month. The final amount was negotiated and settled with KiK under the auspices of a tripartite ILO mechanism in 2018. The auditing firm RINA, through its Pakistani affiliate, had certified the Ali Enterprise factory as safe only three weeks prior to the fire. Criminal proceedings were initiated in Italy and a complaint was filed against the Italian parent company at the OECD National Contact Point at the Ministry for Economic Development in Rome. In another unprecedented occurrence following the disaster, the two owners of the Ali Enterprises factory were put under criminal investigation, held in pretrial detention for several months, and had their assets frozen.

This book forms part of a larger project to explore the different ways in which transnational human rights litigation, advocacy, and collaboration among different actors can materialise. It therefore maps how various actors collaborated in the aftermath of the Ali Enterprises fire: from the spokesperson of the AEFFAA, Saeeda Khatoon, who lost her only son in the fire, to the NTUF trade unionist Nasir Mansoor, the journalist and activist Zehra Kahn, the lawyer Faisal Siddiqi, and a broad range of lawyers, activists, journalists, and filmmakers from Pakistan, Germany, and beyond. All have played vital roles in building up the momentum needed for redress and, in the long run, change.

The objective of this book is to document and analyse the various interventions—legal, political, and even artistic—that followed the horrendous factory fire in order to illuminate the different substantive and procedural aspects of the legal proceedings and negotiations between the various local and transnational actors implicated in the Ali Enterprises fire, as well as the legal and policy reforms sparked by the incident. This endeavour serves to embed these legal cases and reform efforts in the larger context of human and labour rights protection and global value chain governance. It also offers a concrete case study relevant for ongoing debates around the role of transnational approaches in making human rights litigation, advocacy, and law reform more effective. In this regard, the book interrogates and critically reflects on such legal campaigns and local and transnational reform work with a view to future transformative legal and social activism.

In its scholarly form as a "book", this volume was constrained by both time and resources and is, therefore, neither an exhaustive historiography nor a thorough sociological and anthropological analysis. Rather, it provides a platform for the different actors involved to tell their stories and share (self-)critical insights about their contributions to the post-fire struggles for justice and change. Hence, it attempts to display the wide variety of actors who intervened in the aftermath of the Ali Enterprises fire, with each writing from their own perspective and professional approach. A particular challenge for transnational human rights work is that it feeds off the energy and commitment of local and transnational networks scattered across different arenas. While the knowledge of who engaged, from what perspective, and how in order to secure redress and justice is often shared "in the moment", it is frequently too short-lived to be built on in future interventions. Because they are seldomly recorded, highly valuable reflections on how different actors organised their collaboration often gets lost, and their assessments of interventions aimed at identifying and responding to serious human rights violations, calling for accountability, ensuring fair compensation, and preventing future violations by addressing root causes are rarely available to others as references or resources. Despite this book's inevitable gaps, we hope it will serve as a useful resource for other actors and future struggles yet to come.

Berlin, Germany — Miriam Saage-Maaß
Montreal, QC, Canada — Peer Zumbansen
Berlin, Germany — Michael Bader
Karachi, Pakistan — Palvasha Shahab
15 August 2020

Acknowledgments

We are immensely grateful to the families and survivors organised in the Ali Enterprises Fire Affectees Association as well as the National Trade Union Federation, the Pakistani Institute of Labour Education and Research, the Home Based Women Workers Federation, the Rasheed Razvi Centre for Constitutional and Human Rights, Medico International, and the European Center for Constitutional and Human Rights for their time, insights, and contributions to this book. We are particularly indebted to Karamat Ali, Saeeda Khatoon, Nasir Mansoor, and Zehra Khan for providing their insights into the beauty, complexity, history, politics, and lived realities of Pakistan. We are grateful for their expertise, without which this book project (let alone the transnational development of the legal cases it discusses) could have never been realised. A huge thank you is also due to ECCHR's Corey Barber, Arite Keller, and Allison West for providing their expertise and patience in transforming the book into its current form. We also want to thank Markus Krajewski for making the publication of this book possible, but also more generally for his continuous support of our work. We thank Stiftung Menschenwürde und Arbeitswelt for their generous financial support. And last but not least, we thank ECCHR's Institute for Legal Intervention for support in distributing the book and ECCHR's Business and Human Rights team for sharing with us their expertise, experience, and knowledge, which found their way into the book in one form or another.

Contents

Introduction: Transnational Law and Advocacy Around Labour and Human Rights Litigation 1
Peer Zumbansen

Part I The Ali Enterprises Factory Fire and Its Aftermath: Litigations, Campaigning and Transnational Collaboration

Loss and Legibility: A Conversation with Saeeda Khatoon 15
Palvasha Shahab

Legal Interventions and Transnational Alliances in the Ali Enterprises Case: Struggles for Workers' Rights in Global Supply Chains 25
Miriam Saage-Maaß

Paradoxes of Strategic Labour Rights Litigation: Insights from the Baldia Factory Fire Litigation 59
Faisal Siddiqi

After the Ali Enterprises Fire: Occupational Safety and Health and Workers' Organising—A Conversation with Zehra Khan About Current and Future Struggles 97
Palvasha Shahab

Pakistan's "Industrial 9/11": Transnational Rights-Based Activism in the Garment Industry and Creating Space for Future Global Struggles 107
Nasir Mansoor, Thomas Rudhof-Seibert, and Miriam Saage-Maaß

The Land of Mourning: A Conversation with Adeela Suleman 121
Palvasha Shahab

Four Against KiK: A Conversation with Caspar Dohmen 129
Michael Bader

Part II Labour and Tort Law Aspects of Global Supply Chains

The Rana Plaza Collapse and the Case for Enforceable Agreements with Apparel Brands 137
Ben Vanpeperstraete

Trade Union Approaches to Global Value Chains: The Indonesian Experience 171
Reingard Zimmer

Transnational Labour Law? "Corporate Social Responsibility" and the Law 187
Eva Kocher

Tort Law and Human Rights 209
Gerhard Wagner

Part III Critical Perspectives on Law and Litigation

Confined Employment: Exploring Labor Marginalization in Workplace Safety 237
Palvasha Shahab

The KiK Case: A Critical Perspective from the South 279
Muhammad Azeem

From Strategic Litigation to Juridical Action 299
Andreas Fischer-Lescano

Toward a Strategic Engagement with the Question of the Corporation 313
Michael Bader

Introduction: Transnational Law and Advocacy Around Labour and Human Rights Litigation

Peer Zumbansen

Abstract In this chapter, Peer Zumbansen introduces the book. He contextualizes the Ali Enterprises Factory Fire and the movement building and activism that followed in light of current transnational legal debates as well as global value chain research and subsequently introduces each contribution.

Keywords Transnational law · Rights advocacy · Ali enterprises factory fire · KiK case · Global value chains · Transformative politics

1 Law, Lawyers and the Persistence of Injustice

Today, there is little doubt that the public is more aware of human and labour rights violations in global supply chains than it once was. The factory fires in the Tazreen Fashion and Ali Enterprises factories in 2012, and the collapse of Rana Plaza in 2013 have arguably initiated a surge in public discussion about the human costs associated with "cheap" labour and inexpensive consumer goods. The plight of factory workers has been a constant feature in the Western imperial political economy since well before the advent of globe-spanning value chains, from Friedrich Engels' dissection of English factory workers to harrowing inside accounts of sweatshop labour in Southeast Asian garment factories. Identifying and evaluating inadequate working conditions has long been a cornerstone of labour and human rights advocates' efforts to both improve concrete working environments and transform the broader system in which worker oppression persists.

Where does law come into the picture? And, more specifically, what roles do lawyers assume, whether they work on the "labour" or "employer" side, or in and around the expansive global web of non-governmental organisations and institutions? Both questions—regarding the role of law, on the one hand, and lawyers, on

P. Zumbansen (✉)
McGill University, Faculty of Law, Montreal, QC, Canada

M. Saage-Maaß et al. (eds.), *Transnational Legal Activism in Global Value Chains*, Interdisciplinary Studies in Human Rights 6,
https://doi.org/10.1007/978-3-030-73835-8_1

the other—are potentially open-ended enough to be self-defeating in their immensity. As we see yet another wave of scholars "discovering" the institutional linkages between capitalism and its legal foundations,[1] the complexity of how "law and society" are connected is once again brought into sharp focus. If law, as currently argued by proponents of a recharged "law and political economy" research agenda, is deeply implicated in the facilitation, persistence and immunisation of an individualist social theory and a matching, exploitative, race- and gender-based and socio-economically discriminative economic system, the question of "where to begin" may seem as obvious as it is overwhelming.[2] The current surge in interest around law's role in the societal structures around us points to an ambitious and arguably hopeful yearning for change. Yet, as we bring this volume to print, the coronavirus pandemic is still raging around the globe while conservative, ethnophobic and racialized policies expand, and it is hard to feel optimistic about the future. In this context, regulatory systems reveal their fragility. The desirability and importance of law—of an accessible, invocable legal system—is again a topic of quotidian conversation.

Focusing on law's role and implication in the state of the world "before the pandemic" then forces us to take stock of not only "the law" and its institutional and procedural manifestations, but also of law's operation as a daily, living reality. This, in turn, directs our focus to those in charge of administrating law. Calls for a "return to normal" ring especially hollow, as each new day lays bare the paucity and vulnerability of our "normal" infrastructures. Indeed, the deep levels of inequality, divisiveness and sheer violence sustaining these infrastructures is now more visible than ever. When Nancy Fraser explored the tensions between the emergence of domestic and "global" legal regulatory structures a little over a decade ago, her verdict was a gloomy one.[3] A few years earlier, following the events of 11 September 2001, Jürgen Habermas had lamented the "fall of a monument," warning that prospects for reconstituting the achievements of nation-state-based democratic governance were increasingly uncertain in the shadow of post-9/11 global political rearrangements and the US-led military interventions in Afghanistan and Iraq.[4] Here, too, emotions oscillated between optimism and mistrust in the ability of a "global civil society" to forge post-national institutions for democratic politics and law.[5]

The global coronavirus pandemic of 2020/2021, however, has given these investigations a sharp twist. Following closely on the heels of a breathtaking surge in nationalism, xenophobia, racism and populism in countries across Europe, Latin

[1]Pistor (2019), Deakin et al. (2017), p. 8; Singh Grewal and Purdy (2014).

[2]Singh Grewal and Purdy (2014), p. 8: "The questions that neoliberalism addresses at the deepest level, then, are not How much market?, or How much governance?, but Which interests will enjoy protection, whether as property rights, constitutional immunities, or objects of special regulatory solicitude, and which others will be left vulnerable or neglected?"

[3]Fraser (2008).

[4]Habermas (2003, 2006).

[5]Compare these assessments almost 20 years apart: Kaldor (2003) and Kalm et al. (2019).

America, South Asia and the US,[6] which have been likened to a potentially irreversible identity crisis of "globalisation,"[7] the current pandemic prompts us to reconsider the significance and competence of the sovereign nation-state and its democratic operation. In "waves", the pandemic not only wreaks havoc with human life, it also continues to strip away any remaining sheen on the vestiges of widely privatised or unequally instrumentalized, hollowed-out welfare states. While astute analysts have long chronicled neoliberalism's destructive devouring of minds, infrastructures and political economies,[8] we now stare at the stupefying void and utter disorganisation left behind by the rejection of welfare state policies and their associated political values oriented around the common good.[9]

Worn out, then, between the smouldering ruins of nation-states' public infrastructures and the oxygen-less space of yet-to-be-established transnational policy coordination, those seeking to foster transformative politics across nation-states' once again hostile borders are yearning for an anchor, platform or institutional framework. As public policy thinkers, particularly those in health and migration, play a key role in pushing agendas for a "new social contract," they underline how any such endeavour is inevitably embedded in a more expansive project of investigating the self-destructive trajectories of today's political economies.[10] Resonating with the assertiveness of such pursuits in this moment, crucial connections emerge and cut across seemingly self-standing areas of health policy, social protection, food (in)security, labour rights and political participation. Because we should never 'let a good crisis go to waste,' such work is now more crucial than ever.

2 Global Value Chain Advocacy as a Laboratory of Transformative Politics

The present predicament showcases the fragility and vulnerability of local infrastructures that once enshrined—albeit with varying degrees and orientations in different locations—the state's responsibility to ensure a minimum standard of

[6]Kende and Krekó (2020); University of Washington Task Force (2018) The global implications of populism on democracy, Henry M. Jackson School of International Studies, available at: www.jsis.washington.edu/wordpress/wp-content/uploads/2018/04/Task-Force_C_2018_Pekkanen_robert.pdf (last accessed 1 August 2020).

[7]Cuperus (2017); Cox (2017).

[8]Slobodian (2018), Brown (2019).

[9]Navarro (2020), Saad-Filho (2020).

[10]Crane (2020); Mornia (2020): "Many say this is an entwined health, social and economic crisis of a magnitude probably not seen in most of our lifetimes and with effects still not fully understood. But it can also be an opportunity for a long-due change, as individuals and society, a turning point to revert some of the social ills that afflict us. We can, if we choose to, forge a different path towards a fairer society, a 'new normal'. This will depend largely on the moral and political choices we make, individually and collectively, at this watershed moment in history."

public health and safety. The transnational nature of the threat itself is often met with rhetoric all too familiar since 9/11. The language of "war," "frontlines," and "enemy" beckons for decisive responses to be carried out with determination and vigour, despite the ambiguous nature of the threat. Looking back, the 2001 declaration of the "war on terror," which was triggered by attacks on US territory but otherwise constituted a continuation of premeditated policy strategies,[11] unleashed a chain reaction of state violence that has been uncontainable ever since, ranging from data-driven surveillance to military intervention into minute details of financial regulation.[12] Relevant for the critical analysis in which we are today engaged, this scenario provides the evidentiary background and "proof" that regulatory infrastructures have indeed undergone fundamental, far-reaching changes since the late 1970s and early 1980s. These changes occurred alongside the rise of conservative politics directed not only against "big government," but also against politics of socio-economic redistribution and universalising access to public services.

A core component of these transnational infrastructures is the web of global value chains (GVCs) through which just about any resource, product, good or service—both material and immaterial—is sourced, processed, disseminated and sold.[13] Certainly, GVCs have long attracted a wide variety of critical analysis. Given their expansive nature and the degree to which they encompass a seemingly infinite range of things while also being deeply enmeshed in the socio-economic and political fabric of local communities,[14] GVCs prompt highly varied investigations into their constitution organisation, activities, hidden forces and collateral.[15] While law has not always played a prominent role in analysing value chains, it is a key component of their regulatory constitution.[16] What is remarkable about the growing attention to law in and around GVCs is the multifaceted nature of the analysis. While lawyers are asked to explain the role of law in generating and oiling the GVC machine, they are also increasingly asked to justify law's effective insulation of powerful actors from accountability. The flipside, then, of law's constitutive role is its affirmative, defensive one. Accordingly, it comes as no surprise that critical engagement with the law of GVCs is based on the recognition of an admittedly much larger project of political critique.[17]

---

[11] Behan (2007).

[12] Sullivan (2020); see also Levinson-Waldman (2017) and Thimm (2018).

[13] Antràs (2020).

[14] Knöpfel (2020), Tsing (2009).

[15] Selwyn (2018).

[16] In this regard, see Gereffi et al. (2005) and Eller (2020).

[17] IGLP Working Group (2016): "While references to GVCs have proliferated rapidly in recent years, in both academic and policy circles, our intervention is motivated by the puzzling fact that there is as yet no well-developed account of the role of law in the structure, operation or governance of GVCs. In fact, we observe that law has, for the most part, been neglected by the political economists, sociologists, economic geographers and other social scientists that have pioneered GVCs as a field of study."

As the chapters in this volume illustrate, the critical project of going beyond a mere exploration of law in GVCs to developing transformative intervention strategies is now well under way. Lawyers are already delving into the myriad ways in which law shapes this mesmerising infrastructure so crucial for our globally networked economy, including how it facilitates non-compliance with labour and human rights standards. As Andreas Fischer-Lescano shows in his chapter, it is our ability to think about law in a larger context that will eventually allow us to mobilise its potential. For that to happen, however, we must strike a paradoxical balance between proximity and distance. We must take a step back from a purely doctrinal analysis of contract, tort, corporate law and conflicts of law—the core elements that contribute to GVCs' legal infrastructure, but which inevitably lead us back to frustrating road blocks such as "separate legal entity" or "*forum non conveniens*." We must also contextualise our quest for a not-yet-matured law of GVCs[18] against the backdrop of rich and still-growing experiences in public interest litigation, labour and human rights activism, transformative constitutionalism and movement and coalition building. The complexity of GVCs and their relationship to law must not lead to paralysis nor prompt wishful thinking for a "*sui generis*" legal solution. Instead, the particular contribution made by the authors convened in this volume is to show how the tools for real change are at our disposal, as long as we recognise that legal conflicts cannot be solved in the abject spaces of legal abstraction.

3 Overview of the Volume

This volume is structured in three parts. Part I focuses on the Ali Enterprises factory fire and its aftermath in terms of transnational coalition building, litigation and campaigning. It begins with two conversations between Palvasha Shahab and both Saeeda Khatoon and Zehra Khan, offering first-hand accounts and insights from the ground as the fire raged and events unfolded in its wake. Both interviews commence with the factory fire on 11 September 2012 and take the reader through detailed personal accounts of transformational movement-building in Pakistan over the months and years that followed.

Miriam Saage-Maaß then offers a close-up analysis of how transformative legal and advocacy projects can be developed in the aftermath of such a human rights tragedy. Her chapter highlights the persistence of exploitative working conditions in global supply chains, resulting from the constant need to externalise costs and increase consumption with a view to sustaining the "imperial lifestyle" of people in the Global North. Echoing the findings of legal sociologists and, more recently, law and political economy scholars and legal institutionalists, Saage-Maaß draws our attention to law's crucial role in organising and structuring production in these supply chains. While the law structuring GVCs is designed to secure the economic

[18] Reinke and Zumbansen (2019), Zumbansen (2020).

interests of Global North companies at the top of most such chains, it also bears considerable potential for transformation and empowerment, she argues. As her chapter aptly illustrates, the different legal interventions around the Ali Enterprises factory fire demonstrate that law is not only a direct product of dominant class interests, but can also open up opportunities for resistance and future-oriented emancipatory struggles. From her position as an actor closely involved in the Ali Enterprises case, both in terms of building transnational alliances and the litigation itself, Saage-Maaß critically reflects on the achievements of these legal interventions. She ends by proposing several elements for a more holistic approach to the growing number of "strategic litigation" initiatives in the area of value-chain-related human and labour rights violations.

In the next chapter, Faisal Siddiqi focuses on the legal activism that followed in the wake of the Ali Enterprises factory fire in Pakistan itself. Siddiqi's chapter both documents the legal proceedings pursued in Pakistani courts and reflects on the judicial process' capacity and suitability for attaining justice in struggles for labour and human rights. Siddiqi's rare and immensely valuable inside account of the legal proceedings in Pakistan lays the empirical foundation for the chapter's subsequent theoretical and strategic claims. Based on the litigation and legal advocacy experiences following the fire, Siddiqi explores what he perceives to be the two primary "paradoxes" at the heart of the litigation. The first paradox is the inseparability of the "limited justice" on offer through the litigation process and the "structural injustice" that informs and determines the conditions the litigation seeks to address and transform. The second paradox concerns the inseparability of both law and lawlessness with regards to the legal status of the litigation, advocacy and policy proposal elements in play. These apparently contradictory phenomena, the chapter posits, not only coexist alongside one another, but guarantee each other's existence. Siddiqi's analysis leads him to the conclusion that to better understand and improve such forms of strategic litigation, one must measure success and failure in terms of three distinct but interconnected criteria, namely, the litigation's tactical, strategic and structural impacts. The chapter makes a valuable contribution by rejecting the binary choice between nihilism and idealism, arguing instead for a conception of such legal struggles as a means of building sustainable and fruitful forms of resistance and change.

The first section of the volume concludes with a chapter co-authored by Nasir Mansoor from the Pakistani National Trade Union Federation, Miriam Saage-Maaß from the European Center for Constitutional and Human Rights, and Thomas Rudhof-Seibert from the German humanitarian organisation medico international. Drawing on an internal evaluation of the three organisations' cooperation between 2012 and 2019, their chapter offers invaluable insights into the internal coordination and strategic deliberations of the partners' evolving transnational collaboration to hold the German retail company KiK and Italian social auditing firm RINA to account on behalf of survivors and victims' families of the Ali Enterprises factory fire. The authors elaborate on the multi-dimensional effects and aftermath of the tragedy, and recount the lessons learned from their different perspectives as trade unionists, activists and lawyers based in both Pakistan and Germany. On that basis, the chapter maps additional possible avenues to further support the transnational struggles of workers around the globe. Resonating with the process analysis offered by Siddiqi in the preceding chapter, the authors offer rich insights into the experiences and complex debates ongoing amongst themselves and their respective organisations on how to develop common positions and further enhance their mutual understanding in order to collectively imagine transformative political goals.

Part I concludes with two interviews between actors on the ground in Pakistan and Germany. In the first interview, Palvasha Shabab speaks with renowned Pakistani artist Adeela Suleman about her artistic interventions in the aftermath of the fire and the opportunities art offers for political and social mobilisation. In the second interview, Michael Bader from ECCHR talks with German business journalist and author Caspar Dohmen about the role of media and journalism in the transnational lawsuit against retailer KiK filed in Germany.

Part II of the volume focuses on legal doctrine with regard to labour, tort and human rights law. Ben Vanpeperstraete kicks off the section by zeroing in on the Accord on Fire and Building Safety in Bangladesh (Bangladesh Accord) that grew out of the 2013 Rana Plaza garment factory collapse in Dhaka. For Vanpeperstrate, disasters like Rana Plaza and the Tazreen and Ali Enterprises factory fires painfully demonstrate the limits of state-based models of labour regulation. The rise of multinational corporations and decades of outsourcing and offshoring, he argues, have undermined both the regulatory role of the state and the potential of collective bargaining. Meanwhile, substandard and unsafe working conditions in GVCs continue to accrue. Beyond identifying law's crucial role in bringing about such results, Vanpeperstraete asserts that these disasters provide a textbook example of how worker-driven strategies can be developed in a meaningful way. Such strategies, he suggests, can pursue the goal of bringing transnational corporations "to the table" to critically and productively engage in negotiations over global value chain organisation in a way that more effectively protects weaker parties' interests. Vanpeperstraete's analysis shows how both the Bangladesh Accord and the Rana Plaza Arrangement (as well as the corollary Tazreen and Ali Enterprises compensation agreements) can be studied as sites for counter-hegemonic resistance to globalisation as well as platforms for developing new strategies to advance social justice within GVCs.

In the next chapter, Reingard Zimmer reviews the "evident failure" of voluntary corporate codes of conduct to protect labour and human rights in GVCs. Despite their much discussed "toothless tiger" nature, she notes that such codes' proliferation, along with the rise of assorted public, private and hybrid monitoring processes, has only intensified debates over transnational corporations' purchasing practices and legal accountability. Specifically, Zimmer studies the development of "international framework agreements" as an alternative approach advanced by trade unions to complement state-based and voluntary modes of transnational corporate regulation. Her chapter offers a concise analysis of these instruments, highlighting both their strengths and weaknesses. As a case study, she specifically examines the Indonesian Protocol on Freedom of Association, a special framework agreement concluded between Indonesian trade unions and international sportswear firms to protect freedom of association and trade union rights in the Indonesian textile, garment and footwear industries. Beyond outlining the protocol's content, she offers a rich assessment of the international framework agreement's implementation and monitoring system based on interviews conducted in Indonesia between November 2018 and January 2019. Zimmer identifies several key factors that, in her view, led to the successful promotion of strong trade union rights in the protocol's formation phase, including public awareness following intensive campaigning around a mega sporting event, strong support from different civil society actors and the presence of a neutral facilitator. Overall, Zimmer unpacks the Indonesian Protocol as an example of a bottom-up process that strengthened signatory trade unions and, thus, potentially serves as a constructive model for actors in other countries.

Turning to the forever-intriguing relationship between corporate law and labour law, Eva Kocher's chapter traces the development of transnational concepts of corporate social responsibility (CSR), particularly in relation to the standards developed under the auspices of the International Labour Organization in Geneva. Kocher analyses the relationship between transnational private law instruments on the one hand, and national and international law on the other, exploring both the opportunities and limits of new CSR enforcement mechanisms. Only if CSR instruments become sufficiently effective, she concludes, can law avoid becoming a pawn in corporate strategies.

Gerhard Wagner's contribution explores the relationship between tort law and human rights with the aim of gauging tort law's potential for holding corporations liable for human rights violations within GVCs. The chapter takes the 2013 Rana Plaza collapse in Bangladesh as its starting point, examining the intense debates it aroused around the tort law accountability of those involved in the building's maintenance and of the Global North companies that sourced their goods there. Proceeding in two steps, the chapter first proposes a legal framework for tort liability that would optimise social welfare. Under this optimal liability system, manufacturers would internalise the full cost of production, including harm caused to workers, third parties and the environment. Such a model, Wagner asserts, would differ significantly from the present reality of global tort liability, which is plagued by legal fragmentation and enforcement deficits. These factors explain corporations' wanton externalisation of production risks today, which, in turn, lead to inflated global demand. In principle, Wagner argues, tort law is well suited to offer remedy for corporate harms, as the interests protected by human rights and national tort law broadly overlap. Moreover, the core requirement for shifting losses to others via tort law—the duty of care—is a flexible concept capable of accommodating cross-border human rights policies, which he illustrates with reference to France's landmark 2017 *devoir de vigilance* legislation and recent UK Supreme Court jurisprudence. In a second step, the article warns against selectively imposing such duties in some jurisdictions but not in others, as this would hinder a global application of national tort law. Finally, the chapter comparatively assesses a number of possible tort law enforcement mechanisms, reaching a cautious verdict with regard to tort law's usefulness for further advancing human rights.

Part III, the final section of the book, draws on critical and postcolonial perspectives to assess law's potential for addressing human rights violations in GVCs. In the first chapter of this section, Palvasha Shahab argues that Pakistan has never had a bona fide system of Occupational Safety and Health (OSH) standards, laws, policies or enforcement mechanisms. The present system, she asserts, is divorced from both the resources needed to enforce it and from workers' most urgent needs, effectively leaving them without any protection. Offering a minute account of various actors' actions as the fire occurred and in its aftermath, Shahab identifies key legal shortcomings and OSH violations involved. Her account highlights the gap between the OSH system's deficiencies and the fatalities it caused, outlining what would have been required to prevent the tragedy. By tracing the history of Pakistan's OSH infrastructure back to British colonial rule, her chapter contextualises the larger global economic and political situation in which the Ali Enterprises factory fire should be seen, rendering visible the historical trajectories and factors that have led to workers' persistent exclusion from politico-legal rights. She concludes by offering suggestions for improving OSH infrastructure in Pakistan.

Muhammed Azeem provides further historical context for assessing labour law and regulation in the Global South, highlighting the prevalence of meagre social security protections and the lack of labour representation in domestic legislatures. He begins by situating the Global South's long struggle for labour rights as a struggle oriented towards "distributive justice" with an emphasis on constitutionally protected freedom of association and collective bargaining rights. Azeem shows how, over the course of the last century, labour law has increasingly sought to pit the core values of "distributive justice" against the strictures of "corrective justice" by rejecting what he calls the slippery "ethical basis" of private law in both civil and common law systems. Azeem critically assesses multinational corporations' continuing use of (voluntary) codes of conduct with respect to labour and working conditions on the one hand, while also scrutinising labour and human rights activists' increasing reliance on the private law doctrines of tort and damages on the other. Both approaches, he argues, dilute labour law's focus on distributive justice by aiming to reform but not fundamentally alter a system that has been rigged from the very start. For Azeem, the KiK litigation highlights the tension between these competing approaches and the ultimate aim of achieving distributive justice.

Andreas Fischer-Lescano's chapter reflects on the long history of lawyers and NGOs using strategic and public interest litigation as a means to advance broader socio-political aims. The chapter begins by unpacking what this type of litigation entails, namely activists (a) initiating legally substantiated lawsuits that (b) pursue goals beyond legal "success" in the strict sense and (c) address contentious political issues. As such, he claims, this type of litigation can never be seen in isolation from the larger socio-political struggles in which the actors are engaged. Yet, by fighting for the judicial enforcement of human, environmental, trade union, migrant and refugee rights within the *prima facie* circumscribed framework of litigation, Fischer-Lescano shows that such "strategic" efforts remain, at their core, engaged in a struggle to make the law "better." As the chapter compellingly demonstrates, it is precisely here that the structural limitations of legal mobilisation become apparent. Fischer-Lescano draws parallels between contemporary strategic litigation efforts to combat injustices in GVCs and earlier as well as ongoing efforts to bring about socio-economic and political change through the judicial process.

Finally, Michael Bader's chapter not only concludes this section, but also the book, widening the lens again to critically examine the political objectives of the broad-church project of Business and Human Rights and its prospects for ending decades of corporate impunity and rights abuses. His chapter shows how, in recent years, the fight for corporate accountability under the banner of Business and Human Rights has come to dominate civil society's engagement with the "question of the corporation." He explores the project's gradual translation of case-based struggles into world-making aspirations and assesses evolving efforts to develop a regulatory framework for corporate human rights obligations like the "Legally Binding Instrument" currently under discussion at the United Nations. Using a historical narrative approach to situate the evolution of Business and Human Rights within neoliberal globalisation, Bader points out the "dark side" of this particular strand of human rights activism. By bringing critical legal scholarship on the corporation and human rights into closer conversation with Business and Human Rights, the chapter excavates the latter's structural flaws, namely that it leaves the asymmetries in the global economy and the imperial corporate form unchallenged. Bader problematises Business and Human Rights' presupposition of business as fact and its uncritical embrace of rights as positive change-makers, prompting us to rethink strategic political objectives vis-à-vis corporate rights abuses.

References

Antràs P (2020) Conceptual aspects of global value chains. Harvard University and The World Bank, 4 February 2020. Available at: www.scholar.harvard.edu/files/antras/files/conceptual_aspects_gvcs.pdf. Accessed 1 Aug 2020

Behan RW (2007) The so-called "war on terror". Global Policy Forum, 29 August 2007. Available at: www.globalpolicy.org/component/content/article/154/26817.html. Accessed 1 Aug 2020

Brown W (2019) In the ruins of neoliberalism: the rise of antidemocratic politics in the west. Columbia University Press, New York

Cox M (2017) The rise of populism and the crisis of globalisation: Brexit, Trump and beyond. Ir Stud Int Aff 28:9–17

Crane D (2020) Once the pandemic is over, we'll need a new social contract for Canada. Hill Times, 6 April 2020. Available at: www.hilltimes.com/2020/04/06/242019/242019. Accessed 1 Aug 2020

Cuperus R (2017) The populist revolt against globalization. Clingendael Spectator 71(3). Available at: www.clingendael.org/pub/2017/3/the-populist-revolt-against-globalisation/. Accessed 1 Aug 2020

Deakin S, Gindis D, Hodgson GM, Huang K, Pistor K (2017) Legal institutionalism: capitalism and the constitutive role of law. J Comp Econ 45:188–200

Eller KE (2020) Is "global value chain" a legal concept? Situating contract law in discourses around global production. Eur Rev Contr Law 16(1):3–24

Fraser N (2008) Scales of justice: reimaging political space in a globalizing world. Columbia University Press, New York

Gereffi G, Humphrey J, Sturgeon T (2005) The governance of global value chains. Rev Int Polit Econ 12:78–104

Habermas J (1986) The new obscurity: the crisis of the welfare state and the exhaustion of utopian energies. Philosophy Soc Crit 11(2):1–18

Habermas J (2003) Interpreting the fall of a monument. Germ Law J 7(4):701–708

Habermas J (2006) The Kantian project and the divided west. In: Habermas J (ed) The divided west. Wiley, Hobken, pp 113–192

IGLP Working Group (2016) The role of law in global value chains: a research manifesto. London Rev Int Law 4(1):57–79

Kaldor M (2003) The idea of global civil society. Int Aff 79(3):583–593

Kalm S, Strömbom L, Uhlin A (2019) Civil society democratising global governance? Potentials and limitations of "counter democracy"? Glob Soc 33(4):499–519

Kende A, Krekó P (2020) Xenophobia, prejudice, and right-wing populism in Eastern Europe. Curr Opin Behav Sci 34:29–33

Knöpfel L (2020) An anthropological reimagining of contract in global value chains: the governance of corporate-community relations in the Colombian mining sector. Eur Rev Contr Law 16 (1):118–138

Levinson-Waldman R (2017) NSA-surveillance in the war on terror. In: Gray D, Henderson SE (eds) Cambridge Handbook of Surveillance Law. Cambridge University Press, Cambridge, pp 7–43

Mornia M (2020) Pandemics and a new social contract: the hope of a "new normal" for a future beyond the lockdown. DiscoverSociety, 8 June 2020. Available at: www.discoversociety.org/2020/06/08/pandemics-and-a-renewed-social-contract-the-hope-of-a-new-normal-for-a-future-beyond-lockdown/. Accessed 1 Aug 2020

Navarro V (2020) The consequences of neoliberalism in the current pandemic. Int J Health Serv 50 (3):271–275

Pistor K (2019) The code of capital: how the law creates wealth and inequality. Princeton University Press, Princeton

Reinke B, Zumbansen P (2019) Transnational liability regimes in contract. Tort and corporate law: comparative observations on "global supply chain liability". In: Schiller S (ed) Le devoir de vigilance, pp 157–183

Saad-Filho A (2020) From COVID-19 to the end of neoliberalism. Crit Sociol 46(4–5):477–485

Selwyn B (2018) Poverty chains and global capitalism. Compet Chang 23(1):71–97

Singh Grewal D, Purdy J (2014) Introduction: law and neoliberalism. Law Contemp Probl 77 (1):1–23

Slobodian Q (2018) Globalists: the end of empire and the birth of neoliberalism. Harvard University Press, Cambridge

Sullivan G (2020) The law of the list: UN counterterrorism sanctions and the politics of global security law. Cambridge University Press, Cambridge

Thimm J (2018) From exception to normalcy: the United States and the war on terrorism. SWP Research Paper 2018, 7 October 2018. Available at: www.swp-berlin.org/en/publication/the-united-states-and-the-war-on-terrorism/. Accessed 1 Aug 2020

Tsing A (2009) Supply chains and the human condition. Rethink Marx 21(2):148–176

Zumbansen (2020) Reflections on Economic Law, J. Polit. Econ 1(3), in print

Peer Zumbansen is a private law scholar with a focus on contract law, corporate governance and transnational regulatory theory. In January 2021, he joined McGill University Faculty of Law in Montreal, Canada, as the inaugural holder of the professorship of business law. From 2004 to 2020, he held a research chair and professorship at Osgoode Hall Law School in Toronto, Canada, where he founded and directed the Critical Research Laboratory in Law & Society, and the Collaborative Urban Research Laboratory and launched the SSRN e-journal for the Comparative Research in Law & Political Economy Network. From 2014 to 2018, he served full-time as the inaugural chair in transnational law at King's College London, UK, and inaugural Director of the Dickson Poon Transnational Law Institute. Starting in 2021, Zumbansen will be a Senior Research Fellow at TLI. His recent publications include *The Many Lives of Transnational Law* (Cambridge 2020) and the *Oxford Handbook of Transnational Law* (Oxford 2021).

Part I
The Ali Enterprises Factory Fire and Its Aftermath: Litigations, Campaigning and Transnational Collaboration

Loss and Legibility: A Conversation with Saeeda Khatoon

Palvasha Shahab

Abstract Saeeda Khatoon rose as a prominent figure and main voice of the Ali Enterprises Factory Fire Affectees Association (AEFFAA). She lost her son in the fire of 11 September 2012 and was one of the four petitioners in the German case against KiK. In this interview, she speaks to Palvasha Shahab about the events unfolding from her perspective as well as strategic decisions and collective organizing in light of the transnational lawsuits she was involved in.

Keywords Ali Enterprises factory fire · KiK case · Transnational collaboration · Strategic litigation · Ali Enterprises Factory Fire Affectees Association · AEFFAA

In the aftermath of the 2012 Ali Enterprises factory fire in Karachi, Pakistan, Saeeda Khatoon rose as a prominent figure and one of the main voices of the Ali Enterprises Factory Fire Affectees Association (AEFFAA). She lost her son in the fire on 11 September 2012 and was one of the four petitioners in the German case against KiK Textilien und Non-Food GmbH (KiK). Conversation with her makes one recall the Argentine Mothers of the Plaza de Mayo, her soft and endearing appearance only testifying to the iron resolve, bravery and strength that lies within. For the past 9 years, she has fought systems that she does not even always understand. But to her, understanding them is not the most relevant factor. What is important to her is to fight against the injustice and precarity that she was and still is forced to occupy, along with countless others. It is important for her to do everything she can to render her son's death meaningful.[1]

[1]The interview was conducted in Urdu and later translated into English by Palvasha Shahab. Saeeda Khatoon's recollection of events is not always self-explanatory or chronologically consistent. For

P. Shahab (✉)
Rasheed Razvi Centre for Constitutional and Human Rights (RCCHR), and the Legal Aid Foundation for Victims of Rape and Sexual Assault (LAFRSA), Karachi, Pakistan
e-mail: palvasha.shahab@columbia.edu

M. Saage-Maaß et al. (eds.), *Transnational Legal Activism in Global Value Chains*, Interdisciplinary Studies in Human Rights 6,
https://doi.org/10.1007/978-3-030-73835-8_2

Palvasha Shahab: Can I record you?

Saeeda Khatoon: Of course! My recordings are everywhere. They have to be, because nobody wants to listen to the voice of labour, nobody wants to work with or for labour interests. I have suffered this. They try to stop you: your own neighbours who are tired themselves, or political parties, or factory owners, or others. They even tried to subvert the whole tragedy and politicise it. They say it was a case of political *bhatta* [extortion money, claimed in return for extra-legal protection by political parties], or terrorism, or this or that. All I have to say is, if this is true, why didn't they [factory owners] get help? Why did the owners not address it in any way? Why did they not even increase security in the factory? It has been 8 years, whoever this secret criminal was, why haven't they found him? And in any case, what has that got to do with our children? That is not why they died.

Shahab: Can you tell us about the events of 11 September 2012?

Khatoon: I used to work as a governess in Shakil Hasan, which is a little beyond Hyderi. I used to get done at 4 pm. We lived in Orangi Town, so it used to take me an hour to get home by bus. The first thing I did when I got home was to cook dinner because as soon as my son walked in, his first question used to be: "Is dinner ready?" And his second question was always: "What have you made for dinner?" So, I always used to make dinner and then do everything else. That evening, I had finished cooking the *saalan* [stew or gravy]. The rice we get in the area cooks very well if you soak it for a while, so I had soaked the rice. Several of our children—of us who lived in our neighbourhood—used to work in that [Ali Enterprises] factory, so around 6:30 pm somebody banged on my door and said there had been a fire in the factory where my son works. I turned off the stove, locked the house and went towards the homes of others who worked in the factory to find out if this was true. As I was walking, people were running and they said: "Others have already gone to the factory, whole families have gone. What are you still doing here? Don't go in that direction, don't go upwards, go to the factory!" I panicked, ran up to the bus stop, and from there I took a rickshaw to the factory. The factory was in SITE [Sindh Industrial Trading Estate], which was about an hour away. I had never been to the factory before. I had not even been to the SITE area before.

When I got there, the fire was raging. I could see it from a distance. There were personnel from the police, the navy, the rangers, even the traffic police. I tried to go towards the factory, but they held me back. There was one fire engine, which had water and was fighting the fire, while the other fire engine had run out of water already. I could see people were being taken out of the factory using a crane. I was frantically running about, crying, yelling my son's name, trying to call him on the phone, messaging him, praying for him to just send me one message—just one message. There were quite a few of us from the neighbourhood, relatives, acquaintances, etc. We tried to get together and do something, to go towards the factory and

more detailed accounts of events and lawsuits surrounding the fire and its aftermath, please see the chapters by Faisal Siddiqi and Miriam Saage-Maaß in this volume.

get our family members out, but the police held us back. They even "baton-charged" [colonial term for pushing back crowds or hitting them with batons] us.

At about 11 pm, the authorities said we should go to either the Civil Hospital or Abbasi Shaheed Hospital. I went to the Civil Hospital first and checked every list. His name was not on the list of the injured or the dead. Then I went to Abbasi Shaheed Hospital, where they had taken only 10–15 of the injured, they had not taken any of the dead bodies there. But I found nothing there either. I sat on the steps of the Abbasi Shaheed Hospital and cried and cried. I didn't know what to do. It was 2 am and there was no sign of my son. Then I went back to the Civil Hospital, where dead bodies were coming in now. Then, we also went to the morgue, but I still couldn't find him. My sister and her husband were with me. They told me to wait outside while they went inside and checked. My neighbours said we should go back home and check if anything or anyone had turned up at home. The first dead body arrived in our neighbourhood at 4 am. I got home, had a cup of tea—I couldn't eat—I said my morning *fajr* prayer and tried to think of what to do, of how to find my son. I was at a loss.

Then, I went back to the factory. They were removing only dead bodies from the factory now. They had been removing dead bodies since late at night. But my son used to work in the basement. There were about 40 people in the basement and none of them survived. At about 10 am, they found my son. Some youths had gone into the building with a torch. His body was found at the top of the stairs; he had been protecting his face with a plate. My child was the first of that lot that they got out. I kept saying: "Ayaan, Ayaan, Ayaan. Get Ayaan out." They found that his death was caused primarily by suffocation and, later, by drowning; there were only minor burns. He had drowned in the hot water from the fire engines that drained towards the basement. When we saw his body, blood was coming out of his nose and ears. They took his body to Civil Hospital. They didn't have space to put the dead bodies inside, so they put them outside and covered them with sheets. The authorities would not hand over the dead body to us, as they said there were many bodies and we would have to wait to identify the body. My sister went to them and said, "Just let us see, we will identify it." Some bodies were recognisable, some weren't. As I was requesting that they let us have the dead body, a gust of wind blew off the sheet they had laid on my son's dead body, and I immediately identified it. We finally brought the dead body home at about 1:30 pm.

That day was like the apocalypse. Every house in our neighbourhood seemed to have a dead body on their doorstep. Some homes had two brothers' dead bodies, and some had the bodies of a mother and daughter. There were 17 bodies in my immediate neighbourhood that day, then 24 more bodies arrived the next day. In total, our neighbourhood received 112 dead bodies. About 13 of these were women. It was a day from hell.

Shahab: What happened in the weeks and months following the fire? How did different victims and affectees come together, how was the AEFFAA founded and what were its aims?

Khatoon: After the fire, I tried to wrap my head around what had happened and different affectees tried to gather to seek justice—to make sure that this kind of tragedy does not happen again. The police also called us in for verification during this time, but that was a harrowing experience. They made us sit and wait until 1 am. This was about a week or 10 days after the fire. I went with my sister's husband. There were many of us. They made us wait and wait. I also yelled and said: "We have come from afar, men, women, all sorts. Why are you not doing anything? Do what you have to do and let us go!" Then they called me in and did the verification, where they asked me the name of my son and what time I got the body, and so on, and prepared their report. And then things started moving along a little.

For the next year and a half, I just kept running from office to office, trying to get justice. It was imperative for us that no one else's child should suffer the same fate. There are others like my child. Every factory is unsafe. These 258 children lost their lives due to a lack of safety. Ali Enterprises did not have any safety. We wanted to take up this issue. We had to take up this issue. My child could not come back, but others can be saved.

During the next year and a half, we sought out the Death Grant.[2] When one person would get the call from government offices that would tell them about the grant or pension, then we would all share the information to make sure that everyone gets their due. When we went to their office on Shahrah-e-Faisal Road, they said we should go to Islamabad. We went to Islamabad. There, they said the money is here, but the orders and directions have to come from Karachi. So, we went back to Karachi, to the office on Shahrah-e-Faisal Road. There were times when we filled two buses, one from Orangi Town and one from Baldia Town, to apply pressure to make sure that all of us got their due.

Over the next year and a half, we kept trying to figure out what was the Death Grant, the pension from the Employees Old Age Benefits Institution (EOBI), the social security, and we went from office to office.

There was this lawyer's office in Mashriq Centre [near Gulshan Town, Karachi]. They had an association of some sort. They said if we pay them 30,000 rupees each,[3] then they would get us all the pension and compensation that was due to us. But at the time, the office of the National Trade Union Federation (NTUF) was in the same building. So, they used to see us coming and going. One of those days, about one and a half years after the tragedy, we got talking with Nasir [Mansoor][4] and Zehra [Khan],[5] who used to be at that NTUF office. They then advised us to organise and form an association [AEFFAA]. And it was the best advice, because things became a lot easier once we formed the association. Different offices and departments started recognising us as a whole, as opposed to the scattered many.

Shahab: When did AEFFAA start working with national and international organisations like NTUF, the Pakistan Institute for Labour Education and Research

---

[2]Provided by the Sindh Employees Social Security Institution (SESSI), under Section 37 of the Provincial Employees Social Security Act, 1965.

[3]The monthly minimum wage at the time was 10,000 rupees.

[4]General Secretary of National Trade Union Federation (NTUF).

[5]General Secretary of the Home Based Women Workers Federation.

(PILER), the Home Based Women Workers Federation (HBWWF), the European Center for Constitutional and Human Rights (ECCHR), and the Clean Clothes Campaign (CCC)?

Khatoon: We met Nasir [Mansoor] and Zehra [Khan] after a year and a half. Then, we made the association [AEFFAA] and the first thing we did as an association was file three court cases. And we won them too. Since then, we have worked in solidarity with Nasir and Zehra. They also introduced us, as an association, to the lawyer Faisal Siddiqi, who fought three cases for us, the affectees, and which we won fairly quickly after we formed the association. As a result of these cases, we got our pension settled with EOBI, and those who didn't have social security [registration with SESSI] also got their social security worked out, and then we got the Death Grant as well. Since then, we have been introduced to many organisations and worked with the lawyer Faisal Siddiqi. It was because we made the association that we got all this done.[6]

After that, we met PILER. Then, we met ECCHR. After the cases here [in Pakistan], we brought a case in Germany,[7] against the international brand [KiK]. What happened there was that there were some people, who are our friends now, who had come from Germany in 2014, who wanted to help us. So, they called about a hundred people over to the Mehran Hotel. They said we would like to meet some people from Baldia Town and some from Orangi Town, for a case about this fire. So, we selected a group of 100 people. They had a 3-day long programme in the Mehran Hotel. In those 3 days, they took in-depth interviews from all of us. They asked what happened, who were the family members, how burnt the bodies were, and so forth. After all these interviews, they selected 15 people, in accordance with what they thought might give us the best chance in Court. Then they called these 15 affectees the next day, to interview them further. Then, from those 15, we selected four people. One of them was me, then Muhammed Jabir, Abdul Aziz, and one who had been injured, Muhammed Hanif—he had fainted at some point in the fire, but he was the one who knew most about what had happened inside. Then, after this, we did this case in Germany.[8] Then, this ILO (International Labour Organization) pension has been coming from the Social Department [SESSI] since 2018.

[6]Two of the cases Khatoon refers to were, in fact, initiated within a month of the Ali Enterprises fire. The third was filed in or around January 2013. Please see Faisal Siddiqi's chapter in this volume for details on the court proceedings. However, it is obvious that Saeeda and most of her fellow affectees had been unaware of the court cases and had been struggling for justice on their own. They believed that the cases were filed sometime after the AEFFAA's formation in late 2013 or early 2014. It appears that by making the association, the affectees became legible to the government offices, civil society organisations and lawyers, and vice versa.

[7]*Jabir and others v. KiK Textilien und Non-Food GmbH* (Case No. 7 O 95/15).

[8]See Business and Human Rights Resource Centre, KiK lawsuit (re Pakistan), 7 October 2015, www.business-humanrights.org/en/latest-news/kik-lawsuit-re-pakistan/ (last accessed 7 October 2020).

Shahab: How did you come to lead AEFFAA and what were the difficulties you faced while leading it?

Khatoon: First, I was made vice president, Muhammed Jabir was president, and Abdul Aziz Khan was made general secretary. They were both from the Baldia Town area. But then later, Muhammad Jabir stepped down and I became president. Even though we were not an association before and didn't have a point person as such, we had, in one way or another, struggled from office to office from day one.

After this, in 2015, we did a case in the Labour Department and one in the Compensation Department [could mean the Sindh Employees Social Security Institution, Employees Old-Age Benefits Institution or Workers Welfare Fund]. We had some gratuity remaining and Group Insurance as well. Now, this year [2020], we will win the Group Insurance. The case is fixed for orders and when we get the order, I'll share it with you.[9]

When I struggled to get results, such as at the Compensation Department and Labour Department, I told the AEFFAA members that if they wanted results, they would have to take the trouble to come with me. I had been running around for 6 years, but it was time for a show of strength. In 2018, when the Compensation Department would not proceed with our case, I decided to fill two to three buses with people and show up at their offices. Then, these officers surrounded me, saying "Saeeda Baji, Saeeda Baji, Saeeda Baji!" [*Baji* means elder sister], requesting that I disperse them. I told the officers they should have thought about this when they refused to take action and move things along. Now, I couldn't help them. They said the judge had an accident and would definitely hear us the next day. But a little while later, we found out that the judge was sitting inside. Then, he met with us and told us to come tomorrow. So, the next day, I filled those buses again and showed up and made sure the hearing happened. Since the tragedy, there has not been a single month when I have not attended some hearing or pursued some meeting.

Shahab: What role did the case against KiK in Germany and the complaint against auditor RINA in Italy play in your struggle? What did the transnational collaboration mean to you?

Khatoon: It was a good experience. Our aim was not compensation, it was justice. We needed to fight for our children's safety against the international brand [KiK], to deter them from enabling this again, so that something like this does not happen to other children. It was not compensation we cared about at the time. We needed to

[9]According to Section 12 of the Sindh Terms of Employment (Standing Orders) Act, 2015 [previously the West Pakistan Industrial and Commercial Employment (Standing Orders) Ordinance, 1968] "every industrial establishment and commercial establishment, in which twenty or more workers are employed, the employer shall have all the permanent workers employed by him insured against natural death and disability and death and injury arising out of contingencies not covered by the Workmen's' Compensation Act, 1923 (Act No. VIII of 1923) or the Provincial Employees' Social Security Ordinance, 1965 (W.P.Ord.No.X of 1965)." This is referred to as "Group Insurance" in the side bar margins of the aforesaid Act, 2015. Khatoon is fighting a case for the victims to be processed for Group Insurance and for their heirs to receive this insurance.

make sure that things did not go on as they were. The dead bodies we have seen—the young bodies, 22-year-olds, 15-year-olds—most of them were so young, most of them were unmarried. The sight of those bodies does not leave me, and I cannot bear to think of something like this happening again.

Due to these transnational collaborations, we were able to amplify the incident and talk about it on various platforms. We were able to draw attention to our cause. The money does not mean anything. It is worth nothing against the joy we would have had if our children were still around. What is money? Money gets spent. But these collaborations allowed us to not be forgotten. If we can work to save lives, prevent deaths—that, for us, is the biggest motivation. We hoped it would lead to the factory owners and the international brand being held accountable and would usher in new safety mechanisms. We wanted a big judgement and something that would put an end to this lack of safety.

Shahab: How did you feel when you were not allowed to address the court in Dortmund, even though you had travelled all the way to Germany from Pakistan for the hearing on 26 November 2018?

Khatoon: I did not like it. I was hurt. On the day of the hearing, the judges in Germany got scared. They realised that we had too much support and too many supporters. That is why they delayed the judgement and said they would reserve it. They said they would give us a report on the 10th of the next month and disposed of our case.[10] But they should have given me something. Some report [judgement], some piece of paper to show for all the effort we made. There were two judges—they should have done something at least. They should have taken some steps, some initiative. That day, the lawyers with us requested the judges to let me address the court, but the judges did not allow it. The judges did not even let me speak to them. That day, I was very upset. When Nasir and all went to get lunch after the hearing, I went straight to my room. I did not eat anything that day. It felt very anticlimactic.

Shahab: How much were you able to achieve in the past 9 years?

Khatoon: We were more hopeful in the beginning. But now, we have very little hope from the government or from anyone else. What we won is more or less irrelevant because, despite the passage of 9 years, nothing has changed with respect to safety. Even if all factories within Karachi were not able to achieve perfect safety, it would have meant something if even 50 of these factories had been made safe. But people are still dying. Factories are still catching fire. Other accidents are still happening. I have run in every direction. I have mobilised here in Karachi, I have gone abroad, I have done it all. But to what real avail? Nevertheless, we do not intend to give up. It is difficult, but if we give up, things might become even worse. Maybe

[10] Jabir and others v. KiK Textilien und Non-Food GmbH—Dortmund court dismisses lawsuit, *Focus on Regulation*, 11 January 2019, www.hlregulation.com/2019/01/11/jabir-and-others-v-kik-textilien-und-non-food-gmbh-dortmund-court-dismisses-lawsuit/ (last accessed 7 October 2020).

one day we will have a breakthrough. We will get safety one way or another, whether it is the government or us, we have to get it done.

Shahab: What are the future goals of AEFFAA?

Khatoon: Safety is a big part of what we want to achieve. We have to get the worker to be seen as human. We want to keep mobilising with the workers. We want to be able to help and advise other workers or their families who are suffering. We want to keep doing these awareness programmes, keep pursuing these cases. Also, no one in the assembly [Pakistan's national or provincial parliaments] ever really raises their voice for the workers. No one really thinks of workers as human beings. We want to change that. We need to keep pushing forward, keep pushing along—we cannot rest until workers are treated humanely.

Shahab: What do you think justice would have looked like?

Khatoon: Justice should have been served. If it had been served, the order of priority would have been as follows: first, the factory owners, then second, the international brand [KiK], and then third, the audit company [RINA] would have been held to account.

First, on one hand, the audit company [RINA] mis-stated everything about safety in the factory. What did they see? Three out of four gates were locked, but they issued their license [SA-8000 certificate, issued by Social Accountability International]. If they had not issued the license, the factory may not have been operating. Second, on the other hand, what did the international brand [KiK] see? They made tens of millions and took it away without worrying about the real cost—the human cost and the lives their business endangered. If they cannot create life, they have no right to take away the lives of our children for their profits. If they cannot return those lives to us, the brands cannot take these lives. What did they see? These are the second culprits. And the third category of culprints are, of course, the factory owners. They have started their own stories and made a huge fuss, crying about how the fire was due to the non-payment of a political prevention tax. Even if it were the case, how come they were seen or known to be taking no action? How come they did not close down the factory to assess their situation? How come they put our children at risk, even if, as they say, the fire was caused or initiated by political goons? How dare they risk our children like this?

But we must emphasise that it is irrelevant if the fire was accidental or intentional. There was no safety in the factory. That is why our children died. We sent our children to the factory well and living, and their dead bodies came back to us. It is irrelevant what caused the fire. The only thing that is relevant is that they would have survived if there had been any semblance of safety in the factory. They were so young, they would have survived—they were fit and able-bodied, they would have run, they would have climbed, if only there were a way to do so, if the gates and exits were open. The biggest criminals are truly the factory owners. They must not be spared. If they are spared, an incident like this will happen again. There will be even more impunity than before.

We believe that the factory owner and the workers should have a healthy relationship. They are mutually benefiting each other. They should be like family. But here, we have lost 258 of our children. And here, he [the owner of Ali Enterprises] fled to Dubai and has been gone since. His life was so precious that he fled. But our children's had no value? Know that we are still here. And we will stay here and we will keep fighting. We are here in Karachi and we will keep fighting and raising our voices until our last breath. We will keep trying to save the other children.

Palvasha Shahab was the joint executive director of the Rasheed Razvi Centre for Constitutional and Human Rights, and the Legal Aid Foundation for Victims of Rape and Sexual Assault through September 2020. She now works a consultant for RCCHR, LAFRSA, the Legal Aid Society and the Pakistan Institute for Labour Education and Research. She is on the Law Committee of the Sindh Commission of the Status on Women and advises on upcoming legislation. She is also an advisor to a transnational collaborative project on oral histories and social interventions titled "Karachi Beach Radio." She also teaches undergraduate courses on peace movements and international human rights law at SZABIST, Karachi. Shahab further curates and moderates important public discussions on national platforms such as the Adab Fest and The Second Floor. She holds a Master of Laws from Columbia Law School, New York, US, where she was also a Human Rights Fellow at the Human Rights Institute in 2017–2018.

Legal Interventions and Transnational Alliances in the Ali Enterprises Case: Struggles for Workers' Rights in Global Supply Chains

Miriam Saage-Maaß

Abstract This article highlights the persistence of exploitative working conditions in global supply chains resulting from the constant need to externalise costs and increase consumption with a view to sustaining the "imperial lifestyle" of people in the Global North. While the law structures today's global value chains and is designed to secure the economic interests of Global North companies that sit at the top of most of such chains, it also bears considerable potential for transformation and empowerment. The different legal interventions around the 2012 Ali Enterprises factory fire demonstrate that law is not only a direct product of dominant class interests, but that it can also open up opportunities for resistance and emancipatory struggle. Written from the perspective of one of the actors closely involved in the legal struggle for justice that followed the Ali Enterprises factory fire, both in terms of building transnational alliances as well as in the litigation itself, this chapter critically reflects on the achievements of the legal interventions carried out and also attempts to develop criteria for a holistic approach to what is often called strategic litigation.

Keywords Global value chains · Strategic litigation · Movement lawyering · Marxist critiques of law · Decolonial critiques of law · Transnational law · Human rights · Labour rights · Tort law litigation

---

I want to thank Corina Ajder, Johan Horst, Wolfgang Kaleck, Cannelle Lavite, Franziska Oehm, Christian Schliemann, Faisal Sidiqqi, Palvasha Shahab, Ben Vanpeperstraete and, last but absolutely certainly not least, Michael Bader, for their helpful comments on the text, but also more generally for the many opportunities for discussion and reflection. I also want to thank Carolijn Terwindt who accompanied me on the case for a long time. Her insights are surely also reflected in this text.

M. Saage-Maaß (✉)
European Center for Constitutional and Human Rights, Berlin, Germany
e-mail: saage-maasz@ecchr.eu

M. Saage-Maaß et al. (eds.), *Transnational Legal Activism in Global Value Chains*, Interdisciplinary Studies in Human Rights 6,
https://doi.org/10.1007/978-3-030-73835-8_3

1 Introduction

Human rights litigators and activists around the world often use law and legal proceedings to challenge those in positions of power, whether they be governments or corporate actors, involved in human rights abuses. Using law as a defence against state and corporate oppression is not a recent phenomenon; the anti-slavery movement, the nineteenth and early twentieth-century workers' movement, as well as the women's movement have all used law and litigation as a tool to fight for social change. In a time of globalised neoliberal market economies, communities and individuals have now started to use litigation against multinational corporations as a way to address the many harms they cause. This trend is often called transnational strategic litigation, as it seeks to hold parent companies liable in the jurisdictions in which they are headquartered for violations that have occurred in foreign states, often through the involvement of company subsidiaries. The first lawsuits of this kind were filed in the USA under the Alien Tort Statute (ATS), for example, against British-Dutch oil company Shell for its involvement in the killing of Nigerian activist and writer Ken Saro Wiwa and others in 1996. Also, in the mid-1990s, South African workers started to sue British parent companies in English courts, claiming compensation for occupational health damages like asbestosis.[1]

The strategy of using transnational litigation to address human rights abuses caused by multinational corporations has been picked up by different groups of affected people and rights advocates around the world, using not only civil law, but also other legal claims and procedures.[2] Still, in 2012, when the Ali Enterprises factory fire killed 258 workers and injured tens of others, litigation of this kind was mainly concentrated on challenging corporate involvement in parent-subsidiary relationships and—at least in the US—in grave international crimes like torture, killings, or slave labour.[3] Hardly any lawyers considered challenging supply-chain relationships through litigation as it already seemed hard enough to argue that parent companies bear responsibility for harm caused or contributed to by their foreign subsidiaries. Also, for labour activists, the idea that one might not only use national labour courts to address factory owners' responsibilities, but also to legally challenge the multinational brands buying from these factories, was novel.

This chapter will describe the 2012 Ali Enterprises incident and the related legal interventions that evolved in its wake, contextualising them within the realities of capitalist production in global value chains and law's particular role in securing the profits and interests of transnational business. Coming from a critical legal perspective, it recognises law's many shortcomings and pitfalls, but also its emancipatory

---

[1]Meeran (2011).

[2]For an overview, visit the "legal accountability" section of the Business and Human Rights Resource Centre website: www.business-humanrights.org/en/big-issues/corporate-legal-accountability/ (last accessed 12 September 2020).

[3]This case selection was, and to some extent still is, primarily driven by the legal requirements of the respective causes of action, as the ATS, in particular, requires a violation of the "law of nations."

potential. Indeed, the chapter explores this ambiguity of law by highlighting how affected groups and those supporting their struggle were able to use the legal interventions around the Ali Enterprises incident in a self-empowering way. While legal actions often aim to set legal precedent, there are potential effects beyond the courtroom. This chapter shows that those driving the litigation can intervene in public and legal discourses, and thereby influence the way exploitation and "organised irresponsibility" are created in global value chains. While it is impossible to say that a few legal actions will fundamentally change the daily realities of workers in global value chains, they can and do contribute to broader trajectories of emancipatory change.

2 The Context of the Ali Enterprises Factory Fire Litigation

The litigation against the German company KiK Textil und Non-Food GmbH (KiK) and the Italian firm RINA SpA cannot be fully understood if only viewed as single, isolated instances of transnational strategic litigation. Instead, these legal proceedings should be considered in the context of the broader economic realities of globalised value chains, which are structured according to law.[4] In this context, the legal system plays the role, first and foremost, of protecting business interests and sustaining the Global North's imperial way of life. At the same time, however, the legal system also holds out fora through which the very same system can be challenged.

2.1 The South Asian Textile Industry and Europe's Enduring Imperial Way of Life

The textile industry is paradigmatic of the current neoliberal, globalised economy in that it is based on the continuous exploitation of natural resources and labour.[5] This starts with the agricultural production of cotton, which has major impacts on the environment as well as humans. Described as the birthplace of global capitalism, the cotton industry was a key historical driver of colonialism and the slave trade.[6] Today, it is one of the major drivers behind the growing need for pesticides, with all of their devastating consequences for nature, the climate, and people.[7] The cycle

[4]Scholars have rightly pointed out the need to understand the law of global value chains as a field in itself that transcends the classic disciplinary boundaries of law, just as value chains transcend national borders. Baars et al. (2016).

[5]Lehmann (2012).

[6]Beckert (2014), pp. 98 ff.

[7]Orsenna (2007) and Kumar (2015).

of exploitation continues with cotton processing: from bad working conditions in ginning mills, to dyeing departments where all kinds of hazardous chemicals are used, and on to the actual factories producing ready-made garments for the global market.[8]

Within this production chain, described here only superficially, it is clear that textile factories producing for the international market are not the worst places to work. As industrial workplaces that provide more or less regular salaries, they are relatively less precarious than agricultural or home-based work. Especially in Bangladesh, jobs in garment factories offer an opportunity for young women to have an income independent from their families. But studies have shown that despite the majority of workers being women, gender discrimination is endemic on the factory floor. Hence, to praise such jobs as providing an opportunity for women's emancipation would mean only telling half of the story.[9]

The Ali Enterprises fire was followed by two other factory accidents in Bangladesh: the Tazreen Fashions fire in November 2012, which killed around 100 workers, and the Rana Plaza building collapse in April 2020, which left over 1000 workers dead and even more seriously injured for life.[10] Of course, prior to these incidents, labour rights groups like the Clean Clothes Campaign had been warning about fire and building safety risks in the industry for many years.[11] And still, bad fire and building safety conditions are only one of many symptoms of the exploitative nature of globalised production chains in the textile industry. Wages below the minimum needed to live, excessive overtime, a lack of social benefits, systematic repression of workplace organising and unionisation, as well as gender discrimination and gender-based harassment are the daily realities for many workers in globalised value chains.[12] Although these issues were much discussed by workers' rights groups before the 2012–2013 spate of factory disasters in South Asia, they had been largely ignored by the majority of consumers in the Global North. The three disasters were so emblematic of the industry's systemic problems, however, that they made it impossible for a larger public in Europe and North America to continue to avoid the fact that workers in South Asia and elsewhere risk their lives to produce their clothes.

---

[8]Orsenna (2007).

[9]Hossain (2012). Interestingly, weavers in the cotton mills of nineteenth century Britain were also predominantly women and child labour was common. Beckert (2014), pp. 188 f., 191 f.

[10]Clean Clothes Campaign, Rana Plaza, www.cleanclothes.org/campaigns/past/rana-plaza (last accessed 12 September 2020).

[11]Clean Clothes Campaign (2005).

[12]Anner (2020); Clean Clothes Campaign, Pakistan. Country Report, 2015.

2.2 *The Law of Global Value Chains*

The key feature of our current economic system is the externalisation of costs.[13] Over the last 30 years, the predominant model of the hierarchically structured company with an almost entirely integrated value chain (from the iron mine to the finished automobile), has been replaced by the production model of value chains that arose in the 1980s.[14] Legal obligations to respect labour rights and environmental legislation present as "costs" in this production-model logic, and the law of globalised value chains organises the outsourcing of these costs. On the one hand, international trade law ensures that transnational companies can extract their profits and maintain access to markets and resources. On the other hand, responsibility is reduced and diffused, especially through commercial and company law.

2.2.1 International Trade Law

At the macro level, free trade and liberalisation policies are realised through the international treaty provisions of the World Trade Organization and, increasingly, through regional or bilateral free trade agreements. The reduction and removal of tariffs and trade quotas in the mid-1990s was the determining factor for the rapid increase in textile production that occurred in countries like Bangladesh, India and China. While this enabled these countries to even more grow export-oriented textile industries, it also enabled the EU and US to increasingly outsource their production in order to cut production costs. In this regard, international trade agreements have enabled the access of international buyers to both foreign production sights as well as foreign markets in which to sell their goods. At the same time, a set of laws that includes international investment treaties, intellectual property laws, and international finance regulation, ensures that resources and profits are protected and can be extracted from these foreign markets.[15] This body of international economic law has robust and effective enforcement mechanisms, such as the much criticised arbitration procedures for alleged violations of bilateral investment treaties or patent rights.[16] These laws and arbitration procedures primarily protect the needs of transnational companies for structured trade processes and extensive profit accumulation, while employee and environmental concerns are neglected and even framed as illegal infringements on legitimate property rights. Different authors have shown that this role of international economic law—in enabling access to human labour and natural resources while at the same time protecting the extraction of profits—is a

[13]Brand and Wissen (2017), pp. 30 ff., 63 f.; Lessenich (2018).

[14]Gereffi et al. (2005), pp. 78 ff.; Barrientos et al. (2016), pp. 1214–1219.

[15]Horst (2015), Mgbeoji (2006) and Rahmatian (2009).

[16]An overview can be found at: Kaleck and Saage-Maaß (2016), pp. 49 ff.

continuation of the racist, colonial origins and traditions of international law more broadly.[17]

2.2.2 Commercial and Company Law

While neoliberal thinkers generally claim to advocate for deregulation and the reduction of legal provisions, neoliberal production via global value chains is entirely structured and enabled through law.[18] The law, usually commercial law, organises business practices and, in particular, secures the economic interests of the powerful actors at the top of complex value chains.

Companies organise the global expansion of their activities through the establishment of subsidiaries and a complex system of supply relationships.[19] It is not uncommon today for corporations to have several hundred subsidiaries and even more suppliers. Anything from 100% ownership of subsidiaries to the participation of several other companies and financial investors is an option.

The externalisation of liability risks within a corporate group is primarily achieved through the dogmatic figure of the so-called separation principle, i.e. limited liability.[20] This company law concept exists in almost all legal systems across the globe and establishes that the subsidiaries in a corporate group are to be regarded as legal entities separate from and completely independent of the parent company.[21] This limitation of legal responsibility within the corporate group creates what can be best described as "organised irresponsibility," as local producers often cannot be held to account for harms caused due to practical reasons, while the corporations that hold shares in or exercise a position of economic dominance over the local producing company are, legally, not responsible. In reality, this is often legal fiction. Although an individual group's subsidiaries are, from a legal point of view, independent and not bound by instructions of the group's top management, actual corporate governance structures often entail tight, hierarchical organisation. They also frequently include supervisory and directive powers for the group's board of directors with regard to the group's subsidiaries.

According to the World Bank, roughly 80% of global production is created in supply chains.[22] In this context, another legal fiction becomes relevant, as both

[17]Chimni (2013), pp. 251 ff.; Anghie (2004) shows that investment treaties were closed in the moment that the former colonies gained sovereignty of their resources.

[18]Britton-Purdy et al. (2020). On the particular role of lawyers in this, see Pistor (2019).

[19]For a definition and distinction between supply chains and supplier networks, see Plank et al. (2009).

[20]Baars (2019).

[21]A comprehensive description of the problem can be found in Wagner (2016), pp. 717 ff.

[22]"Global investment and trade are inextricably intertwined through the international production networks of firms investing in productive assets worldwide and trading inputs and outputs in cross-border value chains of various degrees of complexity. Such value chains (intra-firm or inter-firm, regional or global in nature, and commonly referred to as Global Value Chains or GVCs) shaped by

national and international contract law are based on the principle of "equality of the contractual partners."[23] Contractual supply relationships are realised though diverse legal constellations. From long-term business relationships with the manufacturers of highly specialised and technically sophisticated products to volatile order placement via auction platforms, many variants, and also a combination of different supplier relationships, is conceivable.[24] As the organisational set-up of value chains is mainly driven by the goal of cost reduction and profit maximisation, workers' rights to appropriate remuneration, social security, and environmental protection are cost factors left up to the supplier. As a result, neglecting regulations that protect the interests of the common good turns out to be a favourable cost factor in the contractual relationship between local producers and transnational corporations. The interests of employees or communities negatively affected in the process of production would only function as cost-raising factors and have no legal relevance in the contractual relationship.[25]

A recent example of the great social and economic inequality between formally equal contracting parties in global supply chains in the textile industry could be seen when consumer demand dropped drastically due to Covid-19 lockdowns in March and April 2020, and international buyers unilaterally cancelled orders and refused to even pay for already produced goods.[26] Often, these cancellations were not even backed by the international buyers' own contracts, let alone force majeure provisions in national or international contract law.[27] Still, international buyers were able to cancel the orders because they knew their suppliers would hardly object, being in desperate need for the next order once the crisis subsides. As a result, millions of workers in Asia lost their jobs within weeks and were left without savings or social protection schemes. Even if factory owners would have wanted to do otherwise, they work on such tight margins that they were unable to pay workers once the international brands and retailers refused to pay for the already-produced goods.[28] While international buyers make significant profit, they leave so little to their producers and their workers that any friction in market demand leads to social disaster.

TNCs [transnational corporations] account for some 80% of global trade." UNCTAD, World Investment Report (2013), www.unctad.org/en/PublicationsLibrary/wir2013_en.pdf (last accessed 12 September 2020).

[23]Gathii and Odumosu-Ayanu (2015), pp. 70 f.

[24]Gereffi (2005), pp. 1 ff.

[25]Gathii and Odumosu-Ayanu (2015) and Britton-Purdy et al. (2020).

[26]Nova and Zeldenrust (2020); Lane M, 150,000 have lost jobs in Cambodia garment sector. Apparel Insider, 30 June 2020, www.apparelinsider.com/150000-have-lost-jobs-in-cambodia-garment-sector/ (last accessed 12 September 2020); Garment exporter Bangladesh faces $6 billion hit as top retailers cancel. Reuters, 31 March 2020, www.reuters.com/article/health-coronavirus-bangladesh-exports/garment-exporter-bangladesh-faces-6-billion-hit-as-top-retailers-cancel-idUKKBN21I2R9 (last accessed 12 September 2020).

[27]Vogt et al. (2020).

[28]Anner (2020).

2.3 Critical Perspectives on the Law

Law's function in engineering global value chains in the interest of multinational companies and economic elites has been identified as a typical characteristic of law in general and, more specifically, has been the subject of Marxist critiques of law for quite a long time. According to Otto Kirchheimer, for instance, law is a "guarantee of the existing social order."[29] In a similar vein, Franz Neumann asserts that law corresponds with the interests of the ruling classes and the bourgeois way of life, as it safeguards property and private autonomy, and, above all, ensures the calculability of commodity production and trade.[30] Critical legal studies scholars have shown that law disguises exactly these power dynamics, as it creates a notion of neutrality and gives the impression that the existing order is both just and fair.[31] A wide range of authors have also identified the abstract legal subject as problematic.[32] Judith Butler, for example, points out that the limitation of the language of law forces us to describe the abuse of power as a violation of rights, which means that a rights violation can only be framed as an act attributable to an individual subject. Hence, by focusing on the legal subject, the complex institutional structures leading to abuse and harm are made invisible.[33] For Christoph Menke, meanwhile, the pitfall of our current legal system lies more fundamentally in the creation of (individual) rights as such. In his assessment "rights" in bourgeois societies are privatised into something pre-political; they are taken away from the community of citizens and given to the individual.[34]

2.4 Legal Avenues for Those Affected by Human Rights Violations in Global Supply Chains

One can find support for these critical perspectives on the law in the Ali Enterprises case, in which the neutrality of contract law, the fiction of equality between the contractual parties, and the fiction of separate legal entities disguise the actual power imbalance between the international retailers and brands on one side, and their supplying manufacturers and the actual factory workers on the other. The fact that four people had to bring a claim against KiK alleging violations of their individual

[29]Kirchheimer (1976), p. 78.

[30]Neumann (1980), p. 246.

[31]Kennedy (1997), p. 311; Gabel and Harris (1982–1983), p. 372.

[32]Critics range from such diverse authors as the legal theorist of the Russian Revolution, Eugeny Paschukanis, to post-structuralist scholars like Judith Butler.

[33]Butler (2006), p. 125. For more on how law produces the notion of a subject before the law as a naturalised basic assumption and subsequently conceals this production and, thus, its own regulatory hegemony, see Butler (1991), p. 17.

[34]Menke (2018a).

rights clearly neglects the complex social and economic interdependencies in which these rights violations occurred. More fundamentally, the idea of "property" entailing a private right to subject nature and humans to an exploitive production process can be described as the underlying principle of global value chains.

As law creates the externalisation and fragmentation of responsibility in global value chains, it, in turn, creates serious obstacles for affected persons in terms of demanding respect for their labour and human rights. And still, as the production along supply chains creates relationships between actors, like workers in supplying factories and managers in lead firms or auditing companies, new potential claims for workers and other affected groups arise. In the litigation around the Ali Enterprises case, a range of these options were used.

2.4.1 Multiple Jurisdictions

As companies have extended their economic activities across different jurisdictions, affected persons have gained, at least in theory, the ability to take action against the various actors involved in the production process in the different jurisdictions in which they are incorporated. For example, as described by Faisal Siddiqi in this book, complaints about working conditions at a production site can be directed against the actual factory owners, against local authorities responsible for monitoring industrial health and safety standards, or against local certification service providers. Apart from the practical and legal hurdles that workers face in their local legal systems, as Faisal Siddiqi and Palvasha Shahab both describe in their chapters, local courts usually do not have jurisdiction over companies incorporated abroad. Yet, it can also be an option to start legal proceedings in the jurisdiction where the actors along the production process are located. In this case, claims are directed against the parent company of the corporate group, the buying company at the end of the supply chain, or the certification companies located in Europe or North America, as was done in the legal proceedings against KiK in Germany and against RINA in Italy. In these jurisdictions, victims of corporate abuse may choose between civil litigation, to ask for monetary compensation for harm and suffering, and criminal procedures, which will investigate the responsibility of managers and the company as such, and potentially sanction individual corporate managers and the legal entity.[35] Obviously, all of these legal venues are far from easily accessible for potential claimants in global value chains, but they exist at all and that they also give those exploited in supply chains an option for transnational legal interventions.

In line with the general trend towards more flexible forms of regulation and new instruments of implementation in international as well as national law, there are a

[35]Meeran (2011); Kaleck and Saage-Maaß (2010); Tixeire C, Can the Lafarge case be a game changer? French multinational company indicted for international crimes in Syria. Business and Human Rights Centre Blog, www.business-humanrights.org/en/can-the-lafarge-case-be-a-game-changer-french-multinational-company-indicted-for-international-crimes-in-syria (last accessed 12 September 2020).

number of soft law standards and complaint mechanisms that deal with and define companies' responsibilities for human rights in their global value chains.[36] The most important soft law standards are the OECD Guidelines for Multinational Enterprises and the UN Guiding Principles on Business and Human Rights (UNGPs). The OECD guidelines are accompanied by a non-judicial complaint mechanism designed to mediate between complainants and the company. As required by the UNGPs, companies are also increasingly setting up their own internal complaint mechanisms.[37] While the effectiveness of these complaint procedures can be debated, soft law standards and their multiple complaint mechanisms nevertheless extend the range of possible forums that can be used by those affected.[38]

2.4.2 Expansion of the Legal Doctrines on Parent Company and Supply Chain Liability

Despite the dogmatic fictions described above that create a lack of responsibility in global production processes, there is increasing academic debate and case law on extending the tort law liability of transnational companies. The starting point of these discussions are cases in which English courts recognised that parent companies can be liable under tort law for damages caused by subsidiaries abroad, when the harm was foreseeable, when there was sufficient proximity between the parties, and when the imposition of a duty could be seen as fair, just, and reasonable.[39] In the most recent *Vedanta* decision, the UK Supreme Court even held that public corporate social responsibility (CSR) commitments and company policies are relevant in creating and defining the duties a parent company bears with respect to preventing its subsidiary from causing human rights and environmental harms.[40] Subsequently, authors have pointed out that, in accordance with the case law on *Chandler v. Cape*

[36]The term soft law includes resolutions of the UN General Assembly, codes of conduct, guidelines, and recommendations of international organisations, but also declarations and final acts of international organisations.

[37]In doing so, they are following a stipulation of the UNGPs, which also call on companies to introduce complaint mechanisms as part of a "smart mix" of state and private regulations. UN Guiding Principles on Business and Human Rights (UN doc A/HRC/17/31).

[38]Krajewski et al. (2016).

[39]Van Dam (2010), pp. 221 ff.; Meeran (2011).

[40]In Vedanta, the UK Supreme Court held, that "the parent may incur the relevant responsibility to third parties if, in published materials, it holds itself out as exercising that degree of supervision and control of its subsidiaries, even if it does not in fact do so. In such circumstances its very omission may constitute the abdication of a responsibility which it has publicly undertaken." The court also held that "everything depends on the extent to which, and the way in which, the parent availed itself of the opportunity to take over, intervene in, control, supervise or advise the management of the relevant operations (including land use) of the subsidiary. All that the existence of a parent subsidiary relationship demonstrates is that the parent had such an opportunity." *Vedanta Resources PLC v Lungowe* [2019] UKSC20, para. 53 and 49.

plc, *Vedanta*, and others, certain basic assumptions of company law must also be questioned with regard to supplier companies.[41]

2.4.3 Liability of Social Auditors

Social auditing companies belong to the multitude of actors in global value chains. They often replace state-run labour inspections and are a tool for multinational companies to ensure that their codes of conduct on labour rights are adhered to.[42] Corporate codes of conduct have been the textile industry's reaction to consumer campaigns in North America and Europe scandalising the discrepancy between the shiny image of textile and sports brands in the Global North and the horrifying reality of working conditions in the Global South.[43] KiK, just like many other brands and retailers in the textile industry, created a code of conduct in which it declares its commitment to labour standards like health and workplace safety. In order to ensure compliance, brands and retailers usually employ social auditing firms that visit local supplier factories to verify that they respect the code of conduct. These audits often fail to accurately describe the situation in factories, however, due both to the methodological restrictions of their approach, as well as to conflicts of interest and corruption. As such, social audits serve the purpose of diffusing responsibility and giving multinational brands and retailers the possibility of pointing to an audit report to claim that they had done everything in their power to avoid the disaster. The auditing company, in turn, can hide behind the technicalities of their mandate, which restricts their assessment and, hence, their responsibility. This mutual finger-pointing further contributes to the system of organised irresponsibility mentioned above. Currently, it is being discussed whether auditors should be liable under criminal or civil law for audit reports that fail to report adequately or truthfully on workplace safety and labour law violations in supplier companies.[44] In particular, the question has been raised as to whether the concepts of third-party beneficiary rights or other tort law concepts can also be applied to social auditors.[45]

---

[41] Heinen (2018), pp. 96 f.; Heinlein (2018).

[42] As described by Palvasha Shahab in this volume, the international finance institutions' push to systematic privatisation and a slim state has meant that the capacities of labour inspectorates in South Asia have been minimised.

[43] Klein (2005).

[44] Terwindt and Saage-Maaß (2017) On the liability of social auditors in the textile industry. Friedrich-Ebert-Stiftung (ed) International Policy Analysis, www.library.fes.de/pdf-files/iez/13041.pdf (last accessed 12 September 2020).

[45] Glinski and Rott (2019).

3 The Ali Enterprises Factory Disaster and the Litigation That Followed

In the following, I will show how the different legal interventions in the Ali Enterprises case not only exemplify law's shortcomings in protecting the interests of workers in global value chains, but also how they exemplify the various avenues in global supply chains through which workers can demand redress and compensation.

On the evening of 11 September 2012, a fire broke out on the ground floor of the Ali Enterprises factory.[46] It spread quickly to the other floors and many workers were not able to leave the building quickly enough due to the lack of accessible fire exits and the failure of the factory's fire alarm system. At least 258 workers died in the fire and several dozen more were wounded. The main buyer of the factory was the German retailer KiK. According to the company's own claims, it had been purchasing around 70% of the factory's production for a period of 5 years.

The German public came to know about the Ali Enterprises fire mainly through an interview published by *Der Spiegel* with KiK's corporate social responsibility manager.[47] In the interview, the manager—expressing dismay about the disaster—described the relationship between KiK and Ali Enterprises as close and long-lasting. He explained how KiK was keen to exercise its corporate social responsibility through the creation of a code of conduct for its suppliers, expecting them to respect health and safety regulations and other core labour standards. Compliance with these standards was to be ensured through on-site visits of company representatives and social auditing firms. In the course of the litigation after the fire, KiK also produced four social audit reports that had been commissioned by the company between 2007 and 2011. Only the first one in 2007 had shown any concern regarding fire safety, while the others did not reflect any major insufficiencies. Additionally, just a few weeks before the deadly fire broke out, on 21 August 2012, the Italian auditing firm RINA SpA issued the factory a SA-8000 safety certificate, said to be one of leading social certification standards for factories and organisations worldwide. RINA had been hired by the Ali Enterprises factory owners. Its certification of the factory was preceded by an audit report, which was approved by RINA's technical committee on 3 August 2012. RINA had selected and hired the Pakistani service provider RI&CA to conduct the audit. After its verification of the audit report, RINA certified the facility. In the aftermath of the Ali Enterprises fire, the SA-8000 scheme-holder, the Social Accountability Initiative, conducted an

[46]For a detailed reconstruction of the fire see: Forensic Architecture, The Ali Enterprises Factory Fire, www.forensic-architecture.org/investigation/the-ali-enterprises-factory-fire (last accessed 12 September 2020).

[47]Kazim H and Klawitter N, Zuverlässiger Lieferant. Der Spiegel, 22 October 2012, www.spiegel.de/spiegel/print/d-89234400.html (last accessed on 12 September 2020).

investigation into the incident and concluded that there had been several serious shortcomings and even fraudulent behaviour in the certification process.[48]

3.1 The Building of Transnational Alliances

The international labour rights movement's immediate reaction to the Ali Enterprises catastrophe in Pakistan and the two subsequent factory disasters in Bangladesh must be seen in its historic context. Over the last 30 years, the anti-globalisation and consumers' movement has developed into a well-connected network of various trade unions, research and campaigning organisations across Europe, Africa, Asia, and the Americas, with a focus on labour rights in the global textile industry. Over the years, these organisations have cooperated in different constellations on numerous campaigns to scandalise the exploitative labour conditions in textile production,[49] point out the ineffectiveness of corporate social responsibility measures,[50] and call for more robust mechanisms to ensure that brands actually contribute to the improvement of working conditions.[51] The high level of transnational interconnectedness and professionalism already existing between these trade unions and labour organisations in the Global South and Global North allowed them to respond immediately to the major textile industry disasters between September 2012 and April 2013. They quickly mobilised international media attention to the disasters and launched a global campaign demanding international fashion brands and retailers contribute—in the absence of functioning social protection schemes in Pakistan and Bangladesh—to compensation funds for workers. It was their ability to scandalise and raise attention around the issue which created the unprecedented global outcry and the immense pressure on brands that eventually led to the Accord on Fire and Building Safety in Bangladesh and, later on, to the Rana Plaza Compensation Agreement.[52]

At this point in time, the European Center for Constitutional and Human Rights had already done quite some research and thinking about the legal arguments that one would need to make to hold a European company responsible in court for human rights violations in its supply chain.[53] While most European and US litigators had

[48]Social Accountability International (2013), Report Addendum on Fire Safety in Pakistan, p. 16.

[49]Klein (2005), pp. 339 ff.

[50]Locke et al. (2006).

[51]Clean Clothes Campaign (2005).

[52]See chapter by Ben Vanpeperstraete in this volume.

[53]When initially building up its Business and Human Rights program between 2008 and 2010, ECCHR conducted an extensive mapping exercise and held a series of conferences and regional workshops with activists and lawyers from South Asia, Western and Southern Africa, and Latin America. As a conclusion, it determined that labour exploitation in global value chains was one of the most pressing human rights issues where European companies played a major role. Lessons learned from this process can be found in Saage-Maaß (2014).

previously concentrated on holding parent companies liable for the human rights violations committed by their foreign subsidiaries, ECCHR had begun, since 2010, to use different legal tools to approach the topic of labour exploitation in global supply chains. This included filing consumer claims alleging that a company's advertisement of its code of conduct constituted misleading advertisement,[54] and by filing OECD complaints against European cotton trading companies.[55]

After the previously mentioned *Spiegel* article was published in late September 2012, it was clear that the constellation of facts revealed would potentially allow workers to directly go to court in Germany against the retailer KiK. While the Ali Enterprises incident was extraordinary in its cruelty and devastation, it also displayed several crucial factors for a potential legal claim. There was a clear violation of the right to life and health, which translates into civil law as a tort, and an undeniable connection to both the retailer KiK in Germany and the auditing company RINA in Italy, which is often difficult to establish. As KiK had admitted to being the major buyer of the Ali Enterprises factory, there was also a reasonable indication of control on the part of KiK.

In autumn of 2012, ECCHR learned that its partner organisation medico international (medico) was supporting the National Trade Union Federation (NTUF) in Karachi in its efforts to organise the survivors and families of the deceased from the Ali Enterprises fire. Right away, medico, NTUF and ECCHR started discussing the possibilities for a common legal effort to hold the German brand KiK and the Italian firm RINA to account. Representatives of medico and ECCHR travelled to Karachi for the first time in February 2013, where we held long deliberations with NTUF, the Pakistan Institute of Labour Education and Research (PILER), as well as groups of survivors and family members of the deceased. Over the next 5 years, several trips followed, occurring almost every 6 months. As described by Saeeda Khatoon, Zehra Khan, and Nasir Mansoor in their contributions to this book, the surviving workers and family members of the deceased founded the Ali Enterprises Factory Fire Affectees Association (AEFFAA) with the help of NTUF and the Home Based Women Workers Federation (HBWWF).

As a first step in the cooperation, ECCHR assisted initial public interest litigation (PIL) proceedings led by advocate Faisal Siddiqi before the High Court of Sindh by submitting an amicus brief in 2014. The amicus brief outlined Pakistani authorities'

---

[54] ECCHR initiated a civil action brought by Hamburg's consumer protection agency asking Lidl to stop advertising its code of conduct, arguing that it was misleading consumers to believe that products available at Lidl Markets were produced in conditions respecting workers' rights, as proclaimed by the company's code of conduct. ECCHR, Complaint re Fair Working Conditions in Bangladesh. Lidl forced to back down, www.ecchr.eu/en/case/complaint-re-fair-working-conditions-in-bangladesh-lidl-forced-to-back-down/ (last accessed 12 September 2020).

[55] ECCHR filed OECD complaints against seven companies in France, the UK, Germany and Switzerland for their alleged role in trading cotton from Uzbekistan, which was known to be produced through state-organised, forced child labour at that time. ECCHR, The Cases against European Cotton Traders, www.ecchr.eu/en/case/the-cases-against-european-cotton-traders/ (last accessed 12 September 2020).

obligation not only to investigate the responsibility of Pakistani actors, but also the role of the international retail and auditing companies. The next step in building the cooperation involved holding a series of workshops and assemblies with the AEFFAA, in which we discussed the possibilities and risks of a transnational legal claim against KiK and RINA. For the AEFFAA, as well as NTUF, medico and ECCHR, it was clear that the possibility of filing a civil compensation lawsuit was not primarily about gaining the much-needed compensation. Given the cost restraints, only a handful of victims could realistically bring a claim and, as such, it would hardly lead to compensation for all. The option of going to court in Germany against KiK offered the possibility to claim the rights of workers in global value chains rather than asking companies for a humanitarian gesture. It was seen as a chance to make a political claim for justice.

The risks of this approach were also obvious: lengthy procedures and slim chances of actually winning could exhaust the claimants and eventually leave the whole group disillusioned. The claimants would also expose themselves to the public, with all the pressures that this might entail. The decision-making process around whether to pursue the litigation against KiK or not included several meetings and workshops in Karachi and online. In the end, the AEFFAA nominated a group of 10 people who they felt could represent the whole group and their wider claim for justice, and who could also stand the pressure of the legal proceedings.[56] Out of that group, ECCHR selected four people, as it was not possible to cover the litigation costs for all 10. As pre-trial negotiations with KiK stalled in the winter of 2014/2015, the AEFFAA together with ECCHR, NTUF and medico eventually decided to engage in the civil litigation against KiK. In March 2015, the surviving worker Muhammad Hanif, along with Muhammad Jabir, Abdul Aziz, and Saeeda Khatoon, all parents of deceased workers, brought civil action against KiK before the Regional Court of Dortmund, demanding 30,000 euros each in damages for pain and suffering.

While ECCHR, NTUF, medico and AEFFAA engaged in the civil litigation against KiK in Germany, filed a criminal complaint against RINA officials in Italy, and, later on, also lodged an OECD complaint in Italy, other organisations like PILER,[57] the Clean Clothes Campaign, and the IndustriALL Global Union focused their efforts on negotiating a long-term compensation fund in accordance with the standards of the International Labour Organization, along the same lines as the Rana Plaza Compensation Agreement. Controversial discussions occurred between those who saw the ILO negotiations as the best route to pursue and those who preferred to opt for the lawsuit, as some feared the lawsuit would harm the negotiation strategy at the ILO and vice versa. ECCHR made a deliberate decision to

[56]Due to procedural restrictions in Germany, ECCHR did not see it as feasible to represent all 250 families in the civil litigation.

[57]PILER had accomplished an important first step in negotiating with KiK by achieving US $1 million in immediate relief for workers at the end 2012. For more details, see the chapter by Faisal Siddiqi in this volume.

put significant energy into the process of reaching a common understanding among all the different actors. A division among the groups collectively fighting for workers' rights would have been a major defeat of the groups' common ideals and would have weakened the broader struggle of workers to the benefit of companies. After many travels between Europe and Pakistan, and after many meetings and long discussions, all of the parties finally reached an agreement on how to work together in a way that would allow both strategies to mutually reinforce each other.

The "legal route," we decided, would aim to provide an accelerating effect on the ILO negotiations by serving as an implicit incentive for the company to engage in them. The lawsuit deliberately asked only for compensation to cover pain and suffering, while the ILO negotiations demanded compensation to cover the loss of income and medical costs.[58] In this way, the lawsuit in Germany did not provide KiK with an argument for opting out of the ILO compensation talks. Meanwhile, those negotiating with the ILO actively endorsed the legal case as an important additional step.[59] Over time, it seems that the pending lawsuit did indeed enhance KiK's willingness to agree to the terms of compensation suggested by the ILO: one week after the Dortmund court granted legal aid and legal standing to the Pakistani claimants and allowed the case into the discovery phase (*Beweisaufnahme*),[60] KiK agreed to pay an additional US$5.15 million into the ILO Ali Enterprises compensation fund, breaking the almost 2-year deadlock in which the ILO negotiations had been stalled.

3.2 The Litigation Against KiK: Procedure and Key Legal Arguments

According to both Paragraph 17 ZPO (*Zivilprozessordnung*, the German Code on Civil Procedure) and Article 4 of the Brussels I Regulation, the Regional Court of Dortmund (Landgericht Dortmund) had jurisdiction over the case. In accordance with Article 4(1) of the Rome II Regulation, the applicable law in this transborder litigation was Pakistani civil law, which is strongly influenced by Indian and English jurisprudence.[61] Following the established English case law, the claimants argued that KiK breached its duty of care towards the employees of the Ali Enterprises

[58]For more details on the compensation funds see the chapter by Ben Vanpeperstraete in this volume.

[59]See www.media.business-humanrights.org/media/documents/files/documents/PR_Pakistan_KiK_lawsuit_2019_09_10_eng.pdf; Joint Press Release, 29 November 2018: Ben Vanpeperstraete from Clean Clothes Campaign makes clear: "The proceedings against KiK in Germany have contributed significantly to the compensation settlement." www.ecchr.eu/en/press-release/hearing-in-kik-case-in-front-of-regional-court-in-germany/ (last accessed 12 September 2020).

[60]This should not be mistaken with the discovery phase in UK or US law. See: Saage-Maaß (2021).

[61]*Khan v. Haleem*, (2012) CLD (SC) 6 (2011), 8 (Khilji Arif Hssain, J., concurring) (Pak.); *Khanzada v. Sherin*, 1996 CLC 1440 (Peshwar) (Pak.), citing Indian law authoritatively in a case alleging medical malpractice.

factory.[62] The requirements for a duty of care are largely based on the decisions in *Caparo v. Dickman* and *Chandler v. Cape*,[63] according to which, a duty of care is established under the following cumulative conditions: the harm that occurred was foreseeable, there was sufficient proximity between the parties, and the imposition of a duty can be seen as fair, just, and reasonable.[64] The Regional Court of Dortmund was asked to assess the relevant duty of care and thereby had to assess the nature of the relationship between KiK and Ali Enterprises, the applicable industry standards of CSR, the relevant standards for safety audits, and KiK's duty in relation to such audits.[65]

The claimants argued that there was a clear economic dependence between KiK and Ali Enterprises, as KiK had purchased almost three quarters of Ali Enterprises' production output over the 5-year period preceding the fire. The claimants also argued that such an economic dependence created KiK's ability to influence and control the health and fire safety conditions under which Ali Enterprises ought to have conducted its business in Pakistan. The claimants further constructed KiK's obligation through a review of its 2009 code of conduct[66] and a statement by KiK's managing director weeks after the factory fire that "the monitoring of adherence to safety and fire prevention is obligatory for us as a buyer."[67] As KiK's code of conduct was incorporated into the terms and conditions of every purchasing order, the claimants argued that the company's public pledges on safe and ethical working

[62]Terwindt et al. (2018), p. 276.

[63]*Caparo Industries plc v. Dickman* [1992] 2 AC 605; *Chandler v. Cape Plc* [2012] EWCA Civ 525 (25 April 2012).

[64]Paragraph 80 of the *Chandler* appeal's decision provides key indicators of when a duty of care is owed by a multinational corporation parent, namely when: (1) the businesses of the parent and subsidiary are, in a relevant respect, the same; (2) the parent has or ought to have superior knowledge on some relevant aspect of health and safety in the particular industry; (3) the subsidiary's system of work is unsafe, which the parent knew or ought to have known; and (4) the parent knew or ought to have foreseen that the subsidiary or its employees would rely on its using its superior knowledge for the employee's protection. The Court also clarifies that for the purpose of (4), it is not necessary to show that the parent is in the practice of intervening in the health and safety policies of the subsidiary. Instead, the court should look at the relationship between the companies more widely. It may be enough to show that the parent has a practice of intervening in the trading operations of the subsidiary, for example, in production and funding issues.

[65]Terwindt et al. (2018), p. 268.

[66]Here, KiK stated in the section titled "Standard for Employment" in regards to "Health and Safety at Work" in its supply chain that: "The workplace and the practice of the work must not harm the employees' or workers' health and safety. A safe and clean working environment shall be provided. Occupational health and safety practices shall be promoted, which prevent accidents and injury in the course of work or as a result of the operation of employer facilities. These safety practices and procedures must be communicated to the employees as well as the workers; they have to be trained in effective usage [...]." KiK Textilien und Non-Food GmbH, Code of Conduct, revised version, 1 August 2009, p. 3.

[67]KiK Textilien und Non-Food GmbH, Statement on the Panorama Program of 6 December 2012, translation by the author.

conditions caused legal obligations: self-regulation must lead to legal obligation.[68] Finally, the claimants also argued for vicarious liability, which provides for the strict liability of the employer, but also of the principal in a relationship "akin to employment." The concept of vicarious liability under common law is more flexible than it is under German law, as it is not necessarily based on a formal contractual relationship but instead rests on the overall circumstances of a business relationship between two parties examined through a five-factor lens.[69]

KiK defended itself by restating its corporate social responsibility narrative, which presents the company as truly committed to improving working conditions in its suppliers' factories and as taking concrete efforts to achieve this end. At the same time, KiK denied any form of liability, arguing that, as a fully independent legal entity, Ali Enterprises was the only duty bearer for its employees' safety. KiK admitted to having sent its own personnel to visit the production site, to having commissioned several social audits of the Ali Enterprises factory, and to having obliged its suppliers to sign the company's code of conduct. Despite all of this, KiK claimed to have no ability to influence, let alone control, the fire safety standards of the Ali Enterprises factory. Referring to the social audit reports that KiK itself had commissioned, which displayed little to no deficiencies in fire safety, the company additionally claimed that they could not have possibly known about the real state of fire safety and, therefore, could not be legally liable. KiK insisted that corporate social responsibility measures do not imply any legal responsibility. The social audit reports served as a proof of the fact that KiK was under the assumption that general working conditions, and fire safety in particular, were in accordance with their code of conduct. KiK's legal briefs follow the classic industry narrative: "We are concerned about workers' rights and do all we can, but we do all of this purely voluntarily, and take no responsibility."

While the claimants in the KiK case had negotiated a waiver on the statute of limitations in pre-trial negotiations, KiK claimed in the litigation that the case was time-barred under Pakistani law. In a decision based on the expert opinion of a British law professor it had commissioned, the Dortmund court eventually held that the negotiated waiver was invalid because the case was governed by Pakistani law, which does not provide for the possibility of such a waiver. The claimants' attempt to argue that the waiver was governed by German law, because both the representatives of the claimants and the defendant were German lawyers using German legal language, and therefore implicitly agreeing on the application of German law, did not succeed. As a result, the court only superficially dealt with the question of which duties of care a buyer may owe towards the employees of a subsidiary.[70]

---

[68] Beckers (2017), pp. 15 ff.

[69] *E v. English Province of Our Lady of Charity* [2012] EWCA (Civ) 938, [2013] 2 W.L.R. 958, 19, 70 ff.

[70] LG Dortmund, 7 O 95/15, Beschluss 10 January 2019.

3.3 The Legal Interventions Against the Social Auditing Firm RINA

Parallel to the legal action against KiK, Italian lawyers filed criminal charges against the managing director of RINA on behalf of the AEFFAA, NTUF and ECCHR in 2014. The allegation was that top managers of RINA, who had allowed for the issuance of the SA-8000 certificate weeks before the fire in 2012, were liable under Italian criminal law for the crime of giving false certification and falsification of documents.[71] The investigating judge in Turin opened the criminal proceedings and ordered expert opinions on the causes of the fire, but then handed the case over to the public prosecutor in Genoa for jurisdictional reasons. There, the investigative judge closed the proceeding in December 2018 after an appeal,[72] holding that it would be hard to argue in court that the issuing of the SA-8000 certificate had been causal to the fire. In her view, RINA Services could not have prevented the factory's continued operation in the absence of adequate safety conditions for workers, and therefore RINA could not have prevented the fire. With regard to the RINA top manager under investigation, the judge did not see sufficient evidence to indicate that he had been aware of the alleged falsification of the audit report, which was the basis for the issuance of the SA-8000 certificate. Furthermore, in her assessment, RINA managers did not commit the crime of giving a "false statement," as the certification was not legally mandatory, but only issued upon the voluntary request of individual companies, mostly driven by market demand.

As RINA's activities are not only subject to Italian criminal jurisdiction, but also to the OECD Guidelines for Multinational Enterprises because Italy is an OECD member state, the above-mentioned organisations, together with a broader international coalition, filed a complaint against RINA with the OECD National Contact Point in Italy in September 2018. While the National Contact Point treated the complaint in a very swift but thorough manner, RINA management also proved to be very reluctant to accept any responsibility under the soft law standard of the OECD guidelines. The parties, therefore, did not reach an agreement in the negotiations.

---

[71] Art. 477 Codice Penale (Italian Criminal Code): falsità materiale; Art. 479, 480, 481, 482 Codice Penale: falsità ideologica.

[72] Tribunale de Genova, Ufficio del Guidice per le Indagini Preliminari, Decreto di Fissazione dell' Undienza a seguito di opposozione—art. 409 c2 c3 c.p.p., N 3240/16/N 10400/16, 11 December 2018.

4 Objectives and Achievements of the Transnational Legal Interventions in the Wake of the Ali Enterprises Fire

So, what were the effects of the transnational litigation in the wake of the 2012 Ali Enterprises fire? What did the surviving workers of the Ali Enterprises fire and the family members of the deceased achieve? Did the transnational legal interventions change any legal, social, or political realities to the advantage of workers in globalised value chains?

The self-defined objectives of those engaged with the litigation offer perhaps the best benchmark against which to measure the litigation's effects in this regard. As Saeeda Khatoon, the mother of one of the fire's victims and a representative of the AEFFAA, describes the goals of the litigation against KiK: "Our aim was not compensation, it was justice. We needed to fight for our children's safety against the international brand [KiK], to deter them from enabling this again. So that something like this does not happen to other children."[73] Meanwhile, NTUF, medico, and ECCHR claim that "in conceptualising the legal case against KiK in Germany, [they] agreed to promote the factory fire affectees' demand for compensation as a right in itself. From the beginning, we sought to frame the court case against KiK in Germany as a political statement, not just a legal dispute."[74] NTUF also sought to stress the point that working conditions in factories producing for the international market are just as exploitive as elsewhere, meaning that the struggle to organise and demand workers' rights must be fought in all workplaces throughout Pakistan. In sum, the KiK case was not just designed as legal case in the technical sense, but as a case with the wider political aim of challenging corporate irresponsibility in today's globalised capitalist economy by making the legal argument that lead firms like KiK do in fact bear legal responsibility for conditions that prevail in their supply chains.

Despite the abundance of literature describing the relationship between law, litigation, and social change, it is still difficult to find adequate parameters for measuring the effects or impact of human rights litigation.[75] Many authors describe at least three effects of strategic litigation. First, the most obvious effect is precedence-setting: when court decisions change the reading of the law and its application in the way intended by the litigators. Unlike in the continental European setting where courts have the ability to change the interpretation and application of laws, in Anglo-American legal systems court can even create law.[76] Second, court cases can help movement-building and strengthen civil society

[73]See the interview with Saeeda Khatoon by Palvasha Shahab in this volume.

[74]See chapter by Mansoor et al. in this Volume.

[75]Duffy (2018), Marshall and Hale (2014), McCann (2008) and Lobel (2003).

[76]Next to this practice of using emblematic cases to set precedents before the higher courts, Ulrike Müller has pointed out that clients can also be strategically represented in more ordinary cases, not aimed at precedence-setting, but rather serving as acts of resistance, like cases of police violence against protestors or asylum cases. Müller (2019), pp. 50–51.

organisations that pursue wider goals of social change, beyond the individual litigation.[77] Within the context of international crimes, self-empowerment is often described as a positive effect of strategic litigation, as the harmed party can regain control over the narrative of the crimes suffered and actively demand justice.[78] Finally, strategic litigation cannot only help shape legal discourses, but it can also spur wider public debates. Independent from whether a case is won or lost, filing a lawsuit can create a sense of injustice among the public, a sense that something needs to be corrected, if not through the courts then by parliamentarian action and legal reform.[79]

4.1 Self-empowerment

In September 2012, the surviving workers and the families of the deceased from the Ali Enterprises fire were not organised in any way. The one thing that connected them was the tragic experience of a workplace disaster that, for many, resulted in the loss of a family member. With the help of NTUF, however, they started to organise and support each other, both in the daily struggles of families having lost their breadwinners, and in more political work demanding justice and changes in Pakistani labour law.[80] While in the Rana Plaza incident, the affected workers did not organise in a way that would allow an organisation to speak for the wider group, the AEFFAA became, over the course of the last 8 years, an organisation recognised by the ILO, the Pakistani government, and global unions as the legitimate representative of the people affected by the Ali Enterprises fire. Although media and humanitarian relief efforts have often treated workers as passive victims and recipients of charitable assistance only interested in financial compensation,[81] the fact that the workers in the Ali Enterprises incident drove their own legal proceedings as an organisation, both on the domestic and the transnational level, helped others to see them differently, as people acting on their own behalf, refusing to be mere objects of others' policy considerations. Indeed, after the filing of the lawsuit in Germany, the AEFFAA was part of the compensation negotiations at the ILO and was able to exert substantial influence over how the negotiations developed.

Through the civil litigation against KiK in Germany, the four claimants, all workers from Pakistan, were able to force the transnational company KiK to listen

[77] McCann (2008).

[78] Duffy (2018), pp. 48–50.

[79] McCann (2008) and Lobel (2003). On the societal level, the goal behind instigating criminal trials against an alleged perpetrator of international crimes is often to create a narrative that acknowledges the grave crimes that were committed, which then enables a society to transition to a fair and just, peaceful society.

[80] See the interview with Saeeda Khatoon by Palsvahsa Shahab in this volume.

[81] Sumon et al. (2017).

and respond to their claims—simply through the exchange of legal briefs and arguments. The four Pakistani claimants became unavoidable for KiK; its CEO and other managers had to hire expensive law firms to deal with the arguments they brought forth. KiK clearly needed to be forced into this engagement and still did everything possible to avoid personal interaction. On the day of the oral hearing in Dortmund, no KiK manager showed up in the courtroom, only their legal representatives. To this day, KiK still denies Khatoon and the rest of the AEFFAA the respect of meeting with them in person.

Equally disappointing is the situation in Pakistan, where the criminal procedure around the Ali Enterprises fire obtained a first instance judgement in autumn of 2020, in which the factory owners were acquitted from responsibility and all of the criminal charges were put on clandestine criminals for arson.[82] This has shifted the public narrative in Pakistan away from workers' rights to a focus on a "terrorist attack" in which the factory owners are portrayed as the victims. On the one hand, this is a clear insult to all that the AEFFAA and others involved in the struggle for justice stand for. On the other hand, however, this verdict was based on weak evidence and included the handing down of a death sentence by one of Pakistan's notorious and much-criticised Anti-Terrorism Courts,[83] which could potentially delegitimise the whole endeavour of those trying to shift the narrative away from workers' rights.

While it is too early to determine how the narrative about the Ali Enterprises factory fire will eventually be shaped in Pakistan, it is important to note that those deprived of dignity through industrial exploitation were able to act in self-determination. They became actors in Pakistan and internationally who could no longer be ignored by those driving economic decisions in global value chains as well as in international compensation processes. For the main organisations involved in the case and the cooperation that evolved around it, the experience also had empowering effects. NTUF has reported that engaging in transnational cooperation, and in transnational litigation in particular, has helped to raise its profile in the Pakistani context, which helps it have more influence in the workers' rights movement in Pakistan. For medico and ECCHR in Germany, the chance to work so closely with the Ali Enterprises fire survivors and family members of the deceased, as well as those directly supporting them in Pakistan, not only helped guide the work on the legal case, but also gave legitimacy to the political arguments they raised.

[82] Judgement 22 September 2020, In the Anti-Terrorism Court No: VII, Central, Prison, at Karachi. (Special case No: 11 (vii)/2017) EX. No: 492, Document Code: 68D2CAF5EDFA415A0FFB9436A587BF78.

[83] Yusuf (2010).

4.2 Intervention in the Legal Discourse

The most obvious result of the strategic use of legal proceedings is to set legal precedence. To some extent, the litigation before the civil court in Dortmund did set precedence procedurally, as for the first time in Germany a court granted legal standing and legal aid to workers suing a retailer for damages that occurred in a suppliers' factory outside of Europe.[84] The fact that workers from Pakistan came to German courts asking for compensation from a well-known German retailer was perceived both by media as well as legal scholars as a novelty, and therefore, in a less technical sense, as precedence-setting. The litigation against KiK was also rather novel on an international level given that, up until this point, litigation against transnational corporations had primarily targeted parent companies for rights violations in subsidiaries. To legally hold a lead firm responsible for labour rights violations in its supply chain still remains rare.[85]

Still, several points prevent an overly positive assessment of the case's legal success. First, the merits were never decided on, as the court dismissed the case as time-barred and, hence, never dealt with the question of KiK's duties of care. Therefore, precedence could not be established on the question of international buyers' liability for rights violations in their supply chains. In addition to this, there were also downsides with regard to the claimants' access to justice. Saeeda Khatoon was the only one of the four claimants who was able to attend the first and only oral hearing before the Dortmund court in person. The other claimants were either denied visa, as EU policies aim to keep young working-class men from Pakistan out of Europe, or they were hindered from traveling by old age. In the courtroom, the presiding judge denied Khatoon the chance to speak, as he felt she would not have anything "relevant" to contribute to the legal question of statutes of limitation. As this was within the procedural rules, the legal case was debated among the legal experts before the Dortmund court. German civil procedural law allowed the case to be discussed without the voice of those affected and, in the end, offered very little material success to the four claimants from Pakistan.

One aspect that turns the analysis of the lawsuit once again to a more positive note, is that it had positive effects on KiK's willingness to engage in the ILO compensation negotiations and, eventually, to pay the workers a substantial amount

[84]A few months after the KiK case, another important case was filed: a Peruvian farmer brought a civil action against the energy corporation RWE claiming that it needed to pay for the damage on his property stemming from climate change. The case was declared admissible and went into the trail stage in November 2017, where it is still pending. OLG Hamm, I-5 U 15/17, Hinweis- und Beweisbeschluss 30 November 2017.

[85]Lobslaw, which had a supplier factory in the Rana Plaza Building, and Bureau Veritas, which audited the factory, were sued in Canada by Bangladeshi survivors of the Rana Plaza building collapse only a few weeks after the case against KiK was filed in 2015. The Ontario appeals court dismissed the case in December 2018. *Das v. George Weston Limited*, 2018 ONCA 1053 (CanLII) www.canlii.org/en/on/onca/doc/2018/2018onca1053/2018onca1053.html (last accessed 12 September 2020).

of money. The negotiation route gave the company an opportunity to showcase its commitment to corporate social responsibility without acknowledging liability. So, even if the court cases did not deliver compensation, the claimants and all other affected persons eventually received further compensation from KiK, though without recognition of legal responsibility, of course.

Further, the lawsuit in Germany had a visible impact on German legal debate. Even though the case against KiK was lost, it brought up several paradigmatic problems of liability in global value chains and made clear that more cases of this kind raising similar questions of liability are likely to come.[86] The KiK litigation also contributed to ongoing scholarly debates in which the strict application of the principle of limited liability to constellations of transnational human rights violations caused by subsidiaries is increasingly called into question, with a plea made to extend liability standards within the corporate group.[87] Authors increasingly point out that soft law standards such as the OECD guidelines or the UNGPs and their implementation in corporate practice can concretise companies' tortious duties of care also with regard to liability for damages occurring in supplier companies.[88] In particular, authors dispute which actual and normative factors constitute liability and the standards according to which the extent of liability should be determined.[89] Several authors are also working to further develop the reasoning on parent companies and lead firms' potential duties of care with regard to their foreign subsidiaries and suppliers.[90]

4.3 *Intervention in the Public Discourse*

From early on, the AEFFAA engaged with NTUF in political work, as they sought to "prevent such disasters" from happening again.[91] For many members of the AEFFAA, the transnational litigation against KiK offered a possibility to bring forth their demands for structural changes regarding workplace safety and workers' rights in local and national politics. As Khatoon reflected:

---

[86]Osieka (2014), Wagner (2016), Weller et al. (2016), Weller and Thomale (2017), Thiede and Bell (2017), Thomale and Hübner (2017), König (2017), Mansel (2018), Nordhues (2019), Wendelstein (2019), Haider (2019), Von Falkenhausen (2020) and Habersack and Ehrl (2019), two of four articles in the special issue "Human Rights Violations in Global Supply Chains" of the Journal of European Tort Law start their discussion with the example of the litigation against KiK: Spitzer (2019), pp. 95–107; Geistfeld (2019), pp. 130–165.

[87]Wagner (2016), p. 717; Wagner (2017), para. 99; König (2017), p. 611; Schall (2018), p. 479, Habersack and Ehrl (2019).

[88]Segger (2018), pp. 47 ff.; Heinen (2018), p. 87; Thomale and Hübner (2017), p. 394.

[89]Leader and Vastardis (2018), Improving Paths to Business Accountability for Human Rights Abuses: A Legal Guide. University of Essex Business and Human Rights Project.

[90]Heinen (2018), pp. 96 f.

[91]See above footnote 74.

> Due to these transnational collaborations, we were able to project the incident and talk about it on various platforms. We were able to draw attention to our cause. The money does not mean anything. It is worth nothing against the joy we would have had if our children were still around. What is money? Money gets spent. But these collaborations allowed us to not be forgotten. If we can work to save lives, prevent deaths – that, for us is the biggest motivation.[92]

NTUF, medico and ECCHR similarly saw the European public discourse as an important field of intervention and, accordingly, looked for ways to make the story of the Ali Enterprises fire and the workers' claims for justice prominent beyond the actual legal procedure. For example, they organised two speakers' tours for the plaintiffs in Germany, Geneva, and Italy in 2016 and 2018. In 2016, Saeeda Khatoon and Abdul Aziz spoke with German members of parliament in Berlin and with a secretary of state from the ministry of development. They also spoke in townhall meetings and to high school classes around Dortmund and Düsseldorf. The goal of this tour was to give journalists, politicians, and an interested public the opportunity to meet the claimants in person and to hear their claims in a direct encounter.

In the process of reaching out to a wider public to gain support for the cause of the workers and families of the AEFFAA, artists played an important role, as did journalists.[93] For example, Forensic Architecture,[94] a multidisciplinary research and media group based at Goldsmiths University of London that uses architectural techniques and technologies to investigate cases of human rights violations, created a visual reconstruction of the Ali Enterprises fire incident that helped to underline the credibility of the legal case and the legitimacy of the AEFFAA's demands.[95] The reconstruction was based on all available official records from Pakistan and used new evidentiary techniques and advanced architectural and media research. The final product was a 20-minute video that reconstructed the events at the Ali Enterprises factory on 11 September 2012, and simulated how many workers could have been evacuated if only basic fire safety precautions had been respected. The narrative of the factory fire being a terrorist attack, which caught on among the public in Pakistan,[96] never really gained traction in Germany or Europe.

In anticipation that the Dortmund court might not decide in favour of the claimants and that, ultimately, the case would not be won in court, NTUF, medico and ECCHR organised a "Week of Justice" around the oral hearing in Dortmund in

---

[92]See the interview with Saeeda Khatoon by Palsvasha Shahab in this volume.

[93]See the interview with Adeela Suleman by Palvasha Shahab in this volume for the perspective of a Pakistani artist.

[94]Forensic Architecture, www.forensic-architecture.org/ (last accessed 16 September 2020).

[95]For the film, see footnote 46; one of the major German TV channels (ZDF) broadcasted part of the reconstruction on 1 February 2020 in its 5 pm news show. Several newspapers also reported on it, for example: Dohmen C, Simulation eines Infernos. Süddeutsche Zeitung, 31 January 2018, www.sueddeutsche.de/wirtschaft/unglueck-von-karatschi-2012-simulation-eines-infernos-1.3848299?reduced=true (last accessed 16 September 2020).

[96]See chapter by Faisal Siddiqi in this volume.

November 2018.[97] The Week of Justice sought to make the claim for justice visible in the public domain beyond the courtroom, using the media attention the court procedure would raise. Khatoon spoke in this week at one of the opening plenary sessions of the UN Forum on Business and Human Rights in Geneva,[98] at press conferences in Dortmund and Rome, at an event at the Theatre of Dortmund on the Ali Enterprises case, and in a symposium at the University of Bochum on questions of "Corporate Liability in Global Supply Chains."

Through Khatoon's testimony and those of other workers like Mohammed Hanif and Abdul Aziz, the deceased and surviving workers of the Ali Enterprises factory, who usually remain anonymous, became real people with whom the German public could relate.[99] The Pakistani workers embodied the essence of human dignity in confronting the European public with the inequalities and injustice of the global economy. This can help explain the growing interest of a wider public in Germany in the case against KiK, but also in the issue of exploitative working conditions in global supply chains more broadly since 2012. The fact that the claimants lost the case was perceived as "unjust" by a wide range of commentators in print media, as well as on television. From left-leaning newspapers to the prestigious conservatives, all took up the narrative that the case against KiK highlighted the problem of exploitation in global value chains and that retailers like KiK should bear responsibility.[100] When the case was lost, most journalists concluded that the existing law obviously falls short, if claimants could not get justice in such a case.

There is also reason to believe that the legal and public debates around the KiK case influenced a law reform process in Germany. The first formal proposal for a supply chain liability law in Germany was published just a few weeks after the KiK case was dismissed. In continuing debates around the so-called supply chain law (*Lieferkettengesetz*), the KiK case is often cited as a reference point, as the case's

---

[97]ECCHR, One Week of Justice, www.ecchr.eu/en/event/one-week-of-justice/ (last accessed 12 September 2020).

[98]Panel on Voices from the Ground—Forum on Business and Human Rights 2018, www.webtv.un.org/watch/panel-on-voices-from-the-ground-forum-on-business-and-human-rights-2018/5971600547001/ (last accessed 12 September 2020).

[99]Christopher Patz, Discount Workers www.youtu.be/_sXuvORQkqc (last accessed 12 September 2020).

[100]Klage gegen Kik abgewiesen. Frankfurter Allgemeine Zeitung, 11 January 2019, p. 20, "Deutsche Unternehmen aller Branche hätten die Klage gegen Kik genau verfolgt, stellte Miriam Saage-Maaß von der Bürgerrechtsorganisation ECCHR fest: Allen ist klar: Das aktuelle Recht wird der globalisierten Wirtschaft nicht gerecht."; Kein Urteil gegen KiK, Tageszeitung, 10 January 2019, "Die Kläger wollen erreichen, dass die Arbeitsbedingungen in der ausgelagerten Textilproduktion in armen Ländern grundsätzlich besser werden." www.taz.de/Prozess-wegen-Fabrikbrand/!5561365/ (last accessed 12 September 2020); Böker C, KiK muss pakistanischen Arbeitern kein Schmerzensgeld zahlen. Das ändert nichts daran, dass sich die Textilindustrie ändern muss. Denn der Kunde ist schwach. ZEIT ONLINE, 10 January 2019, www.zeit.de/zeit-magazin/mode-design/2019-01/fast-fashion-kik-fabrikbrand-pakistan-textilbuendnis (last accessed 12 September 2020).

dismissal proves the point that law reform is needed.[101] For example, the civil society campaign for a supply chain law in Germany, but also its counterpart at the EU level, refer to the case as a "real-life" example in which a duty of care should be clearly established by law.[102] Nasir Mansoor of NTUF and Saeeda Khatoon of the AEFFAA contributed a video statement in support of law reform in Germany for the launch of the civil society campaign and also spoke before the European Parliament.[103] Studies commissioned by both the European Commission and European Parliament assessing the need for law reform have also made reference to the KiK litigation.[104]

To sum up, in a narrow legal sense, the effects of the cases against KiK and RINA were restricted to procedure: the cases confirmed that workers from outside the EU have legal standing and can apply for legal aid to bring civil claims for compensation or criminal complaints against retailers and auditing companies in European jurisdictions. The merits were not decided upon, leaving the issue of corporations' duty of care towards their supply chains an open question that will need to be addressed through future cases. The litigation created a space in which those affected could raise their voices to a wider public, report on their experiences, and formulate claims in the EU and on the international level. It was not only the court proceedings, through the filing of legal briefs, that allowed the claimants to raise their demands, but equally important was that the "news" of Pakistani workers suing a German

---

[101]Misereor, Dismissal of complaint in KiK case shows serious gaps in the German legal system, 10 January 2019, www.misereor.de/presse/pressemeldungen-misereor/klageabweisung-im-kik-fall-zeigt-gravierende-luecken-im-deutschen-rechtssystem/ (last accessed 12 September 2020).

[102]"Angehörige von Todesopfern, wie im KiK-Fall, müssen oft nicht nur den Verlust hinnehmen, sondern stehen auch noch mittellos da. Die Initiative Lieferkettengesetz will, dass Betroffene auch vor deutschen Gerichten Entschädigung einklagen können, wenn ein Unternehmen seinen menschenrechtlichen Pflichten nicht nachgekommen ist.", Initiative Lieferkettengesetz, Warum wir ein Lieferkettengesetz brauchen, 4 September 2019, www.lieferkettengesetz.de/wp-content/uploads/2019/09/Initiative_Lieferkettengesetz_Basisflyer_148x148_SCREEN.pdf (last accessed 12 September 2020); Anti Slavery International and European Coalition for Corporate Justice, What if? Case studies of human rights abuses and environmental harm linked to EU companies, and how EU due diligence laws could help protect people and the planet, 11 September 2020, www.corporatejustice.org/eccj-publications/16830-what-if-case-studies-of-human-rights-abuses-and-environmental-harm-linked-to-eu-companies-and-how-eu-due-diligence-laws-could-help-protect-people-and-the-planet (last accessed 19 September 2020), pp. 11–13.

[103]ECCHR, Sieben Jahre nach dem Brand bei KiK-Zulieferer: Betroffene berichten, www.youtube.com/watch?v=PbrqRZMod-A#action=share (last accessed 19 September 2020).

[104]European Commission, Study on due diligence requirements through the supply chain. Final Report, p. 215, www.op.europa.eu/en/publication-detail/-/publication/8ba0a8fd-4c83-11ea-b8b7-01aa75ed71a1/language-en (last accessed 12 September 2020); European Parliament, Study: Access to legal remedies for victims of corporate human rights abuses in third countries, pp. 59–65, www.europarl.europa.eu/RegData/etudes/STUD/2019/603475/EXPO_STU(2019)603475_EN.pdf (last accessed 12 September 2020).

retailer attracted wide public attention, allowing for meaningful interventions into the public discourse.[105]

5 The Emancipatory Potential of Legal Interventions: Towards a Holistic Approach

Law must be understood as a product of societal struggles for hegemony and not only as the "immediate arm of the powerful."[106] While law represents the hegemonic interests of capital and the enduring imperial way of life in the Global North, it also has its own interior logic through which it withdraws from the immediate control of the powerful. On the one hand, law's abstractions and fictions are protective mechanisms against the most egregious assaults on human life and dignity.[107] On the other, the relative autonomy of the law creates space in which to challenge the hegemonic reading and make-up of the law itself. Lawsuits and legal proceedings can therefore be used as one way to engage in counter-hegemonic and emancipatory struggles.[108] Because Wendy Brown rightfully concludes that rights are something we "cannot not want," we must acknowledge the paradoxes of law by finding an emancipatory approach to legal practice, which must be much broader than a narrow focus on legal procedure and rights claims.[109] We need a "power-oriented approach" to legal practice that inherently seeks to challenge repressive power structures.[110] This approach interprets rights in an emancipatory way and, even more, focuses on creating a genuine awareness of the political, social, and economic struggles that underlie any given legal case.

Applying this reasoning to the case against KiK reveals that the plaintiffs both used and countered the inherent logic of the law. They used the inherent logic of the law in the sense that the fiction of procedural equality before the law is what enabled four Pakistanis to go before the Regional Court of Dortmund in Germany to represent the workers of South Asia and demand compensation for the losses they suffered at the hands of a transnational company much more powerful than they are. At the same time, the KiK claim also countered the logic of the law in the sense that the plaintiffs and their lawyers demanded rights that, according to the current tort law doctrines, they cannot claim. In their legal argument the plaintiffs and their lawyers

---

[105]Several members of the AEFFAA are by now also active in the HBWWF, in which they organise themselves and the home-based women workers in their communities. In cooperation with NTUF and HBWWF, they have also managed to achieve some substantial legislative changes in the province of Sindh.

[106]Buckel (2009), p. 19.

[107]Williams (1987).

[108]Buckel (2015), p. 313.

[109]Brown (2000), p. 240.

[110]Gabel and Harris (1982–1983), p. 375; Knuckey et al. (2020), pp. 125 ff.

interpreted the existing Pakistani tort law in a way that acknowledges the rights of workers in global value chains. With this, the organisations and lawyers involved aimed to create a new understanding of legal obligations in economic relationships along globalised supply chains. If the reasoning brought forth by the claimants in the KiK case were to become the dominant reading of the law, companies at the top of supply chains, those that gain most of the profits, would have legal obligations—"duties of care"—towards workers in their supply chains. The legally organised "irresponsibility" of lead firms would be reversed, as lead firms bearing a tort law duty of care towards the workers in their supply chains would need to substantially change their mode of production. If workers could regularly challenge the violation of their rights and hold the most powerful actors along the chain responsible, lead firms would have to find other ways of engaging with their supplier companies, their management, and their workers. They would likely need to change their buying and pricing practices altogether.

Using the language of rights in such a way allows utopian claims to be negotiated in legal forums that are usually subject to current legal systems and designed to preserve the status quo of those in power.[111] The KiK case shows that it is possible to invoke the law as it is, and at the same time, present claims that go beyond the status quo, that anticipate a different law to come.[112] This turns legal practice aimed at resistance into a practice aimed instead at emancipation, reaching for a different future. In the example of Pakistani workers suing KiK for damages, the utopian claim lies in the fact that our current economic system would not exist if textile workers and the international company were truly equal before the law. If textile companies could not externalise the social costs of production, the current economic system would not exist. The very act of Pakistani workers using the current legal system and its fiction of equality before the law challenges the status quo. It shows that the world economy and the legal system that would support their claim must be completely different than the one we have today. This is what others have called the revolutionary potential of human rights.[113]

This kind of lawyering understands legal strategy as only one of the many aspects that determine the overall strategy of the coalition of actors involved in a given emancipatory struggle. It is not centred on legal proceedings as such. Therefore, the lawyers' perspective on which jurisdiction, which course of action, and which legal arguments to use is balanced with other considerations on how to gain momentum in political debates and other forums relevant for the overall struggle. As the KiK case shows, it is particularly those actors who engage with the legal proceeding not as lawyers, but as artists, journalists, activists, and trade unionists that help the litigation to gain the momentum needed to have an impact beyond the courtroom.

---

[111] Bader et al. (2019).

[112] Horst (2019), p. 179; "Nur rechtliche Strategien, die entgegen allem Realismus unterstellen, dass das andere Recht schon da ist, können dazu beitragen, dass es einmal hervorgebracht wird." Menke (2018b), p. 28.

[113] Möller and Raimondi (2015).

Therefore, the kind of lawyering described here pays attention to how different actors engage with each other. The actors in the KiK litigation aimed to create a transnational cooperation conscious of the power dynamics between lawyers and clients, and between organisations from the Global North and the Global South, that seeks to constructively engage these dynamics.[114] Lawyers working and living in the Global North must engage with individuals and groups affected by corporate exploitation in solidarity, using their privileges in a way that is driven by the interests of the affected communities.[115] This requires processes of reflection on different actors' political views and an honest analysis of privileges and power dynamics. It requires the building of a trustful partnership attentive and responsive to cultural, ideological, gender, and class differences.

6 Conclusions

The different legal proceedings against KiK and RINA must be seen in the broader context of the economic, social, and legal realities of globalised value chains. While international and national trade and commercial law generally enable lead firms in the Global North to maximise their profits, with these lead firms, in turn, bearing no legal responsibility for the exploitation of workers or the destruction of the environment, globalised value chains also open up possibilities for legally challenging the status quo. In the litigation against KiK, it was German civil procedure and Pakistani tort law that allowed four Pakistani workers to go to court in Germany to claim that lead firms actually do bear a duty of care for the workers in their globalised supply chains who they usually try to externalise.

Regardless of the proceedings' final outcome, the lawsuit against KiK had emancipatory effects because the efforts of the actors involved were not only focused on winning the legal case itself. All of the actors involved understood the legal case to be an opportunity for building a transnational alliance based on solidarity and a commitment to work together on an equal footing. They anticipated the potential shortcomings of the law and legal procedures and aligned the legal strategies with broader political goals of public outreach campaigning, advocacy efforts, and engagement in alternative political processes. This was only possible due to the cooperation of diverse actors from Pakistan and Germany, collectively comprising a diverse range of perspectives beyond legal expertise.[116] Indeed, it was precisely the non-lawyers who played the most crucial roles, because they helped the legal debate

[114]See chapter by Mansoor et al. in this volume.

[115]Knuckey et al. (2020); Ancheita and Terwindt (2015); Hoffman and Vahlsin (2014); Gabel and Harris (1982–1983), p. 376.

[116]Kaleck W, In the legal struggle for human rights, one must use all opportunities and develop a broad strategy. Open Global Rights, 26 February 2019, www.openglobalrights.org/seizing-opportunities-and-broad-strategy-both-essential-in-human-rights-litigation/?lang=German (last accessed 12 September 2020).

become socially and politically relevant: from the Pakistani workers, who as a group and individually, were prepared to expose themselves and take a public stance, to the courageous trade unions and civil society organisations that accompanied the self-organisation of those affected and had the willingness and skills to enter into the ILO negotiations, to the art and media professionals who made the case and the injustice perceptible to a broader public.

References

Ancheita A, Terwindt C (2015) Towards genuine transnational collaboration. Forschungsjournal Soziale Bewegungen 28:56–61

Anghie A (2004) Imperialism, sovereignty and the making of international law. Cambridge University Press, Cambridge

Anner M (2020) Squeezing workers' rights in global supply chains: purchasing practices in the Bangladesh garment export sector in comparative perspective. Rev Int Polit Econ 27 (2):320–347

Baars G (2019) The corporation, law and capitalism. A radical perspective on the role of law in the global political economy. Haymarket Books, Chicago

Baars G et al (2016) The role of law in global value chains: a research manifesto. London Rev Int Law 4(1):57–79

Bader M, Saage-Maaß M, Terwindt C (2019) Strategic litigation against the misconduct of multinational enterprises: an anatomy of Jabir and Others v KiK. Verfassung und Recht in Übersee 52(2):156–171

Barrientos S, Gereffi G, Pickles J (2016) New dynamics of upgrading in global value chains: shifting terrains for suppliers and workers in the global south. Environ Plann 48:1214–1219

Beckers A (2017) Legalization under the premises of globalization: why and where to enforce corporate social responsibility codes. Indiana J Glob Leg Stud 15:15–43

Beckert S (2014) Empire of cotton. A new history of global capitalism. Penguin, London

Brand U, Wissen M (2017) Imperiale Lebensweise. Zur Ausbeutung von Mensch und Natur im globalen Kapitalismus. Oekom, München

Britton-Purdy J et al (2020) Building a law-and-political-economy framework: beyond the twentieth-century synthesis. Yale Law J 129:1784–1832

Brown W (2000) Suffering rights as paradoxes. Constellations 7(2):230–241

Buckel S (2009) Zwischen Schutz und Maskerade – Kritik(en) des Rechts. RAV Infobrief 102:11–23

Buckel S (2015) Subjektivierung und Kohäsion. Velbrück, Weilerswist-Metternich

Butler J (1991) Unbehagen der Geschlechter. Suhrkamp, Frankfurt am Main

Butler J (2006) Haß spricht – Zur Politik des Performativen. Suhrkamp, Frankfurt am Main

Chimni BS (2013) Critical theory and international economic law: a third world approach to international law (TWAIL) perspective. In: Linarelli J (ed) Research handbook on global justice and international economic law, pp 251–273

Clean Clothes Campaign (2005) Looking for a quick fix – how weak social auditing is keeping workers in sweatshops. Amsterdam

Duffy H (2018) Strategic human rights litigation: understanding and maximising impact. Bloomsbury, Oxford

Gabel P, Harris P (1982–1983) Building power and breaking images: critical legal theory and the practice of law. Rev Law Soc Change 11:369–411

Gathii J, Odumosu-Ayanu I (2015) The turn to contractual responsibility in the global extractive industry. Bus Hum Rights J 1(1):69–94

Geistfeld M (2019) The law and economics of tort liability for human rights violations in global supply chains. J Eur Tort Law 10(2):130–165
Gereffi G, Humphrey J, Sturgeon T (2005) The governance of global value chains. Rev Int Polit Econ 12:78–104
Glinski C, Rott P (2019) Regulating certification bodies in the field of medical devices: the PIP breast implants litigation and beyond. Eur Rev Private Law 27(2):403–428
Habersack M, Ehrl M (2019) Verantwortlichkeit inländischer Unternehmen für Menschenrechtsverletzungen durch ausländische Zulieferer – de lege lata und de lege ferenda. Archiv für die civilistische Praxis 219(2):155–210
Haider K (2019) Haftung von transnationalen Unternehmen und Staaten für Menschenrechtsverletzungen. Nomos, Baden-Baden
Heinen A (2018) Auf dem Weg zu einem transnationalen Deliktsrecht? – Zur Begründung deliktischer Sorgfalts- und Organisationspflichten in globalen Wertschöpfungsketten. In: Krajewski M, Saage-Maaß M (eds) Durchsetzung menschenrechtlicher Sorgfaltspflichten von Unternehmen. Nomos, Baden-Baden, pp 87–124
Heinlein I (2018) Zivilrechtliche Verantwortung transnationaler Unternehmenfür sichere und gesunde Arbeitsbedingungen in den Betrieben ihrer Lieferanten. Neue Zeitschrift für Arbeitsrecht 2018:276–282
Hoffman B, Vahlsin M (2014) Collaborative lawyering in transnational human rights advocacy. Clin Law Rev 21:255–282
Horst J (2015) Lex Financiaria. Das transnationale Finanzmarktrecht der International Swaps and Derivatives Association (ISDA). Archiv des Völkerrechts 53:461–500
Horst J (2019) Transnationale Rechtserzeugung. Elemente einer normativen Theorie der Lex Financiaria. Mohr-Siebeck, Tübingen
Hossain (2012) Exprts, equity, and empowerment: The Effects of readymade garments manufacturing employment on gender equality in angladesh. World Development Report
Kaleck W, Saage-Maaß M (2010) Corporate accountability for human rights violations amounting to international crimes. J Int Crim Just 8:699–724
Kaleck W, Saage-Maaß M (2016) Unternehmen vor Gericht. Wagenbach, Berlin
Kennedy D (1997) A critique of adjudication. Harvard University Press, Cambridge
Kirchheimer O (1976) Reichsgericht und Enteignung: Reichsverfassungswidrigkeit des Preußischen Fluchtliniengesetzes? In: Kirchheimer O, Luthardt W (eds) Von der Weimarer Republik zum Faschismus: Die Auflösung der demokratischen Rechtsordnung. Suhrkamp, Frankfurt am Main, pp 77–90
Klein N (2005) No Logo. Der Kampf der Global Players um die Marktmacht. Riemann, München
Knuckey S et al (2020) Power in human rights advocate and rightsholder relationships: critiques, reforms, and challenges. Harv Hum Rights J 33:101–155
König C (2017) Deliktshaftung von Konzernmuttergesellschaften. Archiv für die civilistische Praxis 217(4-5):611–686
Krajewski M, Bozorgzad M, Heß R (2016) Menschenrechtliche Pflichten von multi-nationalen Unternehmen in den OECD-Leitsätzen: taking human rights more seriously? Zeitschrift für ausländisches öffentliches Recht und Völkerrecht 76:309–340
Kumar (2015) Conditions of paraquat use in India. http://www.pan-india.org/wp-content/uploads/2017/03/BD_paraquat_4-15_def-WEB.pdf Accessed 12 April 2021
Lehmann U (2012) Mode gegen Moderne. In: Rohr et al (eds) Mode: Ein Kulturwissenschaflicher Grundriss. Wilhelm Fink, Munich, pp 23–55
Lessenich S (2018) Neben uns die Sintflut. Wie wir auf Kosten anderer leben. Piper, Munich
Lobel J (2003) Success without victory. New York University Press, New York
Locke R, Qin F, Brause A (2006) Does monitoring improve labour standards? Lessons from Nike. MIT Sloan Research Paper 4612(6)
Mansel HP (2018) Internationales Privatrecht de lege lata wie de lege ferenda und Menschenrechtsverantwortlichkeit deutscher Unternehmen. Zeitschrift für Unternehmens- und Gesellschaftsrecht 47(2-3):439–478

Marshall AM, Hale DC (2014) Cause lawyering. Annu Rev Law Soc Sci 10(1):301–320
McCann M (2008) Litigation and legal mobilization. In: Whittington KE, Kelemen RD, Caldeira GA (eds) The Oxford handbook of law and politics. Oxford University Press, Oxford
Meeran R (2011) Tort litigation against multi-national corporations. City Univ Hong Kong Law Rev 3:1–41
Menke C (2018a) Kritik der Rechte. Suhrkamp, Berlin
Menke C (2018b) Genealogie, Paradoxie, Transformation. Grundelemente einer Kritik der Rechte. In: Fischer-Lescano A, Franzki H, Horst J (eds) Gegenrechte. Recht jenseits des Subjekts. Mohr-Siebeck, Tübingen, pp 13–31
Mgbeoji I (2006) Global biopiracy: patents, plants, and indigenous knowledge. Cornell University Press, Ithaca
Möller K, Raimondi F (2015) Mensch, institution, revolution. Zur Politik der Menschenrechte. Forschungsjournal Soziale Bewegungen 28(4):38–46
Müller U (2019) Begriffe, Ansprüche und deren Wirklichkeiten. Zeitschrift für Rechtssoziologie 39 (19):33–63
Neumann F (1980) Die Herrschaft des Gesetzes. Suhrkamp, Frankfurt am Main
Nordhues S (2019) Die Haftung der Muttergesellschaft und ihres Vorstandes für Menschenrechtsverletzungen im Konzern. Nomos, Baden-Baden
Nova and Zeldenrust (2020) Who will bail out the workers that make our clothes? Workers' rights consortium white paper, Washington D.C.
Orsenna E (2007) Weisse Plantagen. Eine Reise durch unsere globalisierte Welt. C.H. Beck, Munich
Osieka G (2014) Zivilrechtliche Haftung deutscher Unternehmen für menschenrechtsbeeinträchtigende Handlungen ihrer Zulieferer. Peter Lang, Frankfurt am Main
Pistor K (2019) Code of capital. How the law creates wealth and inequality. Princeton University Press, Princeton
Plank et al. (2009) Labour rights in global production networks. An qnalysis of the apparel and electronics sector in romania, Vienna
Rahmatian A (2009) Neo-colonial aspects of global intellectual property protection. J World Intellect Prop 12(1):40–74
Saage-Maaß M (2014) Holding corporations accountable: lessons from transnational human rights litigation. In: ECCHR, Brot für die Welt and Misereor (eds), Berlin
Saage-Maaß M (2021) Tort law litigation in germany. In: Richard Meeran (eds), Human rights litigation against multinationals in practice, Oxford University Press, Oxford
Schall A (2018) Die Mutter-Verantwortlichkeit für Menschenrechtsverletzungen ihrer Auslandstöchter. Zeitschrift für Unternehmens- und Gesellschaftsrecht 47(2-3):479–512
Segger S (2018) Europäisches Haftungsmodell für Menschenrechtsverletzungen von Unternehmen? In: Krajewski M, Saage-Maaß M (eds) Die Durchsetzung menschenrechtlicher Sorgfaltspflichten von Unternehmen. Zivilrechtliche Haftung und Berichterstattung als Steuerungsinstrumente. Nomos, Baden Baden, pp 21–60
Spitzer M (2019) Human rights, global supply chains, and the role of tort. J Eur Tort Law 10 (2):95–107
Sumon M, Shifa N, Gulrukh S (2017) Discourses of compensation and the normalization of negligence: the experience of the Tazreen factory fire. In: Prentice R, De Neve G (eds) Unmaking the global sweatshop: health and safety of the world's garment workers. University of Pennsylvania Press, Pennsylvania, pp 47–172
Terwindt C et al (2018) Supply chain liability: pushing the boundaries of the common law? J Eur Tort Law 8(3):261–296
Thiede T, Bell A (2017) Klagen clever kaufen! Zur Haftung einer deutschen Textilhändlerin für die Opfer eines Brandes in der Fabrik eines pakistanischen Zuliefererbetriebs. Recht der Internationalen Wirtschaft 5:263–272
Thomale C, Hübner L (2017) Zivilgerichtliche Durchsetzung völkerrechtlicher Unternehmensverantwortung. Juristenzeitung 72(8):385–397

Van Dam C (2010) Tort law and human rights: brothers in arms on the role of tortlaw in the area of business and human rights. J Eur Tort Law 3:221–254
Vogt et al (2020) Farce majeure: How global apparel brands are using the COVID-19 pandemic to stiff suppliers and abandon workers, Policy Paper, https://www.ecchr.eu/en/publication/die-ausrede-der-hoeheren-gewalt/. Accessed 12 April 2021
Von Falkenhausen (2020) Menschenrechtsschutz durch deliktsrecht. Unternehmerische pflichten in internationalen lieferketten, Mohr Siebeck, Tübingen
Wagner G (2016) Haftung für Menschenrechtsverletzungen. Rabels Zeitschrift für ausländisches und internationals Privatrecht 80:717–782
Wagner G (2017) § 823. In: von Hein J (ed) Münchener Kommentar zum Bürgerlichen Gesetzbuch, vol 7
Weller MP, Thomale C (2017) Menschenrechtsklagen gegen deutsche Unternehmen. Zeitschrift für Unternehmens- und Gesellschaftsrecht 46(4):509–526
Weller MP, Kaller L, Schulz A (2016) Haftung deutscher Unternehmen für Menschenrechtsverletzungen im Ausland. Archiv für die civilistische Praxis 216(3-4):387–420
Wendelstein C (2019) Menschenrechtliche Verhaltenspflichten im System des Internationalen Privatrechts. Rabels Zeitschrift für ausländisches und internationals Privatrecht 83(1):111–153
Williams P (1987) Alchemical notes: reconstructing ideals from deconstructed rights. Harv Civil Rights Civil Liberties Law Rev 40(22):401–433
Yusuf H (2010) Pakistan's anti-terrorism courts. CTS Sentinel 3(3):22–25

Miriam Saage-Maaß is a lawyer and vice legal director at ECCHR, where she has developed and since several years heads the Business and Human Rights program. She worked on various cases against corporations, including civil proceedings against German retailers regarding labor exploitation in South Asia. Furthermore, she is engaged in criminal proceedings against high-ranking managers for their involvement in international crimes, e.g. arms exports from Europe to Saudi Arabia. She regularly publishes articles on the question of corporate accountability for human rights violations in global supply chains and is an internationally renowned expert for corporate responsibility and human rights. She lectures at Freie Universität Berlin, Germany, and joined the Board of the Bonavero Institute for Human Rights at Oxford University in 2018 and the Stiftung Forum Recht's advisory board in 2020.

Paradoxes of Strategic Labour Rights Litigation: Insights from the Baldia Factory Fire Litigation

Faisal Siddiqi

Abstract This chapter focuses on the legal activism that followed the Ali Enterprises factory fire and its aftermath in Pakistan. This chapter has two purposes: firstly, it documents the legal proceedings that were initiated and pursued in the courts of Pakistan as well as its interconnected developments. Secondly, I aim to use this engagement with the legal proceedings of the Baldia factory fire aftermath as an opportunity for an in-depth reflection on the capacity and, finally, suitability of the judicial process to bring about justice in struggles over human and labour rights. Providing a rare and insider account of the legal proceedings in the Pakistani courts and its interconnected developments, I hope to lay the empirical foundation for the theoretical and strategic claims of this study. It is against the background and based on the experience with the litigation and legal advocacy following the Baldia fire that I examine the two what I perceive as "paradoxes" at the heart of the litigation. The first is the inseparability of the "limited justice" that may result from such litigation on one hand, and the "structural injustice" that informs and determines the conditions the litigation seeks to address—and transform—on the other hand. The second paradox concerns the inseparability of both law and lawlessness as regards the legal context of the litigation, advocacy and policy proposal elements that are here in play.

My argument is that these apparently contradictory phenomena not only coexist alongside one another but that they guarantee each other's existence. This analysis leads me to the conclusion that in order to understand and improve such forms of strategic litigation, it is necessary to measure its success and failure in terms of three distinct but interconnected criteria. These are the *tactical*, *strategic* and *structural* impacts of the litigation. Ultimately, I will argue for rejecting what is often perceived by involved stakeholders to be an unavoidable choice between nihilism, euphoria or incremental reform in this context. But, to the contrary, I will argue for a conception of legal struggles as a means of building sustainable and fruitful forms of resistance and of change based on the recognition and exploitation of these irreconcilable

F. Siddiqi (✉)
Siddiqi, Vawda, Usman and Memon Law Associates, Advocates and Legal Consultants, Karachi, Pakistan

M. Saage-Maaß et al. (eds.), *Transnational Legal Activism in Global Value Chains*, Interdisciplinary Studies in Human Rights 6,
https://doi.org/10.1007/978-3-030-73835-8_4

paradoxes rather than fruitless attempts to ignore or transcend these irreconcilable contradictions.

For 'the law', as a logic of equity, must always seek to transcend the inequalities of class power which, instrumentally, it is harnessed to serve.—EP Thompson[1]

Law and lawlessness, we repeat, are conditions of each other's possibility.—Jean and John Comaroff[2]

Out of the crooked timber of humanity no straight thing was ever made.—Immanuel Kant[3]

1 Introduction

The impact of labour struggles in Pakistan, crystalising, *inter alia*, in the evolution of the trade union movement, well intended labour legislation or pro-labour judicial decisions, has not been historically significant. But on 11 September 2012, Pakistan did make labour history, when at least 255 workers died and 55 were injured in a factory fire at the Ali Enterprises textile factory in the Baldia area of Karachi, Pakistan (Baldia factory fire).[4] It was a historic tragedy because it was the highest number of deaths ever recorded as a result of a factory fire in Pakistan or elsewhere.[5] Interestingly, this bloody tragedy has had the unintended consequence of revealing the paradoxical realities of the nature of law and the state, power imbalances of capital and labour, and the extraordinary exercise of judicial power in Pakistan.[6]

[1]Thompson (1990), p. 268.

[2]Comraroff and Comraroff (2006), p. 21.

[3]Quoted in Berlin (1998), p.16.

[4]These figures are from the Final Report of the Commission, Baldia Factory Fire Incident, Karachi, dated 28 June 2013, submitted before the High Court of Sindh in Constitution Petition No. 3318 of 2012. Although the controversy surrounding the correct number of dead and injured workers or persons in this tragedy has recently been revived because an Anti-Terrorism Court No. VII at Karachi, in Special Case No. 11(vii)/2017, through judgment dated 22 September, 2020, has given judicial findings that there were 264 deaths and 60 injured in the Baldia factory fire. As discussed below in this chapter, this Anti-Terrorism Court conducted the criminal proceedings arising out of this Baldia factory fire incident.

[5]This specifically refers to deaths in factory fires and not deaths in other kinds of factory incidents. Before the Baldia factory fire, the highest number of deaths was around 213 in 1993, in a doll factory fire, Thailand. *See*, Thai Factory Fire's 200 Victims Were Locked Inside, Guards Say. New York Times, 12 May 1993, www.nytimes.com/1993/05/12/world/thai-factory-fire-s-200-victims-were-locked-inside-guards-say.html (last accessed 13 August 2020).

[6]I use the term "capital," "capitalist class" and "capitalist elites" at various places in this chapter as an alternative to the terms "business community" or "textile industry" in order to emphasise that these labour legal struggles are actually struggles against the neo-liberal capitalist system existing in countries like Pakistan.

This chapter analyses the legal struggles arising from the Baldia factory fire, concentrating on the litigation initiated and pursued in the Pakistani courts, as well as its interconnected developments. The chapter's purpose is to answer three basic questions: firstly, what happened in these legal struggles and why? Secondly, what do these legal struggles tell us about the role of the law, judiciary and power structures in relation to labour legal struggles in countries like Pakistan? Thirdly, what can we learn from these legal struggles about the nature, the potential but also the limitations of strategic labour rights litigation as a litigation tool in countries like Pakistan? In order to answer these questions, I have divided this chapter into three parts, each dealing with one question. The first part (Story of the legal proceedings: Hope, victories and disenchantments) deals with the question as to the what and why questions of the legal proceedings in Pakistan. The second part (Strange bedfellows: Law, disorder, power relations and anarchic law) deals with the second question about the implications of these labour legal struggles on our understanding of law, judiciary and power relations. And the third part (Strategic labour rights litigation: Tactical victories, strategic possibilities, structural improbabilities) deals with the utility of strategic labour rights litigation.

Before proceeding further, it is important to clarify the following: as the litigation in Pakistan arising from the Baldia factory fire was primarily conducted by the author and his team of lawyers,[7] the discussion and analysis also makes reference to, and relies on, the author's own experience of conducting this litigation. Therefore, this chapter is more than an intellectual exercise. It is also a remembrance, a celebration of sorts and a recording of the horrors of legal injustice. But most importantly, it is an attempt to arrive at a deeper understanding of these issues, through a rigorous self-critique of legal interventions in labour struggles.

2 Story of the Legal Proceedings: Hope, Victories and Disenchantments

Before analysing the jurisprudential and strategic legal implications of the litigation regarding the Baldia factory fire, it is critically important to describe and to understand the litigation and its interconnected developments. Mere abstract conceptualisations or empirical generalisations on the basis of selective victories or defeats will deprive us both of an understanding of the complexities of these struggles and complex implications for future strategic labour rights litigations. In short, we must confront the positive as well as the uncomfortable truths of these complex legal battles regardless of whether they dampen the celebratory narrative of this struggle or whether they question the *a priori* ideological and theoretical presumptions of a legal nihilism which seems to be constantly suspicious of judicial remedies. Therefore, this section describes and analyses the Baldia factory litigation

[7] I would like to thank my colleague, Muhammad Vawda, for his contribution in this litigation.

and its interconnected developments in three parts: First, the two public interest constitutional petitions ("petition") initiated and pursued at the High Court of Sindh at Karachi, Pakistan ("Sindh High Court").[8] Second, the criminal case initiated by the Sindh government at the criminal courts at Karachi against the owners and management of the Ali Enterprises factory and various government officials.[9] Third, the passage of a new workplace safety law and the settlement agreement regarding long-term compensation for the victims of the Baldia factory fire under the mediation of the International Labour Organization.

2.1 *Public Interest Constitutional Litigations*

The litigation strategy adopted was both unusual and eccentric. Instead of pursuing the remedy of tort claims on behalf of the victims[10] under the Fatal Accidents Act (1855), or pursuing the remedy under the Pakistani labour laws, two constitution petitions were filed before the Sindh High Court, seeking multiple reliefs on behalf of the victims of the factory fire. These two constitution petitions were filed under Article 199 of the Pakistani Constitution of 1973, which allows public-spirited persons and organisations to seek the enforcement of fundamental constitutional rights,[11] such as the right to life and the right to justice,[12] on behalf of a group of aggrieved persons, such as the victims of the Baldia factory fire.[13]

2.1.1 Constitution Petition No. 3318 of 2012[14]

This was the primary case of this Baldia factory litigation but it was an unusual petition in two respects. First, the petitioners in this case were labour union organisations, NGOs and publicly-spirited individuals but none of the petitioners were either victims of the Baldia fire or any organisation or union[15] of workers of the Ali Enterprises factory. In other words, it was a petition for the victims but without the

---

[8]One of the Provincial High Courts in Pakistan.

[9]Provincial government of the province of Sindh, Pakistan.

[10]The use of the word "victims" in this article includes both the legal heirs of the deceased workers and the injured persons.

[11]For an overview of public interest litigation and the expansion of judicial review in Pakistan, see Khan (2014), p. 284; Siddiqi (2015), p. 77.

[12]Articles 4 and 9 of the Constitution of Pakistan, 1973.

[13]Article 199 of the Pakistani Constitution,1973, is a constitutional remedy under which public interest litigations can be initiated for the enforcement of fundamental rights. Fundamental rights are contained in Chapter 1, Part II, of the Constitution, 1973.

[14]The information and documents relied upon in these sections are based on the actual court record of this case.

[15]The Ali Enterprises factory was an unregistered factory with no trade union.

victims. Second, the reliefs sought in this case were multifold and numerous, ranging from seeking a proper investigation into and the assigning of liability for this incident to labour institutional reforms and compensation for the victims. In other words, this petition had a highly ambitious litigation agenda. Why was such a strategy adopted? Three main reasons can be identified. First, in view of the grand scale of this tragedy and urgent needs of the victims, this petition was filed within a week of the factory fire.[16] As a result, only a few organisations and persons were interested in instituting this case in such emergency circumstances. Secondly, although the Pakistan Institute of Labour Education and Research (PILER) and the National Trade Union Federation (NTUF) (both of which were petitioners) were in contact with the victims but no victim family or injured person in those early days could be convinced to become a petitioner in this case. As it became evident later, this lack of interest by the victims was a result of their scepticism about the law and courts and more importantly, the result of fear due to threats as well as incentives received from the Ali Enterprises factory owners. Third, a constitution petition seemed the only effective litigation option available because it was practically and financially impossible to file 310 tort claims on behalf of the families of the deceased and injured in the civil courts.[17] In order to institute such tort claims, the basic task of locating all the legal heirs of the victims and injured was a longer-term undertaking with insurmountable difficulties and also without the prospect of any immediate financial relief being provided to the victims because such tort litigation has a minimum litigation life of 15–20 years. Also, as there was no immediate external funding available for this litigation, the only cost-effective remedy was a constitution petition on behalf of all of the victims.[18] Furthermore, as explained below, the other possible remedies, including remedies under existing labour laws, were either toothless or absent.

2.1.2 Relief

The reliefs that were sought through this petition can be divided into four parts. First, it sought the constitution of a judicial commission to investigate this tragedy, to assign liability, to determine compensation and make recommendations for future prevention of such tragedies, including labour reforms. Second, it sought a declaration that the victims were entitled to compensation from both the owners of the factory and the government. Third, it sought effective prosecution of the criminal

[16]The first hearing of Constitution Petition No. 3318 of 2012 was held in the Sindh High Court on 18 September 2012, that is, within a week of this tragedy.

[17]255 persons dead and 55 injured.

[18]The court fee for instituting such a petition was less than 10 euros but this does not include either the professional fee of lawyers and other miscellaneous expenses of such litigation. Court fee for instituting each tort claim is 15,000 Pakistani rupees (80 euros), a substantial amount in Pakistan especially when multiplied by 310 claims. As Pakistan has no civil legal aid system, the entire cost of the Baldia factory fire litigation was financed by the author himself, through his legal practice.

case against the owners and management of the Ali Enterprises factory and various government officials.[19] Fourth, it sought the inspection and survey of all factories and establishments in the province of Sindh.[20]

2.1.3 Identification of Unclaimed Bodies

As noted above, the scope of this constitution petition was manifold, but the court proceedings came to be dominated by two issues: compensation and the identification of unclaimed bodies, which had paradoxical implications for the wider objectives of this litigation. The Sindh High Court in this case passed various orders to identify over 70 unclaimed victims but in the end, around 16 victims could still not be identified. These unidentified victims were finally buried on the orders of the Sindh High Court.[21] The issue of unclaimed victims became dominant for two main reasons. Firstly, the emotional nature of this issue led the Sindh High Court to give it priority. Secondly, the complete failure of the government to prioritise this sensitive issue was aggravated by the logistical fact that at that relevant time the entire Sindh province did not have a single DNA lab for testing and the samples of these unclaimed victims had to be sent to the capital city, Islamabad. Thirdly, the issue of compensation for the legal heirs of the deceased workers was linked with the identification of their deceased loved ones which meant that where no identification was made possible, no compensation could be claimed. Paradoxically, this issue was not anticipated at the time of the petition's filing nor was there a specific relief or prayer sought regarding this issue in the petition. Nevertheless, this issue came to dominate the court proceedings in comparison to other equally important issues.

2.1.4 Judicial Commission and Compensations

As noted above, the constitution of the judicial commission that was sought through this petition had a broader mandate, namely to investigate this tragedy, to assign liability, to determine compensation and also to make recommendations for labour reforms in order to prevent such tragedies in the future. But the judicial commission constituted by the Sindh High Court, within five months after the filing of this

[19] I do not discuss the various court orders passed regarding the criminal case in this section because they are discussed below in Sect. 2.3 which deals with such criminal proceedings.

[20] Sindh is the second biggest province of Pakistan with a population of over 45 million people. The petitioners prayers for effective criminal prosecution and the inspection and surveying of all factories and establishments was simply about seeking the enforcement of the existing statutory obligations of the state under the Criminal Procedure Code, 1898, and the Factories Act, 1934.

[21] Orders passed in Constitution Petition No. 3318 of 2012 between October 2012 and December 2014.

petition,[22] was limited in its scope to the identification of the victims, their legal heirs and the determination and payment of the compensation to them.

Why were these strategic goals with respect to the broader mandate of the judicial commission abandoned for the tactical goal of expeditious immediate compensation?[23] The following reasons can be identified: firstly, there was an accepted underlying presumption among the parties involved as well as a public perception that limited justice in the form of immediate compensation had priority over the strategic goals of substantive justice and labour reforms. Secondly, as an unintended consequence of PILER spearheading this petition, PILER was able to get KiK Textilien und Non-Food GmbH (KiK) on the negotiating table despite the fact that KiK, which was the main buyer of textile goods from the Ali Enterprises factory, accepted no role and no liability with respect to the fire. Consequently, on behalf of the victims of the factory fire, PILER entered into an agreement with KiK on 21 December 2012, in which KiK, among other things, agreed to provide immediate relief of one million US dollars for the victims. One of the main clauses of this agreement also mandated that the disbursement of this compensation be done through a judicial commission constituted by the Sindh High Court. Furthermore, negotiations regarding the long-term compensation with KiK were also dependent on the successful completion of the disbursement of this initial immediate compensation through the judicial commission. Thirdly, the main reason why all parties to the proceedings (petitioners, factory owners and the government), consented to the constitution of the judicial commission was because of its limited focus on immediate compensation, otherwise any insistence on a judicial commission with a broader mandate might have delayed the expeditious determination and disbursement of this immediate compensation. In other words, in order to expedite the compensation to the victims, a consensual process was adopted and as a result, limited justice in the form of immediate compensation trumped the broader goals of substantive justice and labour reforms. Fourthly, the main reason why the Ali Enterprises factory owners agreed to contributing towards the amount of compensation was because they were confined to jail as a consequence of the criminal case against them. It was a strategic decision by the petitioners to expedite the compensation issue before the owners got out of jail on bail because it was more likely that they may not consent to such a judicial commission if the pressure of the criminal case was lifted on them by the grant of bail.[24] Fifthly, there had already been three investigation and inquiry reports into the Baldia factory fire, namely initial reports by the investigation committee of the police, an investigation report by the Federal

---

[22]Order dated: 1 January 2013, passed in Constitutional Petition No. 3318 of 2012 by the High Court of Sindh, Pakistan.

[23]I discuss the issue of strategic and tactical goals and limited and substantive justice in Sects. 3 and 4 of this chapter.

[24]Based on the author's personal assessment following conversations with the lawyers representing the factory owners, it seems that the owner's thought that giving compensation would increase their chances of getting bail, as this act of "generosity" might create a favourable impression in the perception of the public and the judiciary for the purposes of the grant of bail to them.

Investigation Agency, and a Judicial Tribunal's Report,[25] all of which broadly established the owner's liability and the gross negligence of government officials. In the presence of these reports, it became difficult to convince the Sindh High Court to constitute another inquiry commission. But as the criminal case proceeded, it became obvious that it was a strategic mistake not to insist on another judicial commission of inquiry because a report by such a judicially constituted independent commission might have prevented the eventual subversion of the criminal case, which is analysed below.

The judicial commission constituted by the Sindh High Court was headed by a retired judge of the Supreme Court of Pakistan.[26] The commission submitted its final report on 28 August 2013, i.e. within six months of its constitution. The commission's proceedings and report became the foundational document for all future calculations and procedures of disbursing compensation to the victims.[27] It is important to note three aspects of the commission's proceedings and the report. Firstly, for the first time, it was determined on the basis of concrete evidence that there were 255 deceased persons and 55 injured persons in the fire. Secondly, legal heirs of each deceased person were paid 610,000 Pakistani rupees (3216 euros) in total, each permanently disabled person was also paid 610,000 Pakistani rupees, persons with grievous injury were paid 250,000 Pakistani rupees (1318 euros) and persons with simple injury were paid 125,000 Pakistani rupees (659 euros). Thirdly, a procedure was laid down for the separate disbursement of compensation to each legal heir directly, which was especially important for the women heirs, and the share of the minor legal heirs was deposited with the Sindh High Court until they reach the age of majority. This procedure was adopted in light of the persistent complaints regarding the earlier disbursement of compensation by the government as

[25]This tribunal was constituted by the Sindh government and operated under the chairmanship of a retired judge of the Sindh High Court.

[26]The Supreme Court of Pakistan is the apex court in Pakistan.

[27]The amounts of disbursement by the judicial commission came from two sources, namely, as noted above, 1 million US dollars immediate compensation given by KiK under the Agreement dated 21 December 2012, with PILER and 51,800,000 Pakistani rupees (237,086 euros), along with an additional amount of 10 million Pakistani rupees (52,719 euros), was deposited by the owners of the Ali Enterprise factory. It may be noted here that the principal amount of 51,800,000 Pakistani rupees (237,086 euros) deposited by the owners was not a voluntary contribution but was a liability imposed against the owners through order dated 26 December 2012 by the Commissioner for Workmen Compensation for the 259 deceased workers under the Workmen Compensation Act, 1923, and although the owners contested this adjudicated award of the Commissioner for Workmen Compensation but due to the proceedings in this petition and the criminal case, they strategically decided to consent to deposit this amount with the judicial commission. Therefore, the total amount for disbursement as compensation with the judicial commission was PKR 165,495,000 Pakistani rupees (872,403 euros). Two further points of clarification may be noted. Firstly, it was wrongly assumed at that time that there were 259 deceased and not 255 deceased. The authenticated figures are given in the final report dated 28 August 2013 of the Commission, Baldia Factory Fire incident, Karachi. Secondly, all rupee to euro conversions in this text are according to the exchange rates on 10 July 2020.

having been monopolised by a single male or elderly member of the deceased family, which led to the frequent denial of shares due to the rest of the legal heirs.

Once a firm foundation was laid by the judicial commission, the path was established for further and easier disbursement of compensations to the victims. However, the issue which arose was that there were apparently no additional funds available for further disbursement. But on an examination of the various replies submitted by the government in these court proceedings, we found an ambiguous announcement by the then Prime Minister Yousuf Raza Gilani in the year 2012 about the death grant for each deceased worker from the Workers Welfare Fund.[28] Although a serious legal challenge could have been raised as to the validity of such payments to the victims from the Workers Welfare Fund, the government failed to raise such legal objections and agreed to deposit these death grants.[29] Therefore, the Sindh High Court directed the government to deposit an amount of 129,500,000 Pakistani rupees (682,734 euros) with the office of the Sindh High Court, which was to be disbursed by an officer of the Sindh High Court to the legal heirs of the deceased workers.[30] As a result, 500,000 Pakistani rupees (2636 euros) were disbursed to the legal heirs of each deceased worker following the same procedure as had been laid down by the judicial commission. As compared to the initial disbursement of compensation by the government, the disbursement of the compensation by the Sindh High Court (earlier through the judicial commission and later through an officer of the high court) was based on an objective criterion of entitlement and was also administered through a transparent and verifiable process.

Moreover, regarding the initial disbursement of compensation by the provincial and federal governments, there had been persistent complaints about the actual disbursement of this compensation to the victims.[31] The Sindh High Court directed the government officials to submit a report to verify the disbursement of direct payments by the governments of 700,000 Pakistani rupees (3738 euros) per deceased worker and other amounts disbursed to the injured.[32] Resultantly, the entire record of such payments was filed and the following aspects of this record may be noted. Firstly, payments were made to 252 out of the 255 families of the deceased workers and smaller amounts were disbursed to only nine injured persons. Secondly, the disbursement of the compensation was made to one of the male or to an elderly member of the family, leading to this disbursement being monopolised or misused by the receiving legal heir, which resulted in the frequent denial of shares due to the rest of the legal heirs.

---

[28] This was established under the Workers Welfare Fund Ordinance, 1971.

[29] An example of the anarchy of the law, which I will discuss in Sects. 3 and 4 of this chapter.

[30] Court orders dated 29 April 2014, and dated 19 November 2014. As these were limited to death grants, the injured persons were not disbursed any compensation from this amount.

[31] This was disbursed by the government in the first few months after the Baldia factory fire.

[32] Order dated: 4 April 2014, passed in Constitution Petition No. 3318 of 2012, by the High Court of Sindh, Pakistan.

Furthermore, there were also persistent complaints about the lack of payments by the social security institutions, namely, the Employees' Old-Age Benefits Institution (EOBI) and the Sindh Employees' Social Securities Institution (SESSI), who were not making due payments to the heirs of all the deceased workers.[33] Therefore, in view of the reports sort by the Sindh High Court from EOBI and SESSI regarding these disbursement, there was a manifold increase in the number of pensions granted for the deceased workers. For example, EOBI increased the number of pensioners from 177 to 245. But it is important to note several aspects of these social security payments: firstly, most of the amounts were pathetically low, for example the death grant from SESSI was 5000 Pakistani rupees (43 euros) per a deceased's family. Secondly, the pensions given by the EOBI were time-bound for only five years. Thirdly, although there was improvement in the numbers of the legal heirs getting the social security payments, some claims were still pending in 2016 because of bureaucratic hurdles. Fourthly, even though neither the EOBI or SESSI were parties to this petition nor was any specific relief sought against them in this petition, the Sindh High Court issued directions against them, which these social security institutions complied with without any legal objections. Usually, directions are issued only to parties to the petition.[34]

2.1.5 Inspection and Surveys of Factories and Establishments

At the heart of the Baldia factory fire tragedy was the fact that the Ali Enterprises factory was neither registered with the Labour Department nor had any occupational safety inspection ever been conducted in this factory by the department. One of the petition's strategic labour reform objectives was the large-scale registration and inspection of factories and establishments in the Sindh province. The Sindh High Court directed the registration and inspection of all the factories and establishments in the Sindh province and it ordered the submission of a compliance report to the court regarding this issue.[35] In compliance with the aforementioned court orders, the Labour Department submitted a report in 2012 stating that 813 new factories and establishments had been registered, 180 new inspections had been carried out and the authorities had initiated action against 75 factories. It is important to note that the Labour Department in their comments before the court accepted their inability to enforce the law in registering and inspecting these workplaces. This institutional inability can mainly be explained as a result of the ban on surprise inspections, widespread non-implementation of the building codes, the lack of a specific

[33]EOBI is established under the Employee's Old-Age Benefits Act, 1976, and SESSI was established under the Provincial Employees Social Security Ordinance, 1965 (now repealed and replaced by a new law, the Sindh Employees' Social Security Act, 2016).

[34]Another example of the anarchy of the law, which I will discuss in Sects. 3 and 4 of this chapter.

[35]Orders dated: 5 November 2012 and 13 November 2012, passed in Constitution Petition No. 3318 of 2012, by the High Court of Sindh, Pakistan.

occupational safety law, as well as the insignificant penal consequences for labour law violations, and so forth. In short, the enforcers themselves testified to the legal and institutional breakdown of the framework of labour law. This was indeed a promising start and could have led to a strategic breakthrough in this petition. In the end, however, nothing happened beyond that because of the overwhelming focus in the proceedings on issues of compensation and identification of unclaimed bodies. In short, there was a lack of interest and support among the various stakeholders (i.e. victims, NGOs, judges) in their failure to prioritise labour reform through the registration and inspection of factories and establishment.

At this stage, a few general observations regarding these constitutional petition proceedings are necessary. Firstly, the limited success (reasonable compensation etc.) in this petition cannot be understood without the role played by two individuals, namely Justice Maqbool Baqar, the judge of the Sindh High Court (now serving at Pakistan's Supreme Court) who passed most of the important orders in this petition, and Retired Justice Rahmat Hussein Jafferi, who presided over the judicial commission. Without the contribution of these two judges, the limited success achieved in this petition would not have been possible. Secondly, at least at the initial stage and at various other times, the facilitating role played by the provincial and federal governments in these proceedings proved important.[36] Thirdly, the proceedings' limited success also depended on the disclosure of various information and documents made available to the petitioners through the orders of the Sindh High Court. Therefore, these proceedings became a vehicle for the discovery of the unknown and hidden facts regarding this tragedy and also these key pieces of information contributed to the success of this petition. Fourthly, serious questions regarding the legal maintainability of such a petition were surprisingly never seriously raised by the opponents nor adjudicated upon by the Sindh High Court. As examined below, this anarchy in the law laid the foundation for the victim's substantive compensational victories.

2.2 *Constitution Petition No. 295 of 2013*[37]

In view of new developments and the surfacing of previously unknown facts, a second constitution petition was filed by labour rights organisations, NGOs and public-spirited individuals seeking the following reliefs: firstly, an injunction against the Prime Minister of Pakistan to restrain him from interfering in favour of the owners and management of Ali Enterprises factory in the criminal case instituted

[36]Due to the present constraints of space, the author is unable to discuss and explore whether the state in the postcolony and the Global South have become completely co-opted by the forces of capital or if there is still hope for a progressive state capable of checking anti-labour practices in such countries.

[37]The information and documents relied upon in this section is based on the actual court record of Constitution Petition No. 295 of 2013 filed before the High Court of Sindh, Pakistan.

against them.[38] Secondly, directions were sought against the relevant authorities to initiate proceedings regarding the building code violations in the factory. Thirdly, directions were sought against the Labour Department to initiate proceedings against the factory owners for violations of the labour law. Fourthly, directions were sought against the authorities to initiate proceedings against RINA Services SpA, Italy, and their Pakistani affiliate Regional Inspection & Certification Agency (Pvt) Limited, for issuing the false and faulty SA8000 certification, which deliberately misrepresented and underreported the actual and largely non-existent occupational safety measures in the Ali Enterprises factory.

2.2.1 Labour Law Violations

The bombshell dropped in this case was the disclosure by the Labour Department that the Ali Enterprises factory, which employed more than 1500 workers and was a major exporter of textile goods, had not even been registered with the Labour Department. In short, an export-producing textile factory was operating in the industrial heart land of Karachi and employing hundreds of workers without even being registered with Labour Department. Since it was never registered, it was never subjected to any labour or safety inspection by the Labour Department and this was the legal defense taken by the Labour Department. Incongruously, a small percentage of its workers was actually registered with the social security institutions like the EOBI and SESSI but not with the Labour Department. It appeared like a fictional story, clearly betraying the collusive relationship between the capitalist class and the labour regulators. In other words, the state's defence in this tragedy can be captured by the motto "see no evil" (i.e. no registration and thus, no statutory obligation to regulate) and thus, "cannot prevent any evil" (i.e. no responsibility could be assigned for this industrial tragedy on the Labour Department).

But the tragedy did not end with this nonsensical and Machiavellian defense of the Labour Department as to why it had never inspected or regulated this factory. After the Baldia factory fire, the Labour Department did initiate a case against the Ali Enterprises factory owners under the 1934 Factories Act and the 1975 Sindh Factories Rules promulgated under the 1934 Factories Act, but they were charged for an offence under Section 64 (Penalty for failure to give notice of accidents), which imposed a penalty of 500 Pakistani rupees (2.66 euros).[39] This is a minor violation with an insignificant and laughable penalty for the biggest death toll in a factory fire in human history. In fact, there were no provisions in the labour laws which contained any substantial and deterrent penalties, under which the factory owners could be charged with. In short, the Labour Department was helpless not

[38]In order to understand the significance of the orders passed by the Sindh High Court against the interference by the prime minister, see below Sect. 2.3.2 dealing with the criminal case of this chapter.

[39]Section 64, Factories Act, 1934, which lays down the penalty for failing to report any accidents.

only due to its collusive behaviour but also because the labour laws under which it operated were toothless even in the face of such a grave industrial tragedy.

2.2.2 Building Code Violations

One of the tragic surprises of this case is that one of the main reasons for such a large death toll was caused due to the dangerous conditions created by the violations committed by the owners in the factory's building structure. As the FIA report notes:

> owners of the factory committed flagrant violations of approved building plan. The illegal wooden mezzanine floor between the ground and 1st floor was the main cause of aggravation of fire and its spread to upper floor [...] rapid burning of the illegal mezzanine floor not only blocked the staircase but also made the fire spread quickly to the 1st and 2nd floor through the duct available around the cargo lift.[40]

To confirm these buildings code violations, the Sindh High Court ordered an independent building inspection of the factory and unsurprisingly, multiple violations in the construction of the structure of the factory building were promptly discovered.

Were these violations simply due to the corruption or weakness of the building regulatory regime? This would be too easy an explanation. Rather, the cause of these building violations is much more fundamental. The Ali Enterprises factory was located in the Sindh Industrial Trading Estates (SITE), which is the biggest industrial area in Karachi. The Sindh Building Control Authority (SBCA) took the defence before the court that it had no jurisdiction to check building violations in the SITE area and that it was actually the public duty of the management of SITE to issue building plans and check building infringements. This gave rise to both a legal and an enforcement problem: under what law has the management of SITE been issuing building plans for the factories in its area as it is only a leasing authority and not a building authority; and furthermore, how could SITE enforce the rectification of these building violations as it lacked both the technical infrastructure and legal penal framework including a statutory building code? In Karachi, only the Sindh Building Control Authority had the technical expertise and legal enforcement framework, supported by a statutory building code, to enforce violations of building codes. But it should be noted here that this issue of jurisdiction of the SBCA in the SITE area is still pending before the Sindh High Court in this very petition and has yet to be resolved.

[40]Federal Investigation Agency, Sindh Zone, Karachi, "Enquiry Report: Fire Incident At Ali Enterprise S.I.T.E Karachi On 11th September 2012", 3 October 2012.

2.2.3 RINA and Private Inspections

In view of the suspension of surprise labour inspections in the Sindh province since 2001, and due to the lack of capacity and institutional corruption of the Labour Department to enforce even the minimum occupational safety standards, led to the domination of the smokescreen of voluntary social standards certificates issued by private international inspection companies.

On 3 August 2012, 39 days before the Baldia factory fire, RINA Services SpA from Italy (RINA), issued a certificate that the Ali Enterprises factory was in compliance with the standard SA8000, based on an audit and inspection conducted by its Pakistan affiliate, Regional Inspection & Certification Agency (Pvt) Limited, which falsely certified that among other things health and safety procedures were complied with by the factory. The audit report of the factory falsely stated that fire extinguishers and fire safety buckets were available, accessible exit doors were kept unlocked and there were regular emergency drills and firefighting training conducted at the factory.

The investigation report by the Federal Investigation Agency,[41] the Judicial Tribunal's Report[42] and the reply submitted by the chief fire officer of the local government in this petition, all clearly point out that there was a complete absence and failure of fire safety standards at the Ali Enterprise factory. It follows that the SA8000 certification given by RINA was not simply an example of a factually incorrect report but in fact symbolises a fraudulent system of private inspections. In the replies filed by RINA and its Pakistani affiliate in these proceedings, there was a denial of any responsibility and liability, but two facts still point towards at least an implied acceptance by RINA of this fraudulent system. Firstly, these companies suspended all SA8000 certifications issued in Pakistan. Secondly, both RINA and its Pakistani affiliate were disbanded in Pakistan.

Through various orders passed by the Sindh High Court, this petition achieved two objectives in relation to these private inspections. Firstly, this fraudulent private inspection system was exposed and RINA suspended its activities in Pakistan. Secondly, the Sindh High Court directed RINA to provide a complete list of all entities or companies to which SA8000 certificates had been issued and it further directed the Labour Department to re-inspect all these entities or companies to which RINA had issued these certificates. The Labour Department re-inspected all these factories based in the Sindh province and it informed the Sindh High Court that the violations of labour laws have been communicated to these entities or companies. However, there was no independent means to assess the validity and quality of these inspections conducted by the Labour Department itself.

---

[41]Federal Investigation Agency, Sindh Zone, Karachi, "Enquiry Report: Fire Incident At Ali Enterprise S.I.T.E Karachi On 11th September 2012", 3 October 2012.

[42]This tribunal was constituted by the Sindh government under the chairmanship of a retired judge of the Sindh High Court.

On the crucial question as to whether any action could be taken against RINA and its Pakistani affiliate, the Labour Department demonstrated its complete helplessness since there was no law which mandated or regulated private certifications like SA8000 nor were such certificates submitted to and vetted by any statutory authority. Resultantly, RINA and its Pakistani affiliate had actually violated no law by giving a false report. At best, they could be found guilty of violating their contractual obligation towards their clients, e.g. Ali Enterprises. But their clients stood to benefit from such fraudulent inspections and could hardly complain. Therefore, the absence in the law of an effective occupational safety law, the institutional weakness of the Labour Department to enforce even the weak law that existed and the complete non-regulation by the state of these private inspections led to this grave tragedy.

The above narratives of the lack of effective labour laws, ineffective building laws and lack of regulation of a private inspection system share a common theme: in order to avoid detection and rectification of illegalities, there was a deliberate invention of legal vacuums, legal confusions and a deliberate weakening of the enforcement structures. In other words, this deliberate lawlessness and anarchy of the law was not accidental but deliberate as it served the interest of capitalist class.[43]

2.3 *Criminal Case: A Comedy of Horrors*[44]

With the hope for holding accountable the owners and management of Ali Enterprises factory and their colluding and negligent government officials, under the labour or regulatory laws, dwindling and disappearing, the only legal option available for such accountability was through the criminal law, i.e. the imposition of criminal liability for gross criminal negligence under the Pakistan Penal Code, 1860, (PPC).[45] But like a tragic comedy, a cruel drama of injustice was in the process of being performed through the criminal justice system, which would destroy any semblance of accountability and instead tragically further strengthen the impunity from accountability of the capitalist class by facilitating the legal, moral and social rehabilitation of the owners of Ali Enterprises factory.[46]

[43]These notions of lawlessness and anarchy are examined in Sects. 3 and 4 in this chapter.

[44]The information and documents relied upon in this section are based on the actual court record of this case.

[45]PPC is the main criminal statute in Pakistan, which contains the main criminal offences.

[46]As explained in detail in Sect. 2.3 below, the owners emerged also as the victims of this tragedy as they were substituted in the criminal case from being accused persons to becoming victims and innocent witnesses of this tragedy by the prosecutors and as a result, this restored the owners' moral and social position in society.

2.3.1 Act 1: The Illusive Hope

A criminal case was initiated when the first information report (FIR) No. 343 of 2012,[47] was registered by the Pakistani state itself against the owners and management of the Ali Enterprises factory and various government officials, including officials of the Labour Department, SITE, Social Security Department etc. The police investigation report and the Federal Investigation Agency report that were mentioned above had concentrated more on the broader question as to why there was such a large number of deaths from the fire rather than the narrow question of how the fire started. In short, the real issue became as to the cause of the mass deaths resulting from the fire within the context of unsafe working conditions, labour law and building law violations, and as to who was individually and institutionally criminally liable for these unsafe conditions and legal violations. As explained in these reports, the cause of these mass death was identified in the following major acts of commission and omissions:

(a) Safety measures and firefighting measures in the factory were highly inadequate, i.e. there were no smoke alarms due to which the workers were alerted late, hydrants were non-functional and the staff was not trained to use such hydrants. Even otherwise, no attempt was made to extinguish the fire by the factory management.
(b) Rapid burning of the illegally constructed wooden mezzanine floor accelerated the fire and blocked the staircase.
(c) Due to alleged threat of theft, two exit doors of the second floor were permanently sealed by the factory owners and management. This sealing was fatal as most of the workers were gathered on the second floor because it was pay day and once the electricity went off it was extremely difficult for the workers to find their way in the dark.
(d) Due to alleged threat of theft, the windows were permanently sealed with steel grills. Thus, the workers could not even escape through the windows, considering the exit doors had also been sealed.
(e) The factory which employed over 1500 workers and was situated in the biggest industrial area of Karachi, was neither registered nor inspected for fire safety purposes by the Labour Department. Even the Social Security Departments had registered less than 270 workers. Therefore, the collusion and the negligence of these government departments was clear.

As far as the cause of the fire is concerned, the investigations concluded that it was an accidental fire either caused by a localised short circuit or by some negligent act of a worker. The investigation further concluded that although the possibility of mischief could not be ruled out, there was no evidence at all to suggest that the fire was caused due to mischief, sabotage or terrorism. As we will examine below, it is

[47]The first stage of the initiation of criminal case under the Criminal Procedure Code, 1898, is the FIR. The FIR was registered on 12 September 2012 (i.e. a day after the fire).

this unresolved mystery about the cause of the fire which provided the opportunity to sabotage the accountability in this case. What was quite interesting about this initial phase was that the public prosecutor and police acted swiftly and decisively in this case identifying the culprits and taking a broader institutional view of the criminal liability for the mass deaths in the fire, rather than simply focusing on the traditional narrow view of identifying the individual liability in causing the fire.

Furthermore, three important judicial developments happened. Firstly, the magistrate court rejected the bail applications of the owners and management of Ali Enterprises factory and sent the owners and management staff to jail.[48] The unthinkable had happened in a country where corporate actors are hardly ever held accountable, let alone criminally liable. Secondly, the magistrate court froze 80% of the funds in the bank account of the Ali Enterprises factory owners. This provided an avenue for the availability of funds for compensation to be disbursed to the fire's victims.[49] Thirdly, the magistrate court refused the request of the investigation officer to withdraw the prosecution in this case against the negligent and colluding government officials.[50] Therefore, the hope of institutional accountability was kept alive but as the events unfolded, this hope for accountability could not withstand the power of capitalist elite and its strategic partnership with the authoritarian Pakistani state.

2.3.2 Act 2: The Comedy

It quickly became apparent that the initial accountability-seeking actions of the Pakistani state against the owners and managements of Ali Enterprises factory and the colluding government officials turned out to be tactical victories at best. The structural and strategic alliance between the capitalist elite and the authoritarian Pakistani state were revealed in a dramatic manner in a speech delivered by no less than the Prime Minister of Pakistan, Raja Pervaz Ashraf, at a function organised by the Karachi Chamber of Commerce and Industry, in which he declared that: "It is not the incumbent government's policy to harass businessmen. Authorities should reinvestigate the case and provide justice to the employers of Ali Enterprises if a wrong case has been registered against the factory owners under Section 302."[51]

---

[48]The initial stage of the criminal case is conducted by the magistrate but the bail applications are heard by the session judge and it is the session judge who rejected the bail application of the owners and management of Ali Enterprises Factory through order dated 6 October 2012.

[49]Order dated: 14 November 2012, in the criminal case under FIR No. 343 of 2012, passed by the magistrate court.

[50]Order dated 14 November 2012, in the criminal case under FIR No. 343 of 2012, passed by the magistrate court.

[51]This speech was delivered on 29 December 2012. Quelling concerns: PM promises on-time and transparent elections: Premier Ashraf directs authorities to reinvestigate Baldia Town factory fire case. Express Tribune, 30 December 2012, www.tribune.com.pk/story/486571/quelling-concerns-pm-promises-on-time-and-transparent-elections (last accessed 20 July 2020); Section 302 is a penal

It is important to recollect the context of this incredible statement by the prime minister: bodies of all the victims of the Baldia factory fire had still not been identified, the victims had yet to be paid all the compensation and no one had been held accountable for this historic tragedy. But at the same time, the prime minister was attending dinners by the very group of the local capitalist elites which was responsible for such tragedies and the prime minister was "distressed" about providing "justice to the employers of Ali Enterprises." In other words, even in the midst of this historic industrial tragedy, the anguish of these so-called suffering capitalists dominated the mindset of the Islamic Republic of Pakistan instead of the trauma and problems of the families of hundreds of working class dead and injured of the factory fire tragedy.

Constitution Petition No. 295 of 2013 was filed, partly to challenge this interference in a criminal case by the prime minister, and the Sindh High Court was pleased to declare that such interference as not legally permissible.[52] However, such formal orders became irrelevant as through this prime minister's speech the intended message had already been conveyed to the concerned investigation officer of the Baldia factory case: *find a way to get the owners and management out on bail and to dilute the substantial criminal charge against them.*

With the brotherhood between the country's capitalist elite and the Pakistani state reignited, things moved at great speed on two critical fronts, namely investigation and bail proceedings. Magically, in the supplementary investigation report, the investigation officer suddenly discovered that the owners and management were not guilty of the substantive offence under Section 300 PPC, that is, the offence of gross criminal negligence amounting to murder but were rather guilty of the lesser offence under Section 322 PPC, of accidental death. While the former carries a prison sentence, the latter carries no such sentence.[53] But as the owners and the management were in pre-trial detention, the more dramatic reversal took place in the bail proceedings before the Sindh High Court.

In a highly unusual instance during these bail proceedings, the investigation officer himself requested the court to grant bail to the owners and management persons whereas the public prosecutor representing the investigation officer and the State *opposed* the grant of bail. In short, one arm of the state (i.e. investigation officer) was opposing another arm of the state (i.e. prosecutor) on this issue. It is precisely because of this confusion and conflict within the prosecution team regarding the offences for which the accused were proposed to be charged that led to the Sindh High Court granting bail to the owners and the management personnel.

---

provision providing the punishment for murder in the main criminal statute, that is, the Pakistan Penal Code, 1860.

[52]Order dated 15 February 2013, passed in Constitution Petition No. 295 of 2013, by the High Court of Sindh, Pakistan.

[53]Supplementary charge sheet or investigation report in the criminal case under FIR No. 343 of 2012 was submitted on 6 January 2013.

But these bail proceedings were made more bizarre by the court atmosphere. In an interview, I had recalled this court atmosphere as follows: "On the day they were granted bail in court, the entire. . .I mean, what was amazing was that. . .255 people have been burnt alive so you would imagine that the court would be full with victims and their families. But the entire court room. . .There were about 50, 60 people in the court room, and they were all industrialists and supporters of these people. And they were clapping."[54]

Even though the Sindh High Court had ordered in Constitution Petition No. 3818 of 2012 that the criminal case should conclude within one year the battle for accountability had already been lost because on one hand, the capitalist elite and the Pakistani state were bent upon providing relief to the factory owners and management, and on the other hand, only a very few victims family members were willing to pursue the criminal case.[55] On top of this, the witnesses against the owners and management were rapidly turning hostile by retracting their earlier testimony.[56] But what we did not realise at that stage was that matters were going to get bizarrely worse and this comedy of a criminal case was, by design, being converted into an irredeemable tragedy.

2.3.3 Act 3: The Tragedy

One of the valuable but tragic lessons learnt from this litigation was that unlike the poor who were divided, disillusioned and lacked clarity about their collective interest, the capitalist elite had remarkable clarity about *their* collective interest.

In the year 2013, a military intelligence-led police operation had started against the Muttahida Qaumi Movement (MQM), a party which dominated the politics in Karachi using militant means. During an interrogation of one of its activists, Muhammad Rizwan Qureshi, it was revealed that someone had told him that the fire at the Baldia factory fire was the alleged result of the extortion demand made by certain members of the MQM.[57] This was clearly hearsay evidence as he neither was a witness to this so-called arson attack nor did the so-called arson attackers directly inform him about this extortion and arson plan. But soon after this interrogation report became public in 2015, both the capitalist elites and the state took the common stance that certain members of the MQM were responsible for deliberately starting the Baldia factory fire for the purposes of extortion. Therefore, in a god-sent opportunity, both the interest of the Pakistani state to diminish the power of the

[54]Gayer (2019), p. 309.

[55]Even these few families later lost interest in the criminal prosecution.

[56]The witnesses' turning hostile and lack of the interest of the victim families to pursue the criminal cases was clearly indicative of the fact that even the victims had come to accept the entrenched power of the capitalist elites and had understood that the directions of the winds of justice was firmly in favour of the owners and management.

[57]The interrogation by the police and intelligence services took place on 22 June 2013.

MQM through this police operation and the rekindling of the state's strategic relationship with the capitalist elites were achieved through the oldest trick in Pakistani politics: a wild conspiracy theory thrust upon an impressionable, fear-induced and chaotic public discourse.

A new investigation team was formed in 2015, which promptly declared the owners of the Ali Enterprises factory as innocent and further declared that the Baldia fire was the result of a terrorist attack by the MQM for the purposes of extortion. An examination of the criminal charge framed by the Anti-Terrorism Court against the new accused persons reveals the farcical nature of this *new* case.[58] According to the indictment, the fire erupted due to chemical substance thrown by the accused persons; the presence of such chemical substance was remarkably discovered by a lab test conducted on samples collected 3 years after the fire and the extortion was allegedly proven by the payments made by the factory owners to members of the MQM, not before but after the fire. Strangely, the fire tragedy now had two things in common with the attacks of 9/11 in the US: both happened on 9/11 and both were terrorist attacks.

In September 2020, and after converting and transposing the initial accused persons in the criminal case, namely the owners and management of Ali Enterprises factory and the negligent government officials into victims and witnesses, the Anti-Terrorism Court No. VII, at Karachi, in Special Case No. 11(vii)/2017, through judgment dated 22 September 2020, delivered a bizarre but predictably tragic judgment convicting eight persons for the murder of 264 persons and 60 injured persons for various offences including but not limited to deliberating starting the fire at the Ali Enterprise factory for the purposes of extortion and such acts were declared as an act of terrorism. As a result of these convictions, two persons were sentenced to death and the rest of the four persons were sentenced to life imprisonment.[59] An examination of this judgment shows that its extremity in awarding the death sentences and life imprisonment is only matched by the absurdity of its reasoning because these sentences have been awarded on the basis of contradictory, inadmissible or no evidence at all. This is because primarily, there was no reliable forensic evidence to prove that the fire was started deliberately by the convicted persons by throwing chemicals because two of the three laboratory reports did not confirm the presence of any chemical from the crime scene whereas the third laboratory report from a government laboratory surprisingly confirms the presence of such chemicals on the basis of samples obtained three years after the factory fire. Furthermore, the sentences were based on unreliable and coerced confessions, flimsy eye witnesses and dubious circumstantial evidence.[60]

[58]Framing of Charge dated: 14 February 2018, in Special Case No. 11(vii)/2017 before the Anti-Terrorism Court No. VII, at Karachi, Pakistan.

[59]Most of the convicted persons were workers or sympathisers of the MQM and most of them worked in the Ali Enterprises factory.

[60]Due to space constraints, the author is unable to conduct a detailed examination of the said judgment in Special Case No. 11(vii)/2017 before the Anti-Terrorism Court No. VII, at Karachi, Pakistan.

What do these dramatic developments tell us? The above relief of bail provided to, and a diluted and lesser criminal charge imposed on, the owners and management of Ali Enterprises factory and the colluding government officials, were not enough to protect the interest of the capitalist elites. Rather, the entire process of accountability underlining this criminal case of the factory fire needed a complete reversal in order to ensure a devastating blow to any possibility of labour reform. In other words, regardless of the dilution of the criminal charge, the very existence of the criminal case against the owners and management of the Ali Enterprises factory and its colluding government officials was an existential threat to the collective interest of the capitalist elite. A case which began with questioning the unsafe labour practices of the Pakistani textile industry had ended with the textile factory owners and the negligent government officials being declared as victims and by the conversion of the very nature of the criminal case into a terrorist act had resulted in forgoing any possibility of raising uncomfortable questions about unsafe labour practices in Pakistan with reference to this tragedy. This was the ultimate insult to all the hundreds of workers who lost their lives in this tragic fire and a devastating blow to the possibility of labour reform in the textile industry. Therefore, the real existing conditions of the majesty of injustice and lawlessness of the modern legal system in countries such as Pakistan had been fully exposed with blatant shamelessness by the remanufacturing and re-imagination of the criminal liability of the capitalist elite into a fictional case of terrorism.

2.4 *Labour Law Reform, ILO Settlement and Socio-Cultural Mobilisation: The Irresistibility of Hope*

With the prospect of accountability in ruin, with little hope for labour reform and with the possibility of long-term compensation exhausted, there was little scope for optimism among the victims and their families, the lawyers and activist organisations involved in this Baldia factory fire struggles. But then the "Arrangement for the settlement of the funding gap for the compensation to be delivered to the victims of the fire at the Ali Enterprises in Baldia, Pakistan on 11 September 2012" (ILO settlement agreement),[61] came through under the auspices of the International Labour Organization, which gave fresh impetus to this struggle for justice.

As discussed above, as a result of the initiation of the abovementioned Constitution Petition No. 3318 of 2012 by PILER and other organisations, PILER and the German company KiK entered into an agreement on 21 December 2012 for the "Relief for the Victims of the Ali Enterprises Fire Case." This agreement obligated KiK to provide one million US dollars as immediate relief but more importantly, obligated them to contribute towards long term compensation for the victims, quantum of which was to be determined through future negotiation. This agreement

[61] Signed on 9 September 2016.

was legally eccentric for two basic reasons. Firstly, KiK had always denied any liability regarding this tragic fire but now had contractually obligated itself towards accepting at least implied responsibility. Secondly, this was a sketchy document comprised of only two pages and a reading of this agreement showed that no lawyer had vetted it before it was signed. The reason I point this out is because if KiK had sought legal advice on this agreement, it most probably would never have been signed it, or at least the text of the agreement would have been much more detailed and inclined in favour of KiK because it was KiK which was giving the money and so was in a position to dictate the terms of the agreement. Therefore, the absence of lawyers is, at times, quite beneficial for weaker victims like those of the Baldia factory fire and as events would prove, this agreement became KiK's Achilles heel. In other words, the absence of lawyers in drafting and vetting this foundational document directly benefited the interest of justice for the weak.

Negotiations between PILER and KiK on long term compensation became stalled for a number of years. But under the auspices of the ILO, a settlement agreement for providing long-term compensation to the victims of the Baldia factory fire in the sum of 5.1 million US dollars was finally signed between KiK on the one hand and Clean Clothes Campaign and IndustriALL Global Union, representing the victims, on the other hand. This agreement was novel for a number of reasons. Firstly, it based the compensation on the ILO Employment Injury Benefits Compensation, 1964 (C121) and thus provided a higher amount of pensionary benefits than under Pakistani law. Secondly, it provided for a lifelong pension scheme for the victims. Thirdly, this pension scheme was to be implemented through the government run social security institution, SESSI, and was to be monitored by an oversight committee of various stakeholders.

This ILO settlement agreement was a consequence of a number of factors. Firstly, the foundation was laid by the initial agreement between PILER and KiK, which was the consequence of the constitutional litigation initiated in Pakistan. Secondly, the socio-cultural mobilisation, both in Pakistan but especially in Europe by the Ali Enterprises Factory Fire Affectees Association, Clean Clothes Campaign, the European Center for Constitutional and Human Rights, IndustriALL, NTUF and PILER, lead to public awareness and pressure regarding supply chain responsibility of multinational corporations. Thirdly, the pressure generated as a result of the initiation of litigation in Germany, in the case of *Jabir and others v. KiK* filed through efforts of ECCHR. Lastly, the role of the ILO as a trusted mediator and also the background support from the German government.

This agreement breathed new oxygen to an irresistible desire for hope in these dark times. But was this a beginning of supply chain accountability and a resurrection of responsibility by the Pakistani government by administering this pension scheme through SESSI and an implementation of a beneficial international conventions like C-121? A closer examination of this ILO settlement agreement shows that it is simply a voluntary agreement, an ad-hoc acceptance of responsibility by the Pakistani government with no obligation towards any labour reforms regarding pensionary benefits for such tragedies and no international acceptance of any supply chain liability by international buyers. In short, this much-lauded agreement turned out to be both a landmark settlement for the victims of this tragedy but also mere tactical success without any future prospect of supply chain responsibility, accountability of the local textile industry and social security reform. Like the above legal proceedings in Pakistan, this ILO settlement agreement seemed more like a beneficial distraction from the long-term task of reforming the global textile industry and its supply chains.

Together, the ILO settlement agreement, socio-cultural mobilisation and Baldia factory fire cases provided the impetus and pressure which led to the passage of a new workplace safety law called The Sindh Occupational Safety and Health Act, 2017.[62] Was the passage of an exclusive new work place safety law a strategic breakthrough? Apparently it did create the strategic possibility of a more effective regulation of work places but the fact is there has been no implementation of this law (e.g. no increase in number of inspectors or inspections) despite the passage of nearly three years from its enactment. Why is this lack of implementation? Firstly, the Baldia factory fire cases failed to prioritise registration and inspections of work places as a key goal and as a consequence failed to generate any socio-political momentum in favour of effective regulation of workplaces. Secondly, these laws have become like pacifier lollypops with the strategic purpose to distract and deflect real and substantive changes on the ground. This is because a demand for reform is usually satisfied by the passage of laws with full knowledge of all stakeholders that it will take many years (if not decades) to implement these laws. Even otherwise, there always exist many legal loopholes in these laws for the capitalist elite to subvert their effective implementation.[63] But regardless of these problems, the irresistible desire for hope was kept alive by this new law.

3 Strange Bedfellows: Law, Disorder, Power Relations and Anarchic Justice

The above legal narrative about the Baldia factory cases is a complex story of law and the judicial process as a manifestation of law and disorder, the extraordinary power imbalances between capital and labour and the limited justice achieved by the victims as a result of the anarchy of law.[64] One of the central paradoxes at the heart of these legal proceedings is that on the one hand, limited justice is achieved by the

[62]PILER played a critical role in the drafting of this new law.

[63]Since the focus of this article is not this new law, these loopholes are not discussed.

[64]Limited justice is used here as a contrast to substantive justice. Substantive justice is achieved when the main objectives (not all) of the labour legal struggles are achieved, for example, substantive compensation as a right (not voluntary) and accountability. This contrast between limited and substantive justice will become clearer as this analysis develops.

victims in the form of reasonable compensation[65] but on the other hand, this limited justice is linked with the lack of substantive justice, and more so, linked with structural injustice, both manifesting itself in the lack of accountability and the lack of effective labour reform. So, how do we conceptually understand this paradox, and how do we understand and operationalise these concepts of limited and substantive justice, of structural injustice and the anarchy of the law?

Before moving onto questions about the effectiveness of legal remedies, such as strategic labour rights litigation and how to measure their effectiveness for the purposes of reform or transformation through the courts, we need to ask a much more basic question—not in generic jurisprudential terms but within the context of labour rights cases like this. Does law, with its promises of rights, especially human rights and binding legal and constitutional obligations, have the ideological and institutional potential to bring about reform or transformation, especially in the power-infused arena of in-egalitarian labour relations? If the answer to this question is neither a simple "yes" nor a "no" but rather an ambiguous and contradictory answer, then the question arises as to what do these ambiguities and contradictions tell us about the limitations and potentialities of the law for the attainment of substantive justice and for reform or transformation through the law?[66]

In relation to the legal cases against the Ali Enterprises factory owners and KiK, one type of response to the above questions is given by the lawyers who initiated and conducted the *Jabir and others v. KiK* case in Germany. This answer is what I call the "revolutionary potential" view and is expressed in the following terms:

> The principle of equality before the law develops rare momentum, when marginalized workers are able to force the MNE responsible for their losses and injuries to abide by civil procedure rules and to explain its legal position is lengthy writs to the courts. In this regard, claiming rights through legal proceedings can realize the *"revolutionary potential" inherent to human* rights [. . . .] Although the law has its constraints as a driver of social change, strategic interventions bear a *revolutionary potential* [emphasis added].[67]

The above revolutionary potential view does recognise the formidable structural and societal obstacles to the implementation of human rights. Despite recognising these formidable obstacles, it still sees the revolutionary potential inherent in strategic human rights litigation.

Taking a different view from the revolutionary potential view, Laurent Gayer in his study of the Baldia factory fire litigation questions as to why "the trial of

---

[65]Compensation paid to the victims was reasonable but all the compensation or damages actually due to the victims was never adjudicated by the courts nor paid to the victims. For example, the owners of Ali Enterprises factory only paid the minimum statutory amount of death compensation and some voluntary contributions and the civil claim against KiK in Germany was dismissed on a preliminary objection based on the statute of limitation.

[66]It is important to note here that the theoretical assertions made in this section are in the context of countries of the Global South and new constitutional democracies like Pakistan and may have limited implications for countries of the Global North.

[67]Bader et al. (2019), pp. 169, 171.

Karachi's industrial capitalism did not happen."[68] His analysis emphasises the contradictory intertwining of justice and injustice in this litigation:[69]

> Through a detailed study of these judicial proceedings and their successive bifurcations, this chapter aims to grasp the relations of inter-dependence between a distinctly unbridled blend of capitalism, a turbulent urban environment and *a state torn between the strength of the law and the "justice" of the powerful* [....] In the face of a society and economy where the display of might is generally deemed to prevail over the assertion of rights, Thompson's work is a useful reminder that *the effectiveness of the law as an instrument of domination in the service of the powerful rests on its apparent universality and impartiality* [....] What the Baldia factory fire case also exemplifies is that outcome of these battles can never be taken for granted. Even as they serve the strategies of domination of the powerful and generate their own forms of coercion, as well as their own illegalities, legal proceedings always retain a contingent part – the historical and individual 'circumstances' [...] which introduces some indeterminacy in the game and, as such, contributes to its reproduction. This was exemplified in the Baldia factory fire case by a handful of lawyers and judges, who, in the name of social justice did not hesitate to bend the rules. The limited and contested successes of these jurists with a cause therefore obtained less by applying the law by the book – *thus entrapping the dominants into their own rhetoric of self-preservation, as Thompson would suggest – than by twisting the law in order to deliver justice* [emphasis added].[70]

In trying to explain this paradox of limited justice (e.g. reasonable compensation) and structural injustice (e.g. lack of accountability, no effective labour reform), Gayer relies on EP Thompson's examination of the paradoxes of the "rule of law" in his masterly study on the origins and implementation of the Black Act in eighteenth-century England. The present section of this chapter develops Gayer's analysis but also partly disagrees with his analysis. Firstly, this section further explores the structural or systemic logic of the contradiction in this paradox of law as identified by Thompson. Secondly, it argues that Gayer is incorrect to conclude that the limited success achieved in the Baldia factory fire litigation was possible by "bend(ing) the rules" or "twisting the law in order to deliver justice," but rather, as this chapter tries to show that the limited success was achieved by exploiting this paradox of the law and the anarchy of the law as prevalent in countries like Pakistan.

In describing the paradox at the heart of the rule of law, Thompson writes:

> But this is not the same thing as to say that the rulers had need of law, in order to oppress the ruled, while those who were ruled had need of none [...] For as long as it remained possible, the ruled – if they could find a purse and a lawyer – would actually fight for their rights by means of law [....] *If the law is evidently partial and unjust, then it will mask nothing, legitimize nothing, contribute nothing to any class's hegemony. The essential precondition for the effectiveness of law, in its function as ideology, is that it shall display an independence from gross manipulation and shall seem to be just. It cannot seem to be so without upholding its own logic and criteria of equity; indeed, on occasion, by actually being just* [emphasis added].[71]

---

[68] Gayer (2019), p. 288.

[69] Gayer (2019), p. 288. It is important to note here that in his analysis, Gayer also relies on interviews with the present author.

[70] See Gayer (2019), pp. 290, 292, 316, 317.

[71] Thompson (1990), pp. 261, 263.

Without engaging in the debate about whether the rule of law is an "unqualified human good" or in the debates between a Marxist versus liberal understanding of the rule of law,[72] what needs examination is how this paradoxical notion of the rule of law helps us in our understanding of the above described proceedings in the Baldia factory fire litigation. In the context of the factory litigation, Thompson's theoretical insights lead us to the following conclusions: firstly, law in a capitalist society has two contradictory purposes, both to mask, legitimise and contribute to class hegemony of capital but also to uphold the propounded liberal legalities and its foundational principles of equity and universality. But this is not a conflict which only emerges out of the application of the law but rather a systemic contradiction inherent in the very notion of the rule of law. In other words, theses contradictory purposes of the law are a structural or systemic part in the very notion of the rule of law, and this structural contradiction is converted into a legal and social conflict through legal and social mobilisation.[73] Because of this systemic contradiction, the rule of law, in its ideological and institutional manifestations, always contains the possibility of equity, universality and enforcement of rights leading to a limited notion of justice. Therefore, the limited justice achieved in the Baldia factory fire litigation was a result of a substantive rule of liberal legality existing in Pakistan, in the form of labour laws, fundamental rights guaranteed under the constitution and an expansive notion of constitutional judicial review. Law may not be a panacea for complete justice in such cases but law does make limited justice possible and achievable. Secondly, this limited justice comes at a high price and is only possible because it serves a macro purpose by systemically linking itself with, rather than undermining, structural injustice. Limited justice and structural injustice are dialectical twins. Therefore, the limited justice (e.g. reasonable compensation, new workplace safety law and judicial activism in favour of the victims) was achievable and tolerated so long as the structural injustice is guaranteed, which structural injustice meant no accountability and no substantive labour reform in the textile sector. As the narrative of the above legal proceedings has shown, the forces of capital, state and the judiciary always presented a stark choice to the helpless victims. Gayer captures this predicament when he notes that:

> as the courts and industrialists colluded to promote compensation as the sole response to the tragedy, these activists came to realise that "public recognition of suffering and the rights of compensation that it entails remains a largely *ad hoc* affair and generates a political program for compensation that keeps particular demands for structural change at bay".[74]

The brilliance of Thompson's analysis lies in his conceptualising of this dialectical nature of justice and injustice inherent in the rule of law in capitalist societies, where justice and injustice survive and thrive on the principle of "mutual assured

[72] Cole (2001), p. 177; Brown (2018), p. 1391.

[73] Mouzelis (1999), pp. 191–195. Here, I rely on the sociological distinction between social and system integration and conflict as developed by the sociologist David Lockwood and Nicos Mouzelis.

[74] Gayer (2019), p. 314.

survival," displaying itself even today in the same force as it did at the time of Thompson's writing. This structural and dialectical notion of justice and injustice should not be confused with the standard radical left critique which claims that to invoke liberal legalism is to win the battle but lose the war[75] because what Thompson is trying to show is somewhat different, namely that liberal legalism in protecting class hegemony also paradoxically pays a price in having to recognise, and to provide, limited justice for the powerless. In short, this injustice works both ways of this power imbalance, both for and against the capitalist elite.

At the same time, what is missing in Thompson's analysis of the rule of law is the importance of disorder and lawlessness surrounding the rule of law in liberal legal and constitutional systems of the postcolony or new constitutional democracies. What exactly is this disorder and what are the paradoxical implications of this disorder surrounding the rule of law? Law and disorder are at the centre of Jean and John Comaroff's work, who conceptualise this paradox as follows:

> Do these two putative tendencies-the excessive disorderliness of post-colonies on the one hand and their fetishism of the law on the other-describe a concrete reality? [. . . .] It is part of a much more troubled dialectic: a dialectic of law and dis/order, framed by neoliberal mechanisms of deregulation and new modes of mediating human transaction at once politico-economic and cultural, moral, and mortal. Under such conditions-and this our key point-criminal violence does not so much repudiate the rule of law or the licit operations of the market as appropriate their forms-and recommission their substance. Its perpetrators create parallel modes of production and profiteering, sometimes even of governance and taxation, thereby establishing simulacra of social order.[76]

This second dialectic twin of law and lawlessness or disorder surrounding the rule of law is explored by Gayer in the following terms:

> Karachi's industrial capitalism can thus be characterised as an *irregular* production system – a type of organization of the manufacture economy resorting heavily to various illegalities *without completely evading legal norms and the regulatory action of the courts*. Rather than by its outwardly criminal nature, this mode of organisation of the economy is thus characterised by its *uneven relationship with the law* [...] the judicial proceedings considered here provide an opportunity to think through the irregular nature of this production system, and more particularly to reflect upon the force of law in a society where it is constantly undermined by the illegalities of "delinquent elites" [emphasis added].[77]

As described above, the manifestations of this law and lawlessness dialectic are clearly present in the Baldia factory fire litigation. On one hand, Pakistan's legal system displayed all the manifestations of a labour market regulated by labour laws, labour inspectors, social security laws and institutions, an elaborate system of legal rights and fundamental rights including the fundamental right to trade unions and an expansive tradition of constitutional judicial review to enforce such rights. But on the other hand, equally present were the following contradictory features such as

[75] Albiston (2011), pp. 76–77.

[76] Comraroff and Comraroff (2006), pp. viii, 5.

[77] Gayer (2019), p. 291.

outdated labour laws without stringent penalties,[78] the banning of surprise inspections and completely inadequate number of inspectors, the abysmal lack of implementation of labour and social security laws, the systemic elimination of trade unions, an authoritarian state closely working with forces of capitalism and finally a judiciary which was suspicious and cautious in the enforcement of legal and fundamental rights relating to labour.[79] No wonder the Baldia factory fire of 2012 and the Triangle Shirtwaist factory fire of 1911 (in New York City, US) have so much in common even though they are over a century apart.[80] For example, the Triangle Shirtwaist factory fire also manifested similar aspects when compared to the Baldia factory fire, namely: 113 persons dead,[81] the permanent locking of doors and lack of fire safety provisions as the leading cause of an excessive number of deaths, lack of unionisation and the factory owners not being held accountable through the judicial process.[82] How can we explain this inseparable existence of the contradictory phenomena of law and lawlessness and its manifestation in the repetition of history of factory fires in the twenty-first century? Comaroff explain this paradox in the following terms: "violence and the law, the lethal and the legal, are constitutive of one another [...] Law and lawlessness, we repeat, are conditions of each other's possibility."[83]

Similar to the logic of the dialectic of justice and injustice, the dialectic of law and lawlessness also exists because it is based on a hidden structural relationship of each other's toleration leading to the continuing and perplexing reality of mutually assured existence of both law and lawlessness. In other words, law is only tolerated because it is never fully implemented and lawlessness continues to exist even if the formality of law exists, mere islands of lawful implementation are tolerated and occasional justice is allowed to flourish. It is precisely due to the inseparability of law and lawlessness that a tragedy similar to the Triangle Shirtwaist factory fire of 1911 repeated itself in the twenty-first century, with its modernised legal architecture of beneficial labour laws and universal human rights.

Can this paradox be resolved? To try to resolve this paradox and the above lack of justice with the presence of continuing lawlessness, the standard liberal solution is to emphasise the enactment of more beneficial labour laws, the strict implementation of laws, more unionisation, a welfare state and a labour-sensitive judiciary. But our analysis of the Baldia factory fire litigation has suggested different conclusions.

---

[78] After the Baldia factory fire, new labour laws have been enacted in the Sindh province, for example, Sindh Factories Act, 2015 and The Sindh Occupational Safety and Health Act, 2017, but despite numerous years, these laws have yet to be implemented on the ground.

[79] In relation to labour rights, this cautious and suspicious judicial attitude is examined below.

[80] See The Triangle Shirtwaist Factory Fire, Occupational Health and Safety Administration, United States Department of Labour, www.osha.gov/aboutosha/40-years/trianglefactoryfire (last accessed 4 August 2020).

[81] At that time, a historical death toll in any factory fire.

[82] The criminal proceedings against the owners was dismissed and they were acquitted whereas the civil proceedings did not end up in any meaningful or real compensation.

[83] Comraroff and Comraroff (2006), p. 21.

These two dialectics of justice and injustice and law and lawlessness has given rise to a recurrent and systemic anarchy of law. This anarchy of law actually is the foundational and structural reality of the legal system and not a mere aberration or exception to it. In other words, one of the existentialist requirements for the rule of law, including its notions of justice, seems to be an inherent anarchy within the genetic makeup of the rule of law. But the question which arises from the Baldia factory fire litigation is whether this institutional and practical reality of the anarchy of law should necessarily be seen as a problem or is it also a strategic opportunity to be exploited? My analysis shows that this anarchy of the law can indeed be strategically exploited by the poor, including the working class. In an interview with Gayer, I described this anarchy of law in the following terms:

> Pakistan faces a huge disjunction between "the law in books" and "the law in practice" – a disjunction which, in his view, "creates anarchy about interpretation and application of the law". In the Pakistan context, the law would not be a rational architecture of legal norms bringing about certainty in matters of government and in dispensation of justice, but a source of unpredictability benefiting the shrewd and the mighty.[84]

In new and transitional constitutional democracies like Pakistan, this anarchy of the law arises both from the uncertainty of evolving interpretations about the scope of various rights, duties and especially the scope of judicial remedies as well as from the lack of implementation of various laws caused by state incapacity and deliberate reluctance, which in turn paradoxically creates the legal space for the limited successes in cases like the Baldia factory fire case. For example, landmark compensation and other reliefs were granted to the victims in unusual and legally questionable constitutional jurisdiction, in which the proceedings' potential legal objections against such litigation were never adjudicated upon.[85] Another example is the implementation of an ILO-negotiated pensionary scheme through SESSI, even though the Sindh Employees Social Security Act, 2016 (which created SESSI) does not envisage such a pensionary scheme.[86] An examination of the jurisprudential debates and comparative judicial history[87] does show that legal interpretational uncertainty is a common problem in all legal systems. However, these uncertainties have acquired another radical dimension in countries of the postcolony and the Global South because such countries have experienced constitutional overthrows, weak constitutionalism and unsettled meanings of legal and constitutional provisions due to relatively short histories of liberal legalism, as well as state incapacity and

---

[84]Gayer (2019), p. 311.

[85]We were expecting these compensation claims to be challenged on the ground that the victims were not a party to these constitutional petitions and that their proper remedy lies in filing civil claims based on tort law.

[86]An examination of the above narrative of the Baldia factory litigation also contains other examples of this anarchy of law.

[87]See Schwartz (1993). Despite the passage of 230 years since the US Supreme Court first sat in 1790, judicial debates are still waging on the interpretation of seven articles and twenty seven amendments of the US Constitution. Compared to this short US constitution, the Pakistani Constitution of 1973 has 280 Articles plus schedules.

breakdown leading to an inconsistent or non-enforcement of the law and thus, creating the space for an aggressive form of judicial activism. For example, compare the legal proceedings in Pakistan with the litigation in Germany: the key difference seems to be the relatively predictable certainty about the law as applicable in such cases under the German judicial system.

I disagree with Gayer's analysis that this limited justice achieved by the victims should simply be seen as a result of the bending or twisting of the law. Rather, these achievements are the result of something much more fundamental because this anarchy of the law is based on interpretational confusions, state breakdown and reluctance, and not merely on the subversion of the law by the victims. In other words, this anarchy of the law exists between the space between legal and illegal, justice and injustice and it is precisely for these reasons that this limited justice is achieved through the exploitation of these grey areas of the law and judicial remedies. Also, this anarchy of law works both in favour of capitalist elites and labour and the strategic question is as who can mobilise, legally strategise and exploit it for their collective interest.[88]

Moreover, the unpredictability and uncertainty about the law, as well as contingent circumstances, also creates space for the creativity of human agency, whether of judges, lawyers or group mobilisation, and frees such litigation from the straight-jackets of legal determinism. Although, space here does not allow the exploration of this debate between structure and agency in legal struggles,[89] but the role of individuals (e.g. Justice Maqbool Baqar and Retired Justice Rahmat Jafferi) as well as the favourable contingent circumstances existing at that time in Pakistan's judicial history[90] needs to be further explored in order to understand the contingency of legal interpretations and judicial remedies resulting in the relatively open ended nature of the trajectory of these legal struggles.

4 Strategic Labour Rights Litigation: Tactical Victories, Strategic Possibilities, Structural Improbabilities

Strategic litigation has been defined as "litigation of a public interest that will have a broad impact on society beyond the specific interest of the parties involved"[91] or lawyering "done in the service of a political or social cause that seeks to rearrange existing state or social power relations."[92] As examined above, the strategy adopted in the Baldia factory fire cases was one of strategic litigation for labour and human

[88]Of course, because of the balance of power, it works more for capitalist elites than for labour.

[89]Mouzelis (2008), chapters 1 and 6.

[90]This historical period was a period of great expansion of judicial review in Pakistan. See Siddiqi (2015), p. 77.

[91]Roa and Klugman (2014), p. 31.

[92]Nejaime (2011), p. 943, footnote 3.

rights enforcement including, but not limited to, justice for the victims. In other words, it can be described as strategic labour rights litigation (SLRL). The basic limitations of such litigation-based reform strategy, including SLRL,[93] should analytically follow from the above examined dialectics of justice and injustice and law and lawlessness and the limited justice achieved due to the anarchy of law. But before further examining the limitations and potentialities of such litigation based reform remedies like SLRL, the first task is to determine the measurement standards of the success and effectiveness of such litigation strategies. Underlying these measurement standards are the objectives or purposes of such litigation strategies.

The debate regarding the effectiveness and success of such litigation centered on reform has responded to the type of critique exemplified by Gerald Rosenberg's classic text *The hollow hope: Can courts bring about social change?*.[94] Rosenberg had concluded that victories in litigations centered on reform are illusionary because either these victories are never effectively and substantively enforced or these judicial wins fail to have any direct or indirect favourable impact on social change or reform. Moreover, such litigation may not merely be unproductive but counter-productive by diverting resources from social and political mobilisation, de-radicalising politics and provoking legal, political and social backlash.[95]

There were various responses to the above "rights myth" or "hollow hope" critique, which rebuttals partly accepted this critique but still emphasised the strategic and symbolic impact of such litigation based reform remedies.[96] Some of these responses are as follows:

(a) We can have "success without victory" if we reject the sharp divide between winning and losing. If success in litigation means a commitment to resist, building movements and resistance litigation becoming part of a community of memory then even defeat in litigation is neither fatal nor the priority.[97]
(b) We can achieve "winning through losing" as judicial setbacks could, counterintuitively, contribute to the process of reform. This can happen if lawyers and activist use litigation loss, internally, to construct organisational identity and mobilise outrage constituents, and also use it externally, to appeal to other state actors to initiate reform and by appealing to the public against an anti-majoritarian judiciary.[98]

[93]As this article concentrates on labour rights enforcement, therefore, the term "strategic labour rights litigation" is used instead of the more general term "strategic litigation."

[94]Rosenberg (2008). However, Rosenberg seems to have modified this pessimistic legal position in a recent jointly edited book on public interest litigation before the Indian Supreme Court. The title of the edited book captures his changed position, *A qualified hope*. See Rosenberg et al. (2019).

[95]Nejaime (2011), p. 941; Albiston (2011), p. 61.

[96]Nejaime (2011), p. 941; Albiston (2011), p. 61.

[97]Lobel (2003).

[98]Nejaime (2011), p. 947.

(c) A rebellious approach to lawyering that has lawyers work with, rather than on behalf of subordinate persons by recognising the power and expertise of subordinated persons as being critical to the dismantling of the structures responsible for their subordination.[99] In other words, both lawyers and litigation are just one of the many actors and tools of social change.
(d) Movement lawyering as an alternative to public interest litigation, with its emphasis on mobilised clients and integrated advocacy. It is a strategy based on an genuine bottom-up participation of marginalised groups and "by deemphasizing the centrality of any one type of legal intervention (like impact litigation) in favor of flexibly coordinating organizational and tactical resources across different institutional spaces-some within formal law making arenas and some outside,"[100] and in this way, achieving the dual purposes of holding lawyers accountable and achieving effective legal interventions producing social change.
(e) The impact of strategic human rights litigation has to be examined at various levels. Firstly, victims and survivors. Secondly, legal change. Thirdly, political, social and practical change and lastly, democracy and rule of law.[101]

The purpose of the above description of the various approaches is not to engage in a comprehensive and critical analysis of this debate but to show how the approach to SLRL adopted in this section both incorporates, and differs from, the above approaches. The approach to SLRL is based on the following premises: firstly, it concentrates on judicial wins and their impact on social change. This does not imply that the concept of "wining through losing" is not important, but the priority of analysis in this chapter is on judicial wins. This is also because the impact of judicial wins is still a largely misunderstood or understudied phenomenon especially in countries of the Global South. Secondly, it lays down specific criteria for measuring the effectiveness of SLRL in terms of certain basic categories. This lack of clarity in the criterion for measurement is one of the main reasons for the lack of understanding about the real impacts of judicial wins. Thirdly, this analysis is based on accepting the limitations of legal labour struggles, which arise out of the constrained social, cultural, economic and political conditions existing in countries like Pakistan.

One of the central problems in analysing the effectiveness of SLRL is the disagreement in the literature over the criteria to measure the impact of judicial wins on social change. This confusion arises because of two main reasons. Firstly, there is no consensus about what social change implies. For example, does anything short of steps towards the overthrow of capitalism or achieving substantive equality between capital and labour come within the definition of social change in a capitalist system? Does social change have the same meaning as structural or revolutionary change? Secondly, even if there are criteria for measuring social change, these are

[99] Lopez (2005), p. 2041; Shah (2017), p. 775.
[100] Cummings (2017), p. 1653.
[101] Duffy (2018).

too vague to measure such social change. For example, vague criteria like disrupting legal and social discourses[102] or abolishing the basic logic of the system.[103] Therefore, this chapter proposes that even if precise criteria of how to measure social or structural change may not be possible, it may be possible to come up with conceptual categories which can at least distinguish between different kinds of impacts of litigation on change.

In thinking about such conceptual criteria of measurements, one of the key distinctions is between strategic and tactical impacts. In an important article on this distinction from a Marxist understanding of legal interventions, Robert Knox explains this distinction:

> strategy concerns the manner in which we achieve and eventually fulfil our long term aims or objectives, whereas tactics concerns the methods through which we achieve our shorter terms aims or objectives [....] the opposition would not be between "using the law" (as a liberal) or "abandoning it" (as a nihilist). Rather the question is on what terms is it possible to use law *without* fatally undermining longer term, structural considerations [....] legal argument is being geared towards the strategic aim of building a movement to overthrow capitalism rather than on its own terms.[104]

Knox makes a number of crucial points. Firstly, he distinguishes between strategic concerns and tactical concerns. Secondly, he argues that tactical concerns should not be achieved at the expense of strategic concerns and that tactical concerns should always keep in mind the strategic objective of transcending capitalism. But there are two limitations in Knox's analysis. Firstly, structural, systemic or revolutionary change is a multi-faceted phenomenon in complex modern societies. Such structural or revolutionary change cannot only be defined or limited in terms of "a movement to overthrow capitalism" or only in anti-capitalist terms.[105] Secondly, he fails to make the distinction between strategic and structural or systemic change and it conflates all strategic change as structural or systemic change.

In complex modern societies, legal struggles for structural or systemic change can target various systems of dominations, for example class inequalities, racial or ethnic or religious discriminations, repressive state institutions (e.g. police, intelligence agencies), military dictatorship, regressive or conservative judiciaries etc. Simply because a particular legal struggle does not target the structures of capitalism does not mean that these particular legal struggles cannot have a structural or systemic impact on the system of domination being targeted. In other words, legal struggles having structural or systemic impact are not reducible to only anti-capitalist struggles. This critique of reductionism is important because legal struggles for structural or systemic change targeting systems of dominations other than class inequalities

---

[102]Bader et al. (2019), p. 171.

[103]Knox (2010), p. 199.

[104]Knox (2010), pp. 197, 215, 225.

[105]It is not suggested that Knox does not recognise the importance of overthrowing other systems of domination other than capitalism but the point being emphasised is that this overwhelming and singular focus on the overthrow of capitalism reduces all other struggles against other systems of domination to secondary struggles.

can also contribute towards creating socio-economic and political spaces for such class struggles. For example, class struggles in Pakistan are strategically linked with struggles against military dictatorships because constitutional democracy provides more political space for class struggles than military dictatorships.

Various issues raised above regarding the specific and macro goals of strategic litigation, measuring legal and non-legal impact of litigation through an integrated advocacy approach and connecting tactical gains with strategic objectives, can now be addressed by measuring the impact of judicial wins in terms of three interconnected but distinct categories, i.e. tactical, strategic and structural impact. In terms of litigation impact, tactical impact would mean any change or impact which is limited to conferring benefits on the victims involved in the litigation or which impact is short-term. Strategic impact would mean any impact or change which has more than tactical impact and less than structural impact but rather it creates the strategic space for substantial justice, effective legal reform and increases the capacity and space for social mobilisation but without changing the structural balance of power in state and society. Structural impact would mean impact or changes in both systemic and social terms leading to changes in the balance of power in state and society. Moreover, even within (not simply between) these three categories, the impact or change may vary in different types litigation depending on the level of success achieved in tactical, strategic and structural terms.

On the basis of the above examination of the Baldia factory fire litigation and its interconnected developments, we argue that these cases resulted in tactical victories, created strategic opportunities and openings but ultimately resulted in strategic failures and at the level of long-term and macro impact, it resulted in structural or systemic defeat.

The tactical victories are substantive and obvious: reasonable compensation for the victims, a pensionary scheme under international mediation, initial steps towards registration and inspection of factories and the collective memory of the Baldia factory fire tragedy kept alive through socio-cultural mobilisations. The issue is not to deny the substantive nature of these victories but rather to examine whether these victories are merely tactical or not? Firstly, all orders for the verification and grant of compensation passed by the Sindh High Court were consent orders or interim orders and cannot strictly be used as judicial precedents. Secondly, the ILO mediated pension scheme was voluntary and sets no legal precedent, domestically and internationally. It is at best a voluntary and moral precedent. Moreover, KiK won the case against the victims of Baldia factory fire in Germany.[106] Thirdly, after the initial orders for registration and inspection of factories throughout Sindh, no further orders or final judgement was passed in this regard by the Sindh High Court. Fourthly, there was not a single large scale demonstration or labour strike in response to the Baldia fire nor has there been any progress towards greater unionisation, even in Karachi, as a consequence of this tragedy.

[106]Bader et al. (2019), p. 156.

Furthermore, these tactical victories were not connected or translated into strategic success. As explained above, the new workplace safety law, the Sindh Occupational Safety and Health Act (2017) remains an unimplemented paper tiger. Secondly, the passage of this new law cannot overshadow the strategic failures suffered in this case, e.g., no accountability, no judicial precedents in favour of labour rights or enforcement of labour laws, no labour reforms regarding greater labour representation and social security. But these strategic failures were not inevitable or pre-determined because if the tactical objectives of immediate compensation had not overshadowed the strategic objectives of accountability and labour reforms and like compensation, the litigation strategy in the Baldia factory fire litigation had equally prioritised accountability and the improvement of labour conditions of the factories, then the strategic openings created by the Baldia factory litigation might have led to precedent-setting accountability decisions and labour reforms in the textile sector. In other words, the reason for the lack of substantive strategic impact or success of the Baldia factory litigation primarily lies in the lack of social and victim mobilisation for accountability and labour reform resulting in the slow disappearance of any macro or strategic vision during this litigation and the lack of evolution of a legal strategy to effectively operational this strategic vision.[107]

As for the systemic or structural change resulting from the Baldia factory fire litigation, the assessment is quite simple: if there is an absence of strategic victories, then structural or systemic change is impossible to achieve. But more tragically, the defeat on the structural or systemic front is near absolute in the Baldia factory fire litigation. The forces of capitalism had the last laugh when they converted the factory fire from a case involving worker safety and labour law violations into an act of terrorism which resulted in converting the owners of the factory and its government collaborators into victims along with, and at the same level, as the 255 dead workers.

In the midst of this above described treacherous landscape of litigation in countries like Pakistan, can SLRL succeed beyond tactical objectives? In the presence of deunionisation, no political or social sympathy for labour rights, a powerful capitalist elite, a compromised state, no rigorous enforcement of human rights and labour laws, victims who prioritise compensation over accountability and labour reform and a judiciary which is ambiguous towards labour issues and provides relief to victims on the basis of the generic right to life basis rather than on the basis of labour rights, the Baldia factory fire teaches us three basic lessons. Firstly, real tactical victories are possible through SLRL and are worth pursuing for the victims and also in order to explore the possibility of strategic impacts. Secondly, such tactical victories can be translated into strategic openings if the victims can be mobilised to think beyond their concerns like immediate compensation, and if the litigation strategy is able to connect tactical issues with strategic issues by

[107] As explained above in the description of the Baldia factory fire litigation, this failure was also due to the fact that the victims prioritised compensation over accountability and labour reform and the fact that there were hardly any victims who were consistently willing to pursue the criminal proceedings against the owners, management and government officials for the purposes of accountability.

prioritising both tactical and strategic objectives simultaneously. But this is not merely a theoretical exercise in strategic thinking but victims, civil society and the political actors have to be convinced and mobilised, and material resources have to be generated, in order for the effective implementation of these linkages between the tactical and strategic objectives. Thirdly, strategic litigation can achieve strategic and structural or systemic impact against other structures of domination.[108] However, when it comes to inegalitarian capital-labour relations and the dominance of the capitalist elites, SLRL is an ineffective remedy and can have no systemic or structural impact. This conclusion about the ineffectiveness of SLRL in terms of systemic or structural impact is based on the constrained socio-economic and political conditions existing in countries like Pakistan as well as on the basis of the above analysis that there is no immediate hope of escaping the dualism of justice and injustice and law and lawlessness in these labour legal struggles.

5 Conclusion

We need to move beyond the dualities of legal nihilism based on theories devoid of evidence from judicial history and legal practice and a legal optimism which celebrates tactical victories without assessing the strategic and long-term impact and damage. Legal struggles are unavoidable because law is omnipresent in modern capitalist societies but law is also strategically addictive for victims and civil society because it does provide justice in labour struggles, however limited it might be. But moving beyond the duality of legal nihilism and optimism does not imply that we can reach some kind of Aristotelian median between them but rather it is to accept the reality of the existence of these irreconcilable contradictions and paradoxes and to build a legal resistance and strategy on the exploitation of these contradictions.[109] Or as Walt Whitman rightly said, "do I contradict myself? Very well, then I contradict myself (I am large, I contain multitudes)."[110]

[108]In the context of Pakistan, see the judgment reported as *Karamat Ali & Others v. Federation of Pakistan & Others* (PLD 2018 Sindh 8) on police reform. The aforementioned judgment can be considered as a successful example of strategic litigation leading to strategic impact as not only a new law on policing was introduced but a more independent and accountable police is slowly emerging as a result of this litigation. Also see the judgments reported as *Chief Justice of Pakistan Iftikhar Muhammad Chaudhry v. President of Pakistan & Others* (PLD 2010 SC 61) and *Sindh High Court Bar Association & Another v. Federation of Pakistan & Others* (PLD 2009 SC 879) on challenges to military domination and establishing judicial independence. The aforementioned judgments can be considered as successful examples of strategic litigation leading to structural or systemic impact as no military rule has been imposed in Pakistan since December 2007 (the longest period of civilian rule in Pakistan's history).

[109]This analysis is also different from such theories of incremental reformism which presume that in the long run, such contradictions can be resolved. This chapter argues for a theory of reformism which accepts the presence of these irreconcilable contradictions.

[110]Whitman (1855).

References

Albiston C (2011) The dark side of litigation as a social movement strategy. Iowa Law Rev 941 (96):61–77

Bader M, Saagee-Maaß M, Terwindt C (2019) Strategic litigation against the misconduct of multinational enterprises: an anatomy of Jabir and Others v KiK. Verfassung und Recht in Übersee 52(2):156–171

Berlin I (1998) The proper study of Mankind, an anthology of essays. Pimlico, London

Brown M (Fall 2018) "An unqualified human good"? On rule of law, globalization, and imperialism. Law Soc Inq J Am Bar Foundat 43(4): 1391–1426

Cole DH (2001) "An unqualified human good": E.P. Thompson and the rule of law. J Law Soc 28 (2):177–203

Comraroff J, Comraroff JL (2006) Law and disorder in the post-colony. University of Chicago Press, Chicago

Cummings S (2017) Movement lawyering. Univ Ill Law Rev 2017(5):1645–1732

Duffy H (2018) Strategic human rights litigation: understanding and maximising impact. Hart, Portland

Gayer L (2019) Putting out the Baldia factory fire: how the trial of Karachi's industrial capitalism did not happen. In: Harriss-White B, Michelutti L (eds) The Wild East. University California Press, Berkeley, pp 288–321

Khan M (2014) Genesis and evolution of public interest litigation in the Supreme Court of Pakistan: towards a dynamic theory of judicialization. Temple Int Comp Law J 28(1):285–359

Knox R (2010) Strategy and tactics. Finnish Yearb Int Law 21:193–199

Lobel J (2003) Success without victory. New York University Press, New York

Lopez G (2005) Living and lawyering rebelliously. Fordham Law Rev 73(5):2041–2054

Mouzelis N (1999) Differentiation and marginalization in late modernity. In: Gough I, Olofsson G (eds) Capitalism and social cohesion. Palgrave Macmillan, London

Mouzelis N (2008) Modern and postmodern social theorizing. Cambridge University Press, Cambridge

Nejaime D (2011) Winning through losing. Iowa Law Rev 96:941–1012

Roa M, Klugman B (2014) Considering strategic litigation as an advocacy tool: a case study of the defence of reproductive rights in Columbia. Reprod Health Matters 22(44):31–41

Rosenberg GN (2008) The hollow hope: can courts bring about social change? University of Chicago Press, Chicago, IL

Rosenberg G, Krishnaswamy S, Bail S (2019) A qualified hope. Cambridge University Press, Cambridge

Schwartz B (1993) A history of the Supreme Court. Oxford University Press, New York, New York

Shah J (2017) Rebellious lawyering in big case clinics. Clin Law Rev 23:775–815

Siddiqi F (2015) Public interest litigation: predicable continuity and radical departures. In: Cheema MH, Gilani IS (eds) The politics and jurisprudence of the Chaudhry Court 2005-2013. Oxford University Press, Oxford

Thompson EP (1990) Whigs and hunters: the origin of the Black Act. Penguin Books, London

Whitman W (1855) Song of myself. In: Leaves of grass. Viking Press, New York

Faisal Siddiqi is a leading constitutional, civil and human rights lawyer who practices at the Supreme Court and High Courts of Pakistan. Siddiqi graduated from the London School of Economics and Political Sciences and read law at the University of Cambridge. He is one of the main founders of the Rasheed Rizvi Centre for Constitutional and Human Rights, and the Legal Aid Foundation for Victims of Rape and Sexual Assault, where he directly oversees the operations of both organisations. Siddiqi is an active member of the board of directors of the Pakistan Institute for Labor Education and Research. He also regularly writes for the Pakistani daily newspaper *Dawn* and has been a visiting fellow at the London School of Economics and Political Science and McGill University in Montreal, Canada.

After the Ali Enterprises Fire: Occupational Safety and Health and Workers' Organising—A Conversation with Zehra Khan About Current and Future Struggles

Palvasha Shahab

Abstract Zehra Khan is a prominent labour activist and journalist who has been working in Karachi, Pakistan, for more than a decade. She is the founder and General Secretary of the Home Based Women Workers Federation of Pakistan (HBWWF). She also works closely with the National Trade Union Federation (NTUF). In this interview, she speaks to Palvasha Shahab about current and future struggles in regards to working conditions in Pakistan.

Keywords Collective organising · Labour movement · Workers struggle · Ali Enterprises factory fire · KiK case

Zehra Khan is a prominent activist and seasoned journalist who has been working in Karachi, Pakistan, for more than a decade. She is the founder and general secretary of the Home Based Women Workers Federation of Pakistan (HBWWF). She has also been a steadfast supporter of and close collaborator with Pakistan's National Trade Union Federation (NTUF), and a vocal ally of the families affected by the 2012 Ali Enterprises factory fire. Her voice has been an important part of the struggle for justice in the aftermath of the Ali Enterprises fire.

Palvasha Shahab: What is your recollection of the day of the Ali Enterprises fire?

Zehra Khan: I was at the NTUF office that day and was on my way home when I heard the news. When I reached home and watched the whole news on TV, I saw it was a terribly aggressive fire. News of the factory fire was aired on TV continuously for 3 days. I heard on Geo News that more than 300 workers had died in the fire incident.[1]

[1]Although the initial news reports cited higher numbers, the total number of deaths was later determined to be 255, established by the Judicial Commission that conducted thorough

P. Shahab (✉)
Rasheed Razvi Centre for Constitutional and Human Rights (RCCHR), and the Legal Aid Foundation for Victims of Rape and Sexual Assault (LAFRSA), Karachi, Pakistan
e-mail: palvasha.shahab@columbia.edu

M. Saage-Maaß et al. (eds.), *Transnational Legal Activism in Global Value Chains*, Interdisciplinary Studies in Human Rights 6,
https://doi.org/10.1007/978-3-030-73835-8_5

The next morning, I arrived at the scene of the fire and there was destruction everywhere. Later that day, we held a protest at the Karachi Press Club. The fire just kept raging and bodies just kept emerging. When we returned to the factory to continue our protest there, we saw that MQM [Muttahida Qaumi Movement, a political party with considerable clout in the area at the time] had organised a vigil, where they were lighting candles and mourning the dead. I walked past the crowd of people that had collected for our protest, past the MQM vigil and the families of those affected. When I got past them, I saw that EOBI [Employees' Old-Age Benefits Institution] had set up their desk and, as bodies were being retrieved from the fire, they were registering dead bodies. They were actually registering workers posthumously for the benefits scheme!

That day, I also crossed the police lines that cordoned off the fire stricken factory, and found some burnt jeans that had the KiK label on them. At the time, I did not know what it was, but I later learnt that it was a German retail brand. One of the photographs that I took was circulated across the internet and news media. I later found out that the factory predominantly manufactured semi-finished and finished products for "OKAY Jeans" for KiK, which is based in Germany. Also later, in my interviews with workers, I found out that the factory employed approximately 2000 workers in different shifts for different jobs, and that a small portion of its production was also for other brands like Go Blue and Diesel.

Shahab: How did you become involved in the longer-term response to the Ali Enterprises Factory Fire?

Khan: A lot of things happened simultaneously. As I mentioned, the very next day, we were at the Karachi Press Club, along with our trade union affiliates, and were protesting under the slogan: "Safety first, the workplace should be safe for all workers!" After the fire, we organised regular meetings with trade unions and especially with home-based women workers, and we mobilised them around safety issues and said that the workplaces will not be safe until there is a big movement. We contacted almost all trade unions, as well as representatives of political parties, civil society, and human rights organisations. We also mobilised workers outside the courts, such as when the [Ali Enterprises] factory owners' bail application was being heard.

Then, on the other hand, in the months following the fire, the Pakistan Institute for Labour Education and Research (PILER)[2] was involved in negotiations with the international brand [KiK]. Near the end of 2012, they settled on immediate relief of US$1 million and the promise of future compensation. However, at the time, we only heard that a local organisation was negotiating with the brand and guessed that it was

investigations, including DNA tests. Report of the Judicial Commission on Baldia Factory Fire Incident, Karachi, 28 August 2013, Court File of Constitutional Petition 3318 of 2012, p. 1379. For earlier reports, please see: Death Toll from Karachi Factory Fire Soars, BBCNews.com, 12 September 2012 www.bbc.com/news/world-asia-19566851 (last accessed 23 September 2020).

[2]A prominent labour rights organisation in Pakistan.

PILER, because most of us were unaware that this was happening. But later, the workers, NTUF, IndustriALL,[3] and the Clean Clothes Campaign, etc. were also involved in the following rounds of negotiation.[4] In early 2013, on behalf of NTUF, I also conducted an initial survey on the fire tragedy. For the survey, I interviewed more than 100 affected families and connected with even more victims' families.

Shahab: How were you involved with the forming of the Ali Enterprises Factory Fire Affectees Association (AEFFAA)?

Khan: Even though we had initially met quite a few affectees in the immediate aftermath of the fire and interviewed them, it was only after we began working with a different, more consistent group of affectees that things picked up steam. About a year and a half after the fire, we met a group of affectees outside the old NTUF office in the Mashriq Centre. When we ran into them, in the building, it turned out that Nasir Mansoor of NTUF knew some of them. That was the group that took the initiative to keep fighting for justice and keep encouraging other affectees to keep fighting; from then onwards that was the group we collaborated with. Upon our [Nasir Mansoor and Zehra Khan] suggestion, they formed the association [the Ali Enterprises Factory Fire Affectees Association (AEFFAA)] almost a year and a half after the fire. So as a result, together with NTUF, I helped the victims and affected families come together in the form of an association and we have been working together ever since.

Shahab: How would you describe the formation of the coalition between the national and international actors? What role did the case in Germany against KiK play in this?

Khan: On the international front, first Nasir Mansoor contacted IndustriALL, with whom NTUF is affiliated. Later the European Center for Constitutional and Human Rights (ECCHR) and the Clean Clothes Campaign (CCC) joined, and so forth, as time went by. When ECCHR wanted to file a case in Germany, we supported that idea. PILER and the lawyer Faisal Siddiqi initially thought it was risky and wanted to pursue litigation in the courts here [in Pakistan] instead. They said that KiK had already promised a second round of negotiations and more compensation, so we should pursue that and focus on the litigation here in Pakistan. They believed it could jeopardise the negotiations which were being facilitated by the International Labour Organization and, if it failed on substantive grounds, it could set an unfavourable legal precedent. Then, when negotiations with KiK hit a roadblock, PILER and Faisal Siddiqi also extended their support to the litigation in Germany in the hope that Kik may be pressurised into returning to the negotiating table.

We, as HBWWF and NTUF, supported and facilitated the idea of litigating abroad from the very beginning. When ECCHR came to Pakistan and discussed this idea with us, we gathered a group of affectees, assisted in the selection of

[3] An international labour union.

[4] As described in the chapters by Faisal Siddiqi and Miriam Saage-Maaß in this volume.

petitioners or plaintiffs, and then helped the Petitioners sign their Powers of Attorney and get their other documents in order. The documentation process was also riddled with difficulties and we ended up repeating the process a few times before everything was in order for filing. We also helped get the necessary expert opinions from Pakistan that could be used for the litigation in Europe.

Shahab: What are the results of the different legal struggles in Pakistan and Germany?

Khan: Regardless of the results of the court case, ECCHR has really managed to keep the issue alive in Europe. The media and lawyers, in general, have really managed to keep this issue alive, both here and in Europe. For the litigation in Pakistan, the results were compensation-oriented. There [in Germany], our main objectives were to create an opportunity for ensuring worker safety while also ensuring that people affected by the fire were involved and included in all decisions being made on their account, such as negotiations, litigation, pensions, compensation, and so forth.

In the end, a Compensation [Judicial] Commission was set up for the distribution of compensation that was being provided by the Government of Sindh, the Federal Government, and through the initial instalment from KiK. The commission was headed by a retired judge and was formed through an order of the High Court of Sindh (SHC). The Compensation [Judicial] Commission distributed compensation money in two rounds. The criteria set up by this commission was also used to administer the ILO pensions that came a few years later in 2018. The Government of Sindh distributed 300,000 Pakistani rupees to the family of each deceased person and 50,000 Pakistani rupees to each injured person. The federal government gave 400,000 Pakistani rupees to the family of each deceased person. The Compensation [Judicial] Commission also prepared criteria for distributing compensation amongst different legal heirs from the same family. This was important because, initially, the male members of the family were keeping all the money, and women, particularly those who had been widowed in the fire, were not being given any share.

In the first round, legal heirs of each deceased worker received a total amount of 500,000 Pakistani rupees. Whereas in the second round, the same legal heirs of each deceased worker will receive a total of 110,000 Pakistani rupees. This commission also distributed compensation money among 55 injured workers. For the injured workers, the commission formed the following criteria to distribute compensation:

Permanently disabled injured workers: 500,000 Pakistani rupees
Gravely injured workers: 250,000 Pakistani rupees
Simply injured workers: 125,000 Pakistani rupees

Shahab: You conducted a study on the Ali Enterprises fire incident on behalf of NTUF in 2013. Could you please elaborate on your findings from this study?

Khan: The survey was very revealing. First, the workers who were interviewed confirmed that the emergency gates were locked on the instruction of the factory management. All windows were blocked permanently with iron grills on the pretext of stopping the theft of merchandise. It was horrifying. It was also the result of criminal negligence. Second, it was also found that this fire incident was not the first in the factory. Two fire accidents had occurred in the same factory earlier in the year, in February and September 2012, respectively. Only, those fires were not as dreadful as this mishap. They had both been caused by electric short-circuiting. Third, both before and after the previous two smaller fires, the factory owners did not take any precautionary measures to secure their workers' lives. The factory management had not even so much as ensured a functional emergency fire alarm or smoke detector alarms to alert the workers to a fire or other emergency so that they could escape during such situations to save their lives. Fourth, the workers didn't have any training or support to cope with emergency situations. Fifth, there was only one entrance and exit point, which was also blocked with materials and merchandise dumped here and there. The three-story garment factory had only one exit and no functioning firefighting equipment. Sixth, it was also revealed, by some surviving workers that, among the workers hired through contractors, children also used to work in Ali Enterprises Factory without any medical clearance as mandated by the Factories Act, 1934. Seventh, the Labour and Human Resources Department of the Government of Sindh also confirmed that Ali Enterprises was not officially registered with them, and its building design was also not approved by the competent Building Control Authority. The factory had been functioning for years in the heart of an industrial zone in Karachi, illegally, without any check. Eighth, hardly any workers had social security, as the majority of the workers didn't have formal appointment letters and most of them were hired through third-party contractors. When workers do not have appointment letters, it is very easy to deny the workers any kind of job security, entitlement to sick leave, health cards, compensation for injury at the workplace, registration with social security schemes, and so forth. The same tactic of recruiting through contactors is adopted by the majority of employers in Pakistani factories, to avoid abiding by the rights guaranteed to workers. This makes workers even more vulnerable to excessive working hours and extremely, even fatally, unsafe conditions.

Shahab: As you report, there has been quite some compensation paid to the victim's families and the surviving workers. What are the issues remaining?

Khan: Firstly, the conditions of workplace safety have not improved and there is still complete impunity for violating safety laws. Moreover, precarious employment continues to be the norm. Workers are hired through third party contractors; they are denied employment letters and denied registration with the Sindh Employees Social Security Institution, EOBI and the Workers Welfare Fund. As a result, they have no safety at the workplace, no job security and no health and pension benefits. Forget informal workplaces, discreet sweatshops and home based workers— even formally registered factories are not following safety laws, rules, regulations, standards or best practices.

Secondly, it is very unfortunate that in an industrial city like Karachi, where more than 65% of the country's revenue is generated, there was no laboratory to conduct DNA tests at the time when the Ali Enterprises fire happened. There was no proper mechanism to collect the DNA samples of the deceased's blood relatives. As a result, the bereaved families endured agony and trauma for many months to get the DNA reports to confirm the identity of unclaimed, unrecognisable bodies lying in the Edhi mortuary of Karachi. A year after the fire, there were still 25 unidentified workers, and 17 of them were buried in the Baldia graveyard of the city. After the fire incident, many workers became unemployed and many of those who were injured due to the fire didn't get proper treatment from the government. Now these families are still facing problems and struggling to make ends meet. The lack of systems and streamlined processes which are responsive to the realities on ground is often the undoing of the working class in particular and of the citizens of Karachi in general.

Thirdly, even more importantly, we found that many of the workers who were employed at the factory were of Bengali or Bihari ethnicity (who are frequently undocumented, and were so in these cases too), and their applications for documentation had either been denied or they had never attempted to make national identity cards (because of the general community-wide belief that their application for national identitiy cards would be denied). Some of them did not even have birth certificates. Later, as the Prime Minister Raja Parvez Ashraf, the Sindh government, and other entities like KiK were announcing compensation, these workers or their families could not access that money because they did not have the requisite identification documents and, hence, also did not have bank accounts. So, we had to try to help them or their families get some kind of documentation or see how they could be paid without bank accounts and documentation —such as in cash. At present, I believe five of the pensions are being given in cash.

Shahab: How do you assess the role of international companies in the Ali Enterprises incident?

Khan: The catastrophic incident itself, and all the investigations and reporting that followed, revealed that not only local manufacturers, but also international companies, brands, and audit certification organisations (such as Social Accountability International, which issues the SA-8000 certificates), are all responsible for the prevailing situation of workers' rights; the poor safety standards at workplaces, and the grievous or fatal accidents and diseases that result from these conditions. International brands and audit certification organisations should implement the international labour standards for safeguarding the rights of workers in producing countries like Pakistan, but sadly, they become the key drivers of exploitative global value chains and local private enterprises become vehicles of this oppressive chain whose participants just want money by hook or by crook.

These multinational companies don't pay any attention to the inhuman working conditions prevailing in workplaces like Ali Enterprises, which provide the products they then sell in European and North American markets. They fully know about the working conditions in Pakistani factories. They are aware that laws are not followed and that genuine unions, that can possibly safeguard the workers and work towards securing their rights, are not allowed to exist, and they benefit from it. The international brand KiK belatedly and only indirectly assumed responsibility for the fire when they agreed to pay compensation— and only after intense pressure from various international and domestic organisations. The factories supplying merchandise, as well as the international brands and retailers, are morally and ethically bound. They should all be legally bound with the threat of liability, to enforce national and international labour standards, as they miserably fail to fulfil their so-called corporate responsibilities.

Shahab: You are heavily involved with home-based workers. What proportion of them are textile and garment workers and what are the difficulties, safety concerns, wage theft or other problems faced by home-based workers? How are these different from the problems of those working in formal factories?

Khan: There are approximately 12 million home-based workers in Pakistan, out of which 3–4 million are living in the province of Sindh. About 60% of home-based workers are engaged with the textile and garment sector, including in stitching, cropping, packing, folding, sorting, patchwork, embroidery, elastic work, button-making, beadwork, etc. And approximately 80% are female workers who work at very cheap rates and uses their home as their workplace. They get work from different contractors and middlemen, without knowing for whom, for which market, and for which brand they are working. Their actual employers are veiled and obscured, due to which they can't get any benefits within the existing legal structure.

Home-based workers are not protected by labour laws in Pakistan. They are not allowed to form unions, their minimum wages are not fixed by law, they are working for very low wages without any social benefits, their jobs are not permanent, and they have no job security. As their terms and conditions of employment are not certain, they end up working long hours and having to invest in and use their own work material and infrastructure, such as sewing machines, electricity, etc. All these things make them even more vulnerable. They have no benefits, despite the fact that they are an important part of the supply chain.

Nevertheless, due to our efforts, Sindh became the first province to recognise and empower home-based workers. The Sindh Home Based Workers Act of 2018 was passed in Sindh on 9 May 2019 by the Sindh Assembly.[5] The minimum wage board has now included home-based bangle workers in their minimum wage gazette for the first time. Moreover, official rules were also formulated under the act and were notified in January 2020. We are hopeful that home-based workers' registration will start with the Labour and Human Resources Department of the Government of Sindh in August 2020.

Shahab: How do you place the tragic fire in the context of the labour struggles in Pakistan?

Khan: The Ali Enterprises factory fire was an emergency siren for worker safety in Pakistan. The incident has changed into a new symbol of workers' resistance, which could eventually help factory workers to secure the right of having a decent working environment and to get rid of social injustice and prevailing modern slavery based on crony capitalism.

The accident forced the government to confront the miserable working conditions in factories and workplaces, or rather, the fire slapped the government in the face

[5]See Yousafzai A, 11-year struggle for home-based workers' rights set to bear fruit this year. The News, 18 January 2019, www.thenews.com.pk/print/420315-11-year-struggle-for-home-based-workers-rights-set-to-bear-fruit-this-year#:~:text=After%20many%20years%20of%20efforts,their%20status%2C%E2%80%9D%20Khan%20said (last accessed 10 September 2020).

with these miserable work conditions. For instance, the government introduced a number of initiatives to improve overall working conditions in factories and work-places. One of these initiatives is an ILO-supported project on occupational safety and health (OSH). Another is the Deutsche Gesellschaft für Internationale Zusammenarbeit (GIZ) pilot project in the Punjab province to improve the working environment through a tripartite mechanism in 10 selected factories. This initiative is also to be extended to Karachi in the near future. The Sindh government has also initiated a number of measures in response to workers' demands, including OSH legislation [The Sindh Occupational Safety and Health Act, 2017], and has declared 11 September as "Health and Safety Day" in the province.

In the years following the fire, the Government of Sindh has finally recognised agricultural labour, including cotton field workers, as workers protected by labour law, and is now more willing to explore ways to extend legal rights and social and economic protections to them. The Government of Sindh also recognises home-based workers as workers who are an integral part of ready-made-garment-sector supply chains.

Shahab: What are the struggles for workers' unions lying ahead?

Khan: Occupational safety and health remains one of the main issues for the workers. Five years after the Ali Enterprises incident, a law, that is, the Sindh Occupational Safety and Health Act, 2017, was passed in Sindh. Now, 3 years later, the implementation of this act is still far away. Pakistan has still not implemented most of the international conventions on OSH that it has signed and ratified.[6] The importance of occupational safety and health hasn't been understood by government departments and employers. Therefore, many factories are still death traps for workers.

Factories are unsafe for workers. Workers' access to the right to freedom of association is still a dream. One of the most dangerous and most common characteristics of textile and garment establishments, especially the units which produce merchandise for international brands, is that the management of these factories often form two or more "yellow" labour unions,[7] with acquiescence from the officials from the Labour and Human Resources Department, to block workers from forming genuine, representative, independent unions. These factories engage in this illegal labour practice to gain superficial credibility or to fulfil the requirements needed to attract orders from international buyers,[8] and these international buyers usually know exactly what is going on. In the meanwhile, many of the workers in the

[6]Pakistan has signed and ratified various ILO conventions on labour administration and inspections, occupational safety and health, social security, working times, and various other issues. Details can be found at: Ratifications for Pakistan, ILO, Normlex www.ilo.org/dyn/normlex/en/f?p=NORMLEXPUB:11200:0::NO::P11200_INSTRUMENT_SORT,P11200_COUNTRY_ID:2,103166#Occupational_safety_and_health (last accessed 10 September 2020).

[7]A "yellow" union is a worker organisation that is dominated or influenced by an employer and is therefore not an independent trade union.

[8]Many transnational corporations have requirements under voluntary corporate social responsibility mechanisms, codes of conduct, or other similar documents. For more details, see the chapter by Michael Bader in this book.

factories often don't even know about the existence of the fake "yellow" unions that are apparently representing them.

Every factory must have a genuine union and the right of collective bargaining, so a constructive dialogue between employers and workers can be started and both parties can mutually understand each other and reach an agreement on working conditions in which every worker can feel safe during work. This environment would also support employers in increasing their work. But unfortunately, in Pakistan, employers are still involved in making dummy unions, where there is no collective bargaining.

Palvasha Shahab was the joint executive director of the Rasheed Razvi Centre for Constitutional and Human Rights, and the Legal Aid Foundation for Victims of Rape and Sexual Assault through September 2020. She now works a consultant for RCCHR, LAFRSA, the Legal Aid Society and the Pakistan Institute for Labour Education and Research. She is on the Law Committee of the Sindh Commission of the Status on Women and advises on upcoming legislation. She is also an advisor to a transnational collaborative project on oral histories and social interventions titled "Karachi Beach Radio." She also teaches undergraduate courses on peace movements and international human rights law at SZABIST, Karachi. Shahab further curates and moderates important public discussions on national platforms such as the Adab Fest and The Second Floor. She holds a Master of Laws from Columbia Law School, New York, US, where she was also a Human Rights Fellow at the Human Rights Institute in 2017–2018.

Pakistan's "Industrial 9/11": Transnational Rights-Based Activism in the Garment Industry and Creating Space for Future Global Struggles

Nasir Mansoor, Thomas Rudhof-Seibert, and Miriam Saage-Maaß

Abstract This chapter is based on an internal evaluation of the of the 2012–2019 cooperation between the Pakistani National Trade Union Federation (NTUF), the German humanitarian organisation medico international, and the Berlin-based European Center for Constitutional and Human Rights (ECCHR). Written from a first-person perspective by three members of these organisations, it offers invaluable insights into the internal coordination and strategic deliberations of the partners' evolving transnational efforts to hold the German retail company KiK and Italian social auditing firm RINA to account on behalf of the survivors and victims' families of the 2012 Ali Enterprises factory fire. The authors elaborate on the multi-dimensional effects and aftermath of the Ali Enterprises tragedy, and recount the lessons learned from their different perspectives as trade unionists, activists, and lawyers based in both Pakistan and Germany. On this basis, the chapter then maps additional possible avenues for supporting the transnational struggles of workers around the globe. All in all, it offers rich insights into the experiences and complex debates ongoing amongst the authors and their organisations on how to develop common positions and further enhance their mutual understanding in order to collectively imagine and work towards transformative political goals.

Keywords Transnational collaboration · Evaluation · Coalition-building · Advocacy · Lobbying · Movement-building · Trade unions · Pakistan · Ali Enterprises factory fire

N. Mansoor · T. Rudhof-Seibert (✉)
medico international e.V., Frankfurt am Main, Germany
e-mail: seibert@medico.de

M. Saage-Maaß
European Center for Constitutional and Human Rights, Berlin, Germany

M. Saage-Maaß et al. (eds.), *Transnational Legal Activism in Global Value Chains*, Interdisciplinary Studies in Human Rights 6,
https://doi.org/10.1007/978-3-030-73835-8_6

1 Introduction

On 11 September 2012, at least 258 people burned to death in the Ali Enterprises garment factory in the Baldia area of Karachi, Pakistan, in what has come to be known locally as Pakistan's "Industrial 9/11." Not long after, two other garment industry catastrophes followed in Bangladesh. On 24 November 2012, a fire broke out at the Tazreen Fashion factory in the Ashulia district on the outskirts of Dhaka, killing over 100 people and injuring hundreds more. On 24 April 2013, structural failure led to the collapse of Rana Plaza in Dhaka's Savar area, an eight-story commercial complex that housed garment factories, a bank, apartments and several shops, killing 1134 people and injuring over 2500. This series of high-profile disasters brought the South Asian garment industry into the international spotlight, spurring new debate on workers' dismal living and working conditions, as well as the toxic role of Western consumerism in driving these conditions in globalised value chains.

Following the Ali Enterprises fire, the National Trade Union Federation in Pakistan immediately threw its weight behind the survivors and families of the deceased workers, supporting them in their efforts to self-organise and wage a strategic fight for justice. When it became clear that the main buyer of over 70% of the Ali Enterprises factory's output was the German retailer KiK, the Germany-based human rights organisation medico international (medico) positioned itself in support of NTUF, providing the federation with political backing and solidarity in the form of an extensive media and public outreach campaign highlighting the Ali Enterprises fire as a symbol of the exploitative character of global production and supply chains, and thus global capitalism on the whole. The European Center for Constitutional and Human Rights, another Germany-based legal human rights group, also joined the alliance to take on KiK's responsibility as a legal topic. While our three organisations worked closely together to support those affected in their demands for criminal investigations against and reparation from the factory owners in Pakistan, and their struggles for compensation from the Pakistani government, they also sought to strategically shift focus towards Europe by waging a rights-based struggle in Germany against retailer KiK.

This text, much of it drawn from an internal evaluation of the 2012–2019 cooperation between NTUF, medico and ECCHR, seeks to provide insight into the nature, internal coordination, and strategic deliberations of the collaborative transnational cooperation as trade unionists, activists and lawyers over the past years. The text recounts the German and Pakistani perspectives on the effects of the Ali Enterprises tragedy, and aims to map a joint way forward in continuing to support the broader transnational struggles of garment industry and other workers around the globe. In addition to offering others insight into our cooperation, we see this text as part of an ongoing political debate amongst ourselves, in which we aim to clarify our positions and further develop our mutual understandings, differences and political visions.

2 Looking Back: The Formation of a Transnational Coalition and the Case Against KiK

In the aftermath of the Ali Enterprises tragedy, NTUF supported the factory fire survivors and families of the deceased in organising themselves as the Ali Enterprises Factory Fire Affectees Association (AEFFAA), which, to this day, represents the majority of affected families. Other actors also supported the group with various forms of solidarity, including the Pakistan Institute of Labour Education and Research (PILER), various local labour organisations and international trade unions, as well as civil society organisations and the media. Notably, the global union IndustriALL and the Clean Clothes Campaign, a global grassroots alliance dedicated to improving working conditions and empowering workers in the global garment and sportswear industries, collaborated with NTUF and PILER to help the AEFFAA demand what eventually became successful compensation negotiations facilitated by the International Labour Organization with the German discount retailer KiK, the main buyer of garments produced at the Ali Enterprises factory.

In September 2016, the AEFFAA finally reached a long-term compensation agreement with KiK as a result of the negotiations between the German company and IndustriALL and CCC at the ILO. Having already paid US$1 million in immediate emergency relief in 2012, KiK agreed to provide an additional US $5.15 million in compensation for lost income, medical costs, as well as rehabilitation. The negotiations took a long and winding road not only due to the difficulty of the matter, but also due to temporary stalling tactics on the part of KiK. In this respect, ECCHR's preparatory activities for a lawsuit against KiK in Germany provided an accelerating effect on the ILO negotiations, serving as an implicit threat to the company. However, ECCHR, medico and NTUF had agreed with AEFFAA and the other groups involved that the lawsuit would only be filed when KiK could no longer use it as an excuse to prematurely break off negotiations at the ILO.

In conceptualising the legal case against KiK in Germany, NTUF, medico and ECCHR agreed to promote the factory fire affectees' demand for compensation as a right in itself. From the beginning, we sought to frame the court case against KiK in Germany as a political statement, not just a legal dispute. For all of us, the legal case was a supplement to the overarching "political case." We saw it as a way to increase transnational public awareness around the factory fire and deplorable conditions in the global garment industry, and as an opportunity to advance a broader justice claim. To ensure consensus between our three organisations and the AEFFAA, we held several consultations in 2013 and 2014, culminating in a two-day meeting in Karachi in September 2014. This meeting was attended by relatives of almost all of the families affected by the Ali Enterprises fire and included extensive discussion of the legal and political possibilities and implications of filing a case against KiK in a German civil court. In the wake of this meeting and after extensive discussion and exchange, AEFFAA selected four members to represent the group as plaintiffs in the court case in Germany. While the four plaintiffs were technically claiming their individual rights through their participation in the case, their main goal was to represent AEFFAA's political demands more broadly.

NTUF, medico and ECCHR's confrontational position against KiK was carefully aligned with the strategies of the other actors in the broader solidarity network, such as PILER and CCC, both of whom sought to negotiate with KiK rather than confront them outright. For these civil society organisations coming from an advocacy and campaigning background, the aim of public action was to influence KiK's decision to pay initial emergency compensation and, then, to participate in the ILO-facilitated talks. As soon as talks at the ILO had started, however, they saw a continued confrontational approach as threatening to disrupt the negotiations, thereby risking their chance to gain additional financial compensation. The families of the AEFFAA, in contrast, made the decision to take legal action against KiK, even if it potentially comprised their prospects for additional financial compensation, which was, in itself, already a strong political stand.[1] These views were merged into a common strategy, in which the lawsuit played the role of exerting the continuous pressure needed for the compensation talks to progress.

With this understanding, NTUF was represented by IndustriALL and CCC in the ILO negotiations, while being equally engaged in the lawsuit. medico and ECCHR, in turn, acted as political and legal supporters rather than negotiators, and were not directly involved in the ILO negotiations. This somewhat external positionality with regards to the ILO negotiations enabled medico and ECCHR to exert pressure on the actors driving the negotiations, in particular KiK and the ILO, to ensure that the AEFFAA, as the primary representative body of the fire survivors and victims' families, continued to play a central role in the negotiations. This strategy played out exactly as intended: after the lawsuit in Germany had been filed against KiK in March 2015, the negotiations at the ILO gained speed. An agreement among the negotiating parties was finally reached a week after the German court allowed the case to proceed to the trial phase at the end of August 2016. In the end, the legal case was lost in court, but from our perspective it played a crucial role in bolstering the self-representation of the AEFFAA and eventually played an important role in the negotiations on compensation at the ILO. With the end of the court proceedings in Germany and the resolution of compensation negotiations at the ILO, the first phase of the struggle came to an end.[2]

[1]KiK paid US$1 million in December 2012 as immediate relief.

[2]See the chapter by Faisal Siddiqi in this volume for a description of the Pakistani court proceedings.

3 Mapping the Effects of Pakistan's "Industrial 9/11" in Germany and Pakistan

We now turn to reflect on what NTUF, medico, and ECCHR have achieved over the course of our transnational cooperation to date, and to discuss future areas of our collective engagement. In describing this process of reflection and decision-making for the future, we must consider each organisation's different positionality and perspectives.

3.1 Changing the Discourse on Exploitation in Global Value Chains: medico and ECCHR's Perspectives from Germany

Together with the two Bangladeshi factory disasters, Pakistan's "Industrial 9/11" marked a turning point in German media and public debate regarding working conditions and exploitation in global supply chains. The degree to which German media covered the Ali Enterprises factory fire and related issues was and continues to confound our expectations. For a short time, millions of Germans were deeply shocked by Pakistan's "Industrial 9/11." In 2020, public concern around the factory fire remains high and German media now routinely covers smaller stories about garment industry working conditions in Pakistan and Bangladesh. At medico, meanwhile, we are regularly invited to local meetings all over Germany to discuss the Ali Enterprises case, larger issues in the global garment industry, and global capitalist production practices more broadly.

Compared to the years before these watershed factory disasters in Pakistan and Bangladesh, medico international has seen an encouraging qualitative shift in the types of discussion taking place in Germany around global capitalism's production and supply chains, even as we recognise that those who really care about working conditions in the garment industry still compose only a small minority of German society. Most participants in the public meetings we attend across the country are deeply convinced that the tragedies and the "normalcy" of the exploitation behind the disasters are not accidental, but rather the result of what in German debates is called "imperial way of life"[3] under contemporary capitalist globalisation. People's horror and anger are increasingly driven by the insight that we cannot seem to escape this vicious cycle: those of us in the Global North are more or less forced to buy and wear clothes made in South Asia, even if we try not to. Changing our individual behaviour as consumers can only hope to effect long-term change, but is otherwise an ineffective means of curbing workers' exploitation and oppression today.

[3]Cf. Ulrich Brand, Markus Wissen, Imperiale Lebensweise. Zur Ausbeutung von Mensch und Natur im globalen Kapitalismus, München (Munich) 2017.

While we see the increasing prevalence of these clear-eyed insights in Germany regarding capitalist production as a positive development, at the same time, they also spur a kind of helplessness. This sense of helplessness becomes even bigger when we consider the situation in South Asia itself, namely that for the vast majority of the South Asian workforce, a garment factory job in a place like Karachi is desirable, despite such poor working conditions. Most other options available are even worse. As capitalist exploitation will only be stopped by a global movement comprising a multitude of actors from various backgrounds across the world, it is more obvious than ever that this movement does not currently exist and must still be built.

Therefore, medico sees its role mainly in sustaining publicity for what has happened and further bolstering the mature, critical insights gained by certain sections of German society. We understand this as a preparatory exercise—to keep publicity and critique itself alive and oriented towards a particular, if still distant, horizon. One of our main goals is to create the sense of a new type of solidarity linked to a common global struggle: a struggle to be shared equally and not primarily driven by self-interest, and a struggle that can only be waged worldwide. We hope to also translate this sense of solidarity into concrete networks with other actors, including media professionals, trade unionists, fair trade shops, movement activists, formal and informal educators, researchers, as well as other campaigning groups and institutions who also question global capitalism its "imperial way of life".

ECCHR, on the other hand, considers itself to have a specific role in designing and carrying out legal interventions in a way that productively engages with and advances political debate and legal frameworks with regard to concrete demands for workers' rights. Our legal casework specifically aims to connect general demands for justice and a better future with concrete emblematic cases. For instance, by addressing how (legal) responsibility in global value chains might be constructed in the context of the Ali Enterprises case, we were able to contribute a small piece in the much larger puzzle of how to imagine and bring about a just alternative to the current global capitalist reality.

3.2 Accessing Transnational Partnerships: NTUF's Perspective from Pakistan

The struggle around the Ali Enterprises fire marks the first time in recent Pakistani labour history that survivors and workers have run a successful campaign themselves. In fact, the response to Pakistan's "Industrial 9/11" was the country's first worker-led labour success in 40 years. One of the crucial factors for this success was that those directly affected both organised and spoke for themselves—something that did not happen in the response to Rana Plaza in Bangladesh. It is exceedingly unfortunate that this success had to be built on the ashes of 258 humans. Before the Ali Enterprises fire, public perception prevalent in Pakistan was that factories producing for international brands were more worker-friendly than local ones. In its work both before and since the fire, NTUF has consciously endeavoured to highlight the fallacy of this assumption. Multinationals and local companies must be equally compelled to respect local, national and international labour standards, as well as other global framework agreements. Organising workers in unions, we believe, is critical to achieving this.

NTUF initially sought to form a transnational coalition with medico and ECCHR as a way to contribute international support to the Pakistani labour and democracy movement. The movement's present weakness traces its roots to suppression under several sequential military dictatorships in Pakistan, socialism's twentieth-century defeat worldwide, and prevailing global power relations today. At NTUF, our expertise lies in organising people, which, in this case, meant fire survivors and family members of those killed. While we brought our local experience and, above all, our close connection with those affected into the transnational alliance with medico and ECCHR, they offered us not only professional expertise, but also facilitated crucial access to international debates and the international public.

Our cooperation was and is based on shared views, not only in relation to the specific Ali Enterprises case, but also in terms of common political visons. Our relationship is a comradely partnership, in which we respect our differences with regard to political background, working styles and opinions, but ultimately agree that our differences are less relevant than our common aims. We all understand that we benefit more when we work together. For us at NTUF, "going global" has been a major outcome of this cooperation. Moving forward, we seek to further expand on this achievement, while ensuring that our work at the global level continues to advance our work on the national and local levels as well.

4 The Path Forward: From Fighting for Corrective Justice in the Tragedy to Challenging the "Normalcy" of Global Exploitation

Many may think that because KiK acknowledged the tragedy and paid compensation, survivors and those affected should now move on with their lives. Just because the legal cases related to the Ali Enterprises factory fire have ended, however, our collective work is far from over. KiK never accepted legal responsibility for its role in the 2012 disaster, and unsafe working conditions continue to exist across the garment industry. Today, jeans and t-shirts worn in the Global North remain soaked in the blood of those who made them. Daily exploitation and unsafe working conditions persist in globalised capitalist value chains in the garment industry and beyond. Hence, highlighting these realities is as urgent as ever. We must continue to work to expose local companies that exploit cheap labour under unbearable conditions, as well as the international companies and brands that profit from them.

In its work on the Ali Enterprises factory fire, NTUF gained the trust of a sizeable number of workers from different industrial sectors in Pakistan. Many workers have since asked us for assistance in forming unions and filing cases in Pakistani labour courts. Since 2012, NTUF has positioned itself at the forefront of a growing number of struggles and campaigns for workers' rights, as well a range of issues related to politics and human rights more generally. NTUF's closest ally, the Home Based Women Workers Federation (HBWWF), has become stronger in all domains and significantly increased its impact. Many of the women involved in the AEFFAA, who lost their husbands, brothers, sisters, daughters and sons in the Ali Enterprises fire, have since joined HBWWF in a political statement of solidarity with all women workers.

Today, NTUF and HBWWF are among a small number of trade unions in Pakistan with comprehensive visions for challenging capitalist globalisation and related political issues affecting the country. Both workers' groups, along with other stakeholders, have engaged in a variety of legal reform processes in Pakistan over the last years, and have made history in achieving legal status for workers in agriculture, fisheries and home-based work in the last decade. Laws are now in place to protect workers in these industries, but further work is still required to ensure their effective implementation. NTUF and its supporters are currently considering possibilities for extending our range of action by entering into different tiers of legislative bodies. In a first phase, we are preparing to support candidates in elections for local legislative offices in several select constituencies, in close cooperation with like-minded groups and parties in the Pakistani province of Sindh.

4.1 Continuing to Push for Better Working Conditions and Challenging the "Imperial Way of Life"

In the future, we must widen our focus and discourse to cover the whole garment industry value chain, from cotton fields and factories in the Global South, to warehouses and retail stores in the Global North. This will lead to concerns beyond garment workers' living and working conditions to a whole range of additional questions and issues: feudalism, rural exodus, urban migration, climate crisis and ecological catastrophe, cultural crises, dialectics of modernity and modernisation, as well as capitalist globalisation and ongoing imperialism. It will also lead to new, urgent questions regarding political, social, and economic rights and their implementation in global value chains.

In the face of the current COVID-19 crisis and its major economic impacts, the dramatic power imbalances in global production dynamics, particularly the co-dependence between companies in the Global North and producing factories in the Global South, have become even more apparent. As consumer demand in the Global North dropped drastically due to COVID-19 lockdowns in the EU and North America, many international brands simply cancelled their contracts with textile factories in the Global South, often without paying for the garments already produced. Within weeks, millions of workers in India, Bangladesh, and Pakistan lost their jobs, many without any access to social safety net protections to fall back on. Once again, the sheer normalcy of how exploitative, precarious work in the Global South enables consumerism in the Global North was on display for all to see. Hence, we not only need dramatic occupational health and safety improvements in the Global South garment industry, but more fundamental change in how global supply chains are run and how rights to social protection, health, workplace safety, and a living wage are protected. We believe the following tactics will help us achieve these goals in our struggle to overturn multinational corporations' relationships with and practices in the Global South.

4.2 *Discursive Intervention: Influencing the Terms of Debate*

As German organisations, medico and ECCHR must continue to influence discourses in Germany and Europe related to the textile industry, multinational corporations, and exploitation in global value chains more broadly. This can take diverse forms and occur in a variety of fora, such as writing and publishing articles, strengthening our presence in social networks, and participating in local townhall meetings and conferences. Aside from political debates, ECCHR particularly sees it as its role to influence legal discourse among scholars and practitioners with regards to questions of legal responsibility in global value chains. We see the legal community—from lawyers and justice system professionals to political and corporate legal advisors—as actors that can make key contributions to the realisation of workers' rights in today's globalised economy. Both organisations must also continue to organise opportunities for Pakistani workers, union leaders, and activists to travel to Germany for speaking events and workshops, as well as for German journalists, lawyers, judges, and trade unionists to travel to Pakistan to become witnesses, mediators and multipliers. Moreover, we must intervene in educational discourse, for example, by organising seminars with universities, research institutes, schools, lawyers' associations, and trade union institutes.

In all of our discursive interventions in Germany and Europe, we must continue to partner with NTUF to ensure that we amplify and communicate the background information, stories and pictures from Pakistan that they share with us in a way that further advances their cause and our common aims. This will include perspectives from the cotton fields, spinners, power looms, tanneries, and textile and garment factories about the living conditions of the workers and their families, their individual everyday experiences, collective dreams and imaginaries, as well as resistance struggles. At the same time, we also understand discourse in terms of the ongoing dialogue between NTUF, medico and ECCHR as organisations and political actors. We must continue to reflect on our different positions, roles, and ways of developing common strategies in a manner that respects our differences, understands and engages with the North-South dynamics between us, but ultimately aims at defining and working towards common goals.

4.3 Advocacy and Lobbying: Moving from Corporate Social Responsibility to Binding Law

NTUF, medico and ECCHR share the firm conviction that the era of corporate social responsibility grounded in voluntary corporate commitments must end. We must fight for the legal codification of binding rights and obligations for all actors involved in global production and supply chains.

At the national level, France's 2017 Corporate Duty of Vigilance Law marks a positive development in this regard, as do current German and Swiss NGO initiatives to develop new human rights due diligence laws in their respective national jurisdictions. While NTUF engaged with HBWWF and other organisations on several law reform initiatives in the Pakistani province of Sindh and achieved remarkable legislative improvements, for us, organising, lobbying and advocacy in Pakistan are not ends in themselves, but means through which to politicise workers' and other groups' struggles. Practically, this requires that NTUF builds closer connections with political movements and organisations (including political parties), as well as human and labour rights organisations.

On the international level, NTUF, medico and ECCHR will closely monitor the activities of the open-ended intergovernmental working group (IGWG) established by a 2014 UN Human Rights Council resolution to elaborate an international legally binding treaty on business and human rights, and which currently includes more than 100 UN member states. The KiK case is an important emblematic reference point in all of these legislative reform debates, as it crystallises key contradictions between global capitalist production practices and prevailing human rights standards. In taking the transnational company KiK to court, Pakistani working-class women revealed many pressing problems, legal gaps, and the limitations of current avenues for redress.

We are aware of the dilemmas of entering into the actual political process of negotiating a UN treaty or a national human rights due diligence law, as compromises will have to be made to win over the majority. Therefore, we believe it necessary to keep a certain distance from these negotiations so we can maintain our strong calls for justice for workers. In doing so, we hope to open up and hold space for the even stronger social and political forces that will be needed to transcend the "bad compromise" in which the negotiations are expected to end. While we are not pure "believers" in the salvation that a UN treaty or any other law may bring, we see valuable potential in talking about how the rights of the least privileged in the current capitalist system might be realised in national and international law. To inscribe workers' demands into the language of a "human rights revolution" does not mean to reduce political demands to juridical demands. Instead, we see it as the other way around: transforming a class struggle into a struggle for human rights represents the transformation of a particular social struggle into a universal political struggle, calling for the political support of everyone. Besides this, it also inscribes a contemporary local struggle reaching out for global acknowledgment into the continuing trajectory of the broader "human rights revolution" initiated by the American,

French and Haitian revolutions, which must be sustained and continually renewed until the rights we declare become fully realised for all across the globe.

4.4 Strengthening Global and Local Trade Unions

One, if not *the* main reason for the weakness of our discourse and actions to date has been the weakness of the German, Pakistani and global trade union movements. As the economy becomes increasingly informal, with precarious work the hallmark of contemporary globalised capitalism, trade unions must respond with "outside-of-the-box" solutions. For example, workers' federations like NTUF should no longer organise workers only at their formal workplaces, but must also serve those working in informal settings, as HBWWF has done for home-based and agricultural workers in Pakistan. If workers' organisations are prohibited from organising in factories, then they must go to workers' localities. If we cannot create lawful unions, then we must establish workers' committees, general workers' unions, or other alternative formations.

NTUF addresses the challenge of the labour movement's general structural weakness by choosing to be strategically open in our hybrid form of activism. As a trade union, we are both more and less than an ordinary union in contemporary Pakistan. We function as less than an ordinary union because we are only based in a few locations and our interventions, therefore, are always exemplary in character. We cannot claim to be capable of mobilising Pakistan's working-class masses. We can only realise improved working conditions in singular instances. At the same time, NTUF is more than an ordinary union because we know that we must also act as a political party of sorts, by using strategic, political interventions to pave the way for the labour movement(s) still yet to come and still yet to gain force. In this sense, we see ourselves as prying open and holding space for other actors and future movements.

At medico, meanwhile, because we cannot significantly change the German trade union movement given the current capacities and resources, we are keen to participate in the evolving experiment of developing a new "type" of organisation through the NTUF-medico partnership. The shape and direction this new kind of organisation will take will continue to unfold and develop as we move towards working on whole production and supply chains in the textile and garment industries—both in our fight for the political, social, economic and human rights of the people working within these global structures, and in our efforts to achieve national and international legal regulation of corporate actors' behaviour across these supply chains. To do this, we will need ECCHR's technical legal expertise in order to engage in efforts seeking concrete legal reforms. NTUF, medico and ECCHR must not only struggle to improve the working and living conditions of exploited workers in the Global South, but we must also address the range of other problems mentioned above in relation to what we term the dialectics of modernity and modernisation. Engaging these dialectics opens up vast possibilities for practising everyday forms of resistance and articulating alternative imaginaries within the broader realm of globalising democracy in the longstanding process of a "human rights revolution."

To bring all this back to practical terms, the Pakistani labour movement has spent years discussing the question of how to overcome the traditional factory-based forms of labour organising in order to build an industrial federation covering entire value chains. This cannot be done by NTUF alone, but requires a broad alliance, for example, to lobby national and provincial governments, and advocate with open-minded political parties and other institutions. NTUF will continue to intensify our commitment to basic organising procedures: organising all workers who request assistance and organising workers in all areas of production. The next fundamental step forward will be attempting to organise textile and garment workers in Karachi into one general workers' union, whether the law allows it or not.

The struggle to create, enforce and implement rights on the local, national and international levels forms the umbrella for all of our activities. As the legal action against KiK has shown, emblematic cases are important in advancing workers' struggles for justice and better regulation. The option must always be open, therefore, to take up specific legal cases when it suits the needs of those affected and the general cause. Hence, ECCHR, in particular, must continue to track evolving legal discourse and debates around workers' exploitation in global value chains in order to develop new ideas for potential legal interventions. These ideas would then have to be discussed among our three organisations and our wider network to determine how and in which regard a legal intervention might contribute to our broader goals.

5 Conclusions: The Task of Holding Space for Those Yet to Come

Looking back over the last years, the most disturbing phenomenon we have noticed in the wake of the Ali Enterprises factory fire is not that most local and transnational companies were and remain willing to literally walk over dead bodies to boost their bottom line. Capitalism, after all, has always been all about profit. It is the fundamental lack of solidarity with exploited workers, rather, that alarms us most. Pakistan's "Industrial 9/11" was widely reported in Pakistan and abroad, and shocked many. In the days following the tragedy, however, Karachi saw no spontaneous mass demonstrations to demand justice. In Germany, meanwhile, solidarity came only from the fringes of society, not from those at the heart of capitalist production and consumerism, those responsible for keeping it running.

Since 2012, professional media staff not otherwise known for taking a critical approach to neoliberal capitalism have continued to report on working conditions in global supply chains. Despite this consistent news coverage, the serious lack of effective solidarity has been surprising, as such solidarity could potentially hold the power to change things both in terms of discourse and on the ground. The German justice system was obviously not equipped to grasp the magnitude of the legal case against KiK, opting instead to escape a ruling on the merits of the case by detouring into procedural questions. While the debate around companies' legal responsibility for their supply chains has significantly developed among academics and legislators in Germany over the last few years, it remains to be seen whether it will effectively alter the status quo of corporate social responsibility.

The reasons for the lack of fundamental and powerful opposition against the current global production system are manifold, and we must face and address them as such. The first reason, of course, is the still lasting hegemony not only of neoliberal ideology, but also of its impact on the imaginations of both individuals and the masses. This is not only the case for those already participating in everyday "imperial way of life", but also for those aspiring to become part of this way of life, especially those who must survive in places like Karachi or Dhaka. The second reason goes along with and, indeed, paved the way for today's neoliberal hegemony: the twentieth century failure of socialist transformation that dashed the hopes of millions who had committed their lives and dreams to it over the course of the last centuries. Finally, the third reason is one immediately connected to the present age: both the lack of solidarity and its enduring necessity are as varied and manifold as the struggles by which this solidarity is lived. The most urgent need, therefore, is determining the form under which these manifold struggles, solidarities, and dreams can coalesce around and collectively head towards a common horizon.

As far as this horizon can be considered the horizon of justice, the most important lesson NTUF, medico and ECCHR learned from this experience is that we continue to lead our struggle as a struggle directed towards rights, as a struggle already based on rights. We understand rights, both those rights already achieved and those still in the process of being achieved, as having the power to provide and hold space for struggles still yet to come—no more, but also no less. And by rights, we are not only talking about labour rights or a binding treaty to regulate the behaviour of transnational corporations and other business enterprises. We are talking about all human rights. We are talking about Article 28 of the Universal Declaration of Human Rights in its entirety: "Everyone is entitled to a social and international order in which the rights and freedoms set forth in this Declaration can be fully realized." Fully, not partially. This is the goal for which we will continue to hold space, by all means necessary.

Nasir Mansoor is secretary general of the National Trade Union Federation of Pakistan, and has been an anti-capitalist political activist for the past several decades. He is member of the governing body of Sindh Social Security Institute (SESSI) and the Sindh Tripartite Committee for Implementation of Labor Laws, a tripartite body of workers, employers and government representatives. Mansoor is a marine engineer and holds a Master in International Relations from the University of Sindh, Pakistan.

Thomas Rudhof-Seibert is a human rights advisor and responsible for South Asia in the public relations department of the German-based civil society organisation medico international. Philosopher, author and political activist Rudhof-Seibert is also the spokesman of the board of the Institut für Solidarische Moderne.

Miriam Saage-Maaß is a lawyer and vice legal director at ECCHR, where she coordinates the Business and Human Rights programme. She has worked on various cases against corporations, including proceedings against German retailer Lidl relating to the exploitation of workers in Bangladesh and Pakistan, and against companies trading cotton picked with forced child labour in Uzbekistan. She regularly publishes articles on the legal liability of corporations for human rights violations in global supply chains and is internationally consulted as an expert in the area of corporate responsibility and human rights. She is a temporary lecturer at the Free University of Berlin, and has been a member of the Stiftung Forum Recht's advisory board since 2020.

The Land of Mourning: A Conversation with Adeela Suleman

Palvasha Shahab

Abstract Adeela Suleman is a globally celebrated artist and sculptor. She was front and centre of the artists' response to the Ali Enterprises Factory Fire of 2012. Under her leadership, the Vasl Artists' Association sent out a call for submissions to artists across Pakistan and the overwhelming response was curated in the form of the exhibition titled: 'Awaaz Baldia Factory Inferno: Artists Respond' which was hosted by the Arts Council of Pakistan in February 2013. Her monument dedicated to those who lost their lives in the fire was also part of the one year anniversary of the fire has been placed at the Pakistan Institute of Labour Education and Research (PILER). She also facilitated several international collaborations and artists intending to engage with the fire. Palvasha Shahab sat down with her to explore her thoughts about the role that art and artists play in the face of calamities and social injustices, her relationship to Karachi and her own response to the fire.

Keywords Labour rights · Factory fire · Social justice · Political art · Interdisciplinary perspectives · Karachi · Global south

Adeela Suleman is a globally celebrated artist and sculptor. She is an Associate Professor, and was the Head of Department for Fine Arts, at the Indus Valley School of Art and Architecture in Karachi from 2008 till 2019. She is also the founding member and director of the Vasl Artists' Association, an artist led residency program part of Triangle network, UK, that regularly hosts artists from around the world. She was a key voice in the artists' response to the Ali Enterprises Factory Fire of 2012 and her work features prominently amongst responses to the Fire. Along other artists, her work was very important in drawing global attention to the human societal loss caused by the fire.

P. Shahab (✉)
Rasheed Razvi Centre for Constitutional and Human Rights (RCCHR), Karachi, Pakistan

Legal Aid Foundation for Victims of Rape and Sexual Assault (LAFRSA), Karachi, Pakistan
e-mail: palvasha.shahab@columbia.edu

M. Saage-Maaß et al. (eds.), *Transnational Legal Activism in Global Value Chains*, Interdisciplinary Studies in Human Rights 6,
https://doi.org/10.1007/978-3-030-73835-8_7

Historically, artists have played an important role in labor movements highlighting the plight of workers and bringing it to public attention. American photographer Lewis Hine jarred public and policy makers with his work on the realities of child labour and lack of worker safety in the steel and construction industries. Famous novelist Charles Dickens wrote about the railroad workers in 'Another Railroad Author'; in 'Bleak House and Hard Times' he wrote about mill owners' resistance to measures to ameliorate cruel working conditions. Charles Kingsley's famous work 'The Water Babies' drew attention to the inhumane conditions of chimney sweeps, who were usually young orphan children. Many of these works actually propelled changes in law and practice. Even so, artistic responses are not unidirectional nor are they single-mindedly hurtling to change law and policy.

> Guernica, arguably the most famous and effective work in response to brutal bombing of a village in Spain by the fascist forces of General Franco. Yet, in spite of its historical reference, today the painting is admired and enjoyed foremost being a work of art, which opened up new possibilities in formal elements and aesthetic experiments—Quddus Mirza, *Awaaz Baldia Factory Inferno: Artists Respond (February 2013)*[1]

After the Ali Enterprises Factory Fire, there was no notable workers' strike in Karachi, much less, across Pakistan; even workers' protests were slow to come.[2] There wasn't even an overwhelming and unified response from civil society organizations but the artists seem to have responded overwhelmingly. There were three different types of artistic responses to the Ali Enterprises Factory Fire, including artists in Pakistan and abroad; over 100 works were contributed by artists, including a permanent monument at the Pakistan Institute for Labor Education and Research (PILER).[3] The Vasl Artists' Association, directed by Adeela Suleman, gave out a call for submissions to which artists responded in the Multitudes. This culminated in the exhibit titled: 'Awaaz Baldia Factory Inferno: Artists Respond' [hereinafter 'Awaaz exhibit'] which was hosted at the Arts Council of Pakistan in February 2013 in Karachi. Popular singer and political worker, Jawad Ahmed wrote a song titled 'Sun lo ke hum mazdoor hain' (listen to us, the workers!) which was first

[1]Qudus Mirza is an art critic, artist and independent curator <http://vaslart.org/quddus-mirza/>; 'Awaaz: the Baldia Factory Inferno Artists Respond', February 8–15, 2013, Arts Council of Pakistan, Karachi.

[2]'Labour Unions to hold worldwide protests for Baldia Fire victims', 21 March 2016, https://tribune.com.pk/story/1069544/going-global-labour-unions-to-hold-worldwide-protests-for-baldia-fire-victims/.

[3]'Jawad Ahmed to dedicate his latest song to Baldia's victims', 23 December 2012, https://tribune.com.pk/story/483214/singer-jawad-ahmed-to-dedicate-his-latest-song-to-baldias-victims/; Jawad Ahmed, 'Sun lo ke hum mazdoor hain' (listen to us, the workers!), Love and Revolution (2013), https://www.youtube.com/watch?v=oDMVoCFej7E; 'Artists pay tribute to the Baldia fire victims', 10 February 2013, https://www.dawn.com/news/784929; 'Awaaz: the Baldia Factory Inferno Artists Respond', 8–15 February 2013, Arts Council of Pakistan, Karachi; 'Unique memorial erected for 2012 Baldia factory fire victims', 11 September 2013, https://arynews.tv/en/unique-memorial-erected-for-2012-baldia-factory-fire-victims/; 'German artist relives Baldia factory fire', 24 November 2016, https://tribune.com.pk/story/1242427/bringing-art-life-german-artist-relives-baldia-factory-fire/.

introduced during the Awaaz Exhibit and then videographed with all the families of the victims of the fire at the first anniversary of the fire. The song not only moved everyone but also became an anthem for workers to rally around. It soon began to be sung at meetings of the Ali Enterprises Factory Fire Affectees Association (AEFA), and at other meeting or conferences organized with the aim to improve labour conditions and terms of employment.[4] In 2016, the Vasl Artists' Association also hosted an artist residency centered on the Ali Enterprises Factory Fire, 2012. German artist Miro Cramer participated in the residency and produced work that was exhibited in public market places, various college campuses, such as Indus Valley School of Art and Architecture and Iqra University, across Karachi, and at the Textile Industry Museum in Augsburg, Germany.[5] Since Adeela Suleman was a driving force behind the artists' response to the Ali Enterprises Factory Fire, it was important to bring this conversation to this book.

Palvasha Shahab: There were three different types of artistic responses to the Ali Enterprises Factory Fire, including artists in Pakistan and abroad; over 100 works were contributed by artists, including your permanent monument, which is now installed on the campus for Pakistan Institute for Labor Education and Research (PILER). Why do you think there was such an overwhelming response to the Ali Enterprises Factory Fire from the artists? What do you think were the motivations behind that?

Adeela Suleman: I think people's senses were numb. An event of such magnitude sometimes leads to total silence by the people who are directly affected by it. What is the role of Art in the wake of tragedy? We, as artists, ask this question all the time. It took me 3 months to respond to the catastrophe, the pain was unimaginable. What I experienced—mourning isn't an event; it's a state of mind, always there, shifting forward, staying, withdrawing, always growing, like a shadow, it follows you around. You can't let go of it but one can certainly learn to channel it.

Art also reaffirms why we must never allow something like that to happen again. When we think of art or the artists that respond to tragedy—art on terrorism like 9/11, suicide bombings or art that responds to genocide, such as the millions of pieces that respond to the Holocaust—our assumption is that the art works will be sad, frightening and powerful. This is not necessarily true but they will appeal to

[4]'Singer Jawad Ahmed dedicates his HR Award to labourers, working people', 21 December 2016, https://dailytimes.com.pk/39296/singer-jawad-ahmed-dedicates-his-hr-award-to-labourers-working-people/; 'Six years after the Baldia factory fire, working conditions still not changed', 10 September 2018, https://tribune.com.pk/story/1799215/1-six-years-baldia-factory-fire-working-conditions-still-not-changed/; "Law, Judicial Interventions and Social Change, with a special focus on Labor Law", organized by The Rasheed Razvi Centre for Constitutional and Human Rights (RCCHR), 21st and 22nd September 2019, IBA- City Campus, Karachi, Pakistan https://www.youtube.com/watch?v=LHz4t6zGs_g.

[5]'Artist residency in Pakistan' October–December 2016, https://www.lahorebiennale.org/artist-residency-in-pakistan/; 'German artist relives Baldia factory fire', 24 November, 2016, https://tribune.com.pk/story/1242427/bringing-art-life-german-artist-relives-baldia-factory-fire/.

pathos, reminding us of the emotional horrors, such as of the Holocaust and of people dying through suicide bombings, and reminding us of the work needed to prevent these in the future.

The Exhibition *Awaaz* was evidence that art can, in its distanced way, channel sorrow and even help with the healing process. More than 100 artists designers, creative organizations, individuals responded to the call for work. The Citizens Archive of Pakistan (CAP) presented a two-part exhibit that included a timeline tracing the history of major fires in the country over the past 50 years. The second part was an interactive 'moving exhibit' where the CAP team wore special T-shirts, firemen helmets and carried fire extinguishers to create awareness about fire safety. All material created for the exhibit was displayed with concise fire safety information and emergency phone numbers.

I made a film installation; Muzzumil Ruheel printed black and white faces of all the 256 victims and after numerous prints the prints started to fade, becoming invisible. It was the center piece of the exhibition, it was moving and powerful. Hassan Mustafa and Owais Ahmed Khan also made a three dimensional and a video installation in which they actually got the burnt jeans from the site of the Ali Enterprises Factory—these jeans had been lying around the building. Along with that they made a video collage of the 'breaking news' broadcasts that came on that horrific day. Manizhe Ali made a video in which she sat in front of the dressing table and applying make-up on her self and in the background one could hear the television news covering the incident, ambulance sirens; and she sat there seemingly oblivious of what is happening around her. The exhibition was very powerful and it moved everyone. People had tears in their eyes.

Sohail Zuberi a designer and photographer, made posters to mark the horrific event for next 4 years.

I made a wall monument to mark the first anniversary of the AE fire. It was initially installed at the Arts Council of Pakistan, Karachi. All the family members were invited and they all lit *diyas (traditional clay oil lamps)* to remember their loved ones and placed them in niches in the wall. It was quite an emotional event. I don't have words to describe it—to see so many mourning families together. Each brick had the name of a victim. Later the wall was transported to be permanently installed at the Pakistan Institute of Labour Education & Research (PILER) campus in Karachi.

Palvasha Shahab: How did you perceive the Ali Enterprises Factory Fire? How do you think your contemporaries/fellow artists perceived it? A failure of the State? A human tragedy? A tragedy of the working class? An inevitable result of unchecked capitalism?

Adeela Suleman: I think all of the above—it was a wide-ranging state failure, an unimaginable and inconceivable human disaster, an unbearable and agonizing tragedy for the working class and the inevitable and predictable result of inhuman capitalism. That is why monuments are important—it comes from the Latin words *Moneo* or *Monere* which means 'to advise', 'to remind' or 'to warn'. And this reminder, whether it's in the form of an exhibition like the Awaaz or a permanent monument like the one I installed at Pakistan Institute for Labour Education and

Research (PILER) campus, which I built with bricks representing the 256 victims, or any other form—it serves as a piece of advice and as a warning to the living that this could have been them and/or they have to ensure that this is not repeated again ever.

Through a simple call for works, we received overwhelming response—more than 100 art works, performances, video works were exhibited. Jawad Ahmed's song '*Sun Lo Kay Hum Mazdoor Hain*' (Listen to us, the workers!) was performed at the Ali Enterprises Factory site and then the video was played at the first anniversary against the backdrop of the wall monument I made. It brought tears to the eyes of not just the victims' families but everyone who was present there.

Contemporary artists are the inheritors of a modernist tradition of dealing passionately with calamity. If you observe art history you will find that art and tragedy often walk hand-in-hand. There is a long-standing tradition involving artists who decided to *capture* the tragedies of their time. Artists ranging from Goya to Picasso expressed their outrage over specific tragic events upon canvas—the connection between art and tragedy goes further back and becomes more recent than that. From Homer's tales of Troy to Picasso's '*Guernica*' from Tchaikovksy's symphony '*Pathétique*' to Bill T. Jones's choreographed dance performance '*Still/Here*' for an adaptation of Shakespearean drama to Maya Lin's Vietnam Memorial, artists have always combated grave tragedy with intense beauty. Romantic Spanish painter Francisco Goya traveled from Madrid to Saragossa in 1808 to witness the awful consequences of the French siege. The result was his unequaled suite of etchings, '*The Disasters of War*' in which we see three nude men strung up on a dead tree. Goya also painted the second most famous outcry against the consequences of merciless war, the 13-foot-wide '*The Third of May, 1808*' which depicts, in slashing brushstrokes and dramatic color, the massacre of defenseless civilians by a ruthless military. The words of the British poet Wilfred Owen, written at the front in the First World War, are almost mandatory: "All a poet can do today is warn. That is why the true poets must be truthful." But even that hard-won wisdom may not be enough for an artist trying with all his heart to create a work profound enough to do justice to the horrors the world witnesses.

Palvasha Shahab: It appears that you are deeply embedded in Karachi, and in the city's art milieu; you have produced art here for a long time. What do you think was the significance of your work about the Ali Enterprises Factory Fire? Was this a passing moment in the city's artistic milieu or is the consciousness changing? Are artists in Karachi becoming more engaged with the city? Are they finding new ways to connect with the world? Why do you think this fire was significant to artists from outside Pakistan?

Adeela Suleman: I believe nothing provokes the artistic sensibility like grief. One can even say it's a selfish act because we see someone else's pain and make a visual out of it. But that is the only language we speak, a way to retain our sanity, that is the only way we can respond to such an event, that is the only way we can show the others that we have not forgotten them.

Karachi is a mad city—jarring experiences all around. It's difficult for artists to ignore the atrocities that the city is functioning with. Having been a teacher for almost two decades, I can't remember a single year where my students are not directly responding to this city. It's overwhelming; its impossible not to respond to it.

Like historians, artists visually document the events in their time. They try to narrate their experiences by evoking and generating feelings in the viewers.

Palvasha Shahab: What is the relationship between art and politics, in your opinion? What do you think are the implications of and possibilities of political art? Artists and writers such as Upton Sinclair, Charles Dickens, Lewis Hine have contributed significantly to labor movements, and to other movements for liberation or social justice. In producing works of art in response to tragedies and ruptures like the Ali Enterprises Factory Fire, how do you place yourself and your work within these debates?

Adeela Suleman: Dada poet Hugo Ball says, "*For us, art is not an end in itself... but it is an opportunity for the true perception and criticism of the times we live in.*"

In a country like Pakistan I have personally recently discovered the true immensity of art's power. The visual or image created by artists can jolt the entire establishment, tug at the heartstrings of society, it can stir opinion, and even have global impact.

Art is political—all art forms are political—there is no doubt in that. Art complicates our understandings and insights of the world. It alters the discursive frames within which the political is negotiated. Art is also political because it reinterprets what previously was seen and known so that alternative understandings may emerge. These reinterpretations help reveal existing power relations within society, and reexamine what was previously known and what was deemed worthy of analysis in the first place in the context of what was *not* seen previously and (therefore?) was not known. It also brings to light what *should* be seen or known. I think this is perhaps exemplified by my work titled: '*The Killing Fields of Karachi*', which was installed in the courtyard of the Frere Hall, adjacent to a huge public garden in Karachi. Frere hall was constructed, in 1865, during the British era as a Town Hall—and to me, it is noteworthy feature on Karachi's landscape, a reminder of the British Raj and its unchecked power in the Indian Sub-Continent. The installation had 444 pillars shaped like graves—each standing adjacent to the building becoming part of the surrounding landscape. It represented 444 victims of extra-judicial killings and fake police encounters by a police officer named Rao Anwar, who was covertly known to be a gun for hire. To me he is a symbol of terror and the immense power of capitalism and the deep state. Rao Anwar became well-known after his *encounter* of Naqeebullah Mehsud, a young Pashtun man, whose death fueled the Pashtun Tahafuz Movement (a movement against systemic discrimination against and demonization of people of the Pashtun ethnicity in Pakistan). The '*Killing Fields of Karachi*' interpreted and visually represented Rao Anwar's reality and brought it to the public. Those 444 pillars juxtaposed with the mightly colonial building and the charming public garden scared the establishment, the powers that be, to the extent that the work was shut down within the first 2 h of its unveiling at the Karachi Biennale 2019 (which was a 2-week long event). The work captured the pain, sorrow and loss. The work also depicted the powerlessness and impuissance of the victims and their families.

I think art is a more effective means of communicating the experience of pain than words ever could be. A painful experience goes beyond the actual occurrence of physical pain and it surrounds the entirety of one's life. The best of the art comes out of pain, in one form or another. Pain is universal; this is perhaps a major reason why art can break down barriers and brings people together.

Many artists use their visual language to highlight the grave injustices in their societies. For example, the work of Ai Wei Wei titled: '*Sunflower Seeds*' consists of 100 million ceramic husks created to resemble in size, color and shape their counterparts from nature. The husks were produced for Wei Wei by 1600 artisans who suffered mass unemployment, in Jingdezhen, China, a town where imperial porcelain has been made for over a 1000 years. Francisco de Goya's masterpiece, '*The Third of May 1808*', depicts a long trail of Spanish rebels lining up to be executed by French troops. The viewer's eye is immediately drawn to the rebel figure wearing white, his arms raised, he has a harrowed expression as he faces the French soldiers readying to gun him down. Works of art allow us to forge deeper emotional bonds with the people who actually lived in different times and places, as well as in our own times. These works of art serve as windows to the soul of their times.

Art also forces us to remember. To produce his work, Gerhard Richter looked at the photographs of Andreas Baader, Jan-Carl Raspe, and Gudrun Ensslin from newspaper and their police photographs their television images. Andreas Baader, Jan-Carl Raspe, and Gudrun Ensslin were found dead in their cells in a Stuttgart prison on October 18, 1977. The three were members of the Red Army Faction, a coalition of young political radicals jointly led by Baader and Ulrike Meinhof (who had hung herself in police custody earlier). Having turned to violence in the late 1960s, the Baader-Meinhof group had become Germany's most feared radicals. Although the prisoners' deaths were pronounced suicides, the authorities were suspected of murder. Gerhard Richter's slurred and murky motifs derived from newspapers and police photographs or television images. Shades of gray dominate the work; the absence of color conveys the way these secondhand images from the mass media sublimate their own emotional content. The visual that Richter created made his work the most challenging work of his career, according to him. The almost cinematic repetition gives an impression, as if in slow motion, of the tragedy's inexorable unfolding. Produced during a prosperous, politically conservative era, 11 years after the actual events—the work insisted that this painful and controversial subject be remembered.

Many of us are blind to the realities of loss and mourning until we're confronted with them: a devastating news headline, a live broadcast of war images, a lifeless animal on the side of the road, or the life-altering loss of a loved one. Great art speaks not just to the pain experienced, but also looks toward the day where we are able to move forward or are able to or learn to live with the pain. As Henri Frédéric Amiel, Swiss moral philosopher, poet and critic said, "you desire to know the art of living, my friend? It is contained in one phrase: make use of suffering".

Palvasha Shahab was the joint executive director of the Rasheed Razvi Centre for Constitutional and Human Rights, and the Legal Aid Foundation for Victims of Rape and Sexual Assault through September 2020. She now works a consultant for RCCHR, LAFRSA, the Legal Aid Society and the Pakistan Institute for Labour Education and Research. She is on the Law Committee of the Sindh Commission of the Status on Women and advises on upcoming legislation. She is also an advisor to a transnational collaborative project on oral histories and social interventions titled "Karachi Beach Radio." She also teaches undergraduate courses on peace movements and international human rights law at SZABIST, Karachi. Shahab further curates and moderates important public discussions on national platforms such as the Adab Fest and The Second Floor. She holds a Master of Laws from Columbia Law School, New York, US, where she was also a Human Rights Fellow at the Human Rights Institute in 2017–2018.

Four Against KiK: A Conversation with Caspar Dohmen

Michael Bader

Abstract Caspar Dohmen is a business journalist, author and lecturer living in Berlin. In this interview, he speaks to Michael Bader about the role of the media in raising awareness, transnational activism and strategic litigation claims. Their conversation illuminates the crucial role of journalists regarding inter-connected transnational social struggles, such as global production of textile and garment.

Keywords Journalism · Media · Rana Plaza · KiK case · Ali Enterprises factory fire

Caspar Dohmen is a German business journalist, author and lecturer living in Berlin. He writes feature articles and background reports for the German newspaper *Süddeutsche Zeitung*, and regularly contributes reports to German radio broadcasting networks like Deutschlandfunk, SWR and WDR. He previously worked as an editor for *Süddeutsche Zeitung*, *Handelsblatt* and *Wiesbadener Kurier*, and has written several books dealing with the topic at hand: *Profitgier ohne Grenzen* (*Profit without Borders*), *Das Prinzip Fairtrade* (*The Principle of Fairtrade*) and, most recently, *Schattenwirtschaft* (*Shadow Economy*), which was written together with three researchers about the world of informal work. In this interview, Michael Bader comes in conversation with Caspar Dohmen about the crucial role of media and journalists in transnational activism and strategic litigation claims.

Michael Bader: How did you come to know about the lawsuit against KiK? Why did you choose to write about it?

Caspar Dohmen:[1] For me, the lawsuit against KiK was a journalistic stroke of luck. When I heard about the idea, my curiosity was of course immediately piqued

[1] More information can be found at: www.caspar-dohmen.de.

M. Bader (✉)
European Center for Constitutional and Human Rights, Berlin, Germany
e-mail: bader@ecchr.eu

M. Saage-Maaß et al. (eds.), *Transnational Legal Activism in Global Value Chains*, Interdisciplinary Studies in Human Rights 6,
https://doi.org/10.1007/978-3-030-73835-8_8

because it's a classic David versus Goliath story, which readers and journalists love—and I'm no exception. On one side were the people who had suffered direct damage in the fire at the Ali Enterprises textile factory and the relatives of the at least 258 dead, many of whom had lost their family's breadwinner. On the other side was the textile discounter KiK, a large company from Germany. Those working at a distance were taking aim at a powerful actor in the Global North. This had already occurred before, after previous scandals and grievances in Global South supplier companies, but never before had supply-side workers brought an action against a company in a German court. If they were successful, then it would not only be the company that got convicted but rather the entire business model of our current global division of labour. This is because many companies no longer produce their products themselves, but rather limit their activity to research and development, as well as marketing and sales. In fact, production today is often completely carried out by third parties. This applies equally to clothing, toys, computers and smartphones. The conditions in these global supply chains are dictated by multinational corporations, which pass the pressure on to suppliers, who, in turn, pass it on to their employees. The dogs always bite the last in the chain and it's the workers at the bottom who face dangerous working conditions, starvation wages and excessive working hours as part of their everyday life.

Journalistically, this lawsuit offered an ideal opportunity to bring readers and listeners closer to the conditions along supply chains. The popular narrowing of public discussion after disasters like the Ali Enterprises fire or Rana Plaza collapse, with its 1129 dead, to the question of whether, as a consumer, you should still buy clothes from a cheap brand always seemed absurd to me. Or whether one should still buy clothing from Pakistan or Bangladesh. I had already seen on my first visit to a textile factory in Asia that seamstresses there produce goods for cheap and expensive brands in the same hall. And the seamstresses had told me that they would lose their jobs if consumers boycotted the goods they sewed.

Bader: How did you become interested in questions of global production? What is the personal story behind your writing about topics such as the KiK case?

Dohmen: As a young business journalist, I got to know the so-called value chain model. At the time, in the early 1990s, I worked as an editor for the *Handelsblatt* newspaper and participated in a seminar for young journalists that had been organised by the Bertelsmann Foundation. If you want to understand what strategies companies are pursuing, you have to know the concept, a management consultant explained to us. It's about breaking down entrepreneurial activity and limiting it to the steps a company can take to maximise its profits. Accordingly, companies now outsource activities on a large scale. Local suppliers have taken over canteens, cleaning and plant security, among other services. But more and more activities have also been moved from the Global North to the Global South and Eastern Europe, mainly due to lower wages. Call centres in the Philippines have taken over customer service, software companies in India have taken over system support and accounting, factories in China now manufacture computers and smartphones, and factories in Bangladesh now produce clothing.

After the financial crisis of 2008, as a journalist I dealt with the serious side effects of financial capitalism on a large scale. The collapse of Rana Plaza seemed to me the appropriate moment to address turbo-capitalism's consequences for the global division of labour. Officially, a dozen well-known brands had their goods produced in one of the five textile factories in the multipurpose Rana Plaza complex. KiK was also there, as were Benetton and Mango. When I heard about the plans for the lawsuit against KiK, I thought about how I should approach the issue and it soon became clear to me that I would like to accompany the plaintiffs in their project from start to finish. This proved to be a difficult undertaking, as the proceedings took much longer than I expected.

At SWR, a German regional public broadcaster, I was able to win over an editor for the topic, who in turn inspired other colleagues. This enabled me to realise the radio feature "Tatort Textilfabrik" ("Crime Scene Textile Factory") for German public-service broadcaster ARD. For me, this was the start of a whole cycle of research and stories about the global division of labour. I did research on textile supply chains in Pakistan, India, Bangladesh and El Salvador, and on other supply chains in other countries. My experiences also resulted in a book on business and human rights, *Profitgier ohne Grenzen*, and a learning module, "Am seidenen Faden" ("On a Silken Thread"), for familiarising young journalists with supply chains.

Bader: What do you make of the lawsuit against KiK? What questions did it raise for you?

Dohmen: KiK was not just any client for the Ali Enterprises factory but accounted for at least 70% of its capacity utilisation at the time of the accident. So, was the supplier only independent on paper? Or did their buyer KiK determine what happened? And if so, could the latter be held jointly responsible for the consequences of the fire? Such questions were asked by the European Center for Constitutional Human Rights and I was very interested in the answers. If the plaintiffs were to win in court, I thought it would probably have consequences for many transnational companies with operations in distant countries in pursuit of the lowest possible costs. As KiK explained at the time, any company producing abroad could then be held liable for conditions in factories it did not own. This was unimaginable for them then, just as it was for the Federal Association of German Employers in the summer of 2020. But in the meantime, a whole series of companies, including KiK, have begun calling for a supply chain law. And the German government is now working on such a law. There is no doubt that something has happened and that the lawsuit against KiK and the reporting around it certainly had a part to play in it.

Bader: Did the collapse of Rana Plaza and the fires in the Ali Enterprises and Tazreen Fashion factories in South Asia, as well as the lawsuit against KiK in Germany, alter public perception on questions of global production?

Dohmen: I still write regularly about this topic for *Süddeutsche Zeitung* and report on it for Deutschlandfunk and other ARD radio stations. This is only possible because the demand for such stories has increased. Rana Plaza was the main reason for the topic's rise to prominence on the global public agenda. Just how much so, I only learned later at a workshop hosted by the Fraunhofer Gesellschaft in 2017, where I and a handful of other industry, civil society and trade union experts discussed scenarios for the textile industry's future. The researchers who invited us had combed through databases including around 23,000 press sources looking for links between well-known brand names and terms such as "child labour," "working conditions," "modern slavery" and "living wage" for the period of 1990–2016. The results showed that in 2013 and 2014, the press reported on the topic more than ever before—thus reaching more and more people. The grievances in the global textile industry had already been the subject of discussion for a quarter century before the Ali Enterprises factory burned down and Rana Plaza collapsed. In Europe, the Clean Clothes Campaign has addressed the issue since at least 1989, following a scandal about poor working conditions in a C&A supplier. Since then, the network has grown to include more than 300 organisations from 15 countries, all struggling for better working conditions for seamstresses in the Global South. In the US, a scandal about miserable working conditions in an Indonesian sweatshop that supplied Nike triggered a similar movement in 1990. But on both sides of the Atlantic, the protest against conditions in the global textile industry persisted in social niches and a few milieus, such as universities. In the media, the protest found comparatively little resonance.

This was hardly surprising at that time, as in the early 1990s, the world was preoccupied with the consequences of the fall of the Berlin Wall. It was only then that the conditions were created for more and more companies to transfer their production completely to supply chains. First of all, China and the countries of Central and Eastern Europe came to organise their economies capitalistically rather than socialistically. Then came a surge of liberalisation in world trade. In 1994, the community of states founded the World Trade Organization. In early 2005, with the expiry of the World Textile Agreement, the last restrictions in industrialised countries on the import of textiles from developing countries fell. Many in the Global South saw the globalisation push as a chance to boost development in their countries, with their big trump card being cheap labour. The calculation worked out for hundreds of millions of people who were able to rise into the middle classes, especially in China and India. But in many places, workers continued to face meagre wages and often inhumane conditions. Today, seamstresses' wages in Asian factories usually fail to meet their basic existential needs. Nevertheless, many workers are happy when they get such jobs. These connections became clear to me when I was on the road for the lawsuit against KiK.

But it was not only the plaintiffs' side that was interested in convincing me, as a journalist, of their point of view. The defendants' side was too. KiK did not stonewall the media, but rather engaged in dialogue. After the disaster, KiK paid aid money to those affected. The company also remained convinced that it had fulfilled its responsibilities prior to the accident. After all, it had demanded that the manufacturer comply with a code of conduct and, at the same time, had had an audit carried out. KiK saw the fact that the factory had been certified to the high SA8000 standard only shortly before the accident as confirming its position. Above all, however, the company wanted to show that under the current legal situation, it could not be held liable for the consequences of the fire at the supplier's premises. The company opened doors for me and provided insights. However, because of the lawsuit, many other companies also began to take a serious look at the situation in their supply chains.

Bader: When you think back and reflect about your own journalistic engagement with the lawsuit against KiK and the underlying conditions of global production it speaks to, did your view or assessment change over time? Would you say the lawsuit had any impact despite being lost in court?

Dohmen: In one respect, I made a mistake in my initial assessment of the complaint. At first, I only thought there were two options. On the one hand, the court could consider the case and dismiss the claim. This, I thought, would be further indication that affected persons' chances to sue in German courts are limited. On the other hand, the judges could award damages to those affected, which would have drastic consequences both because it would directly help the affected persons who suffered harm and, from a broader perspective, because it would open up important legal avenues for workers in supply chains connected to Germany. Such a decision would, above all, have consequences for the current system of the global division of labour. After all, if corporations were to be held liable for violations at their suppliers under certain circumstances, they would have to change a number of things. They would likely urge that grievances be really recognised and remedied, and they would perhaps even start producing in their own factories again and thus take full responsibility for labour and production practices, as was normal in the past. In the beginning, I had not considered that the court might not make any decision on the matter whatsoever. But that is exactly what happened. According to the Dortmund Regional Court, the case was time-barred under Pakistani law. This left the central question unanswered as to whether a company could be held liable for conditions at its supplier.

Nevertheless, the proceedings made a great deal of difference. Above all, the public attention around the lawsuit contributed momentum to the discussion about a binding supply chain law in Germany. When the German government adopted a National Action Plan for Business and Human Rights in 2016, it was still based on the principle of voluntarism. It asked companies to fulfil their human rights due diligence obligations in their supply chains but did not prescribe it. According to the results of two surveys conducted by the German government, only about every fifth company did so. Currently, in the summer of 2020, the *Eckpunkte für ein Lieferkettengesetz* ("Cornerstones for a Supply Chain Law") presented by two German Federal Ministers sit on my desk. On the aspect of enforcement, they read:

> The law will be designed in such a way that the requirements of an "obligatory norm" under EU law are met. This means that German law is applicable in this respect (as the law of the place of action where the supply chain management takes place) and supersedes the law of the country of production (the law of the place where the damage occurs), which is usually applicable in cross-border cases. In this respect, it will no longer be necessary to obtain time-consuming and costly legal opinions in order to determine the content of the foreign law.

What the Federal Minister of Economic Cooperation and Development Gerd Müller (CSU) and Federal Minister of Labour Hubertus Heil (SPD) are planning here would considerably simplify lawsuits such as the past case against KiK. If the law had been in place at the time of the Ali Enterprises fire, it would have greatly benefitted the four plaintiffs and their supporters. Of course, they have had their complaint and cannot repeat it because of the statute of limitations, but should this law pass, they will have helped to facilitate access to German courts for plaintiffs in other cases. In this sense, the four will have been successful after all: Muhammad Hanif, who started as a factory worker at the age of nine and survived the fire by a hair's breadth; Muhammad Jabbir, the widower who lost his son Muhammad Jahanzab Abdul Aziz Khan; Yousuf Zai, who found his dead son Attaullah Nabeel in the ruins; and Saeeda Khatoon, who was able to immediately identify the corpse of her son Ijaz Ahmed because he had shielded his face with a plate, leaving it recognisable.

Michael Bader studied law at Humboldt University in Berlin, Germany, and holds a Master of Laws (LLM) in Law, Development and Globalisation from SOAS, University of London. Bader joined the European Center for Constitutional and Human Rights in September 2019 as a Research Fellow in the Business and Human Rights programme with a focus on corporate exploitation in global supply chains. Since September 2020, he has been supporting ECCHR's Institute for Legal Intervention as a Bertha Justice Fellow.

Part II
Labour and Tort Law Aspects of Global Supply Chains

The Rana Plaza Collapse and the Case for Enforceable Agreements with Apparel Brands

Ben Vanpeperstraete

Abstract Disasters like the Rana Plaza collapse and the Tazreen Fashions and Ali Enterprises fires painfully demonstrate the limits of conventional models of labour regulation in global supply chains. Buyer-driven markets characterised by outsourcing, subcontracting and offshoring, and the price pressure that results from them, undermines both the regulatory role of the state and the potential for collective bargaining. As a result, poor and unsafe working conditions prevail in transnational corporate supply chains in the garment industry. The aforementioned disasters offer a textbook example of the challenges facing the current clothing industry and the limits of the dominant "Corporate Social Responsibility" (CSR) model used to address labour rights abuses.

Yet, the responses to these disasters also provide fertile ground for alternative "worker-driven" strategies, where worker organisations enter into negotiated supply chain agreements with transnational corporations and hold the latter to account. The Bangladesh Accord and Rana Plaza Arrangement, as well as the corollary Tazreen Compensation Agreement and Ali Enterprises Compensation Agreement attempt to develop a counter-hegemonic alternative to dominant CSR practices and offer new strategies for social justice within global supply chains. This chapter describes and contextualises these agreements in a broader trajectory of labour organisations bargaining and negotiating such agreements with lead firms, highlighting how the post-Rana Plaza momentum made significant strides possible in terms of the depth, scope and enforceability of these negotiated agreements. The chapter identifies the strengths of these developments, but also identifies room for improvement for future negotiated enforceable agreements with apparel brands.

Keywords Enforceable Brand Agreements (EBAs) · Private governance · Labour standards · Global supply chains · Apparel · Freedom of association · Corporate social responsibility · Workers' rights · South Asia

---

B. Vanpeperstraete (✉)
ECCHR, Berlin, Germany
e-mail: vanpeperstraete@ecchr.eu

M. Saage-Maaß et al. (eds.), *Transnational Legal Activism in Global Value Chains*, Interdisciplinary Studies in Human Rights 6,
https://doi.org/10.1007/978-3-030-73835-8_9

1 Introduction

After the 2012 Ali Enterprises fire in Baldia Town (Karachi, Pakistan) killed at least 258 workers, survivors and labour rights groups immediately focused on establishing responsibility and securing financial compensation for the survivors and families of the deceased.[1] After a struggle comprised of legal action and campaigning—which took the better half of a decade—long-term compensation was finally agreed with the factory's biggest buyer, the German lead firm[2] KiK. The resulting Ali Enterprises Arrangement borrowed heavily from the previously concluded Rana Plaza Arrangement.

After securing compensation, both Pakistani and global unions as well as other labour rights groups have increasingly turned to advocacy to ensure that similar tragedies are avoided in the future.[3] Indeed, the problems that led to the Baldia tragedy are endemic to the entire South Asian, and by extension the global, garment industry. Amidst all of the possible policy options for preventing similar tragedies from occurring again, the Bangladesh Accord on Fire and Building Safety represents one example of an instrument designed to achieve such an objective. Recent calls for a similar Pakistan Accord and even calls for an agreement on wages demonstrate the inspiration that the Bangladesh Accord brings to labour rights groups for worker-driven alternatives.

This chapter contextualises the achievements regarding compensation and calls for prevention through negotiated agreements between worker organisations and transnational corporations (lead firms) within a broader trajectory of social movement strategies for improving labour rights in global supply chains. It first provides a succinct overview of the globalised garment industry in South Asia, where mainstream "Corporate Social Responsibility" (CSR) efforts have only minimally addressed the challenges of ensuring labour rights in globalised supply chains. Secondly, it explores direct agreements between worker organisations and lead firms as a distinct counterstrategy to the dominant CSR approach proposed by lead firms. Although based on conventional labour management approaches adapted to a supply chain context, the nascent practice of enforceable supply chain agreements has been taken to the next level with the adoption of the Bangladesh Accord[4] and the

[1]See also chapters by Miriam Saage-Maaß, by Saage-Maaß et al. and by Faisal Siddiqi in this book.

[2]For consistency, the paper uses the term "lead firms" to refer to what is commonly known in the context of the garment industry as brands and retailers, but which can also cover other dominant market parties that do not necessarily have a consumer-focused brand. These transnational companies often design textile, clothing and/or shoes, and market and sell them, while contracting out the actual production. The word brand is used occasionally for stylistic purposes.

[3]IndustriALL, Pakistan's Garment Workers Need a Safety Accord, www.industriall-union.org/safety-is-our-right-not-a-privilege (last accessed 30 August 2020).

[4]Accord on Fire and Building Safety in Bangladesh, www.bangladesh.wpengine.com/wp-content/uploads/2018/08/2013-Accord.pdf (last accessed 30 August 2020) and 2018 Accord on Fire and Building Safety in Bangladesh, www.bangladesh.wpengine.com/wp-content/uploads/2018/08/2018-Accord.pdf (last accessed 30 August 2020).

conclusion of the Rana Plaza Arrangement.[5] While the post-Rana Plaza momentum has made significant strides possible in terms of the depth, scope and enforceability of these negotiated agreements, increasing their potential for future application in similar set-ups, advocates have not yet managed to successfully replicate the strategy elsewhere, despite calls from, for example, Pakistan.

2 The Contemporary Garment Industry Worldwide and in South Asia

2.1 The Globalised Garment Industry and Buyer Pressure

The rapid globalisation of the 1980s created a new context for apparel and footwear brands. Facilitated by cheaper, more efficient and faster transportation and communication, as well as the removal of trade barriers, lead firms who previously owned and managed (most of) their own production capacity, began shifting production to contractors based in low-income countries with weaker labour standards, limited collective bargaining coverage, and poor enforcement. Today, apparel production often takes place in independent factories located in regions of the world where labour costs are lower and social and environmental regulations less stringent. Manufacturing has become characterised by complex, multi-tiered and opaque supply chains often stretching across several countries. As lead firms search for ever-lower production costs, producing countries compete against each other to attract orders. As supply chains have internationalised, the so called "race to the bottom" began.

The emergence of "fast fashion" in the last two decades has meant that lead firms introduce new fashion lines and collections much more frequently and, hence, require quicker inventory renewal. Consequently, lead times for orders to suppliers are no longer planned in months, but rather in weeks. This sourcing model characterised by short lead times on orders frequently results in last-minute changes to product designs and specifications, causing rushes to meet product launches or replenishment. Garment suppliers work on ever-thinner margins and are often forced to sell products to buyers at a price below the production cost. According to an International Labour Organization study into the textile, clothing, leather, and footwear sector, at least 81% of suppliers have sold goods at below cost price, primarily to secure future orders. When statutory minimum wages have increased in production countries, only 25% of buyers were willing to increase payments to

[5] Rana Plaza Arrangement, Understanding for a Practical Arrangement on Payments to the Victims of the Rana Plaza Accident and their Families and Dependents for their Losses (as amended 20 November 2013), www.ranaplaza-arrangement.org/MOU_Practical_Arrangement_FINAL-RanaPlaza-c34d165e591e40d43a603e95ac2b38e9.pdf (last accessed 30 August 2020).

suppliers to cover the increased production cost, and those who did made suppliers wait an average of 12 weeks before doing so.[6]

When studying the hyper-competitive structure of global apparel supply chains, Mark Anner concluded that the garment sector is characterised by a buyer-driven sourcing squeeze that has pushed prices down, shortened lead times, and contributed to low wages, health and safety concerns, and violations of freedom of association rights.[7] In an effort to attract business, investments and trade, both factories and governments of producing countries are disincentivised to protect or respect workers' rights. In turn, working conditions, including wages and working hours, are put further under pressure.[8] Indeed, the pressure exerted by lead firms has a direct negative impact on textile and cut-and-sew workers, in terms of suppressed wages,[9] poor health and safety conditions, irregular working hours and excessive and mandatory overtime, unrealistic performance targets and quotas, precarious employment and the lack of stable, permanent work, and (sexual) harassment and abuse by management and supervisors.[10] Even after the tragic Rana Plaza building collapse in 2013 and commensurate pledges to improve practices, the prices paid by lead firms to suppliers declined by 13% in the following years. Similarly, lead times shrunk by 8.14%, which increased pressure on suppliers and work intensity for workers, leading to forced overtime, diminished working conditions, and a drop in real wages of 6.47% (since the December 2013 wage increase) (Fig. 1).[11]

2.2 *The Garment Industry in Bangladesh and Pakistan*

In Pakistan and Bangladesh, the textile and garment industry is of vital importance for the national economy. Indeed, a significant share of both countries' industrial labour force, export earnings, and total gross domestic product are dependent on garment and textile exports. The European Union and the United States of America

---

[6]ILO, Purchasing Practices and Working Conditions in Global Supply Chains: Global Survey Results, 2016, www.ilo.org/wcmsp5/groups/public/%2D%2D-ed_protect/%2D%2D-protrav/%2D%2D-travail/documents/publication/wcms_556336.pdf (last accessed 30 August 2020).

[7]Anner (2018).

[8]Anner et al. (2012).

[9]ILO, Wages and Working Hours in the Textiles, Clothing, Leather and Footwear Industries, 2014, www.ilo.org/wcmsp5/groups/public/@ed_dialogue/@sector/documents/publication/wcms_300463.pdf (last accessed 30 August 2020); Cowgill and Huynh (2016).

[10]ILO, Purchasing practices and working conditions in global supply chains: Global survey results, 2017, www.ilo.org/wcmsp5/groups/public/%2D%2D-ed_protect/%2D%2D-protrav/%2D%2D-travail/documents/publication/wcms_556336.pdf (last accessed 30 August 2020); Human Rights Watch, "Paying for a Bus Ticket and Expecting to Fly": How Apparel Brand Purchasing Practices Drive Labour Abuses, 2019, www.hrw.org/report/2019/04/23/paying-bus-ticket-and-expecting-fly/how-apparel-brand-purchasing-practices-drive (last accessed 30 August 2020).

[11]Anner (2018).

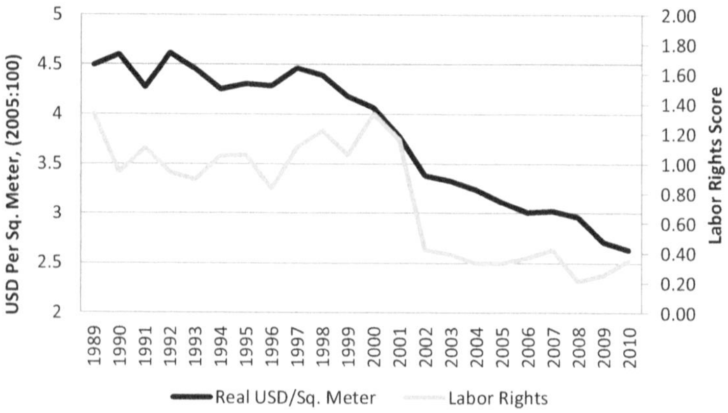

Fig. 1 Labour rights and price per square metre (Source: Anner et al. 2013)

are major export markets for both countries. Bangladesh and Pakistan are the third and fifth biggest garment exporters, respectively, into the EU's single market.[12] Both countries attract foreign buyers in this labour-intensive sector through a strategy of low labour costs, where export growth is coupled with stagnant wages.[13] As a result, regulatory functions for labour have become limited or even non-existent, trade union rights are often violated, and employers strongly resist the unionisation of their employees by resorting to intimidation, dismissal, and blacklisting. Furthermore, workers face unhealthy and hazardous working conditions, often without appropriate protective equipment.[14]

The rapid expansion of these domestic industries in Pakistan and Bangladesh has led to a repurposing of many buildings into factories, often without the required permits. Previously existing factories, meanwhile, have often added extra floors or increased the workforce and machinery to levels beyond the safe capacity of their buildings. Many factories run day and night to meet production targets, under the relentless buyer pressure described above. The establishment of new factories and

[12]See European Commission, Mid-Term Evaluation of the EU's Generalised Scheme of Preferences (GSP), 2018, www.trade.ec.europa.eu/doclib/docs/2018/october/tradoc_157434.pdf (last accessed 30 August 2020); ILO, Decent work country profile: Bangladesh, 2013, www.ilo.org/wcmsp5/groups/public/%2D%2D-dgreports/%2D%2D-integration/documents/publication/wcms_216901.pdf (last accessed 30 August 2020); ILO, Decent work country profile: Pakistan, 2014, www.ilo.org/wcmsp5/groups/public/%2D%2D-asia/%2D%2D-ro-bangkok/%2D%2D-ilo-islamabad/documents/publication/wcms_316668.pdf (last accessed 30 August 2020).

[13]ILO, Wages and productivity in garment sector in Asia and the Pacific and the Arab State, 2016, www.ilo.org/wcmsp5/groups/public/%2D%2D-asia/%2D%2D-ro-bangkok/documents/publication/wcms_534289.pdf (last accessed 30 August 2020); ILO (2014), Cowgill and Huynh (2016).

[14]International Trade Union Confederation, ITUC Global Rights Index, 2020, www.ituc-csi.org/IMG/pdf/ituc_globalrightsindex_2020_en.pdf (last accessed 30 August 2020); International Trade Union Confederation et al., Bangladesh: Complaint to the European Ombudsman, 2018, www.ituc-csi.org/bangladesh-complaint-to-the?lang=en (last accessed 30 August 2020).

conversion of existing buildings into garment factories has often been done as quickly and as cheaply as possible, resulting in widespread safety problems including faulty electrical circuits, unstable buildings, inadequate escape routes, and unsafe equipment. Old and outdated wiring often short-circuits, leading to fire outbreaks, while fire extinguishing facilities, if available at all, are often outdated too.

The price and delivery pressure generated by lead firms in the global apparel industry is not unique to Bangladesh, Pakistan, or even South Asia. Instead, it is a problem facing the global apparel industry. However, it manifests itself in a particularly destructive fashion in Bangladesh and Pakistan, namely in the form of fire and building safety incidents. Indeed, the three most lethal incidents in the globalised garment industry have taken place in Bangladesh and Pakistan, namely the Ali Enterprises fire, the Tazreen Fashions fire, and the Rana Plaza building collapse.[15]

2.3 *South Asia as a Hotspot Demonstrating the Limits of the CSR Industry*

In response to continued disclosures and attention in the public domain by campaigners, NGOs and journalists, lead firms have developed a range of high-profile workplace codes of conduct and industry-driven social responsibility and compliance initiatives. Publicly committing to such codes and their corollary compliance has become a key strategy for lead firms to demonstrate to their customers their commitment and efforts to address labour rights in their supply chains. Yet, this CSR system is either unilaterally defined by lead firms and retailers themselves, or jointly developed in industry-dominated initiatives. To verify risks and track impacts, a severely criticised auditing, certification and CSR compliance industry has also emerged.[16]

[15] See also chapter by Palvasha Shahab in this book, which critically discusses the development, implementation, and enforcement of occupational health and safety (OHS) standards in countries like Pakistan. The author explains in detail why there is little difference in fire and building standards worldwide, as well as the poor capacity for government regulatory enforcement in key production countries. This chapter, however, focusses more on the role and ways to effectively implicate lead firms in OHS. The case of the Bangladesh Accord, which is later discussed, and its focus on fire and building safety, partially challenges classical OHS paradigms themselves, as well as the governance of OHS, as fire and building safety is perceived as a core regulatory role of the state. Nevertheless, as we will see later, the Bangladesh Accord does provide potential solutions on how to finance necessary remediations in a transnational context.

[16] See, for example, Pruett D et al., Looking for a quick fix: How weak social auditing is keeping workers in sweatshops, Clean Clothes Campaign, 2015, www.cleanclothes.org/file-repository/resources-publications-05-quick-fix.pdf/view (last accessed 30 August 2020); Kelly I et al., Fig Leaf for Fashion. How social auditing protects brands and fails workers, Clean Clothes Campaign, 2019, www.cleanclothes.org/file-repository/figleaf-for-fashion.pdf/view (last accessed 30 August 2020); MSI Integrity, Not Fit-for-Purpose: The Grand Experiment of Multi-Stakeholder Initiatives in Corporate Accountability, Human Rights and Global Governance, 2020, www.msi-integrity.org/

Most, if not all, CSR initiatives to date have entirely failed to address poor working conditions in supply chains. At most, they have presented marginal gains that mitigate or render less visible those abuses customers consider to be the most morally repulsive, such as child labour. Especially against the background of continued fire and building safety issues in South Asia it seems clear that the CSR strategies developed and implemented by lead firms have proven to be largely ineffective in addressing the pressures that these same lead firms exert upon their suppliers, which in turn lead to heightened labour and human rights risks and violations. Indeed, the factory collapses and fires across South Asia during 2012 and 2013, preceded by dozens of smaller harmful and deadly incidents for over a decade, combined with an overall lack of demonstrated impact, show the limits of the CSR industry.

All of the factories where major disasters have occurred had been previously and repeatedly audited under prevailing industry audit regimes.[17] Notably, the track record of so-called "third-party" auditing systems is hardly any better than auditing schemes run by lead firms themselves. The Ali Enterprises factory, for example, had received an SA-8000 certificate from RINA, a Social Accountability International (SAI)-accredited auditing firm, only weeks before its lethal fire in September 2012. The factory had also been audited by Worldwide Responsible Accredited Production (WRAP).[18] Two months later, 112 workers died in a fire at Tazreen Fashions in Ashulia, Bangladesh, in a factory that had been audited multiple times by Walmart and by UL Responsible Sourcing. Audits of two factories in the Rana Plaza building in Savar, Bangladesh, one performed by Bureau Veritas for the lead firm Loblaw[19] and another one carried out against the Business Social Compliance Initiative

wp-content/uploads/2020/07/MSI_Not_Fit_For_Purpose_FORWEBSITE.FINAL_.pdf (last accessed 30 August 2020).

[17]For example, the Rana Plaza building passed audits by BSCI and individual lead firms before a collapse killed over 1000 workers. Also, the Hameem/That's It Sportswear factory (29 dead) was directly audited by name brands such as Gap, Abercrombie and Fitch, and Vanity Fair Corporation. The Gharib & Gharib factory (21 dead) was, in turn, audited by H&M. For a more comprehensive overview of the role of auditing, see the previous footnote.

[18]ECCHR, Case Report: RINA certifies safety before factory fire in Pakistan, 2018, www.ecchr.eu/fileadmin/Fallbeschreibungen/CaseReport_KiK_RINA_20181121.pdf (last accessed 30 August 2020); Worker Driven Social Responsibility Network, SA8000: The 'Gold Standard' for Failing Workers?, www.wsr-network.org/resource/sa8000-the-gold-standard-for-failing-workers/ (last accessed 30 August 2020); Walsh D and Greenhouse S, Inspectors Certified Pakistani Factory as Safe Before Disaster. The New York Times, 19 September 2012, www.nytimes.com/2012/09/20/world/asia/pakistan-factory-passed-inspection-before-fire.html (last accessed 30 August 2020); Walsh D and Greenhouse S, Certified Safe, a Factory in Karachi Still Quickly Burned. The New York Times, 7 December 2012, www.nytimes.com/2012/12/08/world/asia/pakistan-factory-fire-shows-flaws-in-monitoring.html (last accessed 30 August 2020).

[19]See *Das v. George Weston Limited*, 2017 ONSC 4129; *Das v. George Weston Limited*, 2018 ONCA 1053; Doorey D, Rana Plaza, Loblaw, and the disconnect between legal formality and corporate social responsibility, 2018, www.ssrn.com/abstract=3265826 (last accessed 30 August 2020).

(BSCI) code of conduct, failed to identify the illegal construction and building flaws that led to the plaza's collapse and the loss of at least 1134 lives.

Despite the disappointing results on the ground, the CSR industry has helped erode the idea initially proffered by lead firms in the garment industry that transnational corporations bear no responsibility for human and labour rights abuses in their supply chains. Initially, lead firms viewed their relationship with their suppliers as one between independent partners, each of whom had freely entered into a business agreement, in which the wellbeing of workers was the sole responsibility of suppliers. By developing codes of conduct and compliance regimes to curb the mounting pressure by civil society groups, and by subjecting their suppliers to social audits, lead firms have gradually implied that they do bear some responsibility for labour and human rights conditions in their supply chains after all. More recently, this view has been captured in key soft law instruments like the 2011 UN Guiding Principles on Business and Human Rights (UNGPs) and the updated 2012 version of the OECD Guidelines on Multinational Enterprises. Both normative instruments express a clear global consensus that businesses have a responsibility to respect human rights, including in their supply chains.

3 Negotiated Brand Agreements

In response to the emergence of the corporate responsibility to respect human rights as the new global standard of expected conduct for businesses and the disappointing results of prevailing CSR and social compliance regimes, advocates have begun calling for greater accountability through legislative frameworks.[20] Proponents of a so-called "smart-mix" see more potential for holding corporations to account for human rights abuses by combining a public regulatory route with private "CSR-style" regulation.[21] While this rightfully brings up associations with the same voluntary regimes developed by lead firms, the field of private regulation may be providing greater means of accountability than perhaps intuitively imagined. Indeed, while private regulatory approaches are diverse and have often produced disappointing outcomes in the past, equally private approaches in which worker organisations enter into enforceable agreements with lead firms deserve further attention and visibility.

---

[20] See, for example, Business and Human Rights Resource Centre, Call for EU human rights and environmental due diligence legislation now supported by over 100 NGOs, trade unions and networks, www.business-humanrights.org/en/latest-news/call-for-eu-human-rights-and-environmental-due-diligence-legislation-now-supported-by-over-100-ngos-trade-unions-and-networks/ (last accessed 30 August 2020).

[21] Locke (2013).

Notably, the garment sector has been one of several sectors[22] in which certain lead firms' concrete supply chain responsibilities have been defined through bargaining structures involving lead firms and worker organisations, usually global unions, national unions, and/or worker-advocacy NGOs.[23] These agreements have so far sought to regulate and protect (a section of) labour rights in workplaces where the lead firms are not the direct employers of the workers.[24] Although private contracts in nature, these agreements enable workers and their representatives to hold lead firms accountable for specific commitments in relation to their supply chains. As rights and obligations are developed through bargaining, worker organisations become partners in a decision-making process, as opposed to passive subjects in a unilaterally defined CSR strategy. This has implications for the framing of specific rights and the ways in which they are implemented and eventually enforced, leading to outcomes that are significantly different to those achieved (or not) when workers and their representatives are mere passive entities within lead firms' individual CSR strategies or lead-firm-dominated monitoring initiatives.

Anner et al. chart the development of this strategy in the garment sector back to early twentieth-century multi-party bargaining agreements, in which lead firms agreed to only contract with suppliers that had entered into an agreement with the union. These so-called "jobbers agreements" were negotiated by the International Ladies Garment Workers Union (ILGWU) with the predecessors of today's apparel brands in New York during the mid-twentieth century, when clothing supply chains still had a domestic character.[25] Yet, this strategy of pursuing contractual agreements

[22]Similarly negotiated supply chain agreements have been concluded between labour organisations and lead brands in other sectors, such as the Fair Food Program agreement concluded between the Coalition of Immokalee Workers (CIW) and food retailers and farmers in Florida, and the Milk With Dignity agreement concluded between the group Migrant Justice and dairy product retailers and farmers in Vermont and New York.

[23]These organisations can be quite diverse and include regional and local unions who represent workers at specific production sites, and local NGOs mandated to act on behalf of workers in the absence of democratic and independent union representation.

[24]Given its focus on enforceable agreements between brands and workers' organisations, this chapter does not explore in depth other forms of instruments in which lead firms, retailers and/or labour meet, such as Global Framework Agreements, Responsible Business Initiatives or Multi-Stakeholder Initiatives. Although a number of these instruments do not enjoy a similar level of enforceability, some GFAs and MSIs do demonstrate modest mechanisms to enforce commitments upon lead firms, sometimes to a greater extent than the instruments discussed here. These other "top down" instruments target one (in the case of GFAs) or several (in the case of MSIs) lead firms with comprehensive regulatory action beyond any single workplace. The agreements covered in this chapter, in contrast, focus on specific topics such as union rights, collective bargaining, factory safety, and compensation. In that sense, they are much more limited in scope, as they do not include other (relevant) labour rights risks, such as poverty wages, overtime, or discrimination. While other instruments focus on a sector-wide approach, the agreements covered here are tailored to specific conditions in a country or to a specific factory incident, and are thus contextualised in local and national circumstances, including laws, norms, practices, the strength of the labour movement, and so on. See, however, Eva Kocher's chapter in this book.

[25]Anner et al. (2013). See also Blasi and Bair (2019).

between labour organisations and brand(s) on one or several issues in a supply chain is equally applicable in the contemporary globalised garment sector. Indeed, in reaction to specific labour rights abuses at factories in the last decades, local trade unions, aided by international allies,[26] have at times successfully compelled lead firms to take regulatory action and implement concrete commitments in their supplier factories.

Past successes in using such private negotiated approaches have included the reinstatement of workers who had faced retaliatory action from factory management for forming or joining a union of their own choosing.[27] However, some of these past wins have been precarious or short-lived, with worker reinstatements quickly overturned when international attention waned.[28] In a few other cases, resolution has managed to go beyond rehiring to include longer-term union recognition and guarantees.[29] Similarly, local unions together with their allies have sometimes managed to go beyond associational issues to address the non-payment of wages

[26]The Clean Clothes Campaign network, through its urgent appeal system, has a track record of campaigning to achieve remedy in specific instances of human rights violations in garment supply chains. See, for example, Den Hond et al. (2014).

[27]IndustriALL Global Union, ITGLWF Commends Goldfame Job Recalls in Cambodia, www.industriall-union.org/archive/icem/itglwf-commends-goldfame-job-recalls-in-cambodia (last accessed 30 August 2020).

[28]See, for example, the River Rich and SL Garment cases in Cambodia, or the Azeem case in Bangladesh. Gregoratti and Miller (2011); Teehan S and Kunthear M, Jubiliation as SL Strike Ends. Phnom Penh Post, 4 December 2013, www.phnompenhpost.com/national/jubilation-sl-strike-ends (last accessed 30 August 2020); IndustriALL Global Union, Cambodian Union Scores Victory at SL Garment, www.industriall-union.org/cambodian-union-scores-victory-at-sl-garment (last accessed 30 August 2020); Odom S, Unions, Bosses Ink Deal to End SL Garment Factory Dispute. The Cambodia Daily, 20 November 2014, www.cambodiadaily.com/archives/unions-bosses-ink-deal-to-end-sl-garment-factory-dispute-72685 (last accessed 30 August 2020); Greenhouse S, Union Leaders Attacked at Bangladesh Garment Factories, Investigations Show. The New York Times, 23 December 2014, www.nytimes.com/2014/12/23/business/international/attacks-on-union-leaders-at-azim-factories-in-bangladesh-are-documented.html (last accessed 30 August 2020).

[29]See, for example, the SF Leather case in Turkey. Clean Clothes Campaign, Turkish workers win case targeting handbag producer Mulberry, www.cleanclothes.org/news/2015/10/19/turkish-workers-win-case-targeting-handbag-producer-mulberry (last accessed 30 August 2020); Clean Clothes Campaign, IndustriALL campaign contributes to Mulberry supplier agreement but struggle continues, www.industriall-union.org/industriall-campaign-contributes-to-mulberry-supplier-agreement-but-struggle-continues (last accessed 30 August 2020).

and overtime,[30] and sometimes even to cover issues at the regional level.[31] However, most campaigns about union recognition, wages or other issues have only addressed a single or a few factories or production sites and have primarily sought to restore or improve *pre-existing* rights. Agreements at the factory level have remained almost exclusively between workers and factory management, meaning their enforcement has relied on national legal systems, while the involvement of buyers (for example financially) has often been without a formal agreement and therefore could not rely on legal enforcement options. Instead, public pressure from international campaign networks has often been needed not only to conclude such agreements, but also to ensure their adequate implementation.

As these cases demonstrate, the lack of structural and institutional power of local unions can, at least partially and occasionally, be compensated by their access to global unions and civil society networks, which can help build leverage to successfully implicate lead firms in resolving workplace incidents.[32] It seems logical, then, that unions and social movements would want to expand on such agreements' depth, duration, coverage, and enforceability. The CGT-Fruit of the Loom Agreement, the Indonesia Freedom of Association Protocol, and the Bangladesh Accord are all efforts to transcend individual factory-level struggles between workers and management. Instead of post hoc or ad hoc interventions in which resolution was finally found after the lead firms sourcing from the relevant facilities intervened, these three agreements have worker organisations enter directly into long-term, pro-active agreements with the relevant lead firms that covered multiple facilities supplying the lead firms and included clear dispute resolution mechanisms. Indeed, these three agreements offer some of the most visible and noteworthy examples of worker organisations entering into contracts with lead firms in order to regulate labour rights in the supply chain. At the same time, these agreements vary significantly, as they operate in different parts of world, cover different thematic issues, and have different institutional arrangements.

---

[30]For example, the Nikomas case in the wake of the Indonesia Freedom of Association protocol which is discussed later. Hodal K, Nike factory to pay $1m to Indonesian workers for overtime. The Guardian, 12 January 2012, www.theguardian.com/world/2012/jan/12/nike-1m-indonesian-workers-overtime (last accessed 30 August 2020); Vaswani K, Nike agrees $1m overtime payment for Indonesian workers. BBC, 12 January 2012, www.bbc.com/news/business-16522992 (last accessed 30 August 2020); Clean Clothes Campaign, Just pay it: Wage compensation for Indonesian Nike workers, www.cleanclothes.org/news/2012/01/12/just-pay-it-wage-compensation-for-indonesian-nike-workers (last accessed 30 August 2020).

[31]Worker Rights Consortium, Remediation of Minimum Wage Violations in Bangalore, 2010, www.workersrights.org/university/memo/120210.html (last accessed 30 August 2020); Worker Rights Consortium, Update on Minimum Wage Violations in Bangalore, 2010, www.workersrights.org/communications-to-affiliates/update-on-minimum-wage-violations-in-bangalore-india/ (last accessed 30 August 2020); Clean Clothes Campaign, Factory Tries to Dodge Inflation Correction, www.cleanclothes.org/ua/2013/cases/gokaldas (last accessed 30 August 2020).

[32]See Nasir Mansoor's part in the chapter by Miriam Saage-Maaß et al. in this book.

3.1 CGT-Fruit of the Loom Agreement (Honduras)

In response to a worker complaint about the closure of the Jerzees de Honduras (JDH) factory that produced garments for the Russell Athletic brand (owned by Fruit of the Loom), the Worker Rights Consortium asserted that the closure was motivated by union hostility and was, in fact, retaliatory. In 2009, following a successful cross-border campaign led by United Students Against Sweatshops (USAS),[33] Fruit of the Loom reached an agreement with the Central General de Trabajadores (CGT) of Honduras and its local affiliate, the Sitrajerzeesh union, in which it committed to open a new factory in the Choloma area, rehire the former JDH factory workers, recognise the union and engage in collective bargaining. The agreement also foresaw the back-paying of workers' wages for the period of the JDH factory's closure, a significant wage increase for the rehired workers, and a commitment that, going forward, factory management would not retaliate against any worker forming or joining a union. It also foresaw joint trainings between the lead firm (Fruit of the Loom) and the CGT aimed at the factory management to this effect.[34]

The company agreed to extend this agreement and the associational rights contained therein beyond this single factory to all of its factories in Honduras. The parties created a structure and mechanism whereby the employers (Fruit of the Loom's representatives and factory management) and the unions (the local confederation and international union partners) would provide governance and ongoing accountability for the agreement. The resulting "Washington Agreement" is grounded in Honduran law and includes an oversight committee where both sides are represented together with a joint appointee, and a dispute resolution mechanism where disputes that are not resolved between the parties can be taken to arbitration in front of an ombudsman.[35]

Three out of the five factories covered by the "Washington Agreement" have Collective Bargaining Agreements (CBAs) with Fruit of the Loom. While a number of conflicts about implementation arose, including the closure of a factory, the oversight committee has been successful in mediating implementation conflict, and as a result it appears that the arbitration option has not yet been tested.[36] Although the factories covered in the agreement are subsidiaries owned by Fruit of the Loom and its brand Russell Athletic, the agreement between the union and Fruit of the Loom remains relevant because "insofar as Russell designs and markets its own brands and sits atop a supply chain that includes independent suppliers as well as

[33]Arengo et al. (2019b); Anner (2013).

[34]Maquila Solidarity Network, Historic Victory: Jerzees de Honduras workers win break-through agreement, www.en.archive.maquilasolidarity.org/node/908 (last accessed 30 August 2020).

[35]Lance Compa of Cornell University has been named as ombudsperson. He was nominated by the union and agreed to by all parties.

[36]Worker Rights Consortium, WRC Factory Investigation: Jerzees Buena Vista, 2016, www.workersrights.org/investigations/jerzees-buena-vista/ (last accessed 30 August 2020).

owned and operated factories, it is much more like a jobber [brand] than a traditional apparel contractor."[37]

3.2 *Indonesia Freedom of Association Protocol*

The Indonesia Freedom of Association (FoA) Protocol[38] was negotiated by an alliance of five Indonesian union federations, six global sportswear brands, and four major Indonesian footwear manufacturers to (partially) redress the power imbalances between supply chain workers and lead firms. The negotiations resulted from pressure generated by the Play Fair campaign, which leveraged the occasion of the 2008 Beijing Olympics to urge sportswear companies to take a series of concrete, measurable actions to improve workers' rights in supply chains, especially around poverty wages, the abuse of short-term contracts, other forms of precarious employment, violations of freedom of association, and factory closures due to industry restructuring.[39] The Play Fair campaign selected Indonesia as the ideal location to start negotiations for a country-level instrument due to the footprint in Indonesia of the major lead firms targeted by the campaign (Nike, adidas, Puma, New Balance, Asics and Pentland, with adidas functioning as a spokesperson), the presence and relative strength of independent unions and federations there,[40] as well as the existence of a broader labour movement in the country with experience in cross-border campaigns. In 2011, after two years of negotiations, an agreement was reached that covered workers' associational rights at all direct suppliers (a major concession for the unions) producing merchandise for the signatory sportswear brands in Indonesia.

Substantively, the agreement outlines the rights of workers and their unions in great detail, provides practical guidelines for organising and collective bargaining, and includes provisions for non-retaliation against trade union officers and limits on employer interference with trade union activities. Especially noticeable is the level of detail with which it covers issues like the release of union representatives from work duties, the use of company materials such as rooms, communication tools, company cars and notice boards, as well as collective bargaining, support from union federations, and the deduction of union fees (see Articles 4–7 of the protocol). In this

---

[37]Anner et al. (2013), p. 34.

[38]For a deeper discussion of the Indonesia Freedom of Association Protocol, see chapter by Reingard Zimmer in this book.

[39]See Maquila Solidarity Network, Clearing the Hurdles: Steps to Improving Wages and Working Conditions in the Global Sportswear Industry, 2008, www.ituc-csi.org/IMG/pdf/Clearing_the_Hurdles.pdf (last accessed 30 August 2020).

[40]The five different Indonesian unions organised themselves under the banner of Play Fair Indonesia. These unions differ in terms of size, political orientation/affiliation, history, and experience in earlier supply chain casework.

regard, the protocol provides much more detail, tangibility and clarity than current Indonesian legislation.[41]

Under Article 6(1) of the protocol, factories and unions must negotiate a collective bargaining agreement within 6 months after signing the protocol. Signatory lead firms, however, have fairly limited obligations, as they are (only) required to supervise and ensure the implementation of the protocol provisions and serve as members of its national Supervision and Dispute Settlement Committee. Moreover, signatory lead firms are only expected to uphold the protocol's articles and provisions at their tier 1 suppliers. If alleged violations of freedom of association cannot be resolved through consensus and deliberations, Article 9(2) of the protocol states that "dispute should be resolved with reference to legal regulations. If a dispute concerning an infringement cannot be resolved via such negotiations, then the matter should be referred to a court of law." Though Article 2 clearly expresses the binding nature of the agreement, stating that the protocol "*binds* the parties in the matter of upholding the right to freedom of association," no provisions are included on how to proceed in legal terms should the parties decide to settle in court.

In November 2012, the dispute settlement architecture was further clarified and refined through the adoption of the Standard Operating Procedure (SOP) for the FoA Protocol Supervision and Dispute Resolution Committee. The SOP foresees the establishment of (bipartite) Factory Committees on freedom of association, which are to oversee and report on the implementation of the protocol provisions at the factory level, as well as a Tripartite National Committee, which is to include trade unions, manufacturers, and brand representation, empowered to deal with conflicts that cannot be solved at the factory level. Since the signing of the protocol, however, no disputes have ever been visibly brought in front of the internal dispute settlement mechanism. In all cases of conflict over implementation (by a supplier of a brand) to date, parties have found an agreement before bringing it to the dispute committee, based on the relationship and opportunity for increased dialogue that the instrument provides.[42]

In conclusion, the Indonesia FoA Protocol is a unique example of a negotiated brand agreement that covers a substantial part of the Indonesian garment sector. Importantly, and in contrast to classic codes of conduct under prevailing CSR regimes, Indonesian union federations involved in negotiating the protocol had substantial power to define what freedom of association means in factories in Indonesia at the drafting stage. A decade later, these same unions continue to enjoy a substantial level of ownership over the instrument. At the same time, the protocol does not guarantee freedom of association overnight, but rather provides important additional and structural leverage for local unions to further their own

---

[41] Indonesia has ratified the ILO Convention 87 on the Freedom of Association and Protection of the Right to Organise (1948) and ILO Convention 98 on the Right to Organise and Collective Bargaining (1949) with a simple instrument of ratification, thus not providing additional prescription on freedom of association or collective bargaining beyond that prescribed in the ILO conventions, which are designed to apply globally in all contexts.

[42] Gardener (2012) and Connor et al. (2016).

strategies for achieving freedom of association. In this sense, the protocol has helped create an enabling environment in which unions can claim their rights, challenge anti-union discrimination, and in some cases, also obtain progress on issues like minimum wage.[43] Hurdles remain in the form of legacy unions, rival unions on the factory floor, and limited organisational capacity on the part of the Indonesian federations to support all factory-level unions and/or to enforce the agreement. Limited organisational capacity of the Indonesian federations is also particularly important when it comes to maintaining the protocol versus attempting to expand it beyond tier 1 suppliers or to cover wages and/or short-term contracts, as initially demanded.

Recent sporting events have shown limited enthusiasm to push for better implementation of the Indonesia FoA Protocol, or to expand its remit beyond tier 1 suppliers or to include issues such as wages and/or short-term contracts.[44] Likewise, there has only been limited public domain activity to push for similar agreements elsewhere. Unlike other instruments such as the Bangladesh Accord, international allies like global unions or labour rights NGOs do not have a defined space or particular role in the (implementation of the) agreement. And yet, the role of these international allies is important to ensure lead firms remain committed to the robust implementation of the protocol, and to possibly extend its scope or establish similar agreements elsewhere. For example, the recent addition of signatories to the Indonesia FoA Protocol was facilitated through the Fair Wear Foundation, a Dutch multi-stakeholder initiative that includes Dutch trade unions and the Clean Clothes Campaign.[45]

3.3 Bangladesh Accord on Fire and Building Safety

The 2013 Rana Plaza collapse in Bangladesh remains the deadliest workplace disaster in the globalised garment industry to date. In its aftermath, over 200 lead firms entered into a legally binding agreement with two global trade unions, UNI Global Union and IndustriALL Global Union, along with eight Bangladeshi trade unions[46]

[43]Connor et al. (2016).

[44]The initial demands in "clearing the hurdles" focused on freedom of association, precarious employment, factory closures, and living wages. See Maquila Solidarity Network, Clearing the Hurdles: Steps to Improving Wages and Working Conditions in the Global Sportswear Industry, 2008, www.ituc-csi.org/IMG/pdf/Clearing_the_Hurdles.pdf (last accessed 30 August 2020).

[45]Fair Wear Foundation, Fair Wear members sign Indonesian FoA protocol, 2017, www.fairwear.org/stories/fwf-members-sign-indonesian-foa-protocol/ (last accessed 30 August 2020).

[46]Bangladesh Textile and Garments Workers League, Bangladesh Independent Garments Workers Union Federation, Bangladesh Garments, Textile & Leather Workers Federation, Bangladesh Garment & Industrial Workers Federation, IndustriALL Bangladesh Council, Bangladesh Revolutionary Garments Workers Federation, National Garments Workers Federation and United Federation of Garments Workers.

and four NGOs that functioned in a witness capacity.[47] Building on the content of the earlier Memorandum of Understanding on Fire and Building Safety in Bangladesh,[48] the final agreement—the Bangladesh Accord on Fire and Building Safety—contains not only unprecedented lead firm participation, but also unprecedented commitments and enforceability. Under the original 5-year agreement, lead firm signatories commit "to the goal of a safe and sustainable Bangladeshi Ready-Made Garment ('RMG') industry in which no worker needs to fear fires, building collapses, or other accidents that could be prevented with reasonable health and safety measures."[49]

The implementation of the Accord is governed through a Steering Committee (SC) which provides equal representation to the signatory lead firms and unions. An ILO representative acts as the SC's neutral and independent chair. The body decides by consensus or through majority votes. Its responsibilities include determining the Accord's budget and financial reporting, appointing the programme's Safety Inspector and Training Coordinator, and managing the dispute resolution process. More concretely, brand signatories agree to finance[50] and implement a collective fire and building safety inspection programme. All facilities producing goods for signatory lead firms (as opposed to facilities that are only directly contracted by the lead firms) are therefore required to allow independent inspections under the direction of the Accord's Chief Safety Inspector. Inspections are comprehensive and include the structural integrity of buildings, the presence and accessibility of emergency exits, stairwell access, and electrical safety, among other details. The inspections done under the Accord are conducted by qualified engineers who are employed or contracted by the Accord as opposed to individual lead firms or social audit companies.[51] If the Chief Safety Inspector determines that a specific building presents a "severe and imminent" danger to worker safety, the factory management, its health and safety committee, worker representatives, the SC, and the union's signatory to the agreement are all immediately informed. If a factory faces (partial) closure for remedial work, the signatories are required to keep the workers and pay their regular wages for a maximum of 6 months.

---

[47]Clean Clothes Campaign, Workers Rights Consortium, Maquila Solidarity Network and International Labor Rights Forum.

[48]First discussions on the Memorandum of Understanding started after the 2010 That's It Sportswear fire. By 2012, Tchibo Gmbh and PvH had signed up to the agreement. For a more detailed account, see Clean Clothes Campaign, Maquila Solidarity Network, The History behind the Bangladesh Fire and Safety Accord, 2013, www.cleanclothes.org/file-repository/resources-background-history-bangladesh-safety-accord (last accessed 30 August 2020).

[49]Preamble, Accord on Fire and Building Safety in Bangladesh, www.bangladesh.wpengine.com/wp-content/uploads/2018/08/2013-Accord.pdf (last accessed 30 August 2020).

[50]The signatory companies must pay an annual fee based on their annual garment production turnover in Bangladesh. Because the Accord is a 5-year agreement between the unions and companies, a company cannot simply unilaterally decide to terminate its commitment to the Accord.

[51]Individual factory CAPs, www.bangladeshaccord.org/factories (last accessed 30 August 2020), aggregated progress reports can be found on www.bangladeshaccord.org/resources/ progress-reports (last accessed 30 August 2020).

The Accord also has a unique level of transparency, especially considering the fact that mainstream social compliance initiatives in the garment sector keep inspection reports private. In contrast to this, Article 11 of the Accord states that the inspection reports will be disclosed to "factory management, the factory's health and safety committee, worker representatives (where one or more unions are present), signatory companies and the SC unions, management and buyers within two weeks, and the public within six weeks." In addition, Article 19(c) requires the release of quarterly aggregate reports "that summarize both aggregated industry compliance data as well as a detailed review of findings, remedial recommendations, and progress on remediation to date for all factories at which inspections have been completed." The Accord also ensures a high level of transparency by publishing all inspection reports (both in English and Bengali, with photos) and corrective action plans online, and publicly tracking progress. All of the 150,000+ safety findings and hazards identified to date, as well as their progress on remediation, are publicly accessible.

Another of the Accord's key components are its provisions directly aimed at empowering workers in factories. Article 16 requires the establishment of "an extensive fire and building safety training program [. . .] with involvement of trade unions and specialized local experts." The aim of the training programme is to both empower workers and support factory owners to jointly take ownership for making and keeping their factories safe. Furthermore, the Accord mandates the establishment of a credible worker-management health and safety committee, with worker-members chosen by their unions and fellow workers. Finally, Article 13 also ensures the right to refuse dangerous work. The Accord further actively involves workers in the process of guarding their own safety through worker trainings, all-staff meetings during which workers are explained their right to refuse unsafe work, and a safety complaints mechanism that is accessible to workers and has managed to resolve direct threats to worker safety, as reported by workers themselves.[52]

Probably the most notable feature of the Accord, and certainly the feature that has garnered the most attention to date, is the fact that the Accord is a legally binding and thus enforceable contract between the parties to the agreement, namely the lead firms and unions. Indeed, lead firm signatories have far reaching obligations under the agreement, namely, to continue their sourcing in Bangladeshi factories[53] and to ensure the financial feasibility of factories making any necessary renovations. Article 22 states that "[e]ach signatory company may, at its option, use alternative means to ensure factories have the financial capacity to comply with remediation requirements, including, but not limited to, joint investments, providing loans, accessing donor or government support, through offering business incentives or through

[52]Arengo et al. (2019a).

[53]Article 23 states that signatories "are committed to maintaining long-term sourcing relationships with Bangladesh," which requires them to "continue business at order volumes comparable to or greater than those that existed in [2012]" for the duration of the Accord (i.e. 5 years).

paying for renovations directly." According to Anner et al., this feature makes the Accord a "buyer responsibility agreement" that establishes joint liability.[54] Although Article 22 is a crucial clause—as it speaks directly to the purchasing pressure which is so characteristic of the sector—it does not stipulate how signatory companies should comply with its requirements. As such a novel obligation, it has proved to be challenging to fully implement and monitor.[55] Alternatively, if a supplier fails to make the necessary renovations, even with financing available, Article 21 requires that participating lead firms cease commercial relations with that supplier.

If company signatories fail to live up to the responsibilities outlined in the Accord, they can be held accountable. Article 5 (and later Article 3 in the 2018 agreement) prescribes that any dispute between the parties shall be presented to the steering committee for resolution, which shall decide the dispute by majority vote within 21 days. The body's decision can be appealed to a "final and binding" arbitration process. Awards resulting from the decision "shall be enforceable in a court of law of the domicile of the signatory against whom enforcement is sought" pursuant to the Convention on the Recognition and Enforcement of Foreign Arbitral Awards,[56] also known as the New York Convention.

Ben Hensler and Jeremy Blasi note that while

> legally enforceable commitments subject to binding arbitration are commonplace in international commercial transactions, the Bangladesh Accord is a major breakthrough because it is the first initiative involving multiple lead firms in which the companies have made detailed, legally enforceable commitments to implement international labor rights protections.[57]

To date, the global union signatories have twice initiated arbitration against brand signatories in 2016–2018 (consolidated in a single proceeding). In both cases, the unions argued that the signatories failed to ensure that remediation occurred within the timeframe required by the Accord, and also failed to negotiate financial terms with the factories that would have allowed them to make the required remediations. In January 2018, a settlement was reached with one of the lead firms for its delay in remediating life-threatening hazards at its suppliers. The settlement included two million US dollars to fix safety hazards like locked gates, structural faults, and lacking fire doors and sprinkler systems in more than 150 factories, as well as

[54]Anner et al. (2013).

[55]On the one hand, factories may be reluctant to ask for financial assistance from commercial partners. On the other hand, in case brands and retailers have offered financial assistance, they still have an incentive to minimise contributions so as not to incentivise their supplier base too much. Finally, it is also important to note that outside of enforcement actions, it is difficult to monitor this requirement.

[56]United Nations Convention on the Recognition and Enforcement of Foreign Arbitral Awards, New York, 10 June 1948, U.N.T.S. 330, p. 3.

[57]Hensler and Blasi (2013).

300,000 US dollars for the unions who brought the case, for their "Supply Chain Worker Support Fund."[58] The other case settled for an undisclosed but allegedly considerable sum of money.[59] However, this also means that no arbitral award was issued and, hence, the full potential of the Accord's arbitration system has still yet to be fully tested.

The enforcement mechanism has arguably worked as an effective incentive for lead firms to take their obligations under the contract seriously. In fact, each step in the enforcement protocol has motivated all company signatories to step up their efforts in requiring and supporting their suppliers to make the necessary renovations, therefore boosting the speed at which safety hazards have been addressed. At the same time, it also needs to be recognised that the timing, costs, procedural complexities, and opacity of the Accord arbitration procedure will still require improvement going forward in the legacy agreement, as well as other who might borrow from this clause. In June 2017, the global union federations of IndustriALL and UNI announced an agreement with lead firms' representatives on the language of a successor Accord on Fire and Building Safety in Bangladesh. The new Accord, which took effect in June 2018 after the original Accord expired, extended the programme for an additional 3 years, adding some improvements for the payment of workers' salaries during required remediation work.[60] In 2020, however, after a protracted legal battle,[61] the functions of the Accord were transferred to a national regulatory body that includes the employer association and the government of Bangladesh next to the lead-firms and unions.

---

[58] IndustriALL, Global unions reach US$2.3 million Bangladesh Accord settlement with multinational brand, www.industriall-union.org/global-unions-reach-us23-million-bangladesh-accord-settlement-with-multinational-brand (last accessed 30 August 2020); Rushe D, Unions reach $2.3m settlement on Bangladesh textile factory safety. The Guardian, 22 January 2018, www.theguardian.com/business/2018/jan/22/bandgladesh-textile-factory-safety-unions-settlement (last accessed 30 August 2020). Another case with a separate brand using more than 200 suppliers was settled under the Accord in December 2017. The details of that settlement, including the amount of the settlement, remains under a strict confidentiality agreement. See IndustriALL, Settlement reached with global fashion brand in Bangladesh Accord arbitration, www.industriall-union.org/settlement-reached-with-global-fashion-brand-in-bangladesh-accord-arbitration (last accessed 30 August 2020).

[59] Anner (2018).

[60] 2018 Accord on Fire and Building Safety in Bangladesh, www.bangladeshaccord.org/wp-content/uploads/2018-Accord-full-text.pdf (last accessed 30 August 2020).

[61] Business and Human Rights Resource Centre, Bangladesh: Accord to continue operations for 281 working days as transition agreement is reached, www.business-humanrights.org/en/latest-news/bangladesh-accord-to-continue-operations-for-281-working-days-as-transition-agreement-is-reached/ (last accessed 30 August 2020).

3.4 Bargaining with Lead Firms

The CGT-Fruit of the Loom Agreement, the Indonesia FoA Protocol, and the Bangladesh Accord are all agreements that are the result of bargaining between lead firms and labour organisations. Although three agreements may be too few to distil a robust typology of the "enforceable" or "negotiated brand agreement", certain apparent features distinguish this type of agreement from general codes of conduct, multi-stakeholder initiatives, or global framework agreements. Whereas the latter three would cover a broad palette of labour rights in their scope, the three negotiated brand agreements discussed above each address a specific set of working conditions (e.g. freedom of association, collective bargaining, and fire and building safety) within a certain geography by involving and ascribing specific and sometimes far-reaching obligations to an otherwise distant yet powerful and crucial actor in workplace relations, namely lead firms.

Unlike the CGT-Fruit of the Loom Agreement, both the Indonesia FoA Protocol and the Bangladesh Accord also include multiple lead firms, from a modest number broadly covering the sports apparel sector in Indonesia to over 200 lead firms spanning a vast part of the garment sector in Bangladesh. For a significant number of factories, the extent of such agreements' lead firm coverage in a sector can be important because they supply to multiple lead firms. The fact that a high percentage of a factory's buyer volume is covered by obligations under an agreement with worker organisations is more likely to compel the ownership and management of the factory to improve practices in line with the agreement's requirements. While sometimes this leverage can be achieved by a single brand, in a number of occasions different signatories can pool their leverage. At the same time, and probably even more in contrast to general codes of conduct, compliance initiatives, multi-stakeholder initiatives, or even global framework agreements, these instruments focus on specific labour rights risks which are adapted and contextualised within a specific geographic context (e.g. Honduras, Indonesia or Bangladesh). This allows these agreements to be sensitive and responsive to the distinct localised settings in which the labour rights are embedded. Unlike more globalised approaches such as MSIs or GFAs, this also allows for much more detailed and targeted interventions.

Many of the human rights risks and violations in the garment industry not only occur in a particular factory but are part of a more general sectoral pattern. For example, the causes of the poor fire and building safety record in Bangladesh cannot be ascribed to an individual factory or lead firm, but are, instead, the logical outcome of a structurally complex garment industry. Yet, while the same purchasing squeeze that leads to many workplace violations is felt throughout the global garment industry, it is specifically in South Asia that this pressure manifests in such widespread fire and building safety issues. Addressing fire and building safety requires a high degree of coordination between actors and tailored incentives for multiple factories, companies, social partners, and government agencies, therefore making it more likely to escape the scope of what is possible within single lead firm initiatives or corporate-dominated initiatives. Perhaps the "meso-level" nature of the three negotiated brand agreements discussed strikes the right balance between necessary scale and not losing focus on concrete, tangible and granular interventions at the workplace.

All three agreements also aim to impose (increasingly) specific commitments upon lead firms, demanding behaviour that they would be unlikely to commit to voluntarily. This includes bringing the behaviour of lead firms, including purchasing practices, into the scope of the agreement which stands in contrast to conventional CSR approaches and social compliance initiatives, where the supplier's behaviour is the exclusive focus of intervention. In the set-up of the agreements themselves, there is also a clear aspiration to establish joint management structures and dispute resolution mechanisms with the aim of allowing labour rights organisations to substantially shape and alter outcomes. In this regard, it is important to highlight that all of these agreements resulted from intense campaigning by activists, trade unions and NGOs, as only a few lead firms would ever enter into such an agreement without some form of public or regulatory pressure. This pressure can be achieved through transnational campaigning, as exemplified by the Honduras and Indonesia agreements, or in conjunction with a significant event and subsequent international media attention, like in the case of the Rana Plaza collapse and the Bangladesh Accord. In each of these three cases, campaigners and activists were crucial in challenging lead firms in their consumption markets on issues in their supply chains, and bargaining (or supporting bargaining) to redress spatially stretched power relations.

The Bangladesh Accord stands out from the other two agreements in terms of its legal enforceability, which represents, as Juliane Reinecke and Jimmy Donaghey note, "a very significant new departure in global supply chain labor governance."[62] While unique, it is important to remember that the Accord's capacity for enforcement still remains new, largely uncharted territory; there are no precedents, and so many details remain unclear and untested. For example, the 2013 Accord failed to spell out how the involved parties should select an arbitrator, choose the applicable jurisdiction or law, or what should happen if they could not come to an agreement. This gave rise to procedural delays when the mechanism was activated and led to arbitration under the Accord requiring considerable time, resources and energy, while remaining relatively opaque.[63] And while the extent of the original arbitration clauses has never been fully tested, it already provided options for how Accord-style arbitration could be further streamlined, as visible in the Accord's 2018 successor agreement. A recent publication also offers model clauses for making such a dispute

[62]Reinecke and Donaghey (2015), p. 32.

[63]The Accord proceedings where in contrast to most arbitral proceedings, relatively transparent with only details that could identify the respondents being omitted. For the procedural clarifications needed, see PCA case no. 2016-37 and PCA case no. 2016-37 Procedural Orders 1-8, which took over a year after commencement of the proceedings, www.pca-cpa.org/en/cases/152/ (last accessed 30 August 2020).

settlement more efficient, transparent and cost-conscious in a way that respects the rights and interests of the different parties.[64]

However, even the Bangladesh Accord, which arguably has the most robust enforcement mechanism and therefore the strongest internal dispute mechanism, has needed to rely on additional public and NGO scrutiny for its implementation. The NGO witness signatories to the Accord, who do not have access to its dispute resolution mechanism, have felt compelled to publicly show their concern on several occasions in relation to delays in remediation. One notable example involved the witness NGO signatories shining a spotlight on H&M,[65] in which they publicly observed that "by now, each of these factories [surveyed] should have already completed all required renovations, with minimal exceptions".[66] By making such a public move, the NGOs successfully pressured H&M and other lead firms to step up their implementation efforts. They also reminded everyone that these negotiated agreements not only come about through public domain pressure, but that they also require continued external pressure to ensure their robust implementation, despite the existence of monitoring capacities and internal dispute mechanisms.

4 Supply Chain Compensation Fund Agreements

While the Rana Plaza collapse was a key event leading to the establishment of the Bangladesh Accord that brought new levels of commitments and enforceability to negotiated brand agreements, a similar impact was also seen on supply chain compensation fund agreements. Following lethal disasters, a significant share of international campaign energy has also focused on the development of ex post facto supply chain compensation fund agreements to provide for the longer-term financial needs of survivors and the families of the deceased. These agreements differ from unilaterally defined contributions offered by lead firms as compensation under their own terms for accidents in their supply chains. Instead, they involve a practice in which worker representatives and lead firms (sometimes together with other stakeholders) reach an agreement over the parameters of the compensation and its implementation.

[64]Clean Clothes Campaign et al., Model Arbitration Clauses for the Resolution of Disputes Under Enforceable Brand Agreements, 2020, www.laborrights.org/publications/model-arbitration-clauses-resolution-disputes-under-enforceable-brand-agreements (last accessed 30 August 2020).

[65]Clean Clothes Campaign et al., Evaluation of H&M Compliance with Safety Action Plans for Strategic Suppliers in Bangladesh, 2016, www.laborrights.org/sites/default/files/publications/H%26M_Bangladesh_September2015_English.pdf (last accessed 30 August 2020).

[66]Clean Clothes Campaign et al., Ongoing Safety Delays at H&M Suppliers in Bangladesh, 2016, www.laborrights.org/sites/default/files/publications/Memo_on_HM_CAPs_1-28-2016.pdf (last accessed 30 August 2020).

The first such fund to be established was proposed following the Spectrum disaster.[67] In April 2005, the Spectrum Sweater factory collapsed in Savar, Bangladesh, killing at least 64 workers and injuring many others. International labour rights groups such as the Clean Clothes Campaign, the ITGLWF (the predecessor of IndustriALL Global Union), and multiple Bangladeshi unions campaigned for the establishment and implementation of a compensation fund. Although only the factory owner and a handful of lead firms (Inditex, KarstadtQuelle, Scapino, New Wave Group, and Solo Invest) contributed, the Spectrum Relief Fund was the first initiative of this kind to be developed in Bangladesh, where an agreement was eventually reached on compensation, pensions, beneficiaries and administration of the scheme. Final pay-outs were made in September 2011.

The same approach was also later applied to the Hameem case. In 2010, the That's It Sportswear factory (part of the Hameem Group) burned down in Bangladesh, leaving 29 dead and 11 seriously injured. In the wake of the fire, the so-called Hameem formula was established, based on the lessons learned from the Spectrum case. The formula provided lump sum compensation for pain and suffering (BDT 500,000)[68] and compensation for loss of income (calculated as 50% of the minimum wage in the garment sector for 25 years with an adjustment for the projected average annual inflation rate). The agreement also offered compensation for injured workers. Perhaps equally important is the fact the Hameem formula also stipulated who should contribute to such a fund, apportioning the financial cost of implementation between lead firms, the factory, the employer association, and the government. Later, a compensation scheme was agreed in the case of the Eurotex and Continental factory disaster along the same lines as the scheme developed in the Hameem case. The Hameem formula was also used as a basis for the Wing Star agreement in Cambodia.[69]

4.1 Rana Plaza Compensation Agreement (Bangladesh)

In the wake of the Rana Plaza collapse, the Rana Plaza Arrangement was established to provide compensation for victims of the disaster and their dependents. In November 2013, a framework agreement was reached by all possible stakeholders, namely the Bangladeshi government, the Bangladesh Garment Manufacturers and Exporters Association, IndustriALL Global Union and the IndustriALL Bangladesh

[67] See for a detailed account Miller (2012).

[68] This constituted a significant upgrade from the BDT 168,000 provided under the Spectrum mechanism, where an initial BDT 100,000 was paid to the families by the employer shortly after the factory collapse.

[69] Clean Clothes Campaign, Bangladesh formula crosses borders to Cambodia, www.cleanclothes.org/ua/2013/cases/wingstar (last accessed 30 August 2020).

Council, the Clean Clothes Campaign, and the Bangladesh Institute of Labour Studies. The agreement foresaw a single process overseen by a Coordinating Committee comprising the signatories' representatives and chaired by the ILO. Among other steps, the committee was tasked with defining a formula for victim compensation and administering the collection and disbursal of funds.[70]

Departing from the Hameem formula, and benefitting from the expertise of the ILO, the agreement was based on principles outlined in ILO Convention 121 on Employment Injury Benefits (1964). The committee established a compensation formula calculated to ensure payments were sufficient to provide an income for the lifetime of all beneficiaries, taking into account different individuals' needs and circumstances. Persons who lost their earnings as a result of injuries sustained in the disaster or dependents of persons killed or missing were eligible to claim compensation. The Rana Plaza Trust Fund was formally established in January 2014, from which time it began accepting contributions that could be made by anyone, including on an anonymous basis. Claims processing and pay-outs began in instalments shortly thereafter.[71]

After an initial assessment of 40 million US dollars, it was finally determined that 30 million US dollars would be needed to satisfy all expected claims. After the initial establishment of the trust fund and the start of its operations, a number of lead firms, the Bangladeshi government, and other stakeholders provided contributions. However, the sum of contributions did not match the total amount needed to enable full minimum compensation for loss of income under the international norm as contained in ILO Convention 121. In the absence of a concrete plan for reaching the required amount, and without a (judicial) route to enforce the MoU, campaign organisations shifted their focus to using public domain pressure to convince lead firms to pay up in order to achieve the required amount. This lack of enforceability was perhaps most clearly illustrated by Benetton's positioning. Citing a lack of clarity in terms of the apportionment for individual lead firm contributions as the main reason,[72] Benetton only contributed to the fund in 2015 after extensive pressure, including an online petition by Avaaz that gathered one million signatures.[73] It was only

[70]Understanding for a Practical Arrangement on Payments to the Victims of the Rana Plaza Accident and their Families and Dependents for their Losses (as amended 20 November 2013), www.ranaplaza-arrangement.org/mou/full-text/MOU_Practical_Arrangement_FINAL-RanaPlaza.pdf (last accessed 30 August 2020).

[71]The Rana Plaza Donors Trust Fund, www.ranaplaza-arrangement.org/fund (last accessed 30 August 2020).

[72]"[S]ince thus far it has not been possible for the RANA PLAZA TRUST FUND, to set forth such principle for any brand," Benetton: Press note—Benetton Group starts global social commitment program for 2015 and launches second phase of support activities for victims of Rana Plaza, www.benettongroup.com/media-press/press-releases-and-statements/press-note-benetton-group-starts-global-social-commitment-program-for-2015-and-launches-second-phase-of-support-activities-for-victims-of-rana-plaza/ (last accessed 30 August 2020).

[73]Butler S, Benetton agrees to contribute to Rana Plaza compensation fund. The Guardian, 20 February 2015, www.theguardian.com/business/2015/feb/20/benetton-agrees-contribute-rana-plaza-compensation-fund (last accessed 30 August 2020).

later in June 2015, after significant public domain pressure, including by governments,[74] and following a significant anonymous contribution, that the ILO could announce that the Rana Plaza Trust Fund had met its 30 million US dollars target and thus had gathered the funds required to enable full payments to all victims.[75] Final disbursements were carried out in the ensuing months.

4.2 *Tazreen Claims Administration Trust (Bangladesh)*

In November 2012, just six months before the Rana Plaza collapse, a massive fire broke out at the Tazreen Fashions factory in Ashulia, Bangladesh, killing 113 workers and injuring nearly 200. Though this disaster occurred before Rana Plaza, negotiations on the Tazreen compensation effort did not conclude until November 2014, when it was finally signed by C&A, the C&A Foundation, IndustriALL Global Union, and the Clean Clothes Campaign. Despite initial unilateral compensation measures by C&A and others, the trust could now equally provide for a single approach. Although the delay in reaching an agreement resulted in significantly delayed compensation for the victims, it also meant that the Tazreen Claims Administration Trust could build and borrow significantly from the gains and expertise of the Rana Plaza Arrangement.[76] Indeed, it used the same actuarial calculations and software, employed the same executive commissioner, and built on other infrastructure developed for the Rana Plaza Arrangement.

Major contributions of one million US dollars were made by the C&A Foundation and the Fung Foundation (Li & Fung had placed orders at Tazreen Fashions on behalf of Sean John's Enyce brand). Smaller contributions were made by KiK, El Corte Ingles, and Walmart, with the latter only contributing 250,000 US dollars. Having achieved full funding, the trust was able to provide compensation to all of the injured workers and dependents of those who had been killed in the fire by July 2016. Recipients included 482 family members of 103 deceased workers and 10 missing workers, and 174 survivors who suffered continuing injuries from the fire. These payments, totalling 2.17 million US dollars, in combination with payments made in the immediate aftermath of the fire by the Bangladeshi government, were sufficient to satisfy the awards for all eligible claimants. An additional 350,000

[74]Trade Union Advisory Committee, 7 OECD Government Ministers call on brands to compensate Rana Plaza victims after strong Trade Union and NGO push, members.tuac.org/en/public/e-docs/00/00/0E/D8/document_news.phtml (last accessed 30 August 2020).

[75]ILO, Rana Plaza victims' compensation scheme secures funds needed to make final payments, 2015, www.ilo.org/global/about-the-ilo/newsroom/news/WCMS_374239/lang%2D%2Den/index.htm (last accessed 30 August 2020); Hoskins T, After two years, the Rana Plaza fund finally reaches its $30m target. The Guardian, 10 June 2015, www.theguardian.com/sustainable-business/2015/jun/10/rana-plaza-fund-reaches-target-compensate-victims (last accessed 30 August 2020).

[76]About the Tazreen Claims Administration Trust, www.tazreenclaimstrust.org/about (last accessed 30 August 2020).

US dollars was set to be transferred to a separate fund to provide ongoing medical treatment for victims of both the Tazreen Fashions fire and Rana Plaza collapse still suffering injuries.[77]

4.3 Ali Enterprises Arrangement (Pakistan)

Preceding both the Rana Plaza collapse and Tazreen Fashions fire, the Ali Enterprises factory burned down on 11 September 2012 in the Baldia Town area of Karachi, Pakistan. Despite numerous documented fire safety failures, the facility received its SA-8000 certification three weeks before the fire, therefore claiming it had fulfilled international standards in areas including health and safety, child labour and minimum wage.[78] The German retailer KiK was the only acknowledged buyer at the Ali Enterprises factory which produced jeans for KiK's Okay Men brand. A public campaign forced KiK to agree to discuss compensation with the Pakistan Institute of Labour Education and Research (PILER), a local labour rights group. These discussions resulted in a 2012 agreement in which KiK committed to making an initial contribution to an immediate relief fund. The lead firm also agreed to engage in good faith negotiations to determine long-term compensation, but these negotiations did not result in an agreement.

Despite the fire occurring eight months prior to the 2013 Rana Plaza collapse, it was only in September 2016 that an agreement was finally reached to provide compensation for income lost by victims of the fire. Indeed, despite initial commitments to good faith negotiations, it took intense public campaigning, a heavily publicised court case,[79] and political pressure for the main buyer, KiK, to sit down at the table and work out an agreement facilitated by the ILO, based on lessons learned in the Rana Plaza and Tazreen compensation models.

Under the agreement, which was signed by the ILO, the lead firm KiK, IndustriALL Global Union, and the Clean Clothes Campaign, KiK agreed to contribute 5.15 million US dollars to fund the compensation scheme, in addition to the one million US dollars it had already paid in emergency funding in December 2012. Pakistan's Sindh Employees' Social Security Institution (SESSI), which also previously contributed funds to employees for loss of income and medical care, would be a central implementing actor for the fund and committed to provide an additional 0.7

[77] Landmark compensation arrangement reached on 4th anniversary of deadly Pakistan factory fire, www.cleanclothes.org/news/press-releases/2016/09/10/press-release-on-ali-enterprises (last accessed 30 August 2020).

[78] ECCHR, Case Report: RINA certifies safety before factory fire in Pakistan, 2018, www.ecchr.eu/fileadmin/Fallbeschreibungen/CaseReport_KiK_RINA_20181121.pdf (last accessed 30 August 2020).

[79] *Jabir et al. v. KiK Textilien und Non-Food GmbH* (Case No. 7 O 95/15, LG Dortmund). See also Terwindt et al. (2017) and chapters by Miriam Saage-Maaß, Faisal Sidiqqi and Saage-Maaß et al. in this volume.

million US dollars as part of the agreement. These funds, totalling 6.6 million US dollars, were determined to be sufficient to meet the requirements for loss of income and medical care for the fire victims and dependents of the deceased under ILO Convention 121, using a proxy "living wage" proposed by the ILO in the absence of direct records of wage rates.[80]

4.4 Delivering Compensation with Lead Firms

The compensation agreements outlined in Sect. 4 of this chapter differ from the other brand negotiated agreements between lead firms and labour organisations discussed in Sect. 3 in their ex post facto nature and their singular focus on one specific form of remedy, namely financial compensation. As in the case of the negotiated brand agreements, the Rana Plaza collapse also elevated the way compensation can be delivered following a deadly factory incident to a new level. Similar to the negotiated brand agreements, the compensation agreements discussed here also resulted from labour organisations and lead firms jointly developing a single process for setting the parameters and, if necessary, building the infrastructure and institutions required to effectively deliver compensation. While there was already an established practice of supply chain compensation fund schemes with the so-called Hameem formula, the scale and scope of the Rana Plaza collapse brought in the expertise and legitimacy of the ILO. This had implications for the use of the Hameem formula by labour advocates or lead firms in their own actuarial methods, as a more sophisticated and legitimate actuarial approach could be found in ILO Convention 121.

In almost every compensation agreement discussed in this section, lead firms had initially tried to provide compensation through a unilaterally defined process. Such a unilateral approach poses problems in terms of rights compatibility, as a discrepancy almost always exists between the kind and amount of compensation the implicated lead firms foresee and the expectations of victims and/or (customary) international rights standards. Both the Tazreen and Rana Plaza cases demonstrate this. Following the fire at Tazreen Fashions, several individual initiatives emerged that tried to provide in-kind services to victims and mobilise donations from apparel companies, local employers, the Bangladesh Garment Manufacturers and Exporters Association (BGMEA), and the Bangladeshi government. Despite the value of these responses, these efforts did not meet an international standard for compensation, such as the customary Hameem formula or the norms enshrined in ILO Convention 121. Indeed, without a coordinated approach, the victims' right to full and fair compensation would remain unfulfilled. Such fulfilment was only made possible when labour

[80] ILO, Compensation arrangement agreed for victims of the Ali Enterprise factory fire in Pakistan, 2016, www.ilo.org/global/about-the-ilo/newsroom/news/WCMS_521510/lang%2D%2Den/index.htm (last accessed 30 August 2020); Payment on claims from survivors of Tazreen factory fire completed, www.laborrights.org/releases/payment-claims-survivors-tazreen-factory-fire-completed (last accessed 30 August 2020).

rights groups and global apparel companies developed a single, coordinated approach to compensation.

A single approach is also necessary from an equity perspective. For example, the Rana Plaza building complex housed five factories. Initially, the Irish fast fashion retailer Primark was quick to react to the tragedy, but only for its approved supplier, the New Wave Bottoms (NWB) factory. It committed to paying long-term compensation to the 581 NWB workers, and nine months' salary to workers and rescue workers regardless of their factory of employment. This generated differentiated compensation for individual workers based on the willingness of lead firms to pay, and the parameters lead firms developed. Indeed, in order to implement its commitment, Primark chose to create its own independent system for calculating and delivering payments to the NWB workers and their family members, de facto creating a separate system of compensation from the other Rana Plaza workers. For these NWB workers, compensation was initially calculated according to the "Bangladesh Scale," which was an approach to disability and vulnerability assessments based on Spanish traffic accident law,[81] as opposed to ILO Convention 121. In response, the Rana Plaza Arrangement decided to compare and adjust amounts under the Primark approach with those that would be offered under ILO Convention 121.

Also important is the amount of learning and institutional transfers possible between the different compensation agreements. The Rana Plaza Arrangement involved an impressive amount of institution building that ranged from developing actuarial parameters to staff and auditing procedures, and included software writing, counselling strategies, etc. The Tazreen Claims Administration Trust and Ali Enterprises Arrangement clearly benefitted from this work, while also learning from and adapting the model. The Tazreen Trust, for instance, deliberately gave a stronger role to local stakeholders in the implementation of the agreement than that provided under the Rana Plaza Arrangement. The Ali Enterprises Arrangement, in turn, addressed up front the issue of low wages that had preceded the lethal tragedy. Both national Employment Injury Insurance Schemes and ILO Convention 121 are *a priori* neutral on the issue of poverty wages prevalent in the garment sector, which under ILO Convention 121, become the reference for calculating compensation benefits. The Rana Plaza Arrangement and Tazreen Trust both tried to mitigate this by retroactively adapting the calculation to use increased garment sector wages and to create a minimum "floor" of compensation payments. The Ali Enterprises Arrangement, meanwhile, used a "living wage" as a reference wage for additional payments under the scheme from the very the start.

All in all, these compensation agreements also reveal a fairly fragile relationship between multinational companies, labour organisations, and states as they work to ensure access to remedy. Whereas the Bangladeshi government was a member of the Rana Plaza Arrangement Coordination Committee, the domestic legal protections in Bangladesh are minimal at best. The Ali Enterprises Arrangement, in contrast, had to

[81]This methodology was developed by Chavier Chercoles, who was also involved in the development of the Spectrum Relief Fund.

take into account but also benefitted from a legal framework being in place and the presence of an implementing authority in the Pakistani province of Sindh. As such, the Ali Enterprises Arrangement carefully bridged the difference between national and international standards on compensation for loss of income, while also providing an opportunity for a strengthened domestic institution to remain in place. Similar to the bargaining agreements described in Sect. 3 in this chapter, the compensation agreements outlined here may are also clearly be sensitive and adapted to distinct localised parameters embedded in local law, social practices or the specific needs of victims.

5 Conclusions

Although the negotiated and enforceable agreements discussed in this chapter are private in nature, worker organisations have managed to successfully use them to contest or at least partially balance indirect and spatially stretched power relations in the globalised garment industry. By entering into such agreements, worker organisations and their allies have been able to establish institutional mechanisms with lead companies that aim to mitigate some of the power asymmetries which characterise globalised value chains and to deliver concrete workplace improvements at a very granular level, adapted to local contexts. At the same time, most of these agreements have been hard fought, not particularly stable, and focused on fundamental rights that should have already been guaranteed in the first place.

The different types of agreements concluded jointly between worker organisations (including workers, unions and NGOs) and lead firms provide an avenue for worker organisations to potentially hold lead firms accountable on specific commitments in relation to their supply chains. Under these agreements, lead firms have specific obligations to compel and incentivise their suppliers toward positive change. These obligations can range from merely encouraging suppliers to providing them with funding or improved commercial terms, or imposing penalties that can even include ceasing the business relationship. These agreements can also include direct lead firm (financial) obligations toward workers, for example, by requiring them to either maintain or compensate for the loss of workers' income.

The crucial point is that the definition, implementation, and monitoring of these commitments is done jointly between worker organisations and lead companies. Most of the agreements discussed in this chapter required the establishment of a governance body to oversee, implement, and/or monitor (parts of) the agreement. In some cases, this required the creation of a joint monitoring committee, tasked with overseeing implementation. In other cases, more significant institution building took place, sometimes including the establishment of new legal entities, the contracting of inspectors, the provision of services, and the developing of specific processes and layers of secondary regulation. While all of the agreements were the result of public domain pressure exerted by broader social movements, they all included internal dispute settlement structures to deal with further issues that might arise under the agreement. These joint bodies consisted of representatives of parties to the agreement, sometimes with participation of a neutral party. The CGT-Fruit of the Loom Agreement and the Bangladesh Accord also provided an external recourse for final and binding arbitration, whereas other agreements would require state-based judicial mechanisms or campaigning to achieve final dispute resolution.

In the case of the supply chain compensation fund agreements, funding shortages often gave rise to disputes and division between participating lead firms, as did certain lead firms' refusal to contribute (yet). To achieve the 30 million US dollars required for the Rana Plaza Arrangement, labour rights groups eventually resorted to other mechanisms, such as public campaigning. To a certain extent, all of the agreements, even those with more robust internal dispute settlement mechanisms and final arbitration provisions, relied on some form of additional public domain pressure for their implementation. Even the success of the Bangladesh Accord, which arguably has the most robust enforcement mechanism, was in part due continuous NGO scrutiny. Nevertheless, there are good reasons to reduce reliance on public campaigning and create stronger enforcement within such agreements' architecture. The Rana Plaza and Ali Enterprises Arrangements have shown that the majority of apparel companies are often too slow in making sufficient contributions, which can, in turn, create harmful delays in payments to workers or their families. Yet, some interventions will always require specific concerted action from lead firm signatories in order to be effective. The Bangladesh Accord, for example, managed to eliminate over 90% of the safety hazards originally identified by the Accord inspectors. These types of targeted and concrete impacts would be impossible to achieve through other corporate responsibility strategies targeting lead companies, such as campaigning or even new legislation.

The Bangladesh Accord and its arbitration mechanisms should therefore be seen as a point of departure from which labour advocates must continue to finetune lessons learned. Although the Accord foresees far-reaching commitments for lead firms, future agreements should ideally contain even clearer obligations and corollary mechanisms for monitoring and enforcing these obligations. Clauses that incentivise suppliers to comply, such as potentially prohibiting future orders in the event of non-compliance or, alternatively, providing financial assistance when needed for remediation efforts, are particularly crucial. Indeed, these clauses are key to (better) aligning the implementation of labour standards with supply chain practices, just as higher prices or other means of paying for improved conditions are crucial to stopping or at least mitigating the downward pressure suppliers face in today's buyer-driven garment supply chains. While a potential withdrawal of orders can be a powerful motivator for suppliers, it is also important to ensure adequate monitoring of lead firms' commitments. Providing suppliers with the ability to raise complaints in the event that signatory companies do not perform in a way that prevents fear of commercial retaliation could provide a powerful balance.

If used as a model for future agreements, the Bangladesh Accord's enforcement mechanism could benefit from further streamlining. For instance, future arbitration clauses could combine due process with rapid timelines to avoid excessive litigiousness, promote transparency, alleviate burdensome costs, and provide final and binding enforcement.[82] In addition to enhanced arbitration clauses, one might also consider expanding the external environment that can support such agreements. Where the Bangladesh Accord arbitrations were previously administered by the Permanent Court of Arbitration in The Hague, an alternative option would be to build a dedicated entity with a roster of arbitrators specialised in these types of agreements, and with standard procedural rules that would not only ensure such rules do not need to be established ad hoc, but that could also provide some procedural coherence and predictability between agreements.

At the same time, it is important to stress that these agreements are not exclusively conflictual in nature. Although arising out of (transnational) conflicts, they also aim to bridge them. More generally, lead firms, suppliers, and workers can potentially gain from taking a robust, practical and rule-based approach to preventing or mitigating specific labour rights risks in textile supply chains. An enforceable agreement with wide participation like the Bangladesh Accord or the Indonesia FoA Protocol encourages competition based on factors other than labour costs. Of course, such agreements also entail a risk of conflicts being created between actors who are party to the agreement and those who are not. While the Sindh government was not a party to the Ali Enterprises Arrangement itself, it agreed to play a central implementing role. The Bangladesh Accord, in contrast, operated in a far more hostile environment in which the government and employer association eventually forced the transfer of the successor agreement's operations into a national entity where the government and employers now enjoy a seat at the table.

Moving forward, it is important to highlight that we have not seen a proliferation of Bangladesh Accord-like instruments or other types of enforceable brand agreements, with the notable exception of an agreement in Lesotho combatting sexual harassment in the workplace.[83] Establishing more of such agreements, as well as further developing them, monitoring them, enforcing them, and managing relations with governments, will require significant resources and coordination of labour organisations across various continents. Any agreement with far-reaching implications on purchasing practices will therefore require a significant amount of sustainable and coordinated pressure to establish it with a decent number of lead firm participants, sufficient depth in terms of company obligations, and robust legal enforceability.

How far can enforceable agreements really go in terms of radically altering purchasing practices and fully aligning them with human rights concerns? On the one hand, they have done far more than other private initiatives to date. On the other hand, however, one can also legitimately argue that they have only managed to partially address the sourcing squeeze at the root of many of the violations in the

---

[82]One such option is offered by the "Model Arbitration Clauses for the Resolution of Disputes under Enforceable Brand Agreements." Clean Clothes Campaign et al. (2020).

[83]Worker Rights Consortium, Landmark Agreements to Combat Gender-based Violence and Harassment in Lesotho's Garment Industry, www.workersrights.org/commentary/landmark-agreements-to-combat-gender-based-violence-and-harassment-in-lesothos-garment-industry/ (last accessed 30 August 2020).

globalised garment supply chains they seek to address. While all of the agreements covered in this chapter did generate specific lead firm behaviour changes that otherwise would not have materialised, and therefore can be said to (sometimes significantly) alter conditions in supply chains, it might be easier to engage lead firms in more targeted agreements that focus on gender-based violence or workplace safety. The safety renovations that were funded through Article 22 of the Bangladesh Accord and other supply chain compensation fund agreements clearly demonstrate that these agreements can force lead firms into punctuated redistributive events. Yet, to what extent enforceable agreements between worker organisations and lead firms can bring about more significant structural, economic shifts like a durable wage increase, for example, remains to be seen.

References

Anner M (2013) Workers' power in global value chains. In: Fairbrother P, Lévesque C, Hennebert M (eds) Transnational trade unionism: building union power. Taylor and Francis, New York, pp 23–41

Anner M (2018) Binding power: the sourcing squeeze, workers' rights, and building safety in Bangladesh since Rana Plaza. Center for Global Workers' Rights, Penn State University

Anner M et al (2012) Buying power, pricing practices and labor outcomes in global supply chains. Institutions Program Working Paper Series, University of Colorado

Anner M et al (2013) Toward joint liability in global supply chains: addressing the root causes of labor violations in international subcontracting networks. Comp Labor Law Policy J 35(1):1–43

Arengo E et al (2019a) Calling for remedy. International Labor Rights Forum

Arengo E et al (2019b) Future of fashion, worker-led strategies for corporate accountability in the global apparel industry. International Labor Rights Forum

Blasi J, Bair J (2019) An analysis of multiparty bargaining models for global supply chains. International Labour Organization

Connor T et al (2016) The freedom of association protocol: a localised non-judicial grievance mechanism for workers' rights in global supply chains. Non-Judicial Redress Mechanisms Report Series 19

Cowgill M, Huynh P (2016) Weak minimum wage compliance in Asia's garment industry. International Labour Organization

Den Hond F et al (2014) A strategic-interaction analysis of an urgent appeal system and its outcomes for garment workers. Mobil Int Q 19(1):83–112

Gardener D (2012) Workers' rights and corporate accountability – the move towards practical, worker-driven change for sportswear workers in Indonesia. Gender Dev 20(1):49–65

Gregoratti C, Miller D (2011) International framework agreements for workers' rights? Insights from River Rich Cambodia. Glob Lab J 2(2):84–105

Hensler B, Blasi J (2013) Making global corporations' labor rights commitments legally enforceable: the Bangladesh breakthrough. Workers Rights Consortium

Locke R (2013) The promise and limits of private power: promoting labor standards in a global economy. Cambridge University Press, New York

Miller D (2012) Last nightshift in Savar: the story of the Spectrum Sweater factory collapse. McNidder & Grace, Alnwick

Reinecke J, Donaghey J (2015) After Rana Plaza: building coalitional power for labour rights between unions and (consumption-based) social movement organisations. Organization 22 (5):720–740

Terwindt C et al (2017) Supply chain liability: pushing the boundaries of the common law? J Eur Tort Law 8(3):261–296

Ben Vanpeperstraete studied sociology and anthropology at the Université Libre de Bruxelles (Free University of Brussels), Belgium. He has worked on the intersection between labour rights, human rights due diligence and international trade, with a focus on the clothing sector. He has supported global unions' work on the legally binding Accord on Fire and Building Safety in Bangladesh and contributed to the Rana Plaza, Tazreen and Ali Enterprises compensation arrangements. Vanpeperstraete has furthermore worked on EU trade policy, especially on the EU Bangladesh Sustainability Compact and the Everything but Arms Cambodia investigation. In spring 2020, he joined ECCHR's Business and Human Rights programme as a senior legal advisor.

Trade Union Approaches to Global Value Chains: The Indonesian Experience

Reingard Zimmer

Abstract The evident failure of voluntary corporate codes of conduct and their monitoring has further intensified debates over the purchasing practices and legal accountability of transnational corporations. This article analyses the development of International Framework Agreements as an alternative approach advanced by trade unions and describes the characteristics of these instruments, pointing out their strengths and weaknesses concerning implementation and monitoring. It specifically focuses on the Indonesian Protocol on Freedom of Association, a special framework agreement concluded between Indonesian trade unions and international sportswear firms to protect freedom of association and trade union rights in the Indonesian textile, garment and footwear industries. After presenting the protocol's content, the article discusses findings concerning the implementation and monitoring of the agreement, based on interviews conducted by the author in Indonesia between November 2018 and January 2019. It identifies several key factors that led to the successful promotion of strong trade union rights in the formation phase of the agreement, namely public awareness due to intensive campaigning around a mega sporting event, strong support from different civil society actors and the presence of a neutral facilitator. Overall, the Indonesian Protocol on Freedom of Association is an example of a bottom-up process that strengthens the signatory trade unions and thus serves as a potential model for actors in other countries.

Keywords International Framework Agreements (IFAs) · Global Framework Agreements · Implementation of IFAs · Monitoring of IFAs · Indonesian Protocol on Freedom of Association · Global Union Federations · Internationalization of industrial relations

---

R. Zimmer (✉)
Berlin School of Economics and Law, Berlin, Germany
e-mail: reingard.zimmer@hwr-berlin.de

M. Saage-Maaß et al. (eds.), *Transnational Legal Activism in Global Value Chains*, Interdisciplinary Studies in Human Rights 6,
https://doi.org/10.1007/978-3-030-73835-8_10

1 Introduction

Safety deficiencies and labour rights violations in Global South (and Global East) factories at the bottom of global value chains, especially in the textile industry, have been criticised time and again.[1] This discussion intensified after "catastrophes" like the Ali Enterprises textile factory fire in Karachi, Pakistan, and the Tazreen Fashion factory fire in Bangladesh in 2012. In both cases, hundreds of workers died and many more were injured.[2] In 2013, the Rana Plaza building near Dhaka, Bangladesh, collapsed, killing more than 1100 workers and injuring many more. In all of these cases, the failure of voluntary codes of conduct and their monitoring instruments became obvious.[3] These incidents showed that profit interests prevailed over workers' safety.

Consequently, a discussion about transnational companies' legal accountability and their purchasing practices intensified. The trade unions' response was not a legal one, however their general understanding is that decent working conditions are a product of collective bargaining processes, and therefore a question of power.[4] From the 1990s on, the global union federations (GUFs) have been developing International Framework Agreements (IFAs), which set minimum working conditions standards based on the International Labour Organization's (ILO) core conventions. Global unions negotiate and conclude these IFAs with transnational companies or corporate groups. This article analyses IFAs' development and implementation, in particular with regards to the situation in Indonesia, where a Protocol on Freedom of Association was established.

---

[1] Altvater and Mahnkopf (2002), p. 12; Chossudovsky (2002), p. 23. For an early analysis, see: Fröbel et al. (1979), pp. 21, 75, 115.

[2] Article of Ali Enterprises factory fire: www.ilo.org/global/about-the-ilo/newsroom/news/WCMS_629839/lang%2D%2Den/index.htm (last accessed 20 April 2020). In Bangladesh, the Tazreen factory fire caused more than 100 deaths, *New York Times* 25 November 2012, online: www.nytimes.com/2012/11/26/world/asia/bangladesh-fire-kills-more-than-100-and-injures-many.html?_r=0 (last accessed 20 April 2020). Many workers died in previous fires in Bangladesh, see: Rubya (2015), pp. 691–692.

[3] Holdcroft (2015), p. 97; Zimmer (2016), p. 2.

[4] Zimmer (2008), p. 158.

2 International Framework Agreements as a Unique Trade Union Approach

The International Transport Workers' Federation (ITF) initiated transnational collective bargaining after World War II, long before the discussion about globalisation began. As a reaction to ship owners' flag of convenience (FOC) policy,[5] the ITF developed a flag of convenience campaign, and started to conclude collective agreements, "which set the wages and working conditions for crews on FOC vessels irrespective of nationality."[6]

Facing globalization's negative outcomes, like lower working condition standards, most of the other global union federations began developing their own policies, concluding International Framework Agreements[7] with transnational companies to ensure adequate working conditions. The United Food, Farm and Hotel Workers Worldwide (IUF) started first, concluding a global agreement already in 1988,[8] from 1995 other GUFs followed.[9] These IFAs established a minimum standard which has to be regarded in national or regional collective bargaining agreements (CBAs). The process of negotiating an IFA takes about 2 years, and marks the starting point of a long-term relationship between the respective GUF and the transnational company.[10] IFAs are mostly concluded with one company, and apply to all of that company's locations worldwide, as well as its subsidiaries and suppliers. It is exceptional to cover the whole value chain, as subcontractors are usually excluded. However, discussions about the necessity to take responsibility for the whole value chain have already started.

IFAs developed over time. Early agreements only included ILO Core Labour Standards. Now IFAs contain more specific provisions to protect workers' rights which go beyond the ILO core conventions, including detailed rules on implementation.[11] Today, there are more than 170 IFAs, which span beyond national boundaries in every sector.[12] The majority are in the metal and electronics industry,

[5]Shipowners started to reflag their vessels after World War II, choosing to register their ships in Global South countries. A flag of convenience vessel is therefore one that flies a different flag than that of the ship's owners.

[6]The FOC campaign is described on ITF's website: www.itfseafarers.org/en/focs/about-the-foc-campaign (last accessed 20 April 2021). For further information see: Lillie (2004), p. 47; Zimmer (2020), pp. 178–179. For legal aspects, see: Däubler (1997); Zimmer (2015), p. 103.

[7]Due to the global scope of application, "Global Framework Agreements" (GFAs) may also be used.

[8]This IFA on social standards was concluded with the French food company BSN (Danone), followed by seven other IFAs with Danone on other topics in subsequent years.

[9]Cf. Telljohann et al. (2009), as well as Sobczak (2012), p. 139.

[10]Drouin (2015), p. 222; Thomas (2011), p. 269 (274); Zimmer (2020), p. 182.

[11]More in-depth: Zimmer (2020), p. 181.

[12]Author's list from February 2020.

concluded by IndustriALL.[13] About 87% of IFAs are concluded with European transnational companies.[14] Few agreements cover just one country. But even these can still be characterised as transnational, since they are signed by various actors. For example, the Accord on Fire and Building Safety in Bangladesh (Bangladesh Accord), an agreement on occupational safety and health, is only applicable in Bangladesh, but was concluded by two GUFs on behalf of workers and 196 transnational companies.[15] Similarly, the Indonesian Protocol on Freedom of Association is limited to Indonesia, but was concluded between Indonesian trade unions and transnational buying companies. These two rather specific agreements may therefore also be characterised as IFAs.[16]

In general, IFAs may be described as a top-down instrument. As a rule, the global unions lead the negotiations, although often European Works Councils or trade unions from (industrialised) countries where parent companies are headquartered, play a central role in negotiations or even lead the process.[17] Global South trade unions representing producers are seldom included in negotiations, which restrains the implementation of the final agreement.

For example, while it is the case that eight Bangladeshi trade unions[18] signed the Bangladesh Accord, due to their rather weak position in Bangladesh,[19] they did not play a major role in negotiations. As usual, GUFs spearheaded the negotiations (in this case, IndustriALL, representing the apparel sector, and UNI Global Union, representing retail), supported by a coalition of NGOs, including the Clean Clothes Campaign.[20] On the one hand, it is clear that global unions have an understanding of transnational affairs, and by mandate, have to bear the interests of all their member organisations in mind, not just those of a particular region. They also have more resources and are often better trained than trade union officials in the Global South.[21]

---

[13]Including the automobile sector and including suppliers.

[14]Author's list from January 2019. Also see: Telljohann et al. (2009), p. 83; Daugareilh (2006), p. 116; Zimmer (2008), p. 160.

[15]Accord on Fire and Building Safety in Bangladesh: www.bangladeshaccord.org/signatories/company-signatories (last accessed 20 April 2020).

[16]IFAs may be characterised as follows: a GUF is involved in the IFA's negotiation and conclusion. The agreement is based upon ILO standards, contain a monitoring mechanism, and often include suppliers. Drouin (2015), p. 222 (218); Zimmer (2020), p. 178 (183 f.).

[17]Zimmer (2013a), pp. 317–318; Zimmer (2013b), p. 249.

[18]The Bangladesh Textile und Garments Workers League; Bangladesh Independent Garments Workers Union Federation; Bangladesh Garments, Textile & Leather Workers Federation; Bangladesh Garment & Industrial Workers Federation; Bangladesh Revolutionary Garments Workers Federation; National Garments Workers Federation; United Federation of Garments Workers; as well as the IndustriALL Bangladesh Council (IBC).

[19]Rubya (2015), pp. 701–702.

[20]Accord on Fire and Building Safety in Bangladesh, available here: www.bangladeshaccord.org/signatories (last accessed 20 April 2021).

[21]Concerning power asymmetries between the GUFs and the affiliated union confederations/trade unions, see: Ter Haar and Keune (2014), p. 12.

On the other hand, the less actors directly affected are involved in negotiations, the more difficult implementing the agreement becomes.[22]

GUFs are aware of previous campaigns' limitations and the fact that it might be difficult for individual factories to stay competitive after significant working condition improvements,[23] making the need for more comprehensive solutions clear. The Bangladesh Accord's binding provisions on factory inspections and trainings is seen as a step towards a more comprehensive approach.[24] Action, Collaboration, Transformation (ACT), an initiative to promote living wages in the garment industry by IndustriALL and 20 transnational companies,[25] go a step further. It promotes the idea that living wages "should be reached through collective bargaining between employers and workers and their representatives at industry level."[26] Promoting collective bargaining at the industry level is considered an opportunity to overcome the risk of companies' social dumping.[27] Another example is the Indonesian Protocol on Freedom of Association, which supports Indonesian trade unions in organising textile, garment and footwear workers, and secures the signing trade unions' access to factories to organise campaigns, as detailed below.

3 Indonesian Freedom of Association Protocol

The Indonesian Protocol on Freedom of Association,[28] an agreement to protect freedom of association and trade union rights in Indonesia's textile, garment and footwear industry was signed in June 2011. It was concluded between five Indonesian trade unions,[29] 35 local suppliers and the transnational sportswear brand companies Adidas (Germany), Asics Corp (Japan), New Balance (US), Nike Inc (US), Pentland Group PLC (Great Britain), and Puma SE (Germany). In the beginning of 2017, three further companies (Haglöfs, Kjus and SuitSupply), members of the multi-stakeholder organisation Fair Wear Foundation, joined the agreement.[30] Its

---

[22]Zimmer (2020), p. 190.

[23]Holdcroft (2015), p. 98.

[24]Holdcroft (2015), p. 99; for more information on the accord, see: Zimmer (2016); Zimmer (2020), p. 197.

[25]Holdcroft (2015), p. 100.

[26]See: ACT initiative: www.actonlivingwages.com/fact-sheet/ (last accessed 20 April 2021).

[27]Holdcroft (2015), p. 101.

[28]This article is partly based upon textual analysis and the author's interviews in Indonesia between November 2018 and January 2019. The author thanks Muthi Muthmainah for her support in this research, and during her stay in Indonesia.

[29]These are: SPN (National Labour Union), KASBI (Indonesian Trade Union Congress), Garteks SBSI (Garment, Textile, Shoe und Leather Union), GSBI (Indonesian Workers' Association), FSPTSK (Association of the Textile, Garment and Leather Trade Unions).

[30]More information is available here: www.fairwear.org/news/fwf-members-sign-indonesian-foa-protocol (last accessed 20 April 2021).

standard operating procedures (SOPs), with provisions on monitoring through a national supervisory committee, were adopted in December 2012.[31] Next, the agreement and the SOPs' content is presented and analysed, as well as factors that enabled the agreement's conclusion and its implementation in practice.

Freedom of association is formally guaranteed in Indonesia in statutory provisions (Article 28 E No. 3 of the constitution,[32] supplemented by the Presidential Decree No. 83 of 1998,[33] and Article 104 para. 1 Law No. 13 of 2003 on Manpower).[34] As statutory provisions, they have to be interpreted and applied to concrete circumstances in practice. Although freedom of association and trade union rights are formally guaranteed in Indonesia, they are constantly violated in practice.[35] Therefore, their specification and implementation through social partners[36] by other means is of vital importance.

3.1 Content of the Freedom of Association Protocol: Protection of Trade Union Rights

The signing parties are obliged to respect freedom of association at factory sites (Article 2 para. 1, p. 1 of the protocol).[37] Upon signing the agreement, brands and suppliers guarantee not to violate trade union rights in Indonesia. Based on Article 4 para. 3, employers guarantee not to interfere in any way with the organisational activities of the trade unions party to the agreement. This provision goes beyond neutrality clauses, which can be found in some IFAs. It entails that the signing trade unions have the right to enter production sites and become registered company trade unions for that factory, and further means that the company cannot prevent any organising campaigns.[38] This applies to all trade union signatories of the agreement therefore ensures plurality of trade unions and non-discrimination against specific trade unions (Article 4 para. 2).

Furthermore, provisions to support trade unions' work within companies are part of the protocol. For instance, trade union representatives have to be released from

[31]The standard operating procedures for the freedom of association protocol supervision and dispute settlement resolution committee.

[32]Article 28 E No. 3 of the Indonesian constitution reads: "Every person shall have the right to the freedom to associate, to assemble and to express opinions".

[33]Presidential Decree No 83 of 1998 on the Ratification of the International Labour Organization Convention No. 87.

[34]Muthmainah (2021), p. 5.

[35]ITUC (2019), p. 10.

[36]The social partners are the organisations representing the workers (trade unions) and capital (employers' organisations).

[37]All following Articles, if not otherwise specified, refer to the Freedom of Association Protocol.

[38]As long as the activities stay within existing law.

their work duties to carry out organisational activities, while the company must respect all rights to which the workers normally are entitled (Article 4 para. 4).[39] Entitlements for paid leave are relative to the factory's size (Article 4 para. 6). In addition, companies have to provide facilities for trade union meetings (Article 5 para. 1(a)), and union representatives "may make use of communication facilities such as telephones, fax and internet within the company as long as such facilities are available," (Article 5 para. 1(a)). Moreover, trade unions are allowed to place their flag at a prominent place in the factory (Article 5 para. 1 (d)), and have the right to display a union signboard on the premises. In addition, several provisions prohibit discrimination, punishing workers because of their trade union affiliation or related work, and hindering the work of trade unions on the factory premises. These rather specific provisions to facilitate trade union work inside factories are not found in other IFAs, although they are common rights of workers' representatives in industrialized countries.

3.2 *Scope of Application*

The protocol Article 2 Paragraph 1, page 2 only covers first-tier suppliers—transnational brands' main supply firms.[40] In the "initial phase," subcontractors are outside the scope of application, and rather have to be "informed and encouraged"[41] to adhere to the agreement's provisions. This "initial phase" has lasted already for 10 years, with no end in sight. Nevertheless, around 300,000 workers are covered[42] as first-tier suppliers' production sites make up a large portion of the overall process.

3.3 *Factors That Promote Strong Trade Union Rights in the Formation Phase*

As the Indonesian protocol contains strong trade union rights and details how to realise them, a central question is: how could such a strong agreement have been achieved?

---

[39]These are further specified in Article 5 and following.

[40]These are suppliers that "produce finished goods for the Brands" (1), "have a direct legal manufacturing contract with the Brands" (2), and "have workplace auditing conducted by the Brand's compliance team" (3), or "have a system whereby all auditing of Codes of Conduct or supplier company workplace standards are conducted by a third-party auditor" (4).

[41]Such wording is used in many IFAs.

[42]Ferenschild (2018), p. 3.

3.3.1 Public Awareness Due to Intensive Campaigning Around a Mega Sports Event

The Indonesian Freedom of Association Protocol was reached after an intense period of negotiations that started in 2009. Different to Bangladesh, there was no catastrophe with numerous dead workers. Nevertheless, in 2008, a coalition of global and European trade union confederations and civil society launched a powerful international campaign for the Beijing Olympics, addressing labour rights violations in sporting goods' global value chains in Southeast Asia. Adidas, Nike, Puma and other brands were called on to take responsibility for labour rights violations along their value chains. A report entitled *Clearing the hurdles* identified central obstacles to overcome: low wages, precarious short-term contract employment, violations of freedom of association, and factory closures due to industry restructuring without compensation pay.[43] In June 2008, the Play Fair Alliance and Indonesian trade unions met with the main transnational sportswear companies for a 3-day conference in Hong Kong. At this conference, the German company Adidas suggested starting a dialogue on working conditions at the national level in Indonesia and tried to get support from other brands.[44]

3.3.2 Why the Topic of Freedom of Association?

Negotiations finally settled on the topic of violations of freedom of association, as extreme "union busting" was a widespread occurrence in Indonesia at the time.[45] Some interviewees[46] explained in addition, that the sportswear brands were more open to the topic of freedom of association than to negotiate wage increases, the termination of precarious short-term contracts, or of unpaid leave due to factory closures—all issues that bear a higher cost on companies.[47] An Adidas representative described his company's motivation, "As there were lots of disputes about trade union rights in Indonesia, an agreement giving concrete guidance (supplementing statutory provisions), was considered as helpful." He frankly admitted that "shareholder interests" were also an important motivation for joining the initiative. If company-level disputes could be prevented, this would be ideal risk-prevention,[48]

[43]Maquila Solidarity Network (2008), p. 47.

[44]Ferenschild (2018), p. 3.

[45]Interview with Sharif Arifin (LIPS) and Iwan Kusmawan (SPN), 2 November 2018.

[46]Interviews conducted with representatives of all signing Indonesian trade unions, Adidas, a supplier, and NGO representatives were between November 2018 and January 2019.

[47]Interviews with Emilia Yanti (GBSBI) on 9 November 2018, and Parto Sumarto (KASBI) on 13 November 2018.

[48]Interview with Harry Nurmansyah (Adidas office in Jakarta) 13 November 2018.

an argument of the employer side, which can be detected as the central motivation for the conclusion of IFAs.[49]

The (Indonesian) unions considered freedom of association a starting point, and acted on the assumption that negotiations over the other three issues would follow. The workers' side has been advocating for a second and third protocol regarding "wages" and "job security," drafts have already been written.[50] Due to employers' reluctance, the conclusion of further agreements is not in sight.

3.3.3 Strong Support from Different Actors

International and national civil society actors, such as NGOs and trade unions, as well as Indonesian trade unions, were involved in and supported the Indonesian negotiation process, which begun in 2009.[51] Oxfam Australia financed the position of a coordinator who facilitated the negotiation process, which the Clean Clothes Campaign took over in 2018. In addition, all actors said consistently, that the Adidas representative played an essential role and took the employer-side lead whenever negotiations stalled.[52]

3.3.4 A Neutral Facilitator as a Central Factor for Success

A coordinator supported the negotiation process, facilitating meetings, actively motivating actors, and coordinating behind the scenes. Everyone interviewed—those representing trade unions, as well as employers—saw the coordinator's neutral role an essential element in the process' success.[53] Nevertheless, the coordinator did not have procedural competences. A stronger coordinator position could have influenced the actors in case of an impasse. It could be beneficial to install someone with broader competences, such as double voting rights, to be even more effective. While the current solution seems to have been more or less effective for this

[49]Zimmer (2008), p. 189 with further references.

[50]Interview with Franky Tan (FSPTSK Reformasi) on 28 November 2018, and Emilia Yanti (GBSBI) on 9 November 2018.

[51]These included: Oxfam Australia, Jakarta Legal Aid Institute, LIPS (Sedane Labour Information Institute), TURC (Trade Union Research Institute), and AKATIGA (Pusat Analisis Sosial). British trade unions invited an Indonesian representative for the Play Fair Campaign, and a ITGWLF representative was also involved.

[52]The interviewees could not elaborate the factors leading to that role.

[53]In interviews with: Sharif Arifin (LIPS) on 2 November 2018; Mimmy Kowel (coordinator of decent work working group) on 7 November 2018; Emilia Yanti (GBSBI) on 9 November 2018; Parto Sumarto (KASBI) on 13 November 2018; Chris Wangkay (formerly OXFAM Australia) on 14 November 2018; Elly Silaban (KSBSI/Garteks) on 21 November 2018; Lilis Usman (former SPN, now KSPN) on 23 November 2018; Franky Tan (FSPTSK Reformasi) on 28 N November 2018 and Indrasani Tjangdraningsih (AKATIGA) on 15 December 2018.

negotiation process, according to the interviewees, it has proven rather ineffective in conflict resolution (in the National Committee).

4 Low Involvement of Global Union Federations

While global unions were hardly involved in the negotiation process (and still are not),[54] labour rights NGOs played a major role. It seems that Indonesian trade unions wanted to run their own affairs, and considered strengthening trade union rights in their country an Indonesian concern.[55] Therefore, they did not maintain the contact with ITGLWF (now IndustriALL), the textile and garment sector GUF. The Indonesian trade unions' focus was on brands fulfilling their promises.[56] Furthermore, not all Indonesian trade unions are members of the respective GUF.[57] Most of the Indonesian trade union leaders involved did not seem aware that in the struggle against transnational companies, the workers' side is stronger the more international actors involved put pressure on the companies. Concerning trade union rights, international NGOs are not strong enough actors on their own.

5 Implementing the Freedom of Association Protocol

Effective implementation of the protocol's comprehensive provisions remains a concern. Therefore, in the following, I turn to the implementation measures laid forth in the protocol and SOPs, and analyse the provisions' functionality in practice to identify problems and positive aspects.

The Indonesian protocol contains wide-ranging implementation mechanisms. The signing parties committed to supervise the implementation of the agreed provisions (Article 3 para. 7). Even though Adidas integrated information about the Freedom of Association Protocol into its local management training and internal audit procedures, it has never offered specific training on freedom of association. The topic seems to be a rather small part of Adidas' programs.[58] The interviewed trade union representatives described supplier firms' local management as poorly informed about and trained in the protocol. Capacity building and training trade

[54]In the beginning, a representative from the former International Textile Garment and Leatherworkers' Federation (ITGWLF, now part of IndustriALL) was shortly involved, as was a British trade union representative.

[55]Interview with Iwan Kusmawan (SPN) on 2 November 2018; Emilia Yanti (GBSBI) on 9 November 2018; Franky Tan (FSPTSK Reformasi) on 28 November 2018.

[56]Interview with Sharif Arifin (LIPS) on 2 November 2018; Mimmy Kowel on 7 November 2018.

[57]Only SPN and KSBSI/Garteks are affiliated with IndustriALL.

[58]Interview with Harry Nurmansyah (Adidas Indonesia) on 13 November 2018.

unionists at the local factory level seems to vary tremendously between organisations, which indicates that also local trade union activists might not all be well informed about the protocol's content.

Supervision and dispute settlement committees were formed (as agreed in Article 7), both on the national level and in most factories. Factory committees are made up of local management and trade union representatives, but seem to operate rather as monitoring bodies than dispute settlement committees, as no (binding) outcome is foreseen in cases of conflict.[59] A National Committee—formed of signing parties' representatives—meet frequently or upon request to take key decisions. Under certain conditions, NGOs may be granted observer status in the committee (Article 3.4 SOP). While the SOPs contain specific provisions pertaining to their operationalisation, the interviewed trade union representatives did not describe the committees as being effective. All interviewees saw a neutral coordinator to facilitate the national committee's meetings as a positive element,[60] although this chair has no procedural power. So far, the National Committee has not been able to take a decision in cases of conflict. Nevertheless, the trade unions described direct contact with the brands through the national committee as positive.

Although violations of trade union rights in factories bound by the protocol are still reported, all interviewed trade unionists described the Freedom of Association Protocol as a "door-opener" to unionise new factories.[61] As not all of the Indonesian union federations seem to be engaged in organising campaigns,[62] and some reported not having any problems with the management at all,[63] it cannot be evaluated exactly how effective the agreement is in this respect. Nevertheless, all interviewed trade unionists stated that in case of a problem, they would call the sourcing brand representative, which in many past cases would have been successful. The protocol (and national committee's work) enabled this direct line of communication.

The protocol acknowledges trade union plurality and assures that specific trade unions will not be discriminated against (Article 4 para. 2). Therefore, especially the more radical (and participation-oriented) trade unions use the document to enter factory premises where the biggest and rather moderate trade union confederation (SPN) already has a presence. In this respect, trade union representatives of the smaller organizations see the Freedom of Association Protocol as a useful instrument.[64] Nevertheless, trade union rights in the Indonesian textile, garment and

[59]The national monitoring committee may make recommendations that have to be followed. Nevertheless, no such recommendations have ever been made.

[60]Interviews with Iwan Kusmawan on 2 November 2018; Emilia Yanti (GBSBI) on 9 November 2018; Parto Sumarto (KASBI) on 13 November 2018; Elly Silaban (KSBSI/Garteks) on 21 November 2018; Lilis Usman (former SPN, now KSPN) on 23 November 2018; Frank Tan (FSPTSK Reformasi) on 28 November 2018.

[61]Interview with Sharif Arifin (LIPS) on 2 November 2018; Chris Wangkay (formerly OXFAM Australia) on 14 November 2018.

[62]Using organising campaigns to enter new factories was documented only for GSBI.

[63]Interview with Iwan Kusmawan (SPN) on 2 November 2018.

[64]Interview with Emilia Yanti (GBSBI) on 9 November 2018; Parto Sumarto (KASBI) on 13 November 2018.

footwear sector are still violated, as some interviewees explained.[65] The interviewees' statements remain rather vague about the extent to which the protocol enables participating trade unions to enter completely new (so far unorganised) factories. However, according to the interviewed trade unionists, in quite a number of factories, management provides a room for trade union affairs, as foreseen in the agreement, and organisers may be excused from their work duties.[66]

In addition, the agreement foresees collective bargaining agreements be concluded within 6 months of a union's formation at the factory level (Article 6 para. 1), and requires companies have an open attitude towards CBA negotiations (Article 6 para. 1 (a)). As no specific CBAs were concluded, the protocol does not seem to facilitate collective bargaining processes. Either trade unions conclude CBAs as discussed and defined in their organisations, or they do not engage in collective bargaining and accept the statutory minimum wage.

6 Conclusions

The Indonesian Protocol on Freedom of Association is an example of a bottom-up process with local (national) trade unions as the driving force in the negotiations process—a central factor for an International Framework Agreements' successful implementation. Local actors' "ownership," commitment and will to make use of the agreement are greatly important to its success.[67] As Indonesian trade unions negotiated the protocol, its contrast to most other IFAs (concluded by a global union federation) is evident. Nevertheless, supplier firms' involvement in the negotiation process could have been intensified. The companies' suppliers "had to" sign the protocol, but do not seem to have been involved in discussions about its content or implementation. In practice, supplier firms' local management is the central employer-side actor in practice. Involving them more in the negotiation of the protocol's content would have been helpful for implementation, as it was partly the case in the ACT initiative process.[68]

Implementation measures do not seem to be particularly efficient. The main benefit for Indonesian textile, garment and leather unions seems to be their contact with the brands, which the agreement enables. Moreover, the parties unanimously described the positive aspect of starting a social dialogue at the national level, which

---

[65] Interview with Sharif Arifin (LIPS) on 2 November 2018; Emilia Yanti (GBSBI) on 9 November 2018; Parto Sumarto (KASBI) on 13 November 2018; Andriko Otang (TURC) on 12 November 2018.

[66] Interview with Iwan Kusmawan (SPN) on 2 November 2018; Emilia Yanti (GBSBI) on 9 November 2018; Parto Sumarto (KASBI) on 13 November 2018.

[67] Zimmer (2020), p. 196; Stevis and Fichter (2012), p. 667.

[68] For further information about the ACT initiative: www.actonlivingwages.com/fact-sheet/ (last accessed 20 April 2020).

did not exist in Indonesia before.[69] In addition, Indonesian trade union confederations' capacity building process started with the signing of the agreement.[70] Still, implementation measures could be intensified with more trainings, but that depends on foreign financial support. In particular, Indonesian trade unions receive at least partial access to factory premises, which is essential for further trade union work, and more than what is achieved elsewhere.

The following aspects warrant improvement: intensified training of local management and workers' representatives would support the agreed provisions' implementation. The national committee's work could be tremendously enhanced by a chair with more competences than in the current solution, a chair who could influence actors in case of an impasse. It would be even more effective to introduce a real and binding conflict-resolution mechanism. This would not have to be the costly UNCITRAL regulation for international commercial arbitration as chosen for the Bangladesh Accord.[71] Other solutions such as an online tribunal with internationally recognised labour law experts would be possible and less costly. In addition, more strongly involving the competent global union federation IndustriALL would significantly support the struggle of Indonesian trade unions.

Overall, the Indonesian Freedom of Association Protocol strengthens the signing trade unions, and is therefore an example for actors in other countries.

References

Altvater E, Mahnkopf B (2002) Globalisierung der Unsicherheit. Arbeit im Schatten, Schmutziges Geld und informelle Politik. Westfälisches Dampfboot, Münster

Chossudovsky M (2002) Global Brutal. Der entfesselte Welthandel, die Armut, der Krieg. Zweitausendeins, Leipzig

Däubler W (1997) Der Kampf um einen weltweiten Tarifvertrag. Nomos, Baden-Baden

Daugareilh I (2006) Les accords cadres internationaux: une réponse européenne à la mondialisation de l'économie. In: Descolognes, Michèle/Saincy, Bernard (Hrsg.), Les nouveaux enjeux de la négociation sociale interntionale, Editions La Découverte, pp 116–129

Drouin RC (2015) Freedom of association in International Framework Agreements. In: Blackett A, Trebilcock A (eds) Research handbook on transnational labour law. Edward Elgar, Cheltenham, pp 217–229

Ferenschild S (2018) Fact Sheet: Nur Papiertiger? Indonesien und Kollektivverhandlungen. Südwind, Bonn

Fröbel F, Heinrichs J, Kreye O (1979) Die Neue internationale Arbeitsteilung. Rowohlt Reinbek, Hamburg

Holdcroft J (2015) Transforming supply chain industrial relations. Int Labour Rev 7:95–104

[69]Interviews with Emilia Yanti (GBSBI) on 9 November 2018; Parto Sumarto (KASBI) on 13 November 2018; Elly Silaban (KSBSI/Garteks) on 21 November 2018; Lilis Usman (former SPN, now KSPN) on 23 November 2018; Frank Tan (FSPTSK Reformasi) on 28 November 2018.

[70]Interview with Amalia Falah Alam on 7 November 2018.

[71]Zimmer (2020), pp. 199, 200; Zimmer (2016), p. 5.

International Trade Union Confederation (2019) 2019 ITUC Global Rights Index. The world's worst countries for workers
Lillie N (2004) Global collective bargaining on flag of convenience shipping. Br J Ind Relat 42 (11):47–67
Maquila Solidarity Network (2008) Clearing the hurdles: steps to improving wages and working conditions in the global sportswear industry
Muthmainah (2021) Muthmainah, Muthi, Vereinigungsfreiheit und Gewerkschaftsrechte in Indonesien, Gastbeitrag in: Zimmer, Reingard, Das indonesische Abkommen zum Schutz von Gewerkschaftsrechten (Freedom of Association Protocol). Ein Vorbild für andere internationale Rahmenabkommen? Düsseldorf 2021
Rubya T (2015) The ready-made garment industry: an analysis of Bangladesh's labor law provisions after the Savar tragedy. Brooklyn J Int Law 40(2):684–718
Sobczak A (2012) Ensuring the effective implementation of transnational company agreements. Eur J Ind Relat 18(2):139–151
Stevis D, Fichter M (2012) International Frameworks Agreements in the United States: escaping, projecting, or globalizing social dialogues? Comp Labor Law Policy J 33(4):667–690
Telljohann V, da Costa I, Müller T, Rehfeld U, Zimmer R (2009) International Frame work Agreements: a stepping stone towards the internationalization of industrial relations? European Foundation for the improvement of the working and living condition, Dublin
Ter Haar B, Keune M (2014) One step forward or more window-dressing? A legal analysis of recent CSR initiatives in the garment industry in Bangladesh. Int J Comp Labour Law Ind Relat 30 (1):5–26
Thomas M (2011) Global industrial relations? Framework agreements and the regulation of international labor standards. Labor Stud J 36(2):269–287
Zimmer R (2008) Soziale Mindeststandards und ihre Durchsetzungsmechanismen. Sicherung sozialer Mindeststandards durch Verhaltenskodizes? Nomos, Baden-Baden
Zimmer R (2013a) European works councils as participants in Euro-wide collective agreements – analysis from a German perspective. Eur Labour Law J 4(4):312–327
Zimmer R (2013b) Entwicklungsperspektiven transnationaler Kollektivverhandlungen in Europa – Schaffung eines rechtlichen Rahmens für transnationale Kollektivverträge in der Europäischen Union. Europäische Zeitschrift für Arbeitsrecht 2:247–259
Zimmer R (2015) EU-Dienstleistungsfreiheit auch für (billig) ausgeflaggte Schiffe. Anmerkung zur EuGH-Entscheidung vom 8. Juli 2014. C-83/13. Arbeit und Recht 3:103–105
Zimmer R (2016) Corporate responsibility in the »Bangladesh Accord«. Which regulations are transferable to other supply chains? Expertise on behalf of the Friedrich-Ebert-Foundation. http://library.fes.de/pdf-files/id-moe/13072.pdf. Accessed Dec 2016
Zimmer R (2020) International Framework Agreements: new developments through better implementation on the basis of an analysis of the Bangladesh Accord and the Indonesian Freedom of Association Protocol. Int Organ Law Rev 17:178–205

Reingard Zimmer is professor of German, European and international labour law at the Berlin School of Economics and Law, Germany. Besides classical labour law courses, she teaches in the program Labour Policy and Globalisation in the German branch of the Global Labour University. She is specialised on collective labour law and transnational issues around social standards. Besides gender analysis, her main research is the internationalisation of collective bargaining. In 2018–2019, she conducted interviews in Indonesia with actors involved in the drafting and supervision of the Indonesian Freedom of Association Protocol. Zimmer is a member of the jury awarding the Hugo-Sinzheimer prize for extraordinary doctoral research in the field of labour law, and serves as an arbitrator for the German Textile Alliance governed by the Federal German Ministry of Economic Cooperation and Development.

Transnational Labour Law? "Corporate Social Responsibility" and the Law

Eva Kocher

Abstract The article traces the development of transnational concepts of corporate social responsibility (CSR), particularly in relation to International Labour Organization (ILO) standards. It analyses the relationship between transnational private law instruments, and national and international law. It points out opportunities and limits of new enforcement mechanisms, emphasising the role of national legal systems: It will only be possible to prevent the law from becoming a pawn in corporate strategies if CSR instruments become sufficiently effective.

Keywords Labour law · Transnational law · Corporate social responsibility · Complaint mechanisms · Postcolonialism · Bangladesh Accord · National arbitration councils · International Labour Organisation · ILO

1 Introduction

The 2012 Ali Enterprises textile factory fire in Karachi, Pakistan, which killed 255 workers and injured 55, some critically, is not only the worst industrial disaster in Pakistan's history. It became a global scandal that gave rise to a variety of legal and quasi-legal actions, which in turn highlighted the impunity, lack of control and diffusion of responsibility between numerous actors that has become a typical feature of global production networks. Responsibility for the disaster could potentially be attributed to the Pakistani company on the ground (Ali Enterprises in

A slightly different German version of this text was published in Kocher (2019), pp. 183–206. This article is the result of longstanding research on these issues. Special thanks go to Professor Sabrina Zajak (Deutsches Zentrum für Integrations- und Migrationsforschung Berlin) for our recent cooperation in researching grievance mechanisms.

E. Kocher (✉)
Europa-Universität Viadrina, Frankfurt (Oder), Germany
e-mail: kocher@europa-uni.de

M. Saage-Maaß et al. (eds.), *Transnational Legal Activism in Global Value Chains*, Interdisciplinary Studies in Human Rights 6,
https://doi.org/10.1007/978-3-030-73835-8_11

Karachi), transnational clients (the German textile company KiK commissioned 70 percent of the production), and private certifiers (the Italian company RINA certified the factory with the SA 8000 standard).

The production's transnational character was mirrored in the legal proceedings. In Pakistan, a criminal investigation was initiated against the owners of the Pakistani factory. At the same time, victims filed two complaints against Pakistani enforcement authorities.[1] In Italy, criminal proceedings were undertaken against the certifier RINA (which were unsuccessful in the end). In Germany, victims and relatives filed an action for damages against KiK, which the Regional Court in Dortmund dismissed in January 2019.[2] Transnational NGOs, such as the Berlin-based European Center for Constitutional and Human Rights (ECCHR) coordinated many of these actions.

Upon first view, these proceedings only refer to national laws. International organisations and their rules only seem to be directly addressed in an NGO complaint against RINA filed with the OECD Italian contact point in autumn 2018. But at closer inspection, human rights and ILO conventions have played an important role in structuring the plurality of conflicts and legal cases' transnationality. The interplay of standards and norms in different legal sources and procedures is described below (Sects. 2 and 3), before the relationship between different sources of law is analysed and evaluated (Sect. 4).

2 Transnational Enterprises, ILO and CSR

The Tripartite Declaration of Principles concerning Multinational Enterprises and Social Policy (MNE Declaration), adopted by the Governing Body of the International Labour Office in November 1977,[3] is an atypical instrument of international law. As stated in Recital 7, it sets out 59 principles "in the fields of employment, training, conditions of work and life, and industrial relations which governments, employers' and workers' organizations and multinational enterprises are recommended to observe on a voluntary basis." The declaration is justified rather defensively with the view that the ILO "with its unique tripartite structure, its competence, and its long-standing experience in the social field, has an essential role to play in evolving principles for the guidance of governments, employers' and workers' organizations, and multinational enterprises themselves."[4] This wording

[1]See chapters by Saage-Maaß and Faisal Siddiqi in this volume for an in-depth description of the proceedings in Pakistan.

[2]LG Dortmund, judgment of 10 January 2019 – 7 O 95/15.

[3]Adopted by the Governing Body of the International Labour Office at its 204th session (Geneva, November 1977), and amended at its 279th (November 2000), 295th (March 2006) and 329th (March 2017) sessions.

[4]www.ilo.org/wcmsp5/groups/public/%2D%2D-ed_emp/%2D%2D-emp_ent/%2D%2D-multi/documents/publication/wcms_094386.pdf (last accessed 31 January 2020).

makes it clear that with this declaration, the ILO cautiously sought to open up a new field of action, in which its authority cannot be taken for granted: regulating the conduct of private companies that are not directly subject to international law.

More than 100 years after the ILO's foundation, and more than 40 years after the adoption of the MNE Declaration, the way these instruments are supposed to work is evidenced in an overview published by the ILO that lists references to the MNE Declaration.[5] The "non-exhaustive" list includes declarations, decisions, guidelines and position papers from the UN, ILO, United Nations Conference on Trade and Development (UNCTAD), OECD, G20, G8, G7, BusinessEurope, European Trade Union Confederation (ETUC), International Trade Union Confederation (ITUC), African Union (AU), ASEAN, Council of Europe, EU, Southern African Development Community (SADC), and Organization of American States (OAS). The main point of the MNE Declaration seems to have become its function as an important point of reference.

This is no coincidence. Although private companies are not traditionally considered subject to international law,[6] it has become rather undisputed that economic activity across state borders nevertheless requires regulation—if necessary, also beyond national law. For these reasons, the ILO's 1977 MNE Declaration still very cautiously points to the facts that "multinational enterprises play an important part in the economies of most countries and in international economic relations" and that "the advances made by multinational enterprises in organizing their operations beyond the national framework may lead to abuse of concentrations of economic power and to conflicts with national policy objectives and with the interest of the workers."[7]

The 2008 Ruggie Report, which forms the basis of the UN Guiding Principles on Business and Human Rights adopted in 2011,[8] is a bit sharper on this point. It posits that the gap between economic global activity's social impact and the steering capacity of politics offers a "permissive environment for wrongful acts by companies of all kinds without adequate sanctioning or reparation."[9]

This difference is an expression of the fact that by the time the Ruggie Report was published, the debate had shifted considerably since the MNE Declaration. Initially,

---

[5]ILO, Overview of references made to ILO MNE Declaration, www.ilo.org/empent/areas/mne-declaration/WCMS_570367/lang%2D%2Den/index.htm (last accessed 31 January 2020).

[6]This is disputed. The mandate of the intergovernmental working group set up by the UN Human Rights Council in 2014 on Ecuador and South Africa's initiative—to draw up a legally binding international agreement on transnational corporations and human rights—is highly controversial (cf. UN Human Rights Council, Resolution 26/9 of 26/6/2014); on the debate: Kanalan (2014), p. 495; Peters (2014); cf. German Federal Constitutional Court (BVerfG), judgment of 25 January 1977, NJW 1977, pp. 1010–1011.

[7]MNE Declaration (fn 4), Recital 1.

[8]*UN Human Rights Council*, Resolution 17/4 of 16/6/2011.

[9]Ruggie, "Promotion and Protection of all Human Rights, Civil, Political, Economic, Social and Cultural Rights, including the Right to Development" ("Ruggie Report"), 7/4/2008, UN Doc. A/HRC/8/5, No. 3.

the declaration had little influence beyond the ILO. It is formulated in terms of development policy, and understands cross-border economic activity as "relations with host countries, especially in the Third World." The term "multinational enterprise" is accordingly defined as "enterprises which own or control production, distribution, service or other facilities outside the country in which they are established."[10]

Since then, new concepts and terms have taken the stage. Firstly, corporate actors in the US developed the term corporate social responsibility in the 1990s, which seeks to address private companies' responsibilities towards society. Secondly, the UN Guidelines for Business and Human Rights have contributed to framing problems as "business and human rights" issues.

2.1 Labour Standards in CSR Policies

In CSR strategies, human rights, sustainability and the global economy are considered compatible within the framework of "three pillars of sustainability:" "profit, people, planet."[11] However, when CSR instruments and policies were first developed,[12] they often focused on environmental concerns.

Regulating working conditions in CSR instruments only became relevant in the second wave of policy development. Sportswear manufacturers that experienced scandals and were targeted subsequently by NGOs, human rights groups and trade union campaigns—such as the anti-sweatshop movement—pioneered in including social and labour standards in CSR.[13] Their corporate social responsibility declarations promised to comply with minimum working hour and health protection standards. As the public paid more attention to working conditions in consumer goods production, not being able to control production standards became a significant reputational risk. Corporate social responsibility can therefore be seen as a reputation management effort.[14]

However, it was only in involving European companies, European works councils and global union federations that trade union rights became an increasingly important element of CSR initiatives.[15] Within the corporate social responsibility framework, international trade union federations promoted transnational collective agreements, so-called international framework agreements (IFAs). These new

[10]ILO, MNE Declaration, www.ilo.org/wcmsp5/groups/public/%2D%2D-ed_emp/%2D%2D-emp_ent/%2D%2D-multi/documents/publication/wcms_094386.pdf (last accessed 31 January 2020).

[11]Elkington (1997).

[12]Kocher (2008b), p. 198. See also, for example, Madhav (2012), p. 267.

[13]Kocher (2008b), p. 198.

[14]Cf. Kocher (2008a), p. 67.

[15]Blecher (2017), p. 437; Kocher (2008b), p. 198.

transnational instruments[16] are explicitly designed to help establish trade union structures and networking, and therefore support collective organising in global production networks.[17]

At the same time, the ILO developed its 1998 Declaration of Core Labour Standards,[18] one of the aims of which was to make some ILO standards more effective, particularly in the transnational sphere, i.e. in directly addressing transnational enterprises. For this purpose, the declaration's standards were described as "fundamental," thus positioned in a human rights context, which has been controversial. The ILO was criticised for implicitly making some of its declarations more important ("fundamental") than others.[19] The debate on the relationship between "labour rights" and "human rights" also warns that focusing on individual rights could marginalise redistribution and collective action as social policy goals and means.[20]

The 1998 declaration focuses on the ILO's constitutional foundations, especially conventions 87 and 98—freedom of association and collective bargaining. In addition, bans on forced and child labour, and freedom from discrimination are part of the declaration. Since the declaration's adoption, CSR policies and international standards on "business and human rights" and "sustainability" have continuously come to refer to these core labour standards as minimum "labour and social affairs" standards. In a similar vein, sustainability clauses in modern trade agreements[21] and the EU Generalised System of Preferences[22] use these minimum standards. The revised OECD Guidelines for Multinational Enterprises also took the 1998 declaration as its starting point.[23]

In retrospect, the 1998 ILO Core Labour Standards Declaration appears to have significantly promoted the anchoring of social standards (including trade union rights) in CSR policies.

2.2 Dissemination of CSR Policies

How can CSR's widespread use be explained? Why have they become an integral part of corporate policies—even beyond sectors of the economy that have to reckon with serious reputation risks in their value chain?

---

[16]Blecher (2017), pp. 454–456; Thüsing (2010), p. 78; Seifert (2006), pp. 205–241.

[17]Kocher (2008a), p. 67; Fichter et al. (2011), p. 68; cf. Mund and Priegnitz (2007), p. 674.

[18]"Declaration on Fundamental Rights and Principles at Work."

[19]For example, the controversy between Alston (2004), p. 457 and Langille (2005), p. 409.

[20]Alston (2004), p. 457; more details on this debate: Kocher (2012), p. 151.

[21]Cf. Zimmer (2011), p. 625.

[22]Ölz (2002), p. 319; Herkommer (2004).

[23]Utz (2011), p. 8.

Competitive strategies use CSR to open up new markets and position brands. Family businesses also use it to promote a certain "corporate culture." Global companies use CSR as part of their branding.

These developments are, however, also driven by spin-off effects, influenced by politics. Corporate social responsibility receives public funding by national governments, the European Union, international organisations, business associations such as the Business Social Compliance Initiative (BSCI), and numerous multi-stakeholder initiatives (such as the Fair Labor Association (FLA), Fair Wear Foundation (FWF), Ethical Trading Initiative (ETI) and Workers Rights Consortium (WRC)).[24] Important bandwagon effects stem from financial markets, where CSR has become an assessment criterion. In the past 20 years, committing to a CSR policy has become the trait of any company wanting to be seen as a global player.[25]

2.3 CSR Instruments and Actors

The keyword CSR denotes private companies as actors that attempt to prevent human rights violations or promote sustainable business practices. Corporate social responsibility therefore usually starts with a company's own actions, its general commitment to certain principles and standards through a unilateral code of conduct and/or an IFA.

One step towards making such voluntary commitments binding are contract clauses with suppliers obliging them to observe certain minimum social standards. In addition, codes of conduct and/or IFAs are often a starting point for national state incentives, as well as international, national, and multi-stakeholder organisation soft law mechanisms.

Since the adoption of the ILO Core Labour Standards Declaration, companies' codes of conduct and private certification companies have taken them as a starting point to define "working condition" minimum standards. OECD Guidelines for Multinational Enterprises have followed. They were revised in 2000, in particular to include ILO core labour standards, but they also contain "employment and industrial relations"—many detailed standards for all areas of working life—in Sect. 5.[26]

Other important international instruments include, among others:

- The UN Global Compact, which claims to "catalyz[e] action, partnerships and collaboration."[27]

---

[24] More on the FLA MacDonald (2011), p. 243; Ruggie (2016); Lukas et al. (2016); Marx (2012).

[25] Kocher (2008b), p. 198; Madhav (2012), p. 267; Gunningham et al. (2009), p. 405 (with a focus on visibility).

[26] Tapiola (2000), p. 9; Fischer-Lescano and Viellechner (2010), p. 23.

[27] www.unglobalcompact.org/what-is-gc/strategy (last accessed 31 January 2020).

- The International Organization for Standardization's ISO 26000 on Social Responsibility and Corporate Social Responsibility strives to translate this into concrete quality standards.
- In Germany, the Sustainability Code[28] "provides support with establishing a sustainable development strategy and offers a way in to sustainability reporting." It is part of the German government's strategy to achieve the Sustainable Development Goals (UN Agenda 2030 for Sustainable Development).
- The German National Action Plan on Business and Human Rights, adopted by the German government at the end of 2016, is intended to "launch a process of creating a road map for the practical implementation of the [UN] Guiding Principles [for Business and Human Rights]."[29]
- The ILO Tokyo 2020 agreement, which aims to promote socially responsible working practices in preparation for the Olympic and Paralympic Games.

2.4 *Beyond ILO Core Labour Standards*

The ILO Core Labour Standards Declaration's success has sometimes led to a peculiar dual strategy of transnational social standards. From the outset, core labour standards do not directly address typical problems in global production networks, such as work time, health and safety, pay or maternity leave. If calls for fair working conditions in such cases refer to the ILO Core Labour Standards, resulting documents will not address specific issues such as health and safety.[30] However, within the discursive framework of sustainability, human rights, and CSR policies in the 2000s, more recent documents give rise to the hope that the labour standards that were not declared "fundamental" in 1998, could play a greater role in future. For example, the broader-based OECD Guidelines, UN Guiding Principles and the ILO's Decent Work Agenda[31] have deepened CSR policies on social standards over the past 10 years.

Against this backdrop, the ILO MNE Declaration was amended in 2000 and 2017 to include core labour standard principles such as forced labour and those in the Decent Work Agenda, including transition from the informal to the formal economy. In addition, the revisions added provisions on legal protection, compensation for victims, and information on due diligence.

---

[28]www.deutscher-nachhaltigkeitskodex.de/en-gb/ (last accessed 31 January 2020).

[29]www.auswaertiges-amt.de/blob/610714/fb740510e8c2fa83dc507afad0b2d7ad/nap-wirtschaft-menschenrechte-engl-data.pdf, p. 5 (last accessed 31 January 2020).

[30]Compa and Vogt (2001), p. 199 mention a very prominent example where the US Congress created its own idiosyncratic definition of "internationally recognized worker rights," without reference to ILO conventions (234).

[31]ILO, "DW4SD Resource Platform" (Decent Work for Sustainable Development), www.ilo.org/global/topics/dw4sd/lang%2D%2Den/index.htm (last accessed 31 January 2020).

The following section concentrates on this last group of rules—control and enforcement. For a long time, the OECD Guidelines for Multinational Enterprises were unique in providing a redress mechanism (i.e. complaints to National Contact Points). Besides emphasising that effective implementation ultimately depends on private companies' institutionalised respect for workers' rights in their corporate and operational processes (i.e. "due diligence"),[32] the UN 2011 Guidelines on Business and Human Rights detail interesting rules on redress and remedies.

3 CSR's Authority and Effectiveness

The recent focus on redress began in the 2000s. The debate has increasingly turned to ensuring CSR policies' authority and effectiveness,[33] or, in other terms, human rights in business and sustainable corporate policies. The terms "authority" and "effectiveness" refer to an approach that identifies a norm as "law" if legitimacy in norm-setting (for example in international law) is institutionally linked with an authority to decide if, in a specific case, the norm has been complied with,[34] in particular by delegating control and enforcement away from norm-setters.[35]

3.1 Monitoring, Auditing and Certification

Control instruments in CSR strategies were developed at an early stage. Monitoring, auditing and certification were concepts first used in managing processes and/or production.[36] In transnational production networks, commissioning companies often require their suppliers to submit to concrete auditing procedures, and/or acquire certification. In some cases, the transnational enterprise monitors and conducts audits. In other cases, external auditors are used. A market of private certification companies has developed around these instruments.

In practice, effectiveness of these enforcement procedures is doubtful. Numerous concrete indications and research show conflicts of interest and other problems in monitoring and auditing procedures.[37] In particular, where collective and trade union rights are concerned, auditing and monitoring have systematically proved unsuitable

[32]For a socio-legal approach: Kocher (2013), p. 41.

[33]For these concepts, cf. Kocher (2014), p. 479.

[34]Cf. Zürn and Koenig-Archibugi (2006), p. 243.

[35]Abbott (2000), p. 408; Zangl and Zürn (2004), p. 21.

[36]For further information: Pries (2010), p. 221.

[37]Sabel et al. (2000); Locke et al. (2007), p. 23; Egels-Zandén and Lindholm (2014); Zajak (2013), p. 178; Estlund (2010), p. 203.

for detecting violations.[38] A particular problem is that the companies that set the standards often have control over, and make decisions about implementation and monitoring.[39] Often, effectiveness problems are not rooted in the process and its results, but in implementation, which mostly remains in the hands of local companies.[40] Overall, the greatest danger to effectiveness lies in management practices to superficially demonstrate "compliance," or "creative compliance." The term "creative compliance" was elaborated in tax evasion models, and indicates "the active response of those subject to the law, not just in political lobbying over legislation but in post hoc manipulation of the law to turn it – no matter what the intentions of the legislators or enforcers – to the service of their own interests and to avoid unwanted control."[41]

In the case of IFAs, this is different, if only slightly. Their implementation and control is usually achieved through dialogue and joint problem-solving between companies, and trade unions or works councils.[42] They are based on mechanisms that enable company employees to identify and report violations. Common mechanisms involve negotiated enforcement through information-sharing and presourcing requirements, which are often the shared responsibility of management and works councils in joint working groups and regular meetings.[43]

Corporate control over monitoring can also be weakened in multi-stakeholder initiatives. An example is the Fair Labor Association (FLA), the oldest such initiative in the textile sector, which offers a CSR fair labour certificate for the textile industry. The FLA was founded as an NGO in the US in 1999. It includes companies such as adidas, Nike and Puma, universities such as Princeton University, and a number of NGOs such as Human Rights First and the Global Fairness Initiative; trade unions are not represented. The FLA audits and monitors the value chain of its member companies, i.e. in their suppliers in the Global South, covering approximately 5000 companies in 60 countries and a total of 3.7 million workers. The association monitors FLA code compliance of its members' supplier factories through independent audit firms that conduct random on-sight inspections of selected factories in the value chain.[44]

However, the FLA has been criticised, for example due to corporate interests' dominance of its organisational structure and its lack of discernible progress in improving working conditions. As a consequence, the organisation has repeatedly changed its procedures, for example, introducing a complaint mechanism for

[38] Anner (2012), p. 609; Egels-Zandén and Lindholm (2014); Terwindt and Saage-Maaß (2017).

[39] Calliess and Zumbansen (2012), p. 59.

[40] Zajak and Kocher (2017), p. 310.

[41] McBarnet and Whelan (1991), p. 848; cf. McBarnet (2007), p. 9.

[42] Blecher (2017), p. 455; Fichter et al. (2011), p. 68; Sciarra (2011), p. 405.

[43] Kocher (2009); Blecher (2017), p. 455.

[44] MacDonald (2011), p. 243.

workers.[45] This is in line with a remarkable development in the CSR field: individual complaint procedures have been suggested as the key to more effective transnational governance in the field of "business and human rights."[46]

3.2 *Complaint Mechanisms in Transnational Production Networks*

Complaint mechanisms make it possible for workers to allege violations and assign responsibility. Unlike auditing and monitoring, complaint mechanisms are not based on processes or structures, but on problems, individual cases and results. This makes them function similarly to individual rights redress and legal remedies. In contrast to the top-down processes of auditing and monitoring, these procedures institutionalise the handling of individual conflicts.

An example of such case-related conflict resolution is the conciliation-like procedure developed by some national contact points in accordance with OECD guidelines.[47] Another quite early example is the "third party complaint process" the Fair Labor Association introduced in 2003.

The UN Guiding Principles now contain an even more generalised call to states and private companies to provide access to effective remedies for violations of standards ("effective remedies"). They offer the following criteria for effective private, out-of-court complaint mechanisms:[48] legitimacy (enabling trust, accountability), accessibility, predictability, access to information, advice and expertise, transparency, "rights compatibility," and continuous learning.

4 CSR in Relation to International and National Law

In language and style, even unilateral corporate codes of conduct predominantly convey the impression of being legal instruments. This is why, independent of their legally binding quality,[49] their "legal" character is such an interesting and important topic. It can be misleading if they look like law without being able to keep the promises inherent in the law. In any case, these forms of transnational "regulation" compete with international and national laws. The following section will therefore elaborate on the relationship of CSR instruments to international and national law.

[45]MacDonald (2011), p. 243.

[46]Ruggie (2016), Lukas et al. (2016) and Marx (2012).

[47]Cf. Calliess and Renner (2009); on effectiveness, see Sanchez (2015), p. 89.

[48]UN Guiding Principles on Business and Human Rights of 2011, No. 31.

[49]See Kocher (2008a), p. 67.

4.1 Privatisation of International Law?

By explicitly referring to international standards such as ILO conventions, private standard-setting in the form of CSR borrows from the legitimacy of these binding norms.[50] However, when an international law norm is translated and transformed into a private law context, it tends to silently change its meaning. CSR declarations and agreements implicitly claim the authority to interpret standards that originally are directed at states for private actors.[51] This is what the term "privatisation of international human rights law" addresses.[52]

This problem of translating norms from one context to another is quite common in law. It also appears if, for example, social clauses in international trade treaties refer to ILO standards. When public actors "own" the norms, there is a way out of the translation dilemma: interpretations of the treaty's social standards could reference those of the ILO Commission of Experts, the Commission on Freedom of Association, or even mandate the ILO's direct monitoring.[53]

However, this is hardly a viable option for private law standards, as the ILO formulates standards for states, not private actors. To get an idea of the problems that arise when a norm is translated from a public to a private law context, we just need to look at the translation of standards that depend on a states' legal guarantees. For example, it is completely unclear what it means when private companies promise to protect freedom of association, trade union and collective bargaining. Free trade union activity is, by definition, an activity that organises interests that conflict with employers' interests. Interviewed company representatives were not able to express clear ideas of what it would mean to promise respect for freedom of association and collective bargaining (for example in China).[54] They mostly pointed to factory committees or grievance mechanisms that give voice to workers' interests, but are not in any way comparable with ILO Conventions 87 and 98. In fact, factory committees and grievance mechanisms often represent potential union competition and, at times, been deliberately established by companies as competition to trade unions.[55] After all, trade union rights require a legal and social framework under the rule of law, which only a state can ensure; a company can at best behave in a non-disturbing or supportive manner.

---

[50]Kocher (2009), p. 409.

[51]Herberg (2001), p. 25.

[52]Blecher (2017), p. 471.

[53]Cabin (2009), pp. 1081, 1088 on the "labor clause" in the Peru-US Trade Promotion Agreement.

[54]Kocher (2009); Trade union rights in China: Cooney et al. (2014), pp. 61–63; cf. Hibbeler and Utz (2010), p. 17.

[55]Kocher (2009), p. 409; cf. Anner (2012), pp. 609–644.

4.2 *The Competition Between Private Standards and National Law in the Global South*

The possible competition between private standards and producing countries' legal systems constitutes a further problem. Codes of conduct and private agreements usually promise to abide by local national laws,[56] while at the same time developing their own control and interpretation mechanisms. Transnational enterprises and multi-stakeholder organisations thus become development policy actors in countries of the Global South.[57]

The resulting coexistence between private standards and national laws entails some ambivalence. On the one hand, there is a danger that these states' legal systems could become caught up in a regulatory "race to the bottom" with private dispute resolution mechanisms.[58] There have been cases in which companies responded to local actors' demands for compliance with national law by referring them to the (lower) "transnational" or company minimum standards.[59]

On the other hand, "ripple effects"[60] or ratcheting-up, i.e. a race to the top, is also possible and, in fact, envisaged.[61] Production sites are often located in countries with deficient (labour) law mobilisation[62] and implementation—due to corruption, entanglement of political and economic elites, weak rule-of-law institutions, weak or divided trade unions or a strong power imbalance between capital and labour—factors that hinder labour laws' effective enforcement.[63] CSR's promotion is often based on the hope that these instruments could serve as a lever for gradually improving working conditions—as additional law enforcement tools or a way to provide human rights with more effective redress mechanisms that could become enshrined in national law.[64]

4.2.1 The Bangladesh Accord on Fire and Building Safety

The Accord on Fire and Building Safety in Bangladesh (Bangladesh Accord) is a good example of some of these contradictions. It was concluded in the aftermath of the Rana Plaza factory collapse in 2013. It is a framework agreement between transnational enterprises in the garment and retail industry and global and local

---

[56] Kocher (2008b), p. 198; McBarnet and Kurkchiyan (2007), p. 59; Hyde (2012), p. 83.

[57] More on labour law and development policies: Ashiagbor (2019).

[58] Hepple (2005), p. 62, referring to arbitration mechanisms in the context of *lex mercatoria*.

[59] Kocher (2009), p. 422.

[60] Compa and Vogt (2001), pp. 204–208.

[61] Sabel et al. (2000).

[62] Cf. Brookes (2013), p. 181; Zajak et al. (2017), p. 899.

[63] Cf. Hepple (2005), p. 87; cf. Körner-Dammann (1991).

[64] Blecher (2017), pp. 437, 440–448.

trade unions, with NGO participation. In the event of a conflict, the agreement provides for arbitration under the rules of the United Nations Commission on International Trade Law (UNCITRAL), and thus a legally enforceable arbitration award.[65] The Bangladesh Accord Foundation that oversees the agreement is based in the Netherlands. An ILO representative serves as the chair of its steering committee.[66]

Bangladesh is one of the most important production countries for textile products worldwide. In 2016, the World Justice Project's listed it in 103rd place out of 113 countries in the Rule of Law Index,[67] with a government described as "hostile to labour rights."[68] The accord operates against this background. It has been of great importance to more effective law enforcement and contributed considerably to the protection of workers' rights through its many inspections[69] and mechanisms to accompany change processes in local companies.

The accord has always competed with other initiatives, most notably the Alliance for Bangladesh Worker Safety, which was founded by the North American enterprises that opposed the accord and does not include binding arbitration mechanisms.[70] At the same time, Bangladesh strengthened the state labour inspectorate by creating the Remediation Coordination Cell (RCC) within the Bangladesh Department of Inspection for Factories and Establishments. The ILO helps coordinate the RCC, and Canada, the Netherlands and the United Kingdom fund it. It stands to reason that the accord spurred these other mechanisms, and they would not be here today without it.

In an attempt to regulate collision between the regimes, the RCC was mandated with inspecting factories not covered by either the accord or the alliance. It seems that this did not keep conflicts at bay. When the accord expired after five years in 2018, the Bangladeshi government slowed down negotiations on a possible extension, insisting on its own sovereignty in occupational safety issues. The accord was extended transitionally by three years, until 2021 (Transition Accord), and the signatories agreed to work with the Bangladeshi government and ILO to transfer the accord's functions to a national government agency.[71]

---

[65] In detail: Zimmer (2016); Salminen (2018), p. 411.

[66] More details by Blecher (2017), pp. 452–453.

[67] WJP Rule of Law Index 2016, p. 39, www.worldjusticeproject.org/sites/default/files/documents/RoLI_Final-Digital_0.pdf (last accessed 31 January 2020).

[68] Vogt (2017), p. 84; ILO, "Report of the High–Level Tripartite Mission to Bangladesh," 2016, www.ilo.org/wcmsp5/groups/public/%2D%2D-ed_norm/%2D%2D-relconf/documents/meetingdocument/wcms_488339.pdf (last accessed 31 January 2020), resulting in a "special paragraph" (marg. 141–145) at the 105th International Labour Conference.

[69] According to the accord, more than 30,000 factories have been inspected since its launch.

[70] In addition, there is the 2013 "Bangladesh Sustainability Compact" with the EU, and the ILO and International Finance Corporation programme "Better Work Bangladesh", Vogt (2017), p. 88.

[71] The accord's website, www.admin.bangladeshaccord.org/wp-content/uploads/2018/08/2018-Accord.pdf (last accessed 31 January 2020).

The Transition Accord agreed that Bangladesh would take over the accord's tasks after fulfilling certain prerequisites.[72] However, the Bangladeshi government ordered the accord to cease operations by November 2018. The Bangladesh Supreme Court issued an interim injunction to prohibit the accord from operating. Then, in May 2019, the government reached an agreement with the Bangladesh Garment Employers Association (BGMEA) to continue the accord's operations for one year.[73] As a consequence, BGMEA, fashion companies and national trade unions have started to create a new organisation, the RMG[74] Sustainability Council (RSC), which should eventually take over the accord's staff and infrastructure. It seems quite doubtful that the Bangladeshi institutions will be able to make significant progress without the accord as a competing mechanism.

4.2.2 Cambodia and Myanmar: National Arbitration Councils

The ILO has focused on strengthening state labour inspection and labour law enforcement.[75] Cambodia, another country that is an important global textile producer, serves as an interesting example of how the ILO has interpreted its role.

As early as 1999, the US concluded a trade agreement with Cambodia which guaranteed the latter better access to the US market, while at the same time obliging Cambodia to improve working conditions in the textile sector. As a result, the ILO created national and regional labour arbitration councils in 2003—tripartite labour dispute arbitration systems to compensate for the lack of independent labour courts and the Cambodian legal system's more general shortcomings. These served as a model for Myanmar's national arbitration council established in 2012—by the Settlement of Labour Disputes Law—a pre-trial, multi-level tripartite labour dispute arbitration system, which arbitrates disputes down to enterprise-level.[76]

The Cambodian Arbitration Council is an independent governmental institution that is funded by Sweden, Switzerland, the US, Australia, the World Bank, the ILO, as well as the transnational enterprises adidas, Levi Strauss and Gap. In Cambodia, these arbitration tribunals have become the central law enforcement instrument in the country's labour law landscape. Its arbitrators have earned great respect and recognition for the way they practice independent adjudication. It is hard to predict the outcome if, as planned, Cambodia adopts and integrates the Cambodian Arbitration Council into its judicial system. It could positively affect the development of the rule of law, or weakening the arbitration system and thereby the rule of law it promotes.

[72]In 2017, an ILO representative in Dhaka estimated several years for this task (according to Vogt 2017, p. 84).

[73]www.business-humanrights.org/en/bangladesh-accord-to-continue-operations-for-281-working-days-as-transition-agreement-is-reached (last accessed 31 January 2020).

[74]This abbreviation refers to the "ready-made garment" industry.

[75]Hofmann (2019), pp. 121–122.

[76]Zajak (2017b); cf. Ediger and Fletcher (2017).

4.3 Transnational Labour Law?

The relationship between different regulatory regimes of cross-border economic activity involving private actors has been discussed as "transnational law." The "transnationalisation" of law, or "transnational law,"[77] refers to a debate about overlapping or competing regulatory regimes, such as international law, national law, European law, private contracts, as well as non-governmental, contractually stipulated rules. These do not have always clear, hierarchical relationships with each other,[78] resulting in "legal pluralism."[79]

So far, however, this debate has focused on areas of the law such as *lex mercatoria*, in which transnational non-state (arbitration) proceedings are functional equivalents of adversarial adjudication.[80] As such procedures guarantee the law's legitimacy and authority, use of the term "law" seems justified.[81] Accordingly, transnational *lex mercatoria*'s general legal character, due to existing transnational arbitration mechanisms, guarantee delegated norm enforcement and control by way of conflict resolution.[82]

With regard to labour law, the existence of a transnational institutional system similar to the law is doubtful to the extent as no equivalent enforcement procedures have been observed.[83] That is why the increasing development of specific transnational complaint mechanisms represents an important step towards labour law's transnationalisation. On the other hand, the fate of the first transnational labour dispute arbitration mechanism, the Bangladesh Accord, shows how unstable competition with national law is in spite of conflict-of-law rules and coordination instruments.[84]

Conflicts of interest and power imbalances in labour law disputes contribute significantly to the fact that labour law's transnationalisation is much less advanced than transnational commercial law. "Creative compliance"[85] corporate strategies are too widespread; too often law-like rules are merely used as strategic competitive resources.[86] As long as private-law corporate standard-setting relies on international and local national law's legitimacy, without being able to guarantee independent authority or effectiveness, it is merely "*ein Spiel mit dem Recht*"—an imitation of the law.[87]

---

[77]Calliess and Maurer (2014); Renner (2014), p. 750. cf. Blackett and Trebilcock (2015).

[78]Viellechner (2013), p. 1.

[79]Merry (1988), p. 869; Teubner (1996), p. 255; Seinecke (2015).

[80]Renner (2014); Viellechner (2013), p. 1.

[81]Kocher (2014), p. 479.

[82]Stein (1995), p. 70; Cutler (2003), p. 26.

[83]Kocher (2014), p. 479; cf. Blackett and Trebilcock (2015); Rogowski (2013).

[84]Teubner (2005), p. 108; Calliess and Zumbansen (2012), p. 19.

[85]McBarnet (2007); McBarnet and Whelan (1991), p. 848.

[86]Cochoy (2007), p. 91.

[87]Kocher (2010), p. 34.

4.4 The Role of National Law in the Global North

Labour law's transnationalisation does not relieve the burden on national law in any way. Rather, it places new regulatory demands on transparency and clarity in consumer and capital markets, such as which legal obligations arise from competition and tort law in transnational commercial activity.[88]

Furthermore, any company can use the term CSR to promote whatever policy they wish. Policymakers, consumers and trade unions cannot differentiate window-dressings from credible efforts to take responsibility. On this backdrop, effective disclosure obligations about companies' CSR measures could help create a more level playing field between companies that use CSR terms and concepts.[89] Such rules have been envisioned by the EU's so-called CSR Directive,[90] which obliges EU member states to require large companies to report "non-financial information." In Germany, the directive was implemented in German Commercial Code (HGB) 289(b-e), which now requires capital market-oriented firms, financial institutions and insurance companies with more than 500 employees to supplement their management report with a section on concepts, results, risks and key performance indicators (HGB 289c(3)) for the "non-financial" aspects mentioned in HGB 289c(2), inter alia employee and social issues, and respect for human rights.

These reporting obligations also require transnational enterprises to report how they exercise human and labour rights "due diligence." This is only an obligation to disclose. If a company has not established due diligence mechanisms, it only needs to say so in its management report (HGB 289c (4)).

A more effective way to increase the credibility of transnational CSR policies would be to legally oblige companies to comply with human rights due diligence obligations in their transnational economic activities. The 2010 US Dodd-Frank Act's section 1502 on use of "conflict minerals" (especially from DRC) is a model for such regulation. French law 2017-399 of 27 March 2017 "on the duty of care of parent companies and controlling companies" goes even further.[91] It adds article L 225-102-4 and -5 to the French Commercial Code (Code de Commerce), obliging companies with least 5000 employees in France, or at least 10,000 employees worldwide, to develop and publish a monitoring plan (*plan de vigilance*), to identify and prevent potential human rights violations arising from their business activities. Subcontractor and supplier activities are also covered, and remedy mechanisms that sanction non-compliance and damages are provided.

---

[88] McBarnet (2007), p. 9; Dilling (2009); Glinski (2005), p. 187; Kocher (2005), p. 647.

[89] McBarnet (2007), p. 9; Kocher et al. (2012); Kocher and Wenckebach (2013), p. 18; Locke et al. (2007), p. 22.

[90] Directive 2014/95/EU of the European Parliament and Council of 22 October 2014 amending Directive 2013/34/EU, as regards disclosure of non-financial and diversity information by certain large undertakings and groups.

[91] "Relative au devoir de vigilance des sociétés mères et des entreprises donneuses d'ordre;" Hoffberger (2017), p. 465.

In Germany, too, such an approach, including transnational enterprises' liability for exploitation in the supply chain, is advocated by NGOs.[92]

5 Summary

Corporate social responsibility instruments and policies are of significant importance to directly address business responsibility for human rights. The ILO's Core Labour Standards Declaration has greatly contributed to making collective rights a central component of, and promoting labour standards in, CSR policies.

At the same time, CSR policies entail a privatisation of law that leads to entangled legal and management logic.[93] CSR standards' competition with norms of national or international law causes further law enforcement and development policy problems. The interaction between state and private actors' "law" requires more than conflict-of-law rules.[94] Globalisation poses a "race to the bottom" danger to labour markets,[95] which can only be countered if national, international and transnational law mutually reinforce one other. This can be achieved through feedback, i.e. sharing experience from local and national levels, which feeds the design of international and transnational instruments, and vice versa.[96]

The ILO is therefore right to re-emphasise the importance of law enforcement mechanisms in countries of the Global South.[97] However, countries in the Global North where many/most of consumers live also face challenges. They will have to create an effective legal framework to sustainably ensure CSR's transparency, credibility and effectiveness.

References

Abbott K, Keohane R, Moravcsik A, Slaughter AM, Snidal D (2000) The concept of legalization. Int Organ 54:401–419

---

[92]For the most recent demands, cf. Initiative Lieferkettengesetz, https://lieferkettengesetz.de/aktuelles/; for the government bill of March 2021: https://www.bmz.de/de/entwicklungspolitik/lieferkettengesetz (both accessed 2021-04-15); also: Kocher et al. (2012); Kocher and Wenckebach (2013), p. 18; contributions in Krajewski and Saage-Maaß (2018); Scheper and Grabosch (2015); Klinger et al. (2016).

[93]Edelman et al. (2001), p. 1589.

[94]Teubner (2005), p. 105; Calliess and Zumbansen (2012), p. 19.

[95]Hepple (1999), p. 360.

[96]Cf. Halliday and Carruthers (2007), p. 1135; Zajak (2017a), p. 530. There is an interesting study on the on translations and retranslations at Bangladesh village courts: Berger (2017); Merry (2006), pp. 38–51.

[97]Hofmann (2019), pp. 121–122.

Alston P (2004) Core labour standards and the transformation of the International Labour Rights Regime. Eur J Int Law 15:457–521
Anner M (2012) Corporate social responsibility and freedom of association rights: the precarious quest for legitimacy and control in global supply chains. Polit Soc 40(4):609–644
Ashiagbor D (2019) Re-Imagining labour law for development. Hart, Oxford
Berger T (2017) Global norms and local courts: translating the rule of law in Bangladesh. Oxford University Press, Oxford
Blackett A, Trebilcock A (2015) Research handbook on transnational labour law. Edward Elgar Publishing, Cheltenham
Blecher L (2017) Codes of conduct: the Trojan Horse of international human rights law? Comp Labor Law Policy J 38:437–476
Brookes M (2013) Varieties of power in transnational labor alliances. An analysis of workers' structural, institutional, and coalitional power in the global economy. Labor Stud J 38 (3):181–200
Cabin M (2009) Labor rights in the Peru Agreement: can vague principles yield concrete change? Columbia Law Rev 109(5):1047–1093
Calliess GP, Maurer A (2014) Transnationales Recht. Eine Einleitung. In: Calliess GP (ed) Transnationales Recht. Stand und Perspektiven. Mohr Siebeck, Tübingen, pp 1–37
Calliess GP, Renner M (2009) From soft law to hard code. The juridification of global governance. Ratio Juris 22(2):260–280
Calliess GP, Zumbansen P (2012) Rough consensus and running code. A theory of transnational private law. Hart, Oxford
Cochoy F (2007) La responsabilité sociale de l'entreprise comme "représentation" de l'èconomie et du droit. Droit et Société 1(65):91–101
Compa L, Vogt J (2001) Labor rights in the generalized system of preferences: a 20-year review. Comp Labor Law Policy J 22:199–238
Cooney S, Mahy P, Mitchell R, Gahan P (2014) The evolution of labor law in three Asian nations: an introductory comparative study. Comp Labor Law Policy J 36(1):23–68
Cutler AC (2003) Private power and global authority. Cambridge University Press, Cambridge
Dilling O (2009) Grenzüberschreitende Produktverantwortung. Nomos, Baden-Baden
Edelman LB, Fuller SR, Mara-Drita I (2001) Diversity rhetoric and the managerialization of law. Am J Sociol 106(6):1589–1641
Ediger L, Fletcher C (2017) Labor disputes in Myanmar: from the workplace to the arbitration council. BSR, San Francisco
Egels-Zandén N, Lindholm H (2014) Do codes of conduct improve worker rights in supply chains? A study of fair wear foundation. J Clean Prod 107(16):31–40
Elkington J (1997) Cannibals with forks: the triple bottom line of 21st century business. New Society Publishers, Gabriola Island
Estlund C (2010) Regoverning the workplace. From self-regulation to co-regulation. Yale University Press, Yale
Fichter M, Helfen M, Sydow J (2011) Regulating labor relations in global production networks. Internationale Politik und Gesellschaft 2:69–86
Fischer-Lescano A, Viellechner L (2010) Globaler Rechtspluralismus. Aus Politik und Zeitgeschichte 34–35:20–26
Glinski C (2005) Produktionsaussagen und Vertrauensschutz im Kauf- und Werberecht. In: Winter G (ed) Die Umweltverantwortung multinationaler Unternehmen: Selbststeuerung und Recht bei Auslandsdirektinvestitionen. Nomos, Baden-Baden, pp 187–230
Gunningham N, Kagan RA, Thormton D (2009) When social norms and pressures are not enough. Environmental performance in the trucking industry. Law Soc Rev 43(2):405–436
Halliday TC, Carruthers BG (2007) The recursivity of law. Global norm making and national lawmaking in the globalization of corporate insolvency regimes. Am J Sociol 112 (4):1135–1202

Hepple B (1999) A race to the top? International investment guidelines and corporate codes of conduct. Comp Labor Law Policy J 20(3):347–363

Hepple B (2005) Labour laws and global trade. Hard, Oxford

Herberg M (2001) Codes of conduct und kommunikative Vernunft. Rechtssoziologische Überlegungen zu den umweltbezogenen Selbstverpflichtungen transnationaler Chemiekonzerne. Zeitschrift für Rechtsoziologie 22(1):25–52

Herkommer V (2004) Die Europäische Sozialklausel. Zollpräferenzen zur Förderung von Kernarbeitsstandards in Entwicklungsländern. Nomos, Baden-Baden

Hibbeler S, Utz B (2010) Die türkische Textil- und Bekleidungsbranche in Zeiten der Krise. Strukturen, Arbeitsbeziehungen, Industriepolitik und Akteursstrategien. Friedrich-Ebert-Stiftung, Berlin/Bonn

Hoffberger E (2017) Das französische Gesetz über die menschenrechtliche due diligence von Muttergesellschaften und Auftrag gebenden Unternehmen. Archiv des Völkerrechts 55 (4):465–486

Hofmann CM (2019) 100 Jahre ILO. Archiv des Völkerrechts 57(2):121–122

Hyde (2012) Legal responsibility for labour conditions down the production chain. In: Fudge J, McCrystal S, Sankaran K (eds) Challenging the legal boundaries of work regulation. Hart, Oxford, pp 83–100

Kanalan I (2014) Extraterritoriale Staatenpflichten jenseits der Hoheitsgewalt. Archiv des Völkerrechts 52(4):495–521

Klinger R, Krajewski M, Krebs D, Hartmann C (2016) Verankerung menschenrechtlicher Sorgfaltspflichten von Unternehmen im deutschen Recht. Germanwatch Nord-Süd Initiative e. V., Bonn

Kocher E (2005) Unternehmerische Selbstverpflichtungen im Wettbewerb. Gewerblicher Rechtschutz und Urheberrecht 107:647–652

Kocher E (2008a) Codes of conduct and framework agreements on social minimum standards – private regulation? In: Dilling O, Herberg M, Winter G (eds) Responsible business: self-governance and law in transnational economic transaction. Hart, Oxford, pp 67–86

Kocher E (2008b) Corporate social responsibility – Instrumente zur Gestaltung transnationaler Arbeitsbeziehungen. WSI-Mitteilungen (4):198–203

Kocher E (2009) Private standards in the North – effective norms for the South? In: Peters A, Koechlin L, Förster T, Fenner Zinkernagel G (eds) Non-state actors as standard setters. Cambridge University Press, Cambridge, pp 409–430

Kocher E (2010) Corporate social responsibility: Eine gelungene Inszenierung? Kritische Justiz 29 (34):29–37

Kocher E (2012) Solidarität und Menschenrechte – Zwei verschiedene Welten? In: Lindemann H, Malaviya N, Hanebeck A, Hanschmann F, Nickel R, Tohidipur T (eds) Erzählungen vom Konstitutionalismus. Festschrift für Günter Frankenberg. Nomos, Baden-Baden, pp 151–162

Kocher E (2013) Unternehmen als Adressaten des Arbeitsrechts. In: Alewell D (ed) Rechtstatsachen und Rechtswirkungen im Arbeits- und Sozialrecht. Reiner Hampp Verlag, München, pp 41–57

Kocher E (2014) Corporate Social Responsibility und transnationales Arbeitsrecht. In: Calliess GP (ed) Transnationales Recht. Stand und Perspektiven. Mohr, Tübingen, pp 479–495

Kocher E (2019) Transnationales Arbeitsrecht? Archiv des Völkerrechts 57(2):183–206

Kocher E, Wenckebach J (2013) Ein Plädoyer für gesetzliche Pflichten von Unternehmen zur Offenlegung ihrer Arbeits- und Beschäftigungsbedingungen. Kritische Justiz 1:18–29

Kocher E, Klose A, Kühn K, Wenckebach J (2012) No accountability without transparency. Legal instruments for corporate duties to disclose working and employment conditions. Friedrich-Ebert-Stiftung, Berlin/Bonn

Körner-Dammann M (1991) Bedeutung und faktische Wirkung von ILO-Standards. Nomos, Baden-Baden

Krajewski M, Saage-Maaß M (2018) Die Durchsetzung menschenrechtlicher Sorgfaltspflichten von Unternehmen. Zivilrechtliche Haftung und Berichterstattung als Steuerungsinstrumente. Nomos, Baden-Baden
Langille B (2005) Core labour rights. The true story. Eur J Int Law 16(3):409–437
Locke R, Kochan T, Romis M, Fei Q (2007) Beyond corporate codes of conduct. Work organization and labour standards at Nike's suppliers. Int Labour Rev 146(1–2):21–40
Lukas K, Linder B, Kutrzeba A, Sprenger C (2016) Corporate accountability: the role and impact of non-judicial grievance mechanisms. Edward Elgar Publishing, Cheltenham
MacDonald K (2011) Fair labor association. In: Hale T, Held D (eds) The handbook of transnational governance: institutions and innovations. Polity, Cambridge, pp 243–251
Madhav R (2012) Corporate codes of conduct in the garment sector in Bangalore. In: Fudge J, McCrystal S, Sankaran K (eds) Challenging the legal boundaries of work regulation. Hart, Oxford, pp 267–284
Marx A (2012) Private transnational governance, legitimacy and dispute settlement. A configurational analysis of private certification systems. Leuven Centre for Global Governance Studies, Leuven
McBarnet D (2007) Corporate social responsibility beyond law, through law, for law. The new corporate accountability. In: McBarnet D, Voiculescu A, Campbell T (eds) The new corporate accountability. Corporate social responsibility and the law. Cambridge University Press, Cambridge, pp 9–58
McBarnet D, Kurkchiyan M (2007) Corporate social responsibility through contractual control? Global supply chains and "other-regulation". In: McBarnet D, Voiculescu A, Campbell T (eds) The new corporate accountability. Corporate social responsibility and the law. Cambridge University Press, Cambridge, pp 59–92
McBarnet D, Whelan C (1991) The elusive spirit of the law: formalism and the struggle for legal control. Mod Law Rev 54(6):848–873
Merry SE (1988) Legal pluralism. Law Soc Rev 22(5):869–896
Merry SE (2006) Transnational human rights and local activism: mapping the middle. Am Anthropol 108(1):38–51
Mund H, Priegnitz K (2007) Soft law – second best solution or a privatisation of social rights? Transfer 13(4):671–678
Ölz M (2002) Die Kernarbeitsnormen der Internationalen Arbeitsorganisation im Licht der neuen handelspolitischen "Sozialklausel" der Europäischen Union. Zeitschrift für internationales und ausländisches Arbeits- und Sozialrecht 16(4):318–358
Peters A (2014) Jenseits der Menschenrechte. Die Rechtsstellung des Individuums im Völkerrecht. Mohr Siebeck, Tübingen
Pries L (2010) Erwerbsregulierung in einer globalisierten Welt. Springer, Berlin
Renner M (2014) Transnationale Wirtschaftsverfassung. Rabels Zeitschrift für ausländisches und internationales Privatrecht 78(4):750–783
Rogowski R (2013) Reflexive labour law in the world society. Edward Elgar Publishing, Cheltenham
Ruggie JG (2016) Hierarchy or ecosystem? Regulating human rights risks of multinational enterprises. In: Rodriguez-Garavito C (ed) Business and human rights: beyond the end of the beginning. Cambridge University Press, Cambridge, pp 11–45
Sabel C, O'Rourke D, Fung A (2000) Ratcheting labor standards. Regulation for continuous improvement in the global workplace. Columbia Law School Public Law Research Paper, New York
Salminen J (2018) The accord on fire and building safety in Bangladesh: a new paradigm for limiting buyers' liability in global supply chains? Am J Comp Law 66(2):411–451
Sanchez JCO (2015) The roles and powers of the OECD National Contact Points regarding complaints on an alleged breach of the OECD guidelines for multinational enterprises by a transnational corporation. Nordic J Int Law 84(1):89–111

Scheper C, Grabosch R (2015) Die menschenrechtliche Sorgfaltspflicht von Unternehmen. Friedrich-Ebert-Stiftung, Berlin/Bonn
Sciarra S (2011) Collective exit strategies: new ideas in transnational labour law. In: Davidov G, Langille B (eds) The idea of labour law. Oxford University Press, Oxford, pp 405–419
Seifert A (2006) Die Schaffung transnationaler Arbeitnehmervertretungen in weltweit tätigen Unternehmen. Zeitschrift für ausländisches und internationales Arbeits-und Sozialrecht 3:205–224
Seinecke R (2015) Das Recht des Rechtspluralismus. Mohr Siebeck, Tübingen
Stein U (1995) Lex mercatoria. Juristische Abhandlungen 28. Vittorio Klostermann Verlag, Frankfurt am Main
Tapiola K (2000) The ILO Declaration on Fundamental Principles and Rights at work and its follow-up. Bull Comp Labour Relat 37:9–16
Terwindt C, Saage-Maaß M (2017) Zur Haftung von Sozialauditor_innen in der Textilindustrie. Friedrich-Ebert-Stiftung, Berlin/Bonn
Teubner G (1996) Globale Bukowina. Zur Emergenz eines transnationalen Rechtspluralismus. Rechtshistorisches Journal 15:255–290
Teubner G (2005) Codes of conduct multinationaler Unternehmen: Unternehmensverfassung jenseits von Corporate Governance und gesetzlicher Mitbestimmung. In: Höland A, Hohmann-Dennhardt C, Seifert A, Schmidt M (eds) Arbeitnehmermitwirkung in einer sich globalisierenden Arbeitswelt. Berliner Wissenschafts-Verlag, Berlin, pp 109–117
Thüsing G (2010) International framework agreements: Rechtliche Grenzen und praktischer Nutzen. Recht der Arbeit 2:78–93
Utz B (2011) Update oder Upgrade? Eine Bilanz zur Revision der OECD-Leitsätze für multinationale Unternehmen. Friedrich-Ebert-Stiftung, Berlin/Bonn
Viellechner L (2013) Transnationalisierung des Rechts. Velbrück, Weilerswist
Vogt JS (2017) The Bangladesh sustainability compact: an effective tool for promoting workers' rights? Polit Gov 5(4):80–92
Zajak S (2013) Transnational private regulation and the transformation of labour rights organisations. Emerging markets: new markets for labour support work in China. J Asian Public Policy 6 (2):178–195
Zajak S (2017a) Channels for workers' voice in the transnational governance of labour rights? Global Pol 8(4):530–539
Zajak S (2017b) Trade Union building in Myanmar. Open Democracy, London
Zajak S, Kocher E (2017) Die Selbstregulierung von Arbeits- und Sozialstandards in transnationalen Wertschöpfungsketten – Rechtsschutz in privaten Beschwerdeverfahren? Kritische Justiz 50(3):310–325
Zajak S, Egels-Zandén N, Piper N (2017) Networks of labour activism: collective action across Asia and beyond. An introduction to the debate. Dev Change 48(5):899–921
Zangl B, Zürn M (2004) Make law, not war: Internationale und transnationale Verrechtlichung als Baustein für Global Governance. In: Zangl B, Zürn M (eds) Verrechtlichung – Baustein für Global Governance? Verlag J.H.W. Dietz, Bonn, pp 12–33
Zimmer R (2011) Sozialklauseln im Freihandelsabkommen der Europäischen Union mit Kolumbien und Peru. Recht der Internationalen Wirtschaft 9:625–631
Zimmer R (2016) Unternehmensverantwortung im "Bangladesh-Accord". Welche Regelungen sind übertragbar auf andere Lieferketten? Friedrich-Ebert-Stiftung, Berlin/Bonn
Zürn M, Koenig-Archibugi M (2006) Modes and dynamics of global governance. In: Koenig-Archibugi M, Zürn M (eds) New modes of governance in the global system. Exploring publicness, delegation and inclusiveness. Palgrave Macmillan, Basingstoke, pp 236–254

Eva Kocher is professor of civil and labour law at the Law Faculty of European University Viadrina in Frankfurt (Oder), Germany. She is the director of the Center for Interdisciplinary Labour Law Research (C*LLaS). Her research focuses on questions of equality, transnational labour law and digitalisation. She coedited *Selbstständige Unselbstständigkeit. Crowdworking zwischen Autonomie und Kontrolle* (Nomos 2019). Kocher's most recent publications include "Die Position der Dritten. Objektivität im bürgerlichen Recht" in *Jahrbuch des öffentlichen Rechts der Gegenwart* (2019) and "Arbeit, Kollektivautonomie und Solidarität" in *Autonomie im Recht – Geschlechtertheoretisch vermessen* (Nomos 2018).

Tort Law and Human Rights

Gerhard Wagner

Abstract The article explores the relationship between tort law and human rights. It explains the potential inherent in holding corporations liable in tort for human rights violations along the supply chain, such as the 2013 Rana Plaza collapse in Bangladesh. On a theoretical level, it devises a legal framework of tort liability that is optimal from the standpoint of social welfare. Such an optimal liability system would make manufacturers internalise the full cost of production, including harm caused to workers, third parties and the environment. In contrast, the present global liability situation is characterised by legal fragmentation and enforcement deficits. These factors provide the explanation for the large-scale externalisation of production risks we witness today, leading to an inflated global demand. In principle, tort law is well suited to offer a remedy, as the interests protected by human rights and national tort law broadly overlap. Furthermore, the duty of care which is the core requirement for shifting losses to others via tort law is a flexible concept that may even be stretched to accommodate cross-border human rights policies. The new French "*devoir de vigilance*," or human rights due diligence, as well the UK Supreme Court's recent jurisprudence, aim to tap this potential. On the other hand, the article raises doubt in relation to the adverse economic incentives and market shifts if such duties are imposed selectively, i.e. only in some jurisdictions, but not in others. After all, private international law often stands in the way of a global application of national tort law. Finally, alternative mechanisms of enforcement are assessed and examined with a view to their comparative effectiveness. This analysis casts doubt on the usefulness of tort law as a means to further the human rights cause.

Keywords Torts · Delict · Entity principle · Duty of care · Human rights due diligence · Strategic litigation · Choice of law · Level playing field · Supply chain liability · Externalities · Cost internalization · Devoir de vigilance

G. Wagner (✉)
Humboldt-Universität zu Berlin, Juristische Fakultät, Berlin, Germany
e-mail: sekretariat.wagner@rewi.hu-berlin.de

M. Saage-Maaß et al. (eds.), *Transnational Legal Activism in Global Value Chains*, Interdisciplinary Studies in Human Rights 6,
https://doi.org/10.1007/978-3-030-73835-8_12

1 Introduction

In spite of the developments of Europeanisation and globalisation, tort law is essentially a domestic affair. Most practical cases involve accidents that are connected to only one legal regime, namely the one in force at the place of injury. Traffic accidents, which account for the bulk of tort cases in courts, are a pertinent example. In recent decades, however, the number of cases that include a foreign element, in the sense that more than one jurisdiction is involved, have grown in number. Even many traffic accidents now involve a party from outside the jurisdiction where the accident occurred. Many products that cause harm in one jurisdiction were produced in other jurisdictions, and so on.

The legal rules for dealing with cases involving a "conflict of laws," where it is not unequivocally clear whether one legal system or another controls, are designed to provide a "level playing field."[1] These rules seek to ensure that the persons who choose to act in a particular jurisdiction play by the same rules. The idea behind ensuring a level playing field is that the safety standards and rules for proper behaviour must be coordinated in order to provide the benefit aimed for, namely reduced accident costs. For example, if a tourist from England decides to drive his car through France while observing the rules of the road of his home jurisdiction, such as driving on the left-hand side of the road, disaster is nearly certain. The conflict-of-law rules providing that the tort law of France applies, and that in any event the safety standards at the place of injury control, ensure that English tourists and French motorists coordinate their behaviour in the interest of safety.[2] Where everybody drives on the same side of the road, the number of accidents is minimised, at least in comparison to any other system of assigning lanes to drivers.

2 Imagine: A Global Legal System

2.1 *Legal Unity, Economic Diversity*

Imagine that all the jurisdictions in the world operated according to the same system of tort law or, alternatively, that the whole world was one single jurisdiction. In this scenario, the courts in Pakistan and Bangladesh would apply the same legal rules and safety standards as the courts in the United Kingdom, France, Germany, or Canada. While the prospect that all countries on the planet merge into one, or that they at least apply identical liability rules, is extravagant already, now stretch your imagination even further to include the enforcement stage. Let us assume not only that the rules

[1] Magnus (2019), para 2; Wagner (2008), pp. 1ff.

[2] Cf. Article 4(1), 17 Regulation (EC) 864/2007 on the law applicable to non-contractual obligations, OJ 2007 L 199/40.

are identical across the globe, but also the frequency of suit, the adequacy of the procedural framework, and the quality of the judicial system.

In such a uniform world, the specific problem addressed by human rights litigation through tort law would not and could not occur. If the systems of tort law, or non-contractual liability more broadly, were identical everywhere and enforcement equally effective, then there would be no disparity between jurisdictions. The "law on the books" and the "law in action" would be the same, regardless of location. In terms of safety levels and, correspondingly, exposure to liability, it would make no difference whether someone acted in Paris, Berlin, Toronto, Karachi or Dhaka. The expected costs of liability would be the same in each of these places.

How would firms that sell goods to consumers behave in such a uniform world? One might expect that firms would always produce "at home" in such a world, in close proximity to their customers. In this scenario, economies would likely resemble those of the mercantilist age, when every nation operated its own closed-shop economy. But this would be a mistake. While expected liability costs are certainly a factor in commercial enterprises' balance sheets, they are not the only factor, let alone the most relevant. Other major factors include raw material costs, which may differ depending on location, and labour costs, which may also vary across jurisdictions, reflecting local differences in supply and demand.

Attempting to eliminate these differences in production factor costs, together with any differences in tort law regimes and their enforcement, would be wrong and wasteful. Economic globalisation has generated huge benefits to the world population in the form of more and better goods and services available at lower prices, largely by expanding the benefits derived from the division of labour to another level. If people in Bangladesh are, on average, more skilled in assembling electronic appliances than people in Germany, then the people in both jurisdictions benefit from an economic system that lets the Bangladeshis run the electronics business, while the Germans focus on other activities in which they enjoy a comparative advantage. In a similar vein, people living in the desert areas of the Middle East and North Africa might enjoy a comparative advantage in the renewable energy sector, simply because there is so much solar power available for collection and transformation into electricity. In short, division of labour is a good thing and would continue to flourish even if human rights standards and their enforcement were identical across the globe.

This thought experiment of a global tort law regime provides a useful backdrop for thinking about the problem of human rights violations. If there were a uniform tort law, applicable and binding around the globe, the scope of liability would be identical across regions and nations. However, diversity and division of labour would persist, as there would still be regional differences in the availability and cost of natural resources as well as talented and skilled labour. Unlike today's reality, tort law would simply be taken out of the equation that defines global competition and economic development.

2.2 The Tort Law Problems of Human Rights Violations

Imagining a world with a uniform tort law raises the question as to the normative underpinnings and principles of such a global regime. More specifically, what uniform rules would govern the human rights violations currently discussed in the present world of legal fragmentation? For this purpose, it is not necessary to develop a rich and nuanced regime of non-contractual liability for any kind of claim and fact pattern. Rather, the thought experiment shall focus on two paradigmatic scenarios for the current discussion on tort law and human rights, both built on widely publicised incidents. One involves the 2013 collapse of a garment factory called Rana Plaza in Dhaka, Bangladesh, which killed 1134 and injured around 2500 of the factory's mostly female workers.[3] As it turned out, the garment factory's owner ignored cracks that had appeared throughout the building and ordered the workers back in before the building collapsed. This case represents a paradigmatic fact pattern characterised by the following features: (1) the victims of the incident are employees who suffered death or personal injuries; (2) the victims' direct employer is a supplier operating in a jurisdiction with poor standards of occupational safety and/or with poor enforcement of these standards; (3) the ultimate buyer of the goods manufactured by the direct employer is a business that sells clothes or other consumer goods under a well-known Western brand; (4) the ultimate buyer is domiciled and sells the goods in a jurisdiction with comparatively high occupational safety standards and with reasonable enforcement of these standards.

The second representative scenario involves injury not to workers, but to third parties, where harm is caused through contamination or deprivation of natural resources. A prominent example of this scenario is the oil contamination of the Niger Delta region in southern Nigeria, involving the Dutch/UK company Royal Dutch Shell and a local subsidiary thereof.[4] From a legal perspective, the crucial elements are: (1) the victims are located in a jurisdiction with poor environmental standards, little or no enforcement of the existing standards, and a weak and/or corrupt government; (2) there is no pre-injury relationship of a contractual or quasi-contractual nature between the victims and the party that allegedly bears responsibility for the harm; (3) part of the harm is caused to private interests, such as health and property, but a major fraction of the harm is caused to public resources, such as soil, water, and the environment at large; (4) the party that, at least initially, bears responsibility for the damage is a local subsidiary of a multinational group of companies; (5) the head of the corporate group is domiciled in a Western jurisdiction

---

[3]ILO, The Rana Plaza incident and its aftermath, www.ilo.org/global/topics/geip/WCMS_614394/lang%2D%2Den/index.htm (last accessed 11 June 2020), see also www.nytimes.com/2013/05/23/world/asia/report-on-bangladesh-building-collapse-finds-widespread-blame.html (last accessed 11 June 2020), www.bbc.com/news/world-asia-22476774 (last accessed 11 June 2020).

[4]Cf. Amnesty International (2017), www.amnesty.at/media/2086/a-criminal-enterprise.pdf (last accessed 11 June 2020).

with a comparatively well-functioning government, comparatively high standards of environmental protection, and reasonable enforcement.

A common feature of both these scenarios is the difference in standards between two jurisdictions. The jurisdiction where the damage occurs is characterised by modest or outrightly insufficient safety standards and enforcement, while another jurisdiction implicated in the incident scores high on these same counts. In both cases, the jurisdictions with the higher standards are similarly situated in countries that import goods from the jurisdictions with the lower standards. A second common feature is the existence of a local entity, usually a corporation, that is domiciled in the low-standard country and which seems to be responsible for the damage as the direct, immediate tortfeasor. In the Bangladesh case, this is the owner and operator of the Rana Plaza garment factory, while in the Nigeria case, it is the Shell Petroleum Development Company of Nigeria Ltd. Both cases involve another party domiciled in a Western country, that is only indirectly connected to the incident, namely major clothing brands like Benetton, Prada, Gucci, Versace, Primark and Walmart in the Rana Plaza case, and Royal Dutch Shell PLC in the Niger Delta case.

2.3 *The Optimal Legal Solution*

If the world was one jurisdiction, what would be the optimal solution to each of the aforementioned cases? This question cannot be answered descriptively, as the law of non-contractual liability differs from country to country. Even comparative legal scholarship cannot provide the answer, as it lacks a normative yardstick to allow the characterisation of one legal system as superior to another.[5] A normative theory is needed to identify the legal system, or rather, the solution, that works best. One such normative theory is the economic approach to law, which aims to maximise society's welfare through an optimal allocation of resources.[6] Applied to the law of non-contractual liability, economic analysis focuses on the incentives of the various actors, namely potential injurers and victims. The goal is to maximise the net surplus from any given activity, meaning that the gains accruing to the potential injurer must outweigh the costs of the respective activity. The costs of any given activity, of course, include the costs of harm caused to third parties. Other than the activity's direct cost, harm to third parties does not figure into the calculus of potential tortfeasors.

Tort law is an instrument to "internalise" costs of an activity that otherwise would be left externalised. The purpose of cost internalisation is not to sanction the activity in question in the sense of punishing the wrongdoer or to suppress the harmful activity altogether, but rather to incentivise potential injurers to balance the costs of precautions against the costs of harm, and against the benefits that the respective

---

[5]For a comparison of national tort law systems cf. van Dam (2013); Wagner (2019), pp. 994ff.

[6]Shavell (2004), pp. 177ff.

activity generates. From an economic point of view, injurers should take precautions and increase the costs of care until they equal the marginal benefit in terms of an associated decrease in the costs of accidents. If optimal care is ensured, the potential injurer should balance the respective activity's total costs, meaning its direct costs, the costs of care, and the costs of the residual harm, i.e. harm that is caused even if optimal care is taken, against the benefits generated by the activity in question. The potential injurer should engage only in activities to the degree where the benefits are at least equal to total costs, including the costs of harm.

These principles apply with particular force to the production and distribution of goods and services.[7] Where product markets are an issue, demand and supply depend on price. The lower the price of a given product, the higher the demand, and the more of the respective good is supplied, that is, manufactured and distributed. The mechanism of supply and demand with price as the crucial variable determining the scale of production works optimally only if the price is set correctly. The price of a product or service must reflect the total costs of production. If some cost items are left out of the equation, the price set for a particular product will be "too low," and consequently, demand will be "too high." The result is that "too much" of the good is produced.

The costs imposed on others in the course of production face a particular risk of being left off manufacturers' balance sheets. The reason for this is simple: Typically, market forces significantly influence how much a manufacturer pays for raw materials and other inputs. No such market forces are at work when it comes to avoiding external harm. When a person other than the manufacturer sustains damage, this loss rests with the victim. The potential victims who stand to suffer from the manufacturing process may be divided into the manufacturer's employees, on the one hand, and external third parties, on the other. Harm to both groups of victims must enter the manufacturer's balance sheet to make him or her face the full social costs of production. Thus, the maxim propagated by an eminent observer of US tort law with a view to workplace injuries makes good sense: "the cost of the production should bear the blood of the workman."[8] The cost of production should also bear the blood of other victims who are not employed by the manufacturer, but external to the manufacturing process and business. Even harm to environmental resources that cannot be captured under the rubric of private property or other private interests should be considered and monetised to avoid their inefficient overuse.

In theory, tort law provides a mechanism to reallocate these costs to the manufacturer, but in reality, this depends on the shape and contents of the applicable tort law rules. More importantly, it also depends on a functioning system of law enforcement, i.e. courts that aim to faithfully apply the law and that are easily accessible to claimants, including potential victims. Finally, where the tortfeasor is unwilling to pay up voluntarily, the victims must be able to credibly threaten the enforcement of a judgment in their favour. This simple and rudimentary sketch of the

[7]Shavell (2004), pp. 207ff.

[8]Keeton et al. (1984), p. 573; cf. Wagner (2012), p. 15.

prerequisites necessary for tort law's proper operation provides an idea of the many pitfalls and intricacies of tort law in practice. Even in well-functioning societies, potential tortfeasors have reasons to discount the costs of harm inflicted on third parties, which, in turn, weakens their incentives to invest in safety measures in order to avoid such harm from occurring.[9] Both effects undermine the functioning of tort law as a means of cost internalisation and depress prices beyond efficient levels. The higher the degree of judicial and other governmental institutions' malfunctioning in a particular jurisdiction, the more serious these consequences will be.

Ignoring the costs of harm caused to third parties is always bad, as the potential injurer has no reason to take precautions against such harm, even if their costs are lower than the damage they would help to avoid. With a view to harm caused in the course of producing goods and services, the additional problem of excessive activity levels is of particular importance. The nexus between the costs of production, demand, and the volume of supply, mediated through the price mechanism, is the reason why the manufacturer's failure to consider all cost items when setting the price for their products results in excessive levels of production and, therefore, excessive levels of harm. If some fraction of the "real" costs of production are ignored, the adverse effects just described ensue, namely, the levels of production and consumption are too high.

3 The Real World: Fragmentation of Legal Systems, Divergent Standards

3.1 Legal Fragmentation

In reality, the world is not a single jurisdiction, but a patchwork of many jurisdictions. The United Nations has close to 200 members, and some member states run federal systems with different tort law regimes. Thus, the number of distinct systems of tort law exceeds 200. Tort law's fragmentation means that a person or legal entity may be liable to redress a particular harm under the tort law rules of one jurisdiction, but not under the rules of another. In reality, such diversity on legal grounds may be rare, as the various tort law systems tend to converge, at least when it comes to the protection of life, bodily integrity, health, and personal property. However, enforcement systems, meaning the quality and accessibility of civil justice systems, vary greatly across jurisdictions. This explains why courts located in well-functioning and comparatively rich countries attract human rights cases that, at least arguably, originate in jurisdictions which are poor and unable to offer high-quality enforcement of legal entitlements.

When a court is confronted with a claim based on a human rights violation that occurred elsewhere, the first step is to identify the applicable law. In doing so, the

---

[9] Polinsky and Shavell (1998), pp. 887ff.

court must consult the private international law of its jurisdiction. International law, in general, is based on the principle of non-interference, meaning that one sovereign must not interfere in the internal affairs of another.[10] In private international law, this principle generates the assumption of equality of legal systems. Private international law does not choose between legal systems based on their inherent merit or functionality. Rather, it assumes that one legal system is as good as another. As a consequence, private international law does not aim to identify the "better law," but rather to identify the "spatially best solution" by choosing the law that is most closely connected to the facts of the case.[11] Whether the legal system that actually has the geographically closest connection to the case provides a solution that is particularly good or bad is irrelevant.[12]

Under this theory of spatial connectedness, it is rather obvious that the legal system of the jurisdiction that imports products manufactured in far-away jurisdictions is not the one that should govern cases involving human rights violations committed in the latter jurisdictions, even if the latter jurisdictions have lower standards and less or no law enforcement. If a garment factory in Bangladesh collapses, or burns down, all the elements of the tort are located in Bangladesh. The harm was sustained there and the behaviour that caused the harm occurred there. In the Rana Plaza case, the workers were ordered back into the building even after cracks in the building's structure had become visible. The incriminating order was issued and received in Bangladesh, the building was located there, and the injuries to life, health, bodily integrity, and private property were sustained within Bangladesh's jurisdiction.

In Europe, the view that the law of the country of production should govern personal injuries and damage to property caused in the course of production is confirmed by Regulation (EC) No. 865/2007 on the law applicable to non-contractual obligations, the so-called Rome II Regulation. The general rule for the choice of law set out in Article 4(1) of the Rome II Regulation provides that "the law applicable to a non-contractual obligation arising out of a tort/delict shall be the law of the country in which the damage occurs ... irrespective of the country or countries in which the indirect consequences of that event occur." Thus, damage claims for personal injuries are governed by the law in force in the jurisdiction where the injury was sustained. In the cases of interest here, this means that the law of the country of production, where the human rights violation occurred, controls. The law of the country to which the goods were ultimately shipped is irrelevant. Even more remote from the choice-of-law analysis is the jurisdiction where the "lead firm" of the supply chain has its headquarters. Thus, if Versace SpA, with its headquarters in Milan, Italy, procures clothes that are produced in a garment factory in Dhaka, Bangladesh, and an accident occurs in this garment factory, then Italian law has nothing to say in this matter. The same is true of French law, assuming it was the

[10] Shaw (2014), p. 832; Shearer (1994), pp. 90ff.

[11] Cf. Hay (2018), pp. 48ff.

[12] Kegel (1964), pp. 184f.

country of destination to which the clothes were shipped. The law that is geographically closest to the accident is the law of Bangladesh.

3.2 *Broad Externalisation*

The fragmentation of the rules on extra-contractual liability, together with the differences in enforcement, provide the explanation for the problem that human rights litigation was designed to address. The existing differences between jurisdictions allow the costs of human rights violations to be externalised, thus generating the adverse effects described above.[13] In short, manufacturers operating in the countries of production omit the costs of harm sustained by employees and third parties in the countries of production in their overall corporate calculus, diminishing incentives to guard against harm. As a consequence, the costs of production in their calculus are "too low" in the sense that they do not reflect the true cost to society for manufacturing the item in question. Hence, the prices quoted for the product in question are also "too low" and, in turn, demand for such products is "too high."

The textile market is an example in point, if one assumes that the incident at Rana Plaza is representative of the current set-up of the garment industry. Publicly available information suggests that the building did not comply with basic safety standards and that the owners of the garment factories operating inside the building ignored their workers' welfare. As no safety measures were taken, the costs associated with such measures did not impact the price of the clothes manufactured at the site. The same is true for the cost of harm incurred by the victims, but only if one assumes that Bangladesh does not offer an effective enforcement mechanism. From this anecdotal evidence, one may conclude that the price of textiles sold in Western markets is not only low, but too low. The normative yardstick against which to measure reality is the hypothetical world in which the price of a fashion item includes the full cost of production, including the costs imposed on workers, third parties, and the environment.

When clothes like t-shirts cost less than 10 dollars or euros, demand often skyrockets in rich countries, where average teenagers with no income can buy large amounts of clothing from the allowance they receive from their parents. Popular brands offering cheap clothes, such as Primark and H&M, put out several product lines per season and dozens of product lines per year. Even without further econometric study, it seems safe to assume that textile prices are artificially low. Demonstrating this, between 1982 and 2020, the US Consumer Price Index (CPI)

[13] Supra, II. 3.

increased by 158.82%,[14] while households' real disposable income rose by 294%.[15] For apparel minus footwear, the CPI rose by a meagre 15.88% during the same period,[16] lagging dramatically behind both rising incomes and the pricing of other consumer goods. This data shows that, with the migration of the garment industry to Asia, relative prices for clothes have drastically decreased.

4 An Easy Fix? Global Application of National Tort Law

4.1 Globalising National Law

An easy fix to the problem of externalisation just described would be the global application of national tort law, together with making the courts in the jurisdictions with well-functioning civil justice systems available to claimants from elsewhere. Both measures would ensure the internalisation of external costs and thus create incentives to take care, compensate victims, and lead to realistic pricing of goods and services. To the extent that a given national tort law system meets these goals, why not opt for its extraterritorial application? Given that tort law pursues the goal of cost internalisation, and further assuming that the legal systems in the countries of production fail to get the job done, it seems to follow easily that the legal and judicial systems of another jurisdiction should pick up the slack and provide the enforcement mechanism lacking abroad.

4.2 The Overlap Between Tort Law and Human Rights

Tort law seems well-equipped to meet this challenge. After all, the interests protected by modern systems of tort law are the same interests protected by human rights.[17] The reason for this broad overlap is not that the private law of torts copied the protected interests from human rights law, but rather the other way around. Historically, the private law of torts offered individuals protection for their basic interests in relation to life, health, bodily integrity, freedom of movement, property, etc., long before human rights law came along and "discovered" these same basic interests for constitutional and international law. While it is true that some forms of

---

[14]Federal Reserve Bank of St. Louis, Economic Research, www.fred.stlouisfed.org/series/CPIAUCSL#0 (last accessed 2 March 2020).

[15]Federal Reserve Bank of St. Louis, Economic Research, www.fred.stlouisfed.org/series/DSPIC96 (last accessed 2 March 2020).

[16]Federal Reserve Bank of St. Louis, Economic Research, www.fred.stlouisfed.org/series/CPIAUCSL#0 (last accessed 2 March 2020).

[17]Van Dam (2011), p. 243; Wagner (2016), pp. 752ff.

human rights violations, such as torture and slavery, constitute exceptionally reprehensible forms of personal injury, they nonetheless fall within the protective parameters of traditional torts.[18] The basic innovation ushered in by human rights law does not lie in expanding the list of protected interests, but in redirecting the protective force of these interests against the sovereign, i.e. the state. It is not without irony that the rhetoric of "tort law and human rights" implies that human rights are new to liability systems.

Another feature of modern tort law amenable to human rights causes is its flexibility. In a long historic development from ancient Roman law to the theoretical cathedrals of natural law and enlightenment, all the way to the challenges of industrialisation, modern liability systems have come to accept a "general clause" of fault-based liability that does not require intentional wrongdoing, but settles with negligence.[19] While aspects of negligence liability are heavily contested between European legal systems and others around the world, particularly with a view to pure financial interests, its core is well established and undisputed. The subjective rights to life, health, bodily integrity, and personal property listed above, which are also the concern of human rights law, are protected against negligent infringements across all legal jurisdictions.[20] The core of a negligence analysis is the violation of a duty of care. The tortfeasor is liable if he or she did not take the safety measures required in the specific situation *ex ante*, at the stage when the decision to take one particular course of action over another was made.

Most tort cases that occupy the dockets of courts around the world centre on the duty of care issue, which can be split up into several sub-issues. A threshold requirement is that the defendant was subject to a duty of care at all, i.e. that the law expected the defendant to avert harm to the plaintiff's interests. The second sub-issue concerns the contents of the duty of care, asking what the defendant should have done or not done in order to comply with the duty of care. Finally, it must be established that the defendant actually breached the duty of care by failing to live up to required safety standards. Hence, the concept of duty of care is potentially broad and flexible enough to ensure adequate protection of human rights.[21] In the context of globalised business practices, a duty of care could be imposed on domestic business enterprises with a view to production abroad, with clearly defined safety measures to be taken in order to comply with such a duty. In this sense, the concept of the duty of care seems to offer a readily available key for developing tort law into an effective tool of human rights policy in the international arena.

---

[18]Cf. the dissent in *Nevsun Resources Ltd. v. Araya*, 2020 SCC 5, www.canlii.ca/t/j5k5j (last accessed 11 June 2020), para. 216: "The point is this: Since all torture is battery (or intentional infliction of emotional distress), albeit a particularly severe form thereof, it does not need to be recognized as a new tort. Our law, as is, furnishes an appropriate cause of action."

[19]Zimmermann (1990), pp. 1031ff; Jansen (2003), pp. 271ff; Wagner (2003), pp. 213ff.

[20]Wagner (2019), pp. 1004ff; Van Dam (2013), pp. 167ff.

[21]Van Dam (2011), pp. 244ff.

Matters are not so easy, however. As will be seen, the large overlap between tort law and human rights carries advantages, but also disadvantages. In essence, tort law's traditional focus on protecting the same interests that are now relabelled as human rights makes it more rather than less difficult to devise tailor-made solutions for the paradigmatic scenarios described above with regards to accountability of subsidiaries or suppliers in far-away jurisdictions for human rights violations. While the duty of care concept is certainly flexible, it has limitations that are not so easy to overcome with a view to these specific cases. The real challenge for tort law with respect to human rights violations caused by third parties in distant jurisdictions is not the protection of basic human interests, but the stretching of duties and liabilities across the borders separating different corporate entities.

4.3 Pathways Towards Global Application

Most systems for dealing with conflict of laws do include pathways towards subjecting domestic firms to domestic liability rules, even with a view to their offshore activities. Take the EU's Rome II Regulation on the application of mandatory provisions of forum law as an example. Article 4(3) of the Rome II Regulation allows the court to avoid the law of the place of injury and to apply the law of another jurisdiction that is manifestly more closely connected with the tort or delict that is the subject matter of the complaint. Hence, one can argue that the law of the jurisdiction where the lead firm of the supply chain has its seat is more closely connected. Another way to evade the application of the *lex loci damni* principle is Article 16 of the Rome II Regulation, which authorises the court to override the law designated by Article 4 of the Rome II Regulation by applying mandatory provisions of *lex fori*. For Article 16 of the Rome II Regulation to apply, one must argue that the tort law at the domicile of the supply chain leader is mandatory in nature, and that the policy decision behind it is strong enough to warrant international application. This is similar to the approach taken by the majority of the Canadian Supreme Court in the *Nevsun v. Araya* case, which classified human rights as "peremptory norms," taking priority over the national law otherwise applicable to the case at hand.[22]

4.4 Discriminatory Liability and the Virtues of Restraint

Whether the pathways outlined above are feasible or not remains a matter for discussion in legal circles and will ultimately be decided by the courts, in the European theatre by the European Court of Justice. However, regardless of this

[22] *Nevsun Resources Ltd. v. Araya*, 2020 SCC 5, www.canlii.ca/t/j5k5j (last accessed 11 June 2020), para. 83ff.

discussion's outcome, the principle of *lex loci damni*, enshrined in Article 4(1) of the Rome II Regulation, will continue to carry weight. From the perspective of international law, it safeguards the sovereignty of the states in which production occurs. From a traditional international law viewpoint, based on the principle of equality of nations, Bangladesh and other countries that manufacture large amounts of consumer goods for markets in the Northern Hemisphere have the right to decide for themselves whether and how to accept and enforce standards of, for example, workplace safety and environmental protection. Other states lack the authority and the legitimacy to impose their standards upon activities that take place in the territory of their peers.

Another concern that points in the same direction of restraint in applying domestic legal standards to activities carried out in other jurisdictions is the fairness of competition, or in other words, the idea of a level playing field for market participants in the economy of the supply chain leader, i.e. in the country that imports the goods or is host to the parent corporation of a multinational group with a subsidiary in the country of production. If only certain jurisdictions recognise and enforce the extraterritorial application of tort law, then corporations domiciled within these jurisdictions that export its tort law face a competitive disadvantage compared to those domiciled elsewhere. In France, for example, lawmakers have imposed a special duty of care on French firms, i.e. on large corporations whose seat is located in France, in the name of protecting human rights.[23] Corporations domiciled in France are now subject to a duty to ensure that human rights are respected elsewhere, i.e. in the countries where their subsidiaries and trading partners operate. Other firms headquartered outside of France are not subject to the same duties. However, the French market remains open to goods and services offered by foreign firms. As a consequence, some participants in the French market are subject to the new corporate "*devoir de vigilance*," while others are not. Assuming, as one must, that raising standards in the countries of origin with a view to workplace safety, environmental, and other concerns is not costless, French firms are burdened with additional costs, while their competitors are free to save these costs, thus distorting competition between them. If a French firm is equally as efficient as a Chinese competitor, for example, the imposition of liability only on the French firm will increase the prices it must charge for its products, thus shifting demand away from the French firm and into the arms of its Chinese competitor. Assuming that the Chinese corporation has access to the French products' markets, its sales will increase, and the revenue of the French firm will decrease. The decline of firms subject to human rights due diligence will not be offset by any benefit in terms of deterrence of violations, and will neither improve production nor compensation of victims.[24] Rather, this will only cause a

[23]Article L 225-102-4 (1) Code de commerce; cf. Cossart et al. (2017), p. 317; Brabant and Savourey (2017), p. 90; Nasse (2019), pp. 789f. More precisely, the law applies to corporations that have been incorporated or registered in France for at least two consecutive fiscal years and employ 5000 persons in France, or 10,000 people worldwide, respectively.

[24]Sykes (2012), pp. 2194f.

shift of demand to the detriment of firms that are domiciled in the jurisdiction imposing strict standards of human rights diligence and serve as chain leaders.

A third problem caused by the unilateral imposition of a duty of care is based on the functions of tort law. In international scholarship, there is broad consensus that tort law not only aims to compensate for damage already incurred, but also aims to avoid harm in the future.[25] In other words, tort law aims to deter wrongful behaviour for the sake of protecting legal entitlements, of course including human rights. The deterrence function of the law requires looking not only at the party that may cause the harm, but also at the victim who stands to suffer. In a causal sense, harmful events are attributable to both parties, not only the injurer: without a victim, there can be no harm. Looking beyond causation, most accidents are bilateral in nature in the sense that both the injurer and the victim were in a position to do something to prevent the harm from occurring. In such bilateral cases, tort law must regulate the behaviour of, or rather address the incentives faced by, both parties. More precisely, tort law must coordinate the behaviour of potential injurers and victims in the interest of safety.

Obviously, the coordination of both parties' behaviour is accomplished if all the actors operating in a certain spatial area are subject to the same standards of behaviour. This is exactly what Article 4(1) of the Rome II Regulation aims for in embracing the principle of *lex loci damni*. Consequently, the deterrence function of tort law suffers if the persons that interact in a given spatial area are not subject to the same standards, as is the case in most jurisdictions where production takes place and from which goods are exported to other countries. If some destination jurisdictions impose tort-based duties of care on firms domiciled there, while others do not, firms and workers in the countries of origin are exposed to divergent legal standards. While this concern is very strong in theory, it may not weigh heavily in the present context, as human rights law seems to aim for minimum protection, a standard that can and should be met anywhere. Matters may look differently when labour law or environmental protection standards enter the picture.

The problems described above counsel against the global application of national tort law, and also against subjecting firms at the top of global supply chains to duties of care and associated liabilities in their domestic jurisdictions, while sparing other firms domiciled elsewhere. In essence, this approach distorts competition in national product markets by only burdening domestic firms with the additional costs of taking care. One remedy against this distortion is to eschew imposing duties of care on domestic enterprises that would require the protection of human rights abroad. Unfortunately, this solution would make it impossible to advance human rights with the help of national tort law.

[25] As to European liability systems: Koziol (2015), pp. 24ff, 115ff, 186ff, 277ff and 379ff; as to US law: Dobbs et al. (2016), pp. 15ff; Geistfeld (2012), p. 383; Geistfeld (2003), pp. 585ff; Goldberg (2003), pp. 513ff. Cf. also Abraham (2017), pp. 16ff.

5 Production Liability as an Alternative Regime of Choice of Law

An alternative to the application of Article 16 of the Rome II Regulation or the peremptory-norms approach of the Canadian Supreme Court turns to product liability for inspiration. This approach marries the goal of improving human rights protection in countries of production and along supply chains to the principles of equal treatment and fair competition. The liability regime for products developed after the Second World War attributes responsibility for the output of the production process, including all inputs procured from other manufacturers along multiple supply chains, to the "ultimate" manufacturer, i.e. the one who markets the product to consumers or other businesses. The ultimate manufacturer thus plays a pivotal role in product liability, bearing full responsibility not only for their own inputs and design choices, but for the product as a whole. This principle, firmly rooted in the liability regime for products, focussing on the *outputs* of the production process, could be transferred, or rather expanded, to apply to the production process itself. The ultimate manufacturer at the top of a supply chain, the "chain leader," would then bear responsibility not only for the processes they organise and control, but for the production process as a whole, including component parts and other inputs procured from third-party suppliers.

Admittedly, the assimilation of human rights liability into product liability does not cure the distortion of the competitive process described above. However, it does provide a clue to a remedy by unlocking the conflict of laws regime for human rights liability. While the rules for conflict of laws in product liability claims differ from jurisdiction to jurisdiction, they have one feature in common: The law applicable to product liability claims is never restricted to products manufactured by firms that are domiciled in the particular jurisdiction, but rather applies to all products sold in a particular market. Take the EU's Rome II Regulation as an example. The relevant provision is Article 5, which supplies an elaborate list of connecting factors that are structured like a "ladder," in that the designation of a legal system by a prong at the top of the hierarchy forecloses steps further down in order to rely on the connecting factors defined on lower prongs. Looking through the complicated array of connecting factors reveals, however, that the general principle behind Article 5 of the Rome II Regulation is simple: All products sold in the market of a particular jurisdiction shall be subject to the law of that jurisdiction.[26]

The product liability version of the equal treatment principle is enshrined in the provision, included in all three variants of Article 5(1) of the Rome II Regulation, that the product must have been marketed within the jurisdiction in question. Only in the rarest of cases, in which the manufacturer did not market the product in any of the jurisdictions listed in Article 5(1) (a)–(c) of the Rome II Regulation, does the law of

[26]Regulation (EC) 864/2007 on the law applicable to non-contractual obligations (Rome II), OJ L 199, 40, Recital 20; Wagner (2008), pp. 6f; Schmid and Pinkel (2015), para. 28; Machnikowski (2019), para. 4.

the habitual residence of the manufacturer apply. The current proposals for human rights liability along supply chains follow the opposite principle of holding manufacturers liable depending upon their seat in one jurisdiction or another. Turning this approach around would lead to a conflict-of-laws rule that imposes liability for human rights violations along the supply chain on any manufacturer who puts a product into circulation within a particular market jurisdiction. In essence, liability for harm caused in the course of production ("production liability") would follow the same principle as liability for harm caused by the outcome of the production process ("product liability").[27]

6 Duties of Care Across the Supply Chain

6.1 The Entity Limitation

A second major roadblock for a vigorous extraterritorial application of tort law in the name of protecting human rights is almost invisible from the black letter law. Even if it is rarely said explicitly, the duties of care imposed by tort law remain confined to the person or entity concerned and do not extend to the behaviour of other persons or entities. This is the tort law version of the so-called "entity principle" in corporate law.[28] Corporate law allows companies to limit liability for contractual obligations, but also for tort-based debts, to the corporate fund. This protects shareholders and managers who are not personally liable for harm caused by the respective corporation. Even before this concept of limited liability developed in corporate law, however, the law of torts limited the liability of actors to their own assets and restricted each actor's duty of care to their own sphere. In general, every person is responsible for their own actions and the things that they control. Rules on vicarious liability, which attribute the wrongful behaviour of employees (traditionally servants) to their employers (traditionally their masters), are the exception to the rule. Vicarious liability means not only that an employer is liable for the torts of their employee, but also that no one bears liability for the torts of someone else who is not their employee.

The high degree of overlap between the scope of protection accorded by tort law and human rights stands in the way of a sweeping solution like attributing wrongs committed by entities within the supply chain to the chain leader. If the owner of a premium clothing brand were liable for harm caused by a supplier in Bangladesh who operates a garment factory there, the same would apply to a supermarket operator and their domestic suppliers of foodstuffs. In effect, everybody could be liable for the harm caused by others with whom they interacted. This outcome is

[27] As to this terminology cf. Bagchi (2019), p. 2501.

[28] Easterbrook and Fischel (1991), pp. 41ff; cf. also Hansmann and Squire (2018), pp. 251ff.

simply untenable as it would destroy the boundaries between different persons and legal entities, which are crucial for an efficient allocation of responsibilities.[29]

Human rights advocates have pointed out that the rules on vicarious liability are not cast in stone, suggesting that it is conceivable to classify a business enterprise incorporated in one jurisdiction as the servant of another corporation with a seat elsewhere. Unfortunately, such a reinterpretation of the traditional rules on vicarious liability could not be confined to human rights violations but would affect tort law as a whole. Moreover, it is doubtful whether it makes sense to classify corporations as servants of another corporation for purposes of holding the latter liable for wrongful behaviour committed by the former. Such a move could easily develop into a general liability of parent companies for torts committed by their subsidiaries. In other words, it threatens to introduce a group-wide liability of parent companies as heads of corporate groups. Traditional doctrines of company law that allow for a piercing of the corporate veil under certain narrowly defined conditions would be pushed aside and rendered meaningless, at least for claims based on tort. However, large segments of the legal system, such as contract law, insolvency law and tax law, as well as the financing of corporations through debt, secured or unsecured, and equity, are built on the entity principle, i.e. on the proposition that different corporations form different legal entities, with each discrete entity being responsible for its own actions and omissions, assets and liabilities. Tort law respects and affirms this structure by addressing duties of care to discrete legal entities, instead of applying them wholesale to corporate groups. This structure cannot be pushed aside for the sole purpose of creating a cause of action for offshore human rights violations.

6.2 Human Rights Due Diligence as an Intermediate Solution

The framers of the UN Guiding Principles on Business and Human Rights acknowledged these difficulties, at least implicitly, by promulgating a duty of care—labelled human rights due diligence—of the firm serving as chain leader regarding the behaviour of every link in the supply chain.[30] This duty is not limited to relationships between parent companies and subsidiaries, but also extends to stand-alone suppliers. While the imposition of a duty of care creates a serious risk of liability for the parent company or chain leader, respectively, it stops short of attributing the actions and omissions of subsidiaries to the parent company. France has adopted the approach of the UN Guiding Principles and translated the duty to take care against human rights violations into a *devoir de vigilance* imposed on large business corporations, provided that their seat is in France.[31]

---

[29]Wagner (2016), pp. 757ff.

[30]UN, Guiding Principles on Business and Human Rights, 2011, Article 15 (b), Article 17.

[31]Article L 225-102-4 (1) Code de commerce, cf. Cossart et al. (2017), p. 317; Brabant and Savourey (2017), p. 90; Nasse (2019), p. 789f.

In the same vein, the UK Supreme Court, in its preliminary judgment in the *Vedanta v. Lungowe* case, clearly distinguished between vicarious liability of parent companies for the torts of their subsidiaries, and liability of a parent company for its own negligence.[32] Liability in negligence requires the breach of the duty of care. The crucial question thus becomes whether the parent company has a duty to prevent careless behaviour on the part of its subsidiary. The general duty of care, designed to protect others from harm to the extent that this is feasible with the help of efficient safety measures, is flexible enough to answer this question in the affirmative. The UK Supreme Court even refused to acknowledge the significance of stretching the duty of care across corporate boundaries. In the eyes of the judges, the tort of negligence was broad enough to allow for the development of a new niche, namely the responsibility of parent companies for the harmful behaviour of their subsidiaries, provided that the parent breached a duty of human rights due diligence incumbent on himself.[33] In doing so, the court placed parent liability for subsidiaries on the same plane as the liability of public authorities for the acts of human agents, as developed in the case of *Dorset Yacht v. Home Office*.[34]

The UK Supreme Court thus downplayed the innovative force of tort-based duties of companies at the top of corporate groups to control their subsidiaries' behaviour. While the conceptual argument that the duty of care is broad and flexible enough to accommodate such an extension is well taken, there is no point in denying the normative weight of such a move. The imposition of a duty of care that cuts across corporate boundaries and reaches businesses that are incorporated as separate legal entities eats away at the entity principle that is not only the basis of corporate law, but also of the law of torts. While the group-wide duty of care still honours the separateness of corporate entities, it creates potential liability of one corporate entity for the acts and omissions of another one. This innovation should not be belittled. The departure from the entity principle of corporate law as well as tort law is particularly striking if the duty of care is triggered by and attached to activities of the parent company or its agents. Notably, in its *Vedanta* decision, the UK Supreme Court went down this route and based the duty of care on a "sufficient level of intervention" of the parent company into the conduct of the subsidiary, together with "published materials" of the parent company in which it assumed responsibility for diligent behaviour of its subsidiaries.[35]

This interpretation of human rights due diligence seems to create highly undesirable incentives. If a parent company's responsibility for harm caused by a subsidiary is contingent on the parent issuing guidelines for diligent behaviour and taking measures to ensure compliance on the part of the subsidiary, then a parent company's efforts to ensure a group-wide policy of human rights protection will be sanctioned,

---

[32] *Vedanta Resources PLC v. Lungowe*, 2019 UKSC 20 para. 44 (per Lord Briggs).

[33] *Vedanta Resources PLC v. Lungowe*, 2019 UKSC 20 para. 54 (per Lord Briggs).

[34] *Dorset Yacht Co Ltd v. Home Office*, 1970 AC 1004.

[35] *Vedanta Resources PLC v. Lungowe*, 2019 UKSC 20 para. 61 (per Lord Briggs); as to the nature of the published materials cf. ibid, para. 58.

rather than rewarded. The parent company that shows indifference vis-à-vis its subsidiaries' behaviour in terms of respect for human rights is more, rather than less, negligent than the one showing a "sufficient level of intervention." However, if the judgment in the *Vedanta* case is taken seriously, the UK Supreme Court attaches liability to the parent's intervention, even though non-intervention would clearly have been worse. The perverse effect of attaching liability to intervention, and not to passivity, will be even more visible in cases involving global supply chains, i.e. where the entity committing the violation is not a subsidiary of the chain leader, but an independent supplier. The passive attitude of firms at the top of the supply chain towards the poor standards of human rights protection prevailing in most countries of production is precisely the problem, and hence, not the cure. This is the behaviour that tort law's duty of care should be designed to discourage. If, however, the duty of care and potential liability hinges on the chain leader taking active measures to control risk, then tort law creates a clear incentive not to do such things, i.e. not to engage in risk management along the supply chain.

The upshot of the preceding analysis is that human rights due diligence cannot settle with sanctioning active measures to control risk. It must also impose affirmative duties to protect human rights on a group-wide scale and across the supply chain. If this is accepted, the problems associated with the rollback of the entity limitation, as explored above, must be confronted in their most poignant form. It is difficult to see how firms at the top of global supply chains could be expected to micro-manage the behaviour of their suppliers located in far-away jurisdictions, while these same firms are not liable for overseeing and controlling their domestic suppliers' behaviour. Tort law simply is not flexible enough to provide nuanced solutions.

7 Enforcement: Public or Private?

As pointed out already, the problems associated with the current fragmentation of liability systems across the globe are not caused by differences of "law on the books," but rather by differences of "law in action." Enforcement is the real problem, not liability rules and legal doctrine. The remedy often employed to compensate for deficient enforcement in various countries of production is the expansion of domestic tort law's territorial reach to cover human rights violations committed in other jurisdictions. As discussed in the previous sections, this approach raises serious concerns. In this section, however, these concerns shall be pushed aside. It will be assumed that the application of domestic liability rules to extraterritorial wrongdoing does not distort competition because it applies equally to all firms selling goods or services in a given market. It will also be assumed that human rights violations committed abroad are not attributable to the firm that serves as the supply chain leader, but that the liability of domestic firms is moderated by the requirement of a breach of a duty of care. With these safeguards in place, the responsibility of firms at the top of the chain of production for human rights violations committed further down the chain may be worth considering.

Under these assumptions, one crucial question remains, namely the one of enforcement within the jurisdiction of the supply chain leader, which is typically an industrialised country that imports goods manufactured in low-cost jurisdictions. While enforcement must be assured within the jurisdiction of the chain leader, it is by no means clear what the preferred means of enforcement should be. As the dissent in the Canadian *Nevsun* case correctly pointed out, the proposition that domestic firms are accountable for human rights violations committed by their subsidiaries as well as independent firms along the supply chain does not, in and of itself, create a private cause of action in damages.[36] Liability in tort certainly counts among the possible remedies for violations of a supply chain leader's human-rights-related duty of care, but it is by no means the only conceivable remedy. The usual alternatives to the liability system, namely criminal law and administrative law, are also options in this context. Typically, criminal and administrative wrongs are prosecuted not by private individuals but by public agencies. Leaving the differences between criminal and administrative sanctions aside for purposes of the present inquiry, the choice is thus between public enforcement and private enforcement.

Disregarding doctrinal and constitutional intricacies, the choice between public and private enforcement is one of policy. Deciding between the two mechanisms requires balancing costs and benefits. Upon first blush, private enforcement of the duty to respect human rights looks attractive. After all, the victims of such violations have a strong incentive to prosecute valid claims, and they typically possess the relevant information needed to assess both liability (fault) and quantum (amount of damages). In contrast, public authorities must expend resources, i.e. taxpayer money, to gather information about human rights violations, including the nature and circumstances of the defendant's wrongdoing and the scope and amount of harm sustained by the victims. Even where the public authority is in command of the relevant information, civil servants may lack the resolve and the financial resources to vigorously prosecute claims against powerful corporations.

Upon second blush, however, private enforcement of human rights, meaning the prosecution of valid claims for redress in response to human rights infringements, is not an easy undertaking. Assuming that the substantive law of torts is up to the task, much depends on the procedural framework for litigating damage claims. A whole array of topics opens up here, such as the availability of funding and the allocation of the costs of litigation; available options to aggregate claims and to litigate collectively; access to information and evidence that is within the possession of the other side, i.e. the potential wrongdoer; and the ways and means to enforce a judgment in favour of the potential claimants. Not all of these issues can be adequately resolved in European jurisdictions where potential claims against corporations at the top of supply chains can be brought. But even assuming that this were the case—that the

---

[36]*Nevsun Resources Ltd. v. Araya*, 2020 SCC 5, www.canlii.ca/t/j5k5j (last accessed 11 June 2020) para. 217ff.

procedural framework provided easy access to justice and ensured a high quality of judicial decisions, based on the true facts of the case—private enforcement would still not be an easy option.

While legal rules and resources may facilitate the enforcement of valid claims, they cannot change the physical and geographical obstacles that often stand in the way of effective cross-border prosecution. Enforcing claims in far-away jurisdictions is never easy, not even for large enterprises experienced in the enforcement market that know how to secure the advice of sophisticated counsel. Empirical studies have confirmed the existence of a "home-town bias" in the enforcement of claims.[37] This bias rests on the realisation that legal proceedings are much easier to initiate and litigation is much more effective and successful within the jurisdiction of one's domicile or seat, where language is no barrier, where representation by one's counsel of choice is possible, and where the substantive and procedural law as well as the members of the judiciary are easily accessible and well-known.

The practical hurdles standing in the way of the effective enforcement of damage claims based on human rights violations that occurred in far-away jurisdictions of the Global South are thus considerable. The typical victim of a human rights violation is in the opposite position of a large corporation. Usually, the potential claimants in human rights cases are poor and without access to the financial resources it takes to successfully launch and prosecute a claim in a court located thousands of kilometres away. In addition, these claimants often lack any legal knowledge and are generally inexperienced in techniques of dispute resolution and, particularly, the art of litigation. The typical respondent in a human rights case is situated at the other end of the spectrum. Corporations that may be the subject of damage claims in their capacity as heads of supply chains are often experienced and sophisticated litigants. They are usually cash-rich or at least enjoy easy access to financial resources. On top of these advantages, corporations are typically sued in their home-country, i.e. in the jurisdiction of their seat, simply because the courts there promise to be friendlier to the victims' cause than the ones in the victims' respective home-country. In light of all these factors, it seems unrealistic to expect that victims located in countries of production in the Global South, such as Pakistan, Bangladesh, Vietnam or Malaysia, will make it into the courtrooms of France, Germany, Switzerland, the UK, or Canada.

Though improbable, human rights litigation does indeed occur in Western courts. However, these cases tend to confirm that the enforcement of claims by the victims is unrealistic. Cases to date have been brought in the name and on behalf of victims, but the victims were usually not the true initiators of the claims. Typically, a human rights organisation or other non-governmental organisation is the real litigant, having recruited the victims, investigated the facts, collected the evidence, explored the applicable substantive law, appointed counsel, and funded the litigation. In essence, the victims only gain access to the courts of the supply chain leader's jurisdiction with the help of an NGO located in the same or a neighbouring

[37] Wagner (2014), pp. 1108ff.

jurisdiction. The enforcement activities taking place in European jurisdictions and elsewhere must therefore be categorised as strategic litigation.[38] Strategic litigation looks far beyond the individual case and its resolution, and instead aims for judicial investigation of the true causes behind accidents and crimes committed in other jurisdictions. It also seeks to raise public awareness of human rights issues.

The fact that NGOs serve as the real litigants in cases involving human rights violations in distant countries of production is nothing to complain about. Civil litigation was not designed to facilitate strategic litigation, but there is nothing illegitimate about using it for this purpose. In the special case of human rights litigation, public interest organisations are needed in order to level the procedural playing field and to provide funding for the claims to proceed. However, the central role played by NGOs raises the question as to whether private enforcement is the optimal remedy. Given that the victims themselves do not have a realistic chance to initiate suits, the enforcement of damage claims relies on public interest organisations operating in the same jurisdiction as the business that stands to be sued. These organisations' activities are not limited to civil litigation, as they can also initiate or participate in criminal or administrative proceedings. If the work is done by an NGO rather than the victims anyway, private litigation loses some of its appeal. It does not lose all of it, however, as damage suits remain an effective and unrivalled tool for achieving deterrence and compensation, at least in comparison to criminal and administrative sanctions.

In relation to litigation's deterrence function, much can be said in favour of criminal and administrative law.[39] To begin with, the question of funding legal proceedings goes away, as criminal and administrative trials are initiated by public authorities, funded by the public purse. Prosecutors and other public authorities command sweeping powers to investigate the facts of an incident and to identify the individuals who bear responsibility. The problem of aggregating claims of several victims into one proceeding does not arise, as criminal and administrative investigations and trials are incident-based, i.e. they relate to a particular accident or crime, and are not tied to individual damage claims growing out of such incidents. Finally, the sanctions meted out by the criminal justice system or administrative law are not tied to the amount of harm sustained by any victim or group of victims. Rather, the overall harm caused by the behaviour in question can be considered, as well as the degree of fault, i.e. whether the harm was caused recklessly, intentionally, or through mere negligence.

Tellingly, French lawmakers, in drafting the law introducing the human-rights-focused *devoir de vigilance*, did not settle for liability in delict as a response to corporations' wrongful behaviour, but also relied upon civil fines as sanctions for wrongful behaviour. The constitutional counsel intervened and held that the

[38]As for the US, see Cummings (2012); for Japan, see Hatano (2019); for Germany and Europe cf. Graser and Helmrich (2019); as for strategic litigation used by businesses, see Nanopoulos and Yotova (2016).

[39]Bagchi (2019), pp. 2535ff.

sanctioning of corporations with the help of civil fines was unconstitutional in the circumstances, as the description of the wrong remained vague und unpredictable.[40] Assuming that these defects can be cured through adequate wording, fines and other criminal sanctions may be a more effective means of deterring domestic corporations' wrongful behaviour than civil liability that is contingent on the enforcement of private damage claims by victims who find themselves at a serious disadvantage vis-à-vis defendant corporations.

8 Conclusions

Tort law is designed to protect the same human interests that also lie at the core of human rights law. However, the globalisation of human rights protection through national tort law creates serious tensions with established legal principles. Legal duties and corresponding liabilities are focussed on particular legal entities and do not cut across such entities. Thus, in principle, parent companies are not responsible for the acts and omissions of their offshore subsidiaries, and firms leading global supply chains are not liable for risks created by direct and indirect suppliers abroad. The entity principle is fundamental to the legal system, relevant not only to the law of torts, but also central to company law, insolvency law, and tax law, to name only a few. Thus, the development of duties of care imposed that cut across legal entities could not be limited to tort law, and would, much rather, affect these fields of law as well.

Further, duties of care designed to protect human rights also cut across national borders and reach subsidiaries and suppliers domiciled in other jurisdictions. Such cross-border duties create problems for private international law as well. The choice of law rules governing non-contractual liability aim to provide a level playing field for people and firms interacting within one particular jurisdiction. If only those firms that are domiciled within the jurisdiction are subjected to human rights due diligence, this will disadvantage them in competition with other firms domiciled outside of this jurisdiction—with the ensuing market shift in favour of the latter hampering the human rights cause. Human-rights-based duties of care thus require a supplement: a choice of law rule that connects them with the products offered in a particular market, regardless of the manufacturer's seat.

Even if these substantive and international law concerns were addressed properly, the fact remains that tort law does not offer an adequate enforcement mechanism for human rights. While the number of claims brought on behalf of offshore claimants in Western jurisdictions is increasing, litigation mostly remains symbolic. The purpose of these claims is not primarily to collect substantial damages on behalf of the victims but to alert the public in the countries where the courts sit to human rights violations. Raising awareness of economic and social problems in other countries is

[40] Conseil constitutionnel, 23 March 2017, Décision n° 2017-750 DC, Rn. 5-14; Mathieu (2017).

certainly a legitimate goal, but not the one tort law was designed to serve. There may be other enforcement mechanisms that are better suited, and that impose lesser costs on firms and society.

References

Abraham KS (2017) The forms and functions of tort law. Foundation Press, St. Paul

Bagchi A (2019) Product liability. Fordham Law Rev 87(6):2501–2538

Brabant S, Savourey E (2017) French law in the corporate duty of vigilance – a practical and multidimensional perspective. Revue International de la Compliance et de l'Étique des Affaires 50:90–95

Cossart S, Chaplier J, Beau de Lemeinie T (2017) The French law on duty of care: a historic step towards making globalization work for all. Bus Hum Rights J 2(2):317–323

Cummings SL (2012) The pursuit of legal rights – and beyond. U.C.L.A. Law Rev 59:506–549

Dobbs DB, Hayden PT, Bublick EM (2016) Hornbook on torts. West Academic Publishing, St. Paul

Easterbrook FH, Fischel DR (1991) The economic structure of corporate law. Harvard University Press, Cambridge

Geistfeld M (2003) Negligence, compensation, and the coherence of tort law. Georgetown Law J 91 (3):585–632

Geistfeld M (2012) The coherence of compensation-deterrence theory in tort law. DePaul Law Rev 61(2):383–418

Goldberg J (2003) Twentieth-century tort theory. Georgetown Law J 91(3):513–584

Graser A, Helmrich C (2019) Strategic Litigation: Begriff und Praxis. Nomos, Baden-Baden

Hansmann H, Squire R (2018) External and internal asset partitioning: corporations and their subsidiaries. In: Gordon JN, Ringe WG (eds) The Oxford handbook of corporate law and governance. Oxford University Press, Oxford, pp 251ff

Hatano A (2019) Can strategic human rights litigation complement social movements? A case study of the movement against racism and hate speech in Japan. Univ Pa Asian Law Rev 14 (2):228–274

Hay P et al (2018) Conflict of laws. West Academic Publishing, St. Paul

Jansen N (2003) Die Struktur des Haftungsrechts: Geschichte, Theorie und Dogmatik außervertraglicher Ansprüche auf Schadensersatz. Mohr Siebeck, Tübingen

Keeton WP et al (1984) Prosser and Keeton on torts. West Publishing Company, St. Paul

Kegel G (1964) The crisis of conflict of laws. Recueil des Cours 112:91–268

Koziol H (2015) Basic questions of tort law from a comparative perspective. Jan Sramek, Wien

Machnikowski P (2019) Article 5 Rome II Regulation. In: Magnus U, Mankowski P (eds) European commentaries on private international law. Dr. Otto Schmidt, Cologne

Magnus U (2019) Article 4 Rome II Regulation. In: Magnus U, Mankowski P (eds) European commentaries on private international law. Dr. Otto Schmidt, Cologne

Mathieu B (2017) Jusque'oú peut-on faire porter sur les entreprises un devoir de vigilance en matière de protection des droits de l'hommes et de l'enviroment? Constitutions 2017:291–295

Nanopoulos E, Yotova R (2016) "Repackaging" plain packaging in Europe: strategic litigation and public interest considerations. J Int Econ Law 19(1):175–210

Nasse L (2019) *Devoir de vigilance* – Die neue Sorgfaltspflicht zur Menschenrechtsverantwortung für Großunternehmen in Frankreich. Zeitschrift für Europäisches Privatrecht 2019(4):774–802

Polinsky AM, Shavell S (1998) Punitive damages: an economic analysis. Harv Law Rev 111 (4):869–962

Schmid C, Pinkel T (2015) Article 5 Rome II Regulation. In: Callies GP (ed) Rome Regulations. Wolters Kluwer, Hürth, pp 127ff

Shavell S (2004) Foundations of economic analysis of law. Harvard University Press, Cambridge
Shaw MN (2014) International law. Cambridge University Press, Cambridge
Shearer IA (1994) Starke's international law. Butterworths, London
Sykes AO (2012) Corporate liability for extraterritorial torts under the alien tort statute and beyond: an economic analysis. Georgetown Law J 100(6):2151–2210
Van Dam C (2011) Tort law and human rights: brothers in arms – on the role of tort law in the area of business and human rights. J Eur Tort Law 2(3):221–254
Van Dam C (2013) European tort law. Oxford University Press, Oxford
Wagner G (2003) Grundstrukturen des Europäischen Deliktsrechts. In: Zimmermann R (ed) Grundstrukturen des Europäischen Deliktsrechts, Nomos, Baden-Baden, pp 189ff
Wagner G (2008) Die neue Rom-II-Verordnung. Praxis des Internationalen Privat- und Verfahrensrechts 2008(1):1–16
Wagner G (2012) Tort, social security, and no-fault schemes: lessons from real-world experiments. Duke J Comp Int Law 23(1):1–61
Wagner G (2014) The dispute resolution market. Buffalo Law Rev 62(5):1085–1158
Wagner G (2016) Haftung für Menschenrechtsverletzungen. Rabels Zeitschrift 80(4):717–782
Wagner G (2019) Comparative tort law. In: Reimann M, Zimmermann R (eds) Oxford handbook of comparative law. Oxford University Press, Oxford, pp 994ff
Zimmermann R (1990) The law of obligations: Roman foundations of the civilian tradition. Juta & Co., Cape Town

Gerhard Wagner holds the chair for private law, commercial law and economic legal analysis in the law faculty of Humboldt University of Berlin, Germany. He is also an external member of the Max Planck Institute of Private Law in Hamburg, Germany. Wagner has published widely in the areas of tort law and liability systems. Another focus of his research is dispute resolution on the national and international level. He is founder and academic director of Humboldt's English-language Master of Laws programme on international dispute resolution. Wagner is coeditor of the two leading scholarly journals on German and European private law. From 2008 to 2011, he was honorary professor at Renmin University School of Law in Beijing, China, and from 2009 to 2014 he also held the position of Erasmus professor of fundamentals of private law at the University of Rotterdam, Netherlands. From 2015 to 2019, he served as president of the academic association of private law scholars.

Part III
Critical Perspectives on Law and Litigation

Confined Employment: Exploring Labor Marginalization in Workplace Safety

Palvasha Shahab

Abstract This chapter argues that Pakistan has never had a bona fide system of occupational safety and health (OSH) laws, policies, standards or enforcement mechanisms ("OSH infrastructure"). Instead, the country's present OSH infrastructure remains divorced from workers' most urgent needs and the country's institutional capacity—effectively leaving workers without protection. This chapter traces the progress of the fire, delineates violations of OSH law and provides an account of the actions and inactions of various actors involved. In doing so, it highlights the gap between the OSH system's deficiencies and the fatalities they caused; outlining what measures were legally required to prevent such a tragedy but they were not in place. Then, it explores the geneology of these illegalities and accompanying apathies as it traces the history of Pakistan's OSH infrastructure back to its origins under British colonial rule and contextualises it with the overarching global (politico-economic) order in which the factory fire should perhaps be seen. Thus, it renders visible the historical trajectories and contemporary political and economic factors that have led to workers' persistent exclusion from the politico-legal sphere, denial of their rights and their dehumanisation—specifically in Pakistan and generally in the Global South. It concludes by identifying some directions that could be taken for a renewed and vitalised mandate to govern the OSH infrastructure in Pakistan.

Keywords Occupational health and safety · Labour · Global South · Modern slavery · Colonialism · Imperialism · Pakistan · Factory fire

---

I would like to express deep appreciation for the thoughtful and acutely constructive feedback provided by Faisal Siddiqi, Miriam Saage-Maaß, Michael Bader and Daniyal Ahmed. I would also like to thank Allison West for her work.

P. Shahab (✉)
Rasheed Razvi Centre for Constitutional and Human Rights (RCCHR), Karachi, Pakistan

Legal Aid Foundation for Victims of Rape and Sexual Assault (LAFRSA), Karachi, Pakistan
e-mail: palvasha.shahab@columbia.edu

M. Saage-Maaß et al. (eds.), *Transnational Legal Activism in Global Value Chains*, Interdisciplinary Studies in Human Rights 6,
https://doi.org/10.1007/978-3-030-73835-8_13

1 Introduction

The 2012 Ali Enterprises factory fire near the Baldia Town area of Karachi, Pakistan, left many orphans, parents, widows, and widowers traumatised. It also left many of them destitute, without their family's main breadwinner. What came to be known as the Baldia factory fire was perhaps the goriest industrial accident in Pakistani history, taking at least 258 lives and injuring 55 others.[1] Following the fire, chaos ensued. Many bodies were burnt beyond recognition and several corpses had melted into each other so indiscernibly that it took the investigation agencies almost a year to identify the victims through DNA tests. In several instances, graves were exhumed to correctly establish who had been laid to rest. The high death toll was due to the factory's lack of adequate health and safety infrastructure. Only two thirds of those present in the building on the day of the fire had been able to escape.[2]

The Ali Enterprises (AE) factory produced garments for export; around 70 percent of the production was for the German company, KiK Textilien und Non-Food GmbH (KiK).[3] The AE factory was situated in the Sindh Industrial Trading Estate (SITE)[4] near the Baldia Town area of Karachi and was owned and operated by a local business family, by the name of Bhailas.[5] With regard to workplace safety standards, three different authorities had jurisdiction over the factory: the Sindh Building Control Authority (SBCA), the SITE Management, and the Labour and Human Resources Department of Sindh (Sindh Labour Department). Yet, none of them had ever inspected the factory building, either before or after its occupation.[6] A staggering 90 percent of the workers employed at the factory were not registered with the Sindh Employees Social Security Institution (SESSI) or any other

---

[1]Report of the Judicial Commission on the Baldia Factory Fire incident, Karachi, 28 August 2013, Court File of Constitutional Petition No. 3318 of 2012, p. 1379.

[2]Forensic Architecture, The Ali Enterprises Factory Fire, 30 January 2018, www.forensic-architecture.org/investigation/the-ali-enterprises-factory-fire (last accessed 15 August 2020).

[3]KiK: Paying the Price for Clothing Production in South Asia/Pakistan Factory Fire Victims Sue German Retailer KiK. ECCHR, www.ecchr.eu/en/case/kik-paying-the-price-for-clothing-production-in-south-asia/ (last accessed 15 August 2020).

[4]SITE was established the very year that Pakistan gained independence, in 1947, as part of efforts to put Pakistan on track for industrialisation. Today, it is the largest industrial trading estate in Asia. www.site.com.pk/wordpress/?page_id=1433 (last accessed 14 August 2020).

[5]Gayer (2019).

[6]At the time of the fire, the Factories Act 1934, prescribed the basic minimum safety standards and stipulated that there be inspectors in every district. However, across the board, inspections have remained haphazard and were often avoided entirely, either as a matter of policy or because there were not enough inspectors, or because factories were simply not registered with the Directorate of Labour or had not notified the Chief Inspectors of their operations as per Section 10 of the Factories Act 1934. For a detailed discussion, please see Sect. 2 of this chapter.

institution like the Workers Welfare Fund (WWF) or the Employees Old-Age Benefits Institution (EOBI).[7]

In the aftermath of the disaster, from 2012 to 2019, lawyer Faisal Siddiqi and his team tirelessly litigated the matter in Pakistan, in the interest of the survivors and the heirs of the deceased, through two separate constitutional petitions before the High Court of Sindh, and the accompanying criminal cases.[8] The European Center for Constitutional and Human Rights also litigated the matter in Germany, filing a lawsuit in the Dortmund Regional Court.[9] Various national and international actors, including but not limited to, the Pakistan Institute for Labour Education and Research (PILER), the National Trade Union Federation (NTUF), the Clean Clothes Campaign and ECCHR, have steadfastly continued to lobby for the survivors and the heirs of the deceased to be compensated, and for measures to ensure safer workplaces in the future.[10] The lawyers, activists, and advocacy experts from these groups have also worked together with the Ali Enterprises Factory Fire Affectees Association (AEFFAA) since its formation. Following negotiations facilitated by the International Labour Organization (ILO), the families of the deceased or permanently injured were awarded lifelong pensions and a compensation whose total amount was unprecedented in Pakistan.[11]

1.1 The Task Ahead

This chapter will show that Pakistan has never had a *bona fide* system of occupational safety and health (OSH) laws, policies, standards or enforcement mechanisms ("OSH infrastructure"). Instead, the country's present OSH infrastructure both lacks the resources and the political will that is needed to enforce it and remains divorced from workers' most urgent needs, effectively leaving them without protection. The chapter begins by identifying all of the actors who either took action or were supposed to take action; to prevent fatalities in the AE factory fire, and in its

[7]Enquiry Report: Fire Incident at Ali Enterprises S.I.T.E Karachi on 11th September 2012. Federal Investigation Agency, Sindh Zone Karachi, 3 October 2012, Court File of Constitutional Petition No. 3318 of 2012, pp. 1291–1333.

[8]Baldia Factory Fire Case Litigation. RCCHR, www.rcchr.com.pk/practice/baldia-factory-fire-case-litigation/ (last accessed 15 July 2020); However, when the criminal case was (controversially) taken into the jurisdiction of the Anti-Terrorism Courts, the court rejected Faisal Siddiqi's application to be allowed to be a party to the proceedings on behalf of the victims.

[9]Kik Lawsuit (Re Pakistan), Business and Human Rights Resource Centre, 7 October 2015, www.business-humanrights.org/en/kik-lawsuit-re-pakistan (last accessed 15 July 2020).

[10]Landmark compensation arrangement reached on 4th anniversary of deadly Pakistan factory fire. IndustriALL, 10 September 2016, www.industriall-union.org/landmark-compensation-arrangement-reached-on-4th-anniversary-of-deadly-pakistan-factory-fire (last accessed 15 July 2020).

[11]ILO, Victims of 2012 Ali Enterprises factory fire receive additional compensation, 20 May 2018, www.ilo.org/global/about-the-ilo/newsroom/news/WCMS_629839/lang%2D%2Den/index.htm (last accessed 14 July 2020).

aftermath. It then re-traces the progression of the fire whilst simultaneously identifying the legal violations involved. In doing so, it will highlight the gap between the OSH infrastructure and its enforcement that resulted in the fatalities of the AE factory fire, outlining shortcomings and what would have been required to prevent such a tragedy. After this, it traces the history of Pakistan's OSH infrastructure back to its origin under British colonial rule, and this is followed by an attempt at contextualising the larger global economic and political situation, in which the AE factory fire should be seen. It thus renders visible the historical trajectories and political and economic factors that have led to workers' persistent exclusion from politico-legal rights in Pakistan, more broadly the Global South (noting that these exclusionary trends are spreading fast to the Global North). It concludes by offering some directions through which the OSH infrastructure in Pakistan can be revitalised.

The chapter also shows how important it is to understand that OSH infrastructures are not static nor are they universal normative edicts that are either applied and enforced; or not. The Pakistani case reveals a rather messy reality in which OSH infrastructure was morphed and applied under colonial rule and later revoked under trade liberalisation, according to the contemporary trade priorities, and according to global demands. In light of this, I argue that the existing OSH infrastructure in Pakistan and the (global) mass contractualisation of labour that has accompanied its development have dehumanised and zombified workers. The workers have become the *homo sacer*, incarcerated in the state of exception, unable to access legal protection and stuck in the limbo between recognised (factual) workers and non-recognised (non-legal) workers; as they are employed through subcontractors, and because they are not in a direct employment relationship with the (local and foreign) employers who profit from their labour and who are or should be responsible for their safety. These workers are unprotected by the legal provisions designed to protect them. Workers provide labour in practice, while labour and safety laws provide protection in theory—the two do not meet to create a politically and legally empowered worker who can demand safe working conditions.

This chapter argues that the distances created by the large-scale outsourcing of production labour—by transnational corporations—and by the factories' or production units' hiring of workers through various subcontractors, all enable the evasion of responsibility for occupational health and safety. National labour laws do not apply to transnational corporations—these transnational corporations go wholly unregulated. They are able to generate vast profits from the labour of workers who are labouring in factories to whom the transnational corporations have outsourced their production work; without having to bear any responsibilities for the workers' safety or other rights.[12] These distances also render inaudible any and all employment and safety-related concerns of the workers. Indeed, the economic and political factors that predetermine OSH failures penetrate so deeply that they cannot be undone with the snap of two fingers. I argue that even if it musters the political will to protect its workers, Pakistan's government cannot simply copy and paste OSH infrastructures from the Global North or hold them up as the invariable

[12]Mende (2020).

universal standard because it does not have the same political autonomy nor the same conditions as the nations in the Global North. OSH must be reimagined in Pakistan (and other similarly placed countries in the Global South) to balance worker safety with the global and local, economic and political, realities that confront and shape it. Moreover, self-regulation by businesses and contract-based OSH solutions are also not a sustainable answer because, as we will shortly see, they are either purely cosmetic or too flimsy to last. Truly workable OSH solutions must incorporate workers' inputs, reflect institutional capacities, and be economically and politically viable. We need workable and effective OSH infrastructure based on realities on the ground, not on colonial or globally ordained standards.

1.2 Homo sacer*: Workers in South Asian Textile Industries*

At the time of the fire, many of the doors in the AE factory had been permanently locked from the outside, by the factory management, while the fire's heat rendered other doors inoperable. As a result, there was only *one* door through which all of the workers present in the factory that day could escape at all.[13] Across both time and geography, factory owners have engaged in the illegal practice of locking doors from the outside whenever and wherever it has been possible to get away with it. The alleged purpose of this practice is to prevent workers from taking extra breaks and stealing merchandise.[14] Workers were locked inside during the 1911 Triangle Shirtwaist Factory fire in New York,[15] the 1991 Hamlet Chicken processing plant fire in North Carolina,[16] the 1993 Kader Toy Factory fire in Thailand,[17] and the 2012 Tazreen Fashions factory fire in Dhaka.[18] Like the Tazreen Fashions fire,[19] the Ali Enterprises fire was further aggravated by negligently stored bales of cloth, which also blocked other possible exits and further trapped workers inside.[20]

[13]Clean Clothes Campaign, The Timeline of the Ali Enterprises Case, www.cleanclothes.org (last accessed 12 August 2020).

[14]Orleck (2018), p. 100.

[15]The Triangle Shirtwaist Factory Fire. Occupational Safety and Health Administration, 2011, www.osha.gov/aboutosha/40-years/trianglefactoryfire (last accessed 2 August 2020).

[16]See Diamond A, The Deadly 1991 Hamlet Fire Exposed the High Cost of "Cheap". Smithsonian Magazine, 8 September 2017, www.smithsonianmag.com/history/deadly-1991-hamlet-fire-exposed-high-cost-cheap-180964816/ (last accessed 30 July 2020); Taylor P, 25 die as fire hits N.C. poultry plant. Washington Post, 4 September 1991, www.washingtonpost.com/archive/politics/1991/09/04/25-die-as-fire-hits-nc-poultry-plant/0fdce6ba-a8e2-46a0-8c48-806012a98938/ (last accessed 30 July 2020).

[17]Thai Factory Fire's 200 Victims Were Locked Inside, Guards Say. New York Times, 12 May 1993, www.nytimes.com/1993/05/12/world/thai-factory-fire-s-200-victims-were-locked-inside-guards-say.html (last accessed 30 July 2020).

[18]The Tazreen Factory Fire occurred on 24 November 2012. Orleck (2018), p. 136.

[19]Orleck (2018), p. 137.

[20]Enquiry Report: Fire Incident at Ali Enterprises S.I.T.E Karachi on 11th September 2012. Federal Investigation Agency, Sindh Zone Karachi, 3 October 2012, Court File of Constitutional Petition

Thus, the AE factory was not uniquely dangerous, but it *was* fatally dangerous. To this day, workers in Pakistan are commonly employed in buildings on the verge of similar disasters, where their safety hangs precariously in the balance.[21] Prison-like conditions also remain common in Pakistani factories, particularly in the textile and garment industry.[22] Laws against unsafe working conditions exist, but they have negligible effect on workers' lived realities, and evidently do not protect them from death at the workplace.[23] I argue that the workers forced to abide by these dangerous conditions are the living dead—the zombified *homo sacer*. The *homo sacer* is understood here as the "the accursed individual"; such a person has been made invisible to the law and has, therefore, lost the rights that were guaranteed to them by virtue of their human-ness; "reduced to the non-human. Denied rights, this person becomes the non-entity."[24] For the *homo sacer*, there is no rule of law; captive outside the kingdom of law, the *homo sacer* is governed only by the needs of the Sovereign.[25]

Through the AE factory fire, many stakeholders, activists and citizens, both in Pakistan and beyond, were shaken out of either ignorance—or perhaps a numbness or resignation that comes from the routinisation of risk. In one sense, the AE factory fire was a rupture.[26] It was a tragedy so big and horrifying that it could not be ignored. The rupture was followed by a degree of momentum for change. It was almost as if in their deaths and injuries the workers had emitted a rallying scream, desperate for the world to pay attention to the sub-human conditions in which they,

No. 3318 of 2012, p. 1313; Forensic Architecture, The Ali Enterprises Factory Fire, 30 January 2018, forensic-architecture.org/investigation/the-ali-enterprises-factory-fire (last accessed 15 August 2020).

[21]Six years after Baldia factory fire, working conditions still not changed. Express Tribune, 10 September 2018, www.tribune.com.pk/story/1799215/1-six-years-baldia-factory-fire-working-conditions-still-not-changed/ (last accessed 12 August 2020).

[22]Six years after Baldia factory fire, working conditions still not changed. Express Tribune, 10 September 2018, www.tribune.com.pk/story/1799215/1-six-years-baldia-factory-fire-working-conditions-still-not-changed/ (last accessed 12 August 2020).

[23]Ijaz S, No Room to Bargain. Human Rights Watch, 23 January 2019, www.hrw.org/report/2019/01/23/no-room-bargain/unfair-and-abusive-labor-practices-pakistan (last accessed 12 August 2020).

[24]Nashef (2017), p. 147; Agamben (1998), p. 86.

[25]For a discussion on the nature and character of the sovereign, see Mbembe (2003) and Elshtain (1991), pp. 1355–1378.

[26]To briefly shed light on what is meant by this, the following quote might be useful: "[R]eality is grounded on a 'void' of 'inconsistent multiplicity', which is at once void and excess. Normally, the state, the count-for-one and the dominant ideology cover up this foundation. But it remains present – imprisoned or kettled, so to speak, at the site of the excluded part. An Event happens when the excluded part appears on the social scene, suddenly and drastically. It ruptures the appearance of normality and opens a space to rethink reality from the standpoint of its real basis in inconsistent multiplicity." McLaverty-Robinson A, An A to Z of Theory. Ceasefire Magazine, 15 December 2014, www.ceasefiremagazine.co.uk/alain-badiou-event/ (last accessed 12 August 2020).

and their counterparts, were and are forced to work, day in and day out.[27] The AE factory fire demanded change in workplace safety in Pakistan, but real change has still yet to come.

Similar working conditions to those in Pakistan also prevail in other parts of the world—predominantly, in the Global South.[28] Across these different locales, a globalised OSH discourse bridges discussions on workplace safety, including building and fire safety.[29] Existing at the intersection of labour law and policy, OSH incorporates aspects of employment law (dangerous buildings, sexual harassment, and mentally or physically abusive environments), health (occupational diseases particular to certain jobs, mental health issues, and the safety of healthcare professionals), building regulation (building approvals and inspections), engineering (building safety), urban planning (zoning considerations such as not placing schools or hospitals near factories), rural development (farming, mining or fishing related accidents and disease control), and even chemistry (effective disposal of chemical waste and hazardous substances) and geology (safe and sustainable mining or agricultural practices). According to statistics from 2003, the ILO/WHO Joint Committee on Occupational Health, estimated that there are between 1.9 to 2.3 million work-related fatalities in the world every year, of which around 355,000 are workplace accidents. The committee also estimates that the cost of all work-related accidents and diseases amounts to about four percent of the world's Gross National Product.[30]

2 A Fire Raging Through Missed Chances: The Persisting Disjunct Between Practical Reality and Legal Fiction

If the laws regarding building and fire safety in force at the time of the Ali Enterprises fire had been abided by and enforced at the factory, it is likely that not a single worker would have died.[31] This section analyses the spread of the fire with respect to the existing laws that were being violated at the factory at the time.

---

[27]Labour safety remains lax seven years after Baldia factory fire. Express Tribune, 12 September 2019, www.tribune.com.pk/story/2054356/1-labour-safety-remains-lax-seven-years-baldia-factory-fire/ (last accessed 12 August 2020); Ashraf Z, Fire breaks out at Gadani shipbreaking yard. Express Tribune, 22 December 2016, www.tribune.com.pk/story/1271626/fire-breaks-gadani-shipbreaking-yard/ (last accessed 3 August 2020); Ali I, Six workers fall to death after Construction lift buckles in Clifton. Daily Dawn, 10 March 2019, www.dawn.com/news/1468611 (last accessed 4 August 2020).

[28]Powell (2014), pp. 109–122.

[29]See Occupational Health. www.who.int/health-topics/occupational-health (last accessed 2 August 2020).

[30]Report of the Thirteenth Session of the Joint ILO/WHO Committee on Occupational Health, JCOH/2003/D.4 (2003), p. 3, www.ilo.org/wcmsp5/groups/public/%2D%2D-ed_protect/%2D%2D-protrav/%2D%2D-safework/documents/publication/wcms_110478.pdf (last accessed 2 August 2020).

[31]Forensic Architecture, The Ali Enterprises Factory Fire, 30 January 2018, www.forensic-architecture.org/investigation/the-ali-enterprises-factory-fire (last accessed 15 August 2020).

2.1 *Legislative and Factual Background of the Ali Enterprises Factory Fire*

In 2012, at the time of the fire, OSH in the Pakistan's Sindh province, where the AE factory fire occurred, was regulated by the Factories Act 1934, the Sindh Factories Rules (1975), and the Sindh Labour Department was responsible for ensuring their implementation. The Ali Enterprises factory was situated in Karachi, where the Sindh Building Control Ordinance (SBCO) 1979, and the Karachi Building and Town Planning Regulations (KBTPR) 2002, governed building safety. The statutory body responsible, for their implementation, is the Sindh Building Control Authority (SBCA). As this chapter traces the progress of the fire and simultaneously identifies relevant OSH violations at the factory, it primarily relies on factual evidence from the report prepared by Pakistan's Federal Investigation Agency (FIA Report), based on the investigation conducted immediately after the fire, which was also submitted before the High Court of Sindh.[32] As a secondary source of factual evidence, it also draws on the Forensic Architecture analysis of the Ali Enterprises factory fire which provides an eye-opening visual aid for reconstructing the fire and was submitted before the Regional Court in Dortmund, Germany, on behalf of ECCHR.[33]

According to the FIA Report, the building that caught fire was Block-A of the Ali Enterprises factory. It covered over 1600 square metres and had five levels: a basement, a ground floor, a mezzanine floor, a first floor and a second floor.[34] The fire started at roughly 6:30 pm[35] on 11 September 2012, and raged until 2:30 pm the next day.[36] The first fire engine reached the factory at approximately 7:00 pm, about half an hour after the fire started, but reinforcements had to be called soon after.[37] According to the Forensic Architecture analysis, there should have been no more than 268 (plus or minus 40) persons present in the building at any given time.

[32]Enquiry Report: Fire Incident at Ali Enterprises S.I.T.E Karachi on 11th September 2012. Federal Investigation Agency, Sindh Zone Karachi, 3 October 2012, Court File of Constitutional Petition No. 3318 of 2012, pp. 1291–1355.

[33]Forensic Architecture, The Ali Enterprises Factory Fire, 30 January 2018, www.forensic-architecture.org/investigation/the-ali-enterprises-factory-fire (last accessed 15 August 2020).

[34]Enquiry Report: Fire Incident at Ali Enterprises S.I.T.E Karachi on 11th September 2012. Federal Investigation Agency, Sindh Zone Karachi, 3 October 2012, Court File of Constitutional Petition No. 3318 of 2012, p. 1301; Forensic Architecture, The Ali Enterprises Factory Fire, 30 January 2018, www.forensic-architecture.org/investigation/the-ali-enterprises-factory-fire (last accessed 15 August 2020).

[35]Enquiry Report: Fire Incident at Ali Enterprises S.I.T.E Karachi on 11th September 2012. Federal Investigation Agency, Sindh Zone Karachi, 3 October 2012, Court File of Constitutional Petition No. 3318 of 2012, pp. 1311, 1313.

[36]Forensic Architecture, The Ali Enterprises Factory Fire, 30 January 2018, www.forensic-architecture.org/investigation/the-ali-enterprises-factory-fire (last accessed 15 August 2020).

[37]Enquiry Report: Fire Incident at Ali Enterprises S.I.T.E Karachi on 11th September 2012. Federal Investigation Agency, Sindh Zone Karachi, 3 October 2012, Court File of Constitutional Petition No. 3318 of 2012, pp. 1301, 1311.

However, on the day of the fire, an estimated 885 people were present in the building: 45 in the basement, 40 on the mezzanine floor, 350 on the first floor and 450 on the second floor. The day of the fire was payday for the workers and, at the time the fire began (around 6:30 pm), as many as 500 to 600 workers were on the second floor of the factory, where their payments were being disbursed at the time.[38]

There was no functional fire alarm in the Ali Enterprises factory and the CCTV footage shows that the workers only became aware of the fire approximately 25 min after it had started.[39] The Factories Act 1934, and the KBTPR 2002, both require that every factory have effective and clearly audible means of giving warning in case of fire, but this was obviously not the case at the Ali Enterprises factory.[40] At 6:56 pm, only a minute or two after the workers realised that there was a fire, the electricity supply was shut off.[41] After this, there was no lighting or emergency markings that could guide the workers to the building's fire exits, despite the fact that this was legally required.[42] There were not even glow-in-the-dark markings pointing towards the exits.[43] Smoke and soot further disoriented workers who were trying to escape though the only available staircase leading to the only functional exit: the only way to escape the fire was through the main entrance on the ground floor, accessible only through the main staircase,[44] which itself was fast disintegrating due to the fire.[45]

---

[38]Enquiry Report: Fire Incident at Ali Enterprises S.I.T.E Karachi on 11th September 2012. Federal Investigation Agency, Sindh Zone Karachi, 3 October 2012, Court File of Constitutional Petition No. 3318 of 2012, pp. 1317, 1337; Forensic Architecture, The Ali Enterprises Factory Fire, 30 January 2018, www.forensic-architecture.org/investigation/the-ali-enterprises-factory-fire (last accessed 15 August 2020).

[39]Enquiry Report: Fire Incident at Ali Enterprises S.I.T.E Karachi on 11th September 2012. Federal Investigation Agency, Sindh Zone Karachi, 3 October 2012, Court File of Constitutional Petition No. 3318 of 2012, p. 1315.

[40]See Section 25 of the Factories Act 1934 and Regulation 13(6.1) of the Karachi Building and Town Planning Regulations 2002. Notably, even when the Factories Act 1934 was updated and re-enacted as the Sindh Factories Act 2015, no specifications for the kind or volume of the fire alarm system to be used were provided, nor were any amendments made in the Sindh Factory Rules 1975.

[41]Enquiry Report: Fire Incident at Ali Enterprises S.I.T.E Karachi on 11th September 2012. Federal Investigation Agency, Sindh Zone Karachi, 3 October 2012, Court File of Constitutional Petition No. 3318 of 2012, p. 1315; Forensic Architecture, The Ali Enterprises Factory Fire, 30 January 2018, www.forensic-architecture.org/investigation/the-ali-enterprises-factory-fire (last accessed 15 August 2020).

[42]Section 19 of the Factories Act 1934 requires that emergency lighting of special points on the factory floors and passages must function automatically in case of a failure of the ordinary electric system.

[43]Section 25 of the Factories Act 1934 and Rule 21 of the Sindh Factory Rules 1975 required that all exits and escape routes be clearly marked in a language understood by the workers and that a free passageway always be maintained to give access to each means of escape in case of fire.

[44]Forensic Architecture, The Ali Enterprises Factory Fire, 30 January 2018, www.forensic-architecture.org/investigation/the-ali-enterprises-factory-fire (last accessed 15 August 2020).

[45]Enquiry Report: Fire Incident at Ali Enterprises S.I.T.E Karachi on 11th September 2012. Federal Investigation Agency, Sindh Zone Karachi, 3 October 2012, Court File of Constitutional Petition No. 3318 of 2012, p. 1303; Forensic Architecture, The Ali Enterprises Factory Fire, 30 January

There were approximately five emergency exit doors in the building, but none of them could be used to escape the fire. The 500 to 600 workers on the second floor were trapped because the two emergency exit doors on the second floor which led to Block-B as well as the two exits to the roof had been permanently locked by factory management.[46] When or if these workers reached the first floor, they found approximately 350 other workers trapped there. The two emergency exit doors on the first floor, which were presumably functional towards the very beginning of the fire, had expanded due to heat and become stuck in their frames by the time more workers became aware of the fire.[47] The exits from the basement only led to the ground floor, which itself was on fire. In the basement, the fire was aggravated and exits were blocked by bales and bales of cloth, which had been wrapped in polyethylene and negligently strewn across the floor.[48] The Factories Act 1934, requires all materials to be stored safely and emergency exits to always be kept clear of any obstruction.[49] Moreover, on the first and second floors, there existed doors that looked like emergency exits that might lead to an escape stairwell, but the emergency staircase itself was missing—one would have had to jump straight out of the first or second floor and some workers did jump.[50] For the most part, the factory's windows had been barred with metal grills, meaning the workers could not jump out of them.[51] The Factories Act of 1934 and the Sindh Factories Rules of 1975 require that the doors affording exit from any room not be locked and to be kept free from obstructions at all times.[52] The Factories Act 1934, also requires that every factory building must have adequate means of escape, accessible from every room of the

2018, www.forensic-architecture.org/investigation/the-ali-enterprises-factory-fire (last accessed 15 August 2020).

[46]Enquiry Report: Fire Incident at Ali Enterprises S.I.T.E Karachi on 11th September 2012. Federal Investigation Agency, Sindh Zone Karachi, 3 October 2012, Court File of Constitutional Petition No. 3318 of 2012, p. 1317.

[47]Enquiry Report: Fire Incident at Ali Enterprises S.I.T.E Karachi on 11th September 2012. Federal Investigation Agency, Sindh Zone Karachi, 3 October 2012, Court File of Constitutional Petition No. 3318 of 2012, p. 1317; Forensic Architecture, The Ali Enterprises Factory Fire, 30 January 2018, www.forensic-architecture.org/investigation/the-ali-enterprises-factory-fire (last accessed 15 August 2020).

[48]Forensic Architecture, The Ali Enterprises Factory Fire, 30 January 2018, www.forensic-architecture.org/investigation/the-ali-enterprises-factory-fire (last accessed 15 August 2020).

[49]Section 25 of the Factories Act 1934; Rule 21 of the Sindh Factories Rules 1975.

[50]Enquiry Report: Fire Incident at Ali Enterprises S.I.T.E Karachi on 11th September 2012. Federal Investigation Agency, Sindh Zone Karachi, 3 October 2012, Court File of Constitutional Petition No. 3318 of 2012, p. 1317.

[51]Enquiry Report: Fire Incident at Ali Enterprises S.I.T.E Karachi on 11th September 2012. Federal Investigation Agency, Sindh Zone Karachi, 3 October 2012, Court File of Constitutional Petition No. 3318 of 2012, p. 1337; Forensic Architecture, The Ali Enterprises Factory Fire, 30 January 2018, www.forensic-architecture.org/investigation/the-ali-enterprises-factory-fire (last accessed 15 August 2020).

[52]Rule 30 of the Sindh Factories Rules 1975.

factory, in case of fire but this was evidently not the case.[53] Moreover, the KBTPR 2002 also requires that all storeys, except for those below the first, should provide direct access for firefighters from the outdoors, but no such access was provided in the AE factory.[54]

There was also an emergency exit on the mezzanine floor, but this mezzanine had a wooden floor that had not been fire-proofed. As a result, it burned down very quickly, casting fiery debris onto the ground floor.[55] For factory buildings of up to 25 feet (7.5 m), the law requires that every element of structure, on the ground floor or any upper storey must be fire resistant for 1.5 h (90 min), and in the basement for 1 h (60 min).[56] It also requires that all steel and metal structures be protected by non-combustible materials.[57] Moreover, the spread of the fire could have been slowed if the floors had been compartmentalised, as is required by the KBTPR 2002.[58] The only part of the factory where there was compartmentalisation was the ground floor. While the warehouse on the ground floor was completely burnt in the fire, only around 10 percent of the washing area on the same floor was affected. The FIA Report noted that this was likely due to the presence of a dividing wall and the absence of readily combustible material.[59]

The second floor of the Ali Enterprises factory was significantly more damaged than the first floor.[60] This was due to the fact that improper ventilation in the

[53]Section 25 of the Factories Act 1934; Moreover, the Sindh Factories Rules 1975 require that all factories of more than one storey must have two sets of stairs. One of the stairways should be external, permanently fixed, made of non-combustible materials, fixed with suitable handrails, accessible, easy to open from inside and have direct and should provide unimpeded access to the ground level from every part of the factory in case of fire (Rule 30 and 52 of the Sindh Factories Rules 1975). Furthermore, the Karachi Building and Town Planning Regulations 2002, require that the staircase inside the building should be a minimum width of 4 feet (1.2 m), and the maximum distance from any point on the floor to the nearest staircase should not be more than 98.4 feet (30 m) (Regulation 9(8.2) of the Karachi Building and Town Planning Regulations 2002).

[54]According to Regulation 14(8) of the Karachi Building and Town Planning Regulations 2002, this access must be provided for every storey whose floor is less than 82 feet (25 m) above ground, and the access bust be at least 3.6 feet (1.1 m) high by 2 feet (0.6 m) wide, with a sill height of not more than 3 feet (0.9 m) above the inside floor.

[55]Enquiry Report: Fire Incident at Ali Enterprises S.I.T.E Karachi on 11th September 2012. Federal Investigation Agency, Sindh Zone Karachi, 3 October 2012, Court File of Constitutional Petition No. 3318 of 2012, pp. 1303, 1313, 1317.

[56]Regulation 14(1.2), Table 14.1, Karachi Building and Town Planning Regulations 2002.

[57]Regulation 14(13.1-13.2), Table 14.1, Karachi Building and Town Planning Regulations 2002.

[58]Regulation 14(5) of the Karachi Building and Town Planning Regulations 2002 also requires that the building floor should be compartmentalised as much as possible by means of appropriate fire-resistant elements/measures (such as firewalls).

[59]Enquiry Report: Fire Incident at Ali Enterprises S.I.T.E Karachi on 11th September 2012. Federal Investigation Agency, Sindh Zone Karachi, 3 October 2012, Court File of Constitutional Petition No. 3318 of 2012, p. 1301.

[60]Enquiry Report: Fire Incident at Ali Enterprises S.I.T.E Karachi on 11th September 2012. Federal Investigation Agency, Sindh Zone Karachi, 3 October 2012, Court File of Constitutional Petition No. 3318 of 2012, p. 1303.

factory's cargo elevator had created an air channel that carried the fire upwards. The elevator shaft, which was located next to the only staircase in the building, also caught fire.[61] The cargo elevator was not properly ventilated and there were gaps in the shaft which created a chimney effect, causing the fire to spread to the first and second floors through the elevator shaft.[62] What was most shocking, however, is that despite the factory building having five storeys, there was only one fire extinguisher in the entire building—which too was empty at the time, and none of the workers knew how to use it.[63] The Sindh Factories Rules 1975, and the KBTPR 2002, both require that there be at least one fire extinguisher on every floor in the building.[64] The Factories Act 1934, also stipulates that all workers should know where the emergency exits are located and should be adequately trained to respond to emergencies, including fires,[65] which was obviously not the case at Ali Enterprises.[66]

Regardless of the fire's cause, if the basic safety precautions and inspections had been conducted, the fatalities at the Ali Enterprises factory could have been minimised and very likely prevented entirely. Nevertheless, the FIA Report explored several possible causes of the fire. It found that the factory's electrical system was errant, unsafe and vulnerable to accidental short-circuiting.[67] Moreover, the burners for the factory's dryers, which were located on the ground floor, used to be lit

[61]Enquiry Report: Fire Incident at Ali Enterprises S.I.T.E Karachi on 11th September 2012. Federal Investigation Agency, Sindh Zone Karachi, 3 October 2012, Court File of Constitutional Petition No. 3318 of 2012, p. 1303; Forensic Architecture, The Ali Enterprises Factory Fire, 30 January 2018, www.forensic-architecture.org/investigation/the-ali-enterprises-factory-fire (last accessed 15 August 2020).

[62]The Karachi Building and Town Planning Regulations 2002 require that the protected shaft containing an elevator must be ventilated; if the opening is at the bottom of the shaft the opening should be as small as practicable and it shall not be constructed of, or lined with, any material which increases the risk of spread of fire. Regulation 14(9.3), Karachi Building and Town Planning Regulations 2002.

[63]Forensic Architecture, The Ali Enterprises Factory Fire, 30 January 2018, www.forensic-architecture.org/investigation/the-ali-enterprises-factory-fire (last accessed 15 August 2020).

[64]Rule 51 of the Sindh Factories Rules (1975) requires that, for floor space up to 6000 square feet, there must be one chemical extinguisher of two-gallon capacity, and there must be an additional extinguisher for each additional 6000 square feet. According to Regulation 13(3.1.5) of the Karachi Building and Town Planning Regulations (2002), all building compartments more than 7000 square feet in covered area that are used to manufacture, display or sell combustible materials and products must have automated sprinkler systems installed. The Ali Enterprises factory, covering an area of 17,222 square feet (according to the FIA Report) and engaged in the manufacture and storage of garments from flammable cotton and synthetic fibres, but it had no such automated sprinkler system installed.

[65]Section 25 of the Factories Act 1934 and Rule 21 of the Sindh Factories Rules 1975.

[66]Enquiry Report: Fire Incident at Ali Enterprises S.I.T.E Karachi on 11th September 2012. Federal Investigation Agency, Sindh Zone Karachi, 3 October 2012, Court File of Constitutional Petition No. 3318 of 2012, p. 1301; Forensic Architecture, The Ali Enterprises Factory Fire, 30 January 2018, www.forensic-architecture.org/investigation/the-ali-enterprises-factory-fire (last accessed 15 August 2020).

[67]For example, the transformer, LT Panel and generators were all installed in the same room as opposed to being in separate rooms. See: Enquiry Report: Fire Incident at Ali Enterprises S.I.T.E

through a very dangerous manual procedure: a worker would dip a metal rod, wrapped in cotton on one end, into a plastic can full of kerosene oil and light it with a matchstick, and then use the flame to fire up the dryer burners. This contraption (consisting of the wrapped rod and kerosene oil) was kept very close to the warehouse, right above which was the wooden floor of the mezzanine, which was completely burnt in the fire. Eyewitness accounts documented in the FIA Report also suggest that fires caused by this dryer-lighting procedure had erupted in the past but had always been successfully extinguished by the staff.[68]

According to the SBCO, all buildings must have their building plans approved by the SBCA. However, only SITE approved the building plan for the Ali Enterprises factory, and it allowed significantly more built-up area than legally permissible. Yet, even the building plan approved by SITE had not envisaged the factory's second floor.[69] Legally, it is only after the proprietors have been granted a "No Objection Certificate" (NOC) for construction by the SBCA that they can start building. The SBCO also stipulates that no building can be occupied before the SBCA has conducted an inspection and issued an "Occupancy Certificate," after an application by the occupant or owner.[70] During the construction, an inspecting engineer or a building supervisor must be engaged and is required to sign off on the building plan.[71] Moreover, the Factories Act 1934, required that every factory be registered with the Chief Inspector in the Sindh Labour Department, to whom any and all accidents in the factory were to be reported.[72]

However, the Ali Enterprises factory never applied for, much less acquired, an NOC or an Occupancy Certificate. It had never been registered with the Chief Inspector as required by the law, nor had previous fires in the factory ever been reported to the Sindh Labour Department.[73] When these lapses became public knowledge and, later, came to the court's attention, the SBCA insisted that SITE

Karachi on 11th September 2012. Federal Investigation Agency, Sindh Zone Karachi, 3 October 2012, Court File of Constitutional Petition No. 3318 of 2012, p. 1327.

[68]Enquiry Report: Fire Incident at Ali Enterprises S.I.T.E Karachi on 11th September 2012. Federal Investigation Agency, Sindh Zone Karachi, 3 October 2012, Court File of Constitutional Petition No. 3318 of 2012, p. 1329.

[69]The total area of the plot F/67, on which the Ali Enterprises factory was built, was 4646.34 square yards (41,817.06 square feet). Legally, it was allowed to have a built-up area of 33,454 square feet (80 percent), but SITE approved a plan for 35,947 square feet, while the factory owners actually built a covered area of 52,569 square feet. Enquiry Report: Fire Incident at Ali Enterprises S.I.T.E Karachi on 11th September 2012. Federal Investigation Agency, Sindh Zone Karachi, 3 October 2012, Court File of Constitutional Petition No. 3318 of 2012, p. 1331.

[70]Section 6 of the Sindh Building Control Ordinance 1979.

[71]If there are defects in the structure, plan and construction, then the SBCA is required to determine the liability of the builder/subcontractor and/or their associates. Section 7 of the Sindh Building Control Ordinance 1979.

[72]Section 11 of the Factories Act 1934.

[73]If there are defects in the structure, plan or construction, then the SBCA is required to determine the liability of the builder/subcontractor and/or their associates. Section 7 of the Sindh Building Control Ordinance 1979.

was responsible, while SITE insisted that the SBCA was also responsible.[74] In reality, neither authority had physically inspected the building or penalised its illegal constructions. The FIA Report notes that if the building had been properly inspected, "large scale" fatalities could have been prevented.[75] While SITE bears responsibility for the oversight of the factories operating within it, the SBCA had the primary responsibility to inspect the building structure, as it is the institution charged with enforcing the Sindh Building Control Ordinance of 1979 and the rules and regulations thereunder, including those listed in the KBTPR of 2002. Nevertheless, in March 2013, the High Court of Sindh directed SITE and the SBCA to conduct a specific investigation to "reveal the deviation from the relevant laws, particularly the rules and the regulations," meaning the building and planning laws.[76] That report also found that the Ali Enterprises factory had never been inspected or approved for occupation, meaning it had deviated from all relevant laws.[77]

Parallel to all these delinquencies, the Ali Enterprises factory and KiK had engaged in certain voluntary regulatory procedures. For instance, a social audit of the factory had been conducted to check the factory for its safety measures etc., and had resulted in the granting of an SA-8000 certification, less than a month before the fire. It is important to note here that the SA-8000 certificate was neither mandated under Pakistani law, nor required by German or European law, under which KiK operates. It was a mere trick to provide the factory with a facade of legitimacy, while it actively violated almost all of the OSH standards required to legally operate in Pakistan,[78] it was merely used to distract from the AE factory's violation of all legally binding OSH regulations.

[74]SITE responsible for Baldia factory building plan, says SBCA. The News, 15 September 2012, www.thenews.com.pk/archive/print/385215-site-responsible-for-baldia-factory-building-plan-says-sbca (last accessed 2 August 2020); Asian Human Rights Commission, Pakistan: Baldia factory fire tragedy – the compensation is not the only solution to deal with such an incident, 10 September 2014, www.humanrights.asia/news/forwarded-news/AHRC-FST-068-2014/ (last accessed 2 August 2020).

[75]Enquiry Report: Fire Incident at Ali Enterprises S.I.T.E Karachi on 11th September 2012. Federal Investigation Agency, Sindh Zone Karachi, 3 October 2012, Court File of Constitutional Petition No. 3318 of 2012, p. 1331.

[76]Order dated: 12 March 2013, passed in Constitutional Petition No. D-295 of 2013, by the High Court of Sindh.

[77]Compliance Report of the Labour and Human Resources Department of the Government of Sindh, submitted pursuant to Order dated 5 November 2012, passed by the High Court of Sindh, in Constitutional Petition No. 3318 of 2012, Court File p. 317.

[78]ECCHR Case Report, RINA certifies safety before factory fire in Pakistan, November 2016, www.ecchr.eu/fileadmin/Fallbeschreibungen/CaseReport_Rina_Pakistan.pdf (last accessed 3 August 2020).

2.2 Recent Developments and Continuing Non-enforcement

During the proceedings regarding the AE factory fire at the High Court of Sindh, it was found that, as of November 2012 (two months after the fire), 7576 factories were registered with the Sindh Labour Department. Of these, 214 factories' registrations (and 180 new Sindh Labour Department inspections) had been prompted by the horrifying fire.[79] Almost eight years later, however, the Sindh Labour Department still lacks a comprehensive registration of factories, any data collection mechanism, as well as any accurate tally of the number of factories, workplaces other than factories or total number of workers in the province of Sindh, or even in the city of Karachi. According to the Sindh Labour Department, as of August 2020, there were 9868 registered factories, though many of them had yet to be inspected due to a chronic shortage of inspectors and a lack of political will for the enforcement of workplace safety laws and standards. Indeed, in August 2020, there were only 22 labour inspectors for all of Sindh.[80] A large proportion of factories also remained unregistered as of August 2020, and no official comprehensive data yet exists for workplaces other than factories, such as construction sites, restaurants, cinemas, etc.[81]

While the Factories Act of 1934 only imposed a penalty fine of 500 rupees (2.82 euros) on the employer for any contravention of its provisions,[82] the purportedly updated Sindh Factories Act of 2015 enhanced and differentiated the penalties, raising them to a range of 10,000 to 50,000 rupees (57.40 to 287 euros).[83] Thus, the total penalty is still exceedingly minimal. This is particularly significant because

[79]Compliance Report of the Labour and Human Resources Department of the Government of Sindh, submitted pursuant to Order dated: 5 November 2012, passed by the High Court of Sindh, in Constitutional Petition No. 3318 of 2012, Court File p. 317.

[80]Interviews conducted with M. Ashraf, Director of the Department of Labour & Human Resources, Government of Sindh, Karachi, 10 January 2020 and 20 August 2020. According to current practice, each inspector (of 22 in total) does eight inspections per month, amounting to around 1800–2000 inspections carried out per year.

[81]Interviews conducted with M. Ashraf, Director of the Department of Labour & Human Resources, Government of Sindh, Karachi, 10 January 2020 and 20 August 2020. 37,000 shops and establishments are registered in Sindh.

[82]Sections 39 and 60 of the Factories Act 1934.

[83]Sections 92–101 of the Sindh Factories Act 2015. At the time of the Ali Enterprises fire, the Factories Act 1934 was still applicable to Sindh as the province had not yet enacted relevant legislation of its own. Over the following years, all four provinces of Pakistan re-enacted the Factories Act (1934) through their own provincial legislatures, more or less without making any substantial changes to the 1934 act. The Government of Sindh passed the Sindh Factories Act (2015), in which Section 114 stipulates that the Sindh Factories Rules 1975 previously enacted under the Factories Act 1934, continue to remain in force. However, further rules are also required to be framed under the Sindh Factories Act 2015, but these have not been framed till date. Therefore, this discussion of the Factories Act 1934 also applies to the Sindh Factories Act 2015 and Sindh Factories Rules 1975 which remain applicable in Sindh today whilst further Rules under the Sindh Factories Act 2015, are awaited.

in the balance of convenience, if enforcing occupational health and safety measures costs an employer any more than the minimal penalties imposed under the inspection regime, it would suit the employers to continue endangering workers. With such low penalties, factory owners essentially lose nothing and anticipate no penal action against themselves if they continue to endanger their workers.

The other mechanism that can potentially enforce a cost on employers is workers' compensation. Under the Workmen's Compensation Act 1923, employers face unqualified liability, with respect to their employees, for any work-related accident, illness, or fatality. However, 87 percent of the Ali Enterprises workers were hired through a third party contractor and were not given any official letter of appointment, even by the contractor.[84] Hence, even if a worker had been injured at the factory, they would not be able to prove an employment relationship with Ali Enterprises or even with the contractor, which would then not be liable for the injury.[85]

In addition to this, the Provincial Employees Social Security Ordinance 1965[86] states that "if an employer fails to observe rules of safety or hygiene prescribed by or under any enactment applicable to his establishment the Commissioner may [...] increase the employer's rate contribution; provided that such increase shall not exceed twenty percent of the contribution otherwise payable."[87] From these provisions, it is quite clear that, even if the workers were officially hired and registered by them, if enforcing OSH measures costs an employer more than 20 percent of the contribution they have to make towards the Social Security Institution, it would be more convenient for them to continue endangering workers instead. And they often do just that. It is also important to highlight that there is no coordination mechanism or overlap between the different bodies overseeing Pakistan's fragmented OSH infrastructure (such as the Sindh Employees Social Security Institution, the Sindh Labour Department, the SBCA, etc.).

In the aftermath of the AE factory fire and following significant lobbying efforts from organisations like PILER and NTUF, as well as individual OSH experts, the Government of Sindh passed a relatively expansive, worker-oriented OSH law: the Sindh Occupational Safety and Health Act 2017 (OSH Act).[88] In addition to this key legislative reform, numerous provincial labour laws were also promulgated after this tragic factory fire, although these were not necessarily in response to it. These new laws were based on the 18th Amendment to the Constitution of Pakistan 1973, which had been passed in 2010 and had removed the subject of labour matters from the federal government and assigned legislative jurisdictions to provincial

[84]Farhat A, Baldia Factory Fire Incident 4 years of successful campaign for justice, PILER, December 2016, www.piler.org.pk/wp-content/uploads/2017/02/Brief_Baldia_Factory_Fire-_Inci dent.pdf (last accessed 12 August 2020).

[85]The problem of contractual labour will be discussed in detail in Sect. 5.

[86]Section 26 of the West Pakistan Employees Social Security Ordinance 1965; Section 27 of the Sindh Employees Social Security Act 2016.

[87]Section 26 of the West Pakistan Employees Social Security Ordinance 1965.

[88]Occupational Safety and Health Act, 2017; The province of Punjab also passed the Punjab Occupational Health and Safety Act 2019 and other provinces are also drafting their own OSH laws.

governments.[89] In Sindh, where the Ali Enterprises factory fire occurred, the Factories Act of 1934 was essentially re-enacted with very few changes, as was passed as the Sindh Factories Act 2015.[90] The West Pakistan Employees Social Security Ordinance 1965 was also re-enacted as the Sindh Employees Social Security Act (SESSI Act) 2016. Although these new acts were passed, they only included minor updates and were not based on any new data or qualitative research.[91]

Nevertheless, Sindh's OSH Act, was the first OSH-specific act passed in the country and it made two significant contributions to OSH infrastructure: it created a mechanism to include workers in informing and enforcing OSH practices, and it created a unified OSH law that is not limited to factories or any particular industry, but it is applicable across Sindh, in all sectors. If the act were to be properly implemented, it would significantly improve the OSH situation in the province. Unfortunately, however, its implementation really has yet to begin. If the OSH Act does get implemented, another noteworthy improvement on the current practices that it would bring is that, all workplaces would have to register themselves with the Directorate of Labour *after* getting approvals from the relevant (building) authority (that is, the SBCA) as well. Indeed, although the OSH Act expressly requires special inspectors, no inspectors have yet even been inducted under the OSH Act.[92] The OSH Act also stipulates that every workplace must either have an elected Health and Safety Representative or a Health and Safety Committee, depending on its size.[93] However, since the provincial government has yet to hire inspectors to monitor and enforce the OSH Act 2017, it can safely be assumed that there has been no implementation of these provisions by the subject workplaces either. The OSH Act further requires the Government of Sindh to make rules under the act and, although drafts have been circulating for a long time, as of mid-2020, no rules have been notified by the Government of Sindh.[94] Finally, the OSH Act also requires that employers allow their occupational safety and health representatives to attend a government-approved health and safety training at least once every two years, for which the employers must bear all of the associated expenses, including paid leave, course fees, room and board, as well as travel expenses.[95] However, the Government of Sindh has yet to operationalise any such training courses. No data has even been collected by the Sindh Labour Department to identify the number of workplaces that

[89] 18th Amendment to the Constitution of Pakistan, 1973, which was passed in 2010.

[90] For example, Section 11 of the Sindh Factories Act 2015 increases the factory registration requirement by adding one more step: factories now need to register with the Chief Inspector *and* the Labour Department.

[91] Interviews conducted with M. Ashraf, Director of the Department of Labour & Human Resources, Government of Sindh, Karachi, 10 January 2020 and 20 August 2020.

[92] Section 22 of the Sindh Occupational Safety and Health Act, 2017.

[93] Section 18 of the Sindh Occupational Safety and Health Act, 2017.

[94] Section 10 of the Sindh Occupational Safety and Health Act, 2017.

[95] Section 13 of the Sindh Occupational Safety and Health Act, 2017.

are operating in Sindh and are evading laws, rules and inspections, despite the passage of eight years since the fire and three years since the OSH Act.[96]

Given the state of affairs described above, it is reiterated that the Ali Enterprises factory was not exceptional in its failure to implement relevant OSH laws. It is regular practice for factories and other workplaces to completely circumvent labour- and safety-related laws. A large proportion of factories in Karachi operate in the realm of illegality.[97]

Why is there such a large disjuncture between the safety standards that are guaranteed by law (regardless of their inadequacies) and the dangerous working conditions prevalent across the garment industry and other industrial sectors? Based on the aforementioned facts, I argue that that despite passage of the OSH Act of 2017 which is itself a relatively promising law, there is still very little impetus for employers to improve workplace safety within the prevailing politico-economic framework in Sindh and generally in Pakistan. In whatever form they exist, laws are divorced from their implementation. This occurs because the purpose of these laws is not truly to ensure worker safety. The purpose of this rigmarole of laws is to give legitimacy to and fulfil the economic and political ends of the sovereign government, may it be the national government and its trade policies or the provincial government. That is, to provide face value. The author tenatively believes that this can be understood more precisely through the work of Giorgio Agamben, on the concept of bare life and the Homo Sacer, who asserts that there exists no *rule of law*, no law "in itself."[98] Instead, there is the rule of the lawmaker, evident through the presence and absence of law. For the law-making sovereign, the worker is *homo sacer*, a zombie whose body is confined and forced to labour, held accountable through the law, but not safeguarded by it. Once this fundamental point is understood in the context of the Ali Enterprises factory fire, it becomes easier to recognise the impediments to workplace safety and then tailor the response accordingly.

3 Colonial Legacy: History of the Factories Act

This section posits that workplace safety in Pakistan may be better reckoned with in light of the history of the Factories Act and global political economy. As noted above, the Factories Act 1934[99] as well as the Workmen's Compensation Act of

---

[96] Interviews conducted with M. Ashraf, Director of the Department of Labour & Human Resources, Government of Sindh, Karachi, 10 January 2020 and 20 August 2020.

[97] When prompted to action, the Labour & Human Resources Department was able to get 214 factories to register with it by November 2012. However, despite the fact that Pakistan's GDP growth rate went from 4 percent in 2012 to 5.5 percent in 2020, only 424 more factories had been registered in Sindh by August 2020. See Country Profile, World Bank, www.wits.worldbank.org/CountryProfile/en/PAK (last accessed 15 August 2020).

[98] Agamben (1998), p. 20.

[99] This factory legislation set up the framework for safety standards and aimed for enforcement through inspections. In addition to the provisions of the Factories Act 1934, that have been

1923, governed OSH in Pakistan at the time of the AE fire. Both these laws were passed under British rule, prior to Pakistan's independence in 1947. The history of the Factories Act is particularly dramatic and important for understanding the evolution of OSH in Pakistan, which was part of a united India and under British rule. Although Indian workers' movements existed and made demands for better working conditions at the time, successive iterations of the Factories Act until the final Factories Act 1934 were passed to facilitate a greater market share for British textile manufacturers in their fight against the manufacturers of British India.[100]

In order to better understand the Factories Act's journey, a brief survey of the history of OSH in Britain is germane (unlike Pakistan). When industrialisation and mass production began gaining a stronghold in England in the mid-1700s, it centred on the cotton and textile industry, and prompted mass urbanisation, as labour was plentiful, cheap and expendable. Much labour at the time was provided by "pauper apprentices" in return for room and board.[101] During this period, factories became increasingly dangerous, and the number of occupational diseases, injuries and fatalities ran high. As a general rule, workers faced long hours and cruel conditions.[102] After much public alarm,[103] the UK parliament passed the Health and

discussed above, Chapter III of this act mandated that provincial governments make rules and standards as to, *inter alia*, the disposal of waste, ventilation, temperature, artificial humidification, lighting, drinking water, latrines and urinals, spittoons, provision of canteens, workforce eye protection, precautions in case of fire, dangerous fumes, explosive dust, fencing, casing, lifting of machinery, work near machinery in motion, shelters for the workforce to rest, provision of first aid, and so forth. In accordance with this, the Sindh Government promulgated the Sindh Factories Rules 1975.

[100]Gilbert (1982), pp. 357–372.

[101]In England, children formed 40 percent of the population around the second half of the 1700s. Many of them were impoverished and/or orphan children, who provided a steady source of cheap and expendable labour. Orphans were sent into factories or other employment by the Poor Law authorities, often very far from their homes. The Poor Law required that every local parish take care of its poor: "A 'poor rate' or local tax paid by parish householders was used to help the poor [. . .] those who were too ill, old, destitute, or who were orphaned children were put into a local 'workhouse' or 'poorhouse'. Those able to work, but whose wages were too low to support their families, received 'relief in aid of wages' in the form of money, food and clothes." Poverty and the Poor Law. Living Heritage/Reforming Society in the 19th Century, UK Parliament, www.parliament.uk/about/living-heritage/transformingsociety/livinglearning/19thcentury/overview/poverty/ (last accessed 20 July 2020).

[102]For example, in 1784, there was a fever outbreak amongst workers at cotton mills, which were the most common type of factory in the late eighteenth century. Young girls working in match factories would regularly develop Phossy Jaw, a condition caused by phosphorous fumes. Workers employed in mines developed and often died of lung cancer before the age of 25. Other accidents causing burns, injuries and even blindness were also increasingly common. History of Workplace Health and Safety, www.staysafeapp.com/blog/2019/12/09/history-workplace-health-safety/ (last accessed 20 July 2020).

[103]This was propelled by a progressive philanthropist and mill-owner, Sir Robert Peel. Early Factory Legislation, Living Heritage/Reforming Society in the 19th Century, UK Parliament, www.parliament.uk/about/living-heritage/transformingsociety/livinglearning/19thcentury/overview/earlyfactorylegislation/ (last accessed 20 July 2020).

Morals of Apprentices Act in 1802, marking the first legislative attempt to regulate health and safety in factories.[104] In 1819, amidst a campaign to ban child labour, it passed the Cotton Mills Act.[105] Then, in response to the Ten Hour Movement, the first Factories Act was passed in 1831.[106] Yet, none of these early legislative efforts were particularly effective in improving workers' health and safety in England, for many of the same reasons responsible for the later failures of the 1934 and 2015 Factories Acts in Pakistan. At first, the laws lacked enforcement mechanisms. Then, after enforcement mechanisms were established, the UK lacked the institutional capacity to effectively operate and guarantee them.

In England, it was the Factories Act 1833, that established the first enforcement mechanism in the form of a four-person inspectorate to oversee approximately 4000 cotton mills. The inspectorate's task was obviously far bigger than its capacity and, hence, employers generally evaded the law and it remained largely unenforced.[107] Subsequent iterations of the Factories Act expanded it in scope to include other industries and tighter inspection regimes,[108] but employers could still avoid

---

[104]This was the first piece of factory legislation and it applied to cotton mills, which were the dominant form of factory in the country. This law required factories to have sufficient ventilation and be kept clean, and to provide adequate clothing and accommodation for apprentices. It also prohibited apprentices under the age of 21 to work longer than 12 h a day. Early Factory Legislation. Living Heritage/Reforming Society in the 19th Century, UK Parliament, www.parliament.uk/about/living-heritage/transformingsociety/livinglearning/19thcentury/overview/earlyfactorylegislation/ (last accessed 20 July 2020).

[105]The 1819 law stipulated that children under nine years could not be employed in cotton mills, and children under 16 years could work a maximum day of 12 h. But once again, the means of enforcing such legislation remained a serious problem. Early Factory Legislation. Living Heritage/Reforming Society in the 19th Century, UK Parliament, www.parliament.uk/about/living-heritage/transformingsociety/livinglearning/19thcentury/overview/earlyfactorylegislation/ (last accessed 20 July 2020).

[106]The Ten Hour Movement was led by philanthropists (including mill owners), workers and writers, calling for a 10-h workday. The 1831 legislation provided that children between the ages of 13 and 18 could work a maximum of 12 h daily. It also extended the ambit of factory legislation to include the wool-producing industry as well. The 1833 Factory Act. Living Heritage/Reforming Society in the 19th Century, UK Parliament, www.parliament.uk/about/living-heritage/transformingsociety/livinglearning/19thcentury/overview/factoryact/ (last accessed 20 July 2020).

[107]Public opinion, influenced in part by popular writers like Charles Dickens, was able to influence subsequent legislation relating to guarding machinery and reporting accidents. Steadily, the number of factory inspectors grew to 35 in 1886. History of Workplace Health and Safety, www.staysafeapp.com/blog/2019/12/09/history-workplace-health-safety/ (last accessed 20 July 2020).

[108]"[T]he Factory Acts (Extension) Act of 1867, took the important step of applying existing legislation to all other factories where 50 or more people were employed. It also brought regulation to other specified industries regardless of numbers employed, namely, blast furnaces, iron and steel mills, glass, paper making, tobacco, printing and bookbinding." The Later Factory Legislation. Living Heritage/Reforming Society in the 19th Century, UK Parliament, www.parliament.uk/about/living-heritage/transformingsociety/livinglearning/19thcentury/overview/laterfactoryleg/ (last accessed 20 July 2020); Other than Factories Acts, the first Chimney Sweeps Act was passed in 1834, and revised in 1840 and in 1863. However, this legislation also lacked enforcement mechanisms, until the Chimney Sweepers Act 1875, was passed and it mandated sweepers to be licensed and made it the duty of the police to enforce all previous legislation. Additionally, the Mines and

responsibility for fatalities, injuries or diseases by simply blaming the affected worker or their fellow worker for any mishap. Accordingly, employers continued to endanger workers with impunity. However, inspection regimes became more potent when they were supplemented by the Workmen's Compensation Act of 1897; this stipulated that in case of any accident, injury or disease, the employer would be responsible for covering costs by default, without the injured person having to prove their case against the employer.[109] By the 1870s, British manufacturers, especially in the cotton and textile industries, had begun to feel the pinch of having to follow health and safety regulations and were ready to do something about it.[110] British cotton and textile factories were also suffering stiff competition from the colonies, particularly from British India.[111]

To counter this threat, British textile interests took two actions. First, they pushed the British government to remove import duties in the name of free trade and trade liberalisation. Second, they pushed for legislation similar to the Factories Act to be adopted in British India in what Marc Gilbert has described as "a cynical proposal that, under the guise of improving working conditions in the subcontinent, would have increased Indian production costs while reducing output, thus making British manufacturers more prevalent and competitively priced in South Asian bazaars."[112] As a result of these efforts, the UK practically abolished Indian import duties in 1879. Following this victory, British textile interests tried to co-opt the Indian Millhands' Association's (and others') appeal for factory reforms, by advocating for stringent regulation of factories in British India. In 1881, pilot Indian factory legislation was passed as the 1881 Indian Factories Act.[113] Encouraged by this, the British textile interests continued to push for enough OSH regulation to rob British India of its competitive advantage.[114]

In the face of British textile interests' adversarial efforts, the Indian Millhands' Association came to agree with Indian factory owners: that factory reform and labour protection were required, but not according to the dictates of British interests.

Collieries Act 1842, was passed in the wake of public outcry at the conditions of women and children employed by the mining industry. Nevertheless, the number of accidents continued to rise until the Coal Mines Regulation Act 1872, stipulated that pit managers must have state certification of their training and miners were given the right to appoint inspectors from amongst themselves. Coal Mines. Living Heritage/Reforming Society in the 19th Century, UK Parliament, www.parliament.uk/about/living-heritage/transformingsociety/livinglearning/19thcentury/overview/coalmines/ (last accessed 20 July 2020).

[109]Poverty and the Poor Law. Living Heritage/Reforming Society in the 19th Century, UK Parliament, www.parliament.uk/about/living-heritage/transformingsociety/livinglearning/19thcentury/overview/poverty/ (last accessed 20 July 2020).

[110]Gilbert (1982), pp. 357–372.

[111]Gilbert (1982), pp. 357–372.

[112]Gilbert (1982), p. 359.

[113]Gilbert (1982), pp. 357–372.

[114]The most influential document in the push for further legislation was the report of the Bombay Factory Commission of 1885, which was prepared during the governorship of Sir James Fergusson, a strong proponent of British textile interests in Asia. Gilbert (1982), pp. 359–360.

Rather, they believed that labour protection should be balanced with the need to protect India's economic integrity.[115] Indian workers, represented by the Indian Millhands' Association, severely criticised the Factory Act of 1881. Though they unequivocally demanded improved working conditions,[116] they did not approve of British manufacturers' suggestions: "We do need factory legislation, but certainly not on the lines indicated by Manchester. We want to encourage and protect the industry and not to hamper it. Manchester is indeed extremely kind to our work people, but it is the kindness that kills."[117] Instead, they demanded improved working conditions that would be economically viable and could ensure long-term job security for workers in India (and could be progressively improved as the Indian economy grew further). Ultimately, the British "decided to apply to India the political formula [they] favored in Europe – the use of more sympathetic administration and the slow but gradual sharing of power with the middle class to co-opt more rapid and radical change."[118]

In March 1890, the International Labour Conference in Berlin (Berlin Labour Conference) passed resolutions with respect to working conditions in Europe, which the British delegates signed.[119] The British textile interests took advantage of this development as an opportunity to reject the new factory legislation being proposed in India at the time, demanding instead that it be aligned with the resolutions of the Berlin Labour Conference. As Gilbert notes, "[t]hese assertions were backed not by appeals from Indian labour or British Progressives but by a letter from the secretary of the Blackburn and District Chamber of Commerce to the Secretary of State for India urging that 'there should not be one law for England and another for India'."[120] Eventually, the Factories Act of 1891[121] was passed in accordance with the Berlin Labour Conference standards with respect to working age and hours of labour, rest and refreshment.[122]

It is apparent that, since the beginning, workers' interests and OSH laws have not been aligned. Although the Indian Millhands' Association raised its voice on behalf of workers, it was not their appeals that led to the promulgation of the law, nor was the voice of British progressives relevant for the implementation or amendment of the law. Rather, it was British textile interests, as allies of the sovereign, who were not only more audible, but more effective in achieving their aims. It also shows that

---

[115]Gilbert (1982), pp. 357–372.

[116]Their key demands included one holiday a week and a midday break period. Gilbert (1982), pp. 357–372.

[117]Gilbert (1982), p. 363.

[118]Gilbert (1982), p. 361.

[119]These established the need for a compulsory holiday every week (on Sunday), fixing the minimum age for children (10), and setting maximum hours of child labour (six with a half-hour rest interval) and female labour (11 with two hours of rest). Gilbert (1982), pp. 357–372.

[120]Gilbert (1982), p. 365.

[121]Act No. XI of 1891.

[122]Gilbert (1982), p. 365.

workers' interests, related to OSH or otherwise, are not universally identical, but may need to be tailored to their particular context. Transnational solidarity among workers should be excepted from this but the top-down enforcement of purportedly universal OSH standards, particularly in this context, can unsettle or counteract ongoing local movements for betterment (of working conditions), and give way to unsustainable or ineffective mechanisms for improvement whilst silencing the most urgent needs. The Berlin Labour Conference was relevant and useful for the European workers, and was the cumulative result of developments in Europe since the eighteenth century.[123] However, applied to Indian workers and factory owners, these same developments threatened to make their conditions worse by possibly costing them their jobs, potential for advancement or more jobs through economic growth. If their voice had not been banished and had their safety been regulated through changes reflective of and responsive to Indian factory owners, the workers and the Indian economy's changing needs and priorities, they may have taken ownership of these regulations. Unlike the gradual but sustained growth of OSH in Britain, various British laws were simply imposed onto the Indian landscape over the course of a few decades. This precluded local ownership of workplace safety, by both workers and employers, from taking root. It co-opted the local movement, and generally thwarted substantive improvements in workplace safety.

Nevertheless, despite the British textile interests' attempt to sabotage it, the Indian textile industry, particularly the Bengal jute industry, continued to compete with British manufacturers. This prompted yet another push for factory legislation, in which British manufacturers demanded improved working conditions for Indian workers. In 1911, a newer, more stringent factory legislation was enacted.[124] A little more than two decades later, the Factories Act 1934 was passed.

Following Pakistan's independence, the Factories Act 1934 has remained applicable across the country. As noted above, it was even re-enacted, without any notable changes, as the Sindh Factories Act 2015, as well as provincial Factories Acts across Pakistan. This continuation of the British law is representative of what Bronwen Manby identifies as the postcolonial states' predilection for half-baked ideas: "The colonial period was both long enough to do very serious damage to pre-existing institutions of government, and too short to create strong new institutions [. . .] post-colonial history shows how difficult it has been to create a functioning polity [. . .] how surprisingly persistent is the attachment to the units created by the colonizers."[125] Additionally, it is also quite possible that the colonial laws were kept in place with a strategic purpose. This also allowed the postcolonial state of Pakistan, which occupies a marginalised position in the global economic and

---

[123]Gilbert (1982), p. 367.

[124]During this period, even editorials in *The Times* newspaper (London) asked point blank if it was "true philanthropy or political immorality for England to interfere with industries which fed millions of men, women, and children." Gilbert (1982), p. 366.

[125]Manby (2009), p. 4.

political order, to protect international trade interests, by continuing to have a *British-approved* OSH law in place. In addition to this, the Factories Act 1934 promised much beyond what new state of Pakistan had the institutional capacity to deliver, hence, it allowed the state to show its *bona fide* intentions without actually attempting to, even progressively, deliver on worker safety. To this day, law in "the postcolonial modern state remains steadfastly a European construction."[126] The postcolonial sovereign imitates the coloniser; it dehumanises its own subjects and, in this instance, betrays the truth about its lowly prioritisation of labour protection and safety.[127] As a result, the OSH infrastructure in Pakistan is disjointed from economic, political, institutional and social realities in that it promises us everything in law, but provides nothing in fact. "Through their uncritical commitment... postcolonial states are complicit" in their own fate and plight.[128]

Perhaps because it was never locally rooted,[129] Pakistan's OSH infrastructure has been easy for the sovereign state to suspend: to make it present or absent as needed. During times of economic or political upheaval, the country's OSH infrastructure is simply abandoned through non-enforcement and fragmentation of the labour force. While the actions of Pakistani organisations like PILER and NTUF, which were able to achieve significant successes in the aftermath of the AE factory fire, are very important and commendable, they are isolated efforts and, ultimately, no substitute for mass labour action. Though such organisations can potentially cajole state institutions and other stakeholders to achieve formal and or isolated successes, they lack the power that comes with mass labour mobilisation.[130] Despite their best intentions, they work within the constraints of the prevailing global order: "the agentic role prescribed to NGOs is [. . .] one that foretells a reworking of democracy in ways that coalesce with global capitalist interests [. . .] NGOs remain trapped within an atheoretical framework of state versus civil society."[131] Neoliberal

---

[126]Otto (1996), pp. 337–338.

[127]Otto (1996), pp. 337–338; Ahmed K, Human Rights and the Non-human Black Body. Sur International Journal on Human Rights, December 2018, www.sur.conectas.org/en/human-rights-and-the-non-human-black-body/ (last accessed 3 August 2020).

[128]Manby (2009), p. 4.

[129]It is important to note that (postcolonial) Pakistan has heavily ostracised and brutalised *bona fide* trade unions. The Trade Unions Act (1926) passed by the British is still in force and has even been supplemented by the Industrial Relations Ordinance (1969). Laws aside, however, practical representation of workers' own voices is extremely limited. This marginalisation of trade unions is part of a global trend, but that discussion is beyond the scope of the present paper. See Khalil and Khan Z, A Profile of Trade Unionism and Industrial Relations in Pakistan. ILO, 2018, www.ilo.org/wcmsp5/groups/public/%2D%2D-asia/%2D%2D-ro-bangkok/%2D%2D-ilo-islamabad/documents/publication/wcms_626921.pdf (last accessed 22 July 2020).

[130]While NTUF is also registered as a trade union with the National Industrial Relations Commission, it primarily operates as an NGO. PILER is an NGO, albeit led by former trade unionists. Both organisations work within the global trend of increasing constraints on NGOs, but both continually work towards strengthening labour movements and facilitating national trade unions that can take power into their own hands.

[131]Kamat (2004), p. 156; See also, Brown et al. (2007), pp. 126–138.

interests view the rise of NGOs as a step towards democracy, but their "ascendancy can be traced to the end of the Cold War and the launch of the global free market."[132]

4 Ruse of Development: Core, Periphery and Global Production

The contemporary global economy is essentially dichotomous.[133] For the purposes of this chapter, I will refer to countries of the Global North as "core" countries/states/ economies, and to countries of the Global South as "peripheral" countries/states/ economies; this terminology is based on the works of Raul Prebisch, Andre Gunder Frank's dependency theory and Immanuel Wallerstein's world-systems analysis.[134] As opposed to the liberal economic theory, which holds sway over the ordering of the contemporary global world order, and claims that liberalised international trade allows countries to benefit from their comparative advantages and hence is advantageous to all,

> the concept of core-periphery views international trade as being an "unequal exchange" with surplus value flowing in one direction only, i.e. from the periphery (the Third world) to the core (the developed world). For the dependency theory, the free trade promoted by the core states and their multinational corporations renders the periphery ever more dependent and results in a "development of underdevelopment".[135]

In a nutshell, the core countries wield political and economic power. The peripheral countries are, as the name suggests, on the margins of global politics and economics. They provide cheap and expendable labour and low-cost manufacturing, thus making vast profits possible for the core economies.[136] This power imbalance allows risk to be outsourced, such as it was to the Ali Enterprises factory, which produced garments for the German company KiK.[137] Through this usage of "core" and "periphery," In using this dichotomous terminology, I also mean to evoke the peripheral existence of *homo sacer*, arguing that workers are the marginalised and

---

[132] Kamat (2004), p. 158.

[133] Chossudovsky (1979), pp. 61–62.

[134] For an overview of this "of core-periphery" terminology's historical development, see Spindler (2013).

[135] Spindler (2013), p. 177.

[136] Hitchings-Hales, Hundreds of H&M and Gap Factory Workers Abused Daily: Report. Global Citizen, 5 June 2018, www.globalcitizen.org/en/content/hm-gap-factory-abuse-fast-fashion-workers/ (last accessed 23 July 2020); Puplampu and Quartey (2012), pp. 151–156.

[137] The dichotomy between the centre economies and the peripheral economies is not a simple binary. There are at least two more variations that disrupt this dichotomy: such as, local manufacturers and profiteers in the peripheral countries (i.e. those who exploit the cheap and expendable labour in their countries), and marginalised workers in the core countries who are deprived of the working conditions associated with and pioneered by the core, and are denied fair wages or the right to association i.e. to form a trade union. See Orleck (2018).

voiceless *homo sacer* within both the global political economy and the peripheral state itself.[138] Gayatri Spivak noted that there is an entire mass of people who are illegible, inaudible and invisible; she referred to them as the "subaltern."[139] Building on this, Diane Otto showed that even when we engage in conversations about the power struggle between core and peripheral states, such as in the Third World Approaches to International Law (TWAIL) discourse, we often ignore the subaltern that resides within these states.[140]

Although they were common in the past,[141] today large industrial disasters and grave workplace hazards are significantly less frequent in core (developed) countries than they are in peripheral countries like Pakistan.[142] Due to improved OSH and labour conditions, manufacturing costs increased over time in core countries, eventually leading to an overwhelming proportion of manufacturing (and hence the risk of workplace accidents and diseases) being outsourced to the peripheral (developing) countries.[143]

---

[138]Otto (1996), pp. 337, 341.

[139]Morris and Spivak (2010). The term "subaltern" was first used by Antonio Gramsci (1971). See also Louai (2012).

[140]Otto (1996), pp. 337–338.

[141]For example, employers in the US consistently endangered workers through the eighteenth century. Although the first factory and railroad commissions were made around 1860–61, they were ineffective and powerless. It took big disasters before employers and government recognised need for safer workplaces, such as the 1860 Pemberton Mill collapse in Massachusetts which took 145 lives and injured another 166 and became a rallying point for improved safety standards and in 1877. Massachusetts was the first state in the US to pass a factory inspection law. The first federal law requiring safety equipment at the workplace, the Safety Appliance Act (applicable only to the railroad system) was passed in 1893. The 1878 Washburn "A" Mill explosion in Minneapolis took 18 lives, but new milling technology and safety standards were introduced thereafter. And it was in the aftermath of the Monongah Mine explosions of 1907, which claimed 361 lives, that the US government established the first United States Bureau of Mines in 1910, to oversee mine safety. After the 1911 Triangle Shirtwaist Factory disaster in New York and the death of 146 workers for the first permanent commission to inspect factory safety to be set up. See MacLaury J, The Job Safety Law of 1970: The Passage Was Perilious. US Department of Labour, March 1981, www.dol.gov/general/aboutdol/history/osha (last accessed 10 May 2020); Workers, and notable journalists, photographers and writers, agitated forcefully during the first 30 years of the twentieth century, resulting which there was widespread adoption of compensation laws which imposed liabilities on employers. In 1908, federal railroad workers, and in 1910, New York State got workmen's compensation law, followed by 44 more states through 1921. During his election campaign, President Woodrow Wilson (1913–1921) was the first to promise safer work conditions to workers and, in 1913, the Department of Labor was established under his government. See Occupational Health and Safety Administration, Can't take no more, 1980, www.youtube.com/watch?v=13gzGkQtVzg (last accessed 6 June 2020).

[142]Workplace accidents are 10 times more likely to occur in a developing country, while fatality rates in workplace accidents that do occur in developed countries are only half that of those that occur in of developing countries. See ILO Estimates Over 1 Million Work Related Fatalities Each Year, ILO, www.ilo.org/global/about-the-ilo/newsroom/news/WCMS_007969/lang%2D%2Den/index.htm (last accessed 9 May 2020).

[143]Feenstra (1998), pp. 499–500.

OSH is usually discussed as a normative concern for developing safe and conscientious workplaces with the support of technical expertise, however, the economic viability of OSH mechanisms plays a key role.[144] For example, in the United States, OSH standards are frequently subjected to a cost-benefit analysis.[145] Indeed, several safety and health regulations proposed by the US Department of Labor have been blocked or influenced due to the consideration of free market guidelines in the decision-making criteria.[146] In Germany, alternatively, OSH standards are primarily set by technical experts, along with the federal and local governments, in a political environment that prevents economics from playing a direct role in standard setting.[147] While OSH standards themselves may remain relatively untainted by economic considerations in Germany, unlike the US, there are no bars in *either* country, or generally in any country in the Global North, against outsourcing OSH risks to other countries like Pakistan, where OSH and labour rights stand abducted.[148] This reinforces the difference between the core and the periphery, as otherwise unbending norms and principles disappear precisely when the core-periphery relation of production comes into being.

[144]Klimnik (1988), pp. 162–165.

[145]Klimnik (1988), pp. 165–167. Historically, US courts have had a key role in determining whether OSH or other labour legislation is enforced or outlawed (based on economic beliefs). Roughly during the same period, from 1897 to 1937, the US Supreme Court was also suffering through what became known as the Lochner Era, where it was striking down any attempts made by the government to regulate the manufacturing processes to make them safer and more just for workers. The Lochner Era is understood to begin with *Allgeyer v. Louisiana*, 165 U.S. 578 (1897), in which the court struck down state legislation prohibiting foreign corporations from doing business in the state because it was deemed to be violating an individual's liberty of contract. It was the first case in which the Supreme Court interpreted the word *liberty* in the Due Process Clause of the Fourteenth Amendment (which was one of the three amendments that abolished slavery and declared all persons born or naturalized on American soil to be equal citizens before the law) to mean economic liberty. This era came to an end with the case of *West Coast Hotel Co. v. Parrish*, 300 U.S. 379 (1937), in which the Supreme Court overturned its own previous decision in *Adkins v. Children's Hospital*, 261 U.S. 525 (1923), and upheld minimum wage legislation, stating that it was valid and did not impinge upon the freedom to contract.

[146]Klimnik (1988), pp. 165, 167 (footnote 135, 136). "The threat of judicial review often eliminates controversial parts of regulations in the United States." Several regulations are delayed for years before they become effective. 167. See *Industrial Union Dep't v. American Petroleum Inst.*, 448 U.S. 607 at 639 (1980) (benzene standard held invalid.) OSHA stayed the publication of lists of potential occupational carcinogens in the wake of the Industrial Union Department. Also See 48 Fed. Reg. 243 (1983); 47 Fed. Reg. 187 (1982). 29 C.F.R. § 1990.121 note (1986).

[147]Klimnik (1988), p. 166.

[148]Meyer (2018), pp. 499–505.

4.1 Pakistan: Postcolony in the Global Political Economy

As a peripheral country, the terms of Pakistan's statehood are determined by the core.[149] Low-cost manufacturing in peripheral (developing) countries is possible because the costs, of safe workplaces and adequately remunerated labour, are avoided. Although laws are in place to ensure both safety and remuneration, there is no enforcement of these laws and the penalties for violating them are minimal.[150] After independence in 1947, Pakistan sought to modernise its economy. This ambition was at its peak during the dictatorship of Field Marshall Ayub Khan (1958–1968); both the economy and the political structure were geared towards earning the favour of the US.[151] In the race to improve economic growth, the liberal "trickle down" approach to prosperity was enthusiastically adopted during the rule of General Ayub Khan.[152] This ambition cost labour protections and safety,[153] as labourers' demands for better protections kept getting pushed further and further to the side lines.[154]

Although workers movements gained some strength after the independence of Pakistan, and various labour-friendly laws were passed during the 1960s and 1970s,[155] their enforcement remained subservient to national economic interests, which sought to catch up with the core economies, that in turn, aimed to instrumentalise these interests. The state's tolerance for labour movements and its willingness to placate workers was intermittent—and laced with its brutalisation of

[149]Otto (1996), p. 337.

[150]Chossudovsky (1979), pp. 61–62. For the garment industry, the rough breakdown is that the foreign companies make 90 percent of the profits, while the local manufacturers get nine percent of the profits and workers get one percent. Orleck (2018), p. 164.

[151]Afzal (2007), p. 725; Child and Kaneda (1975); Ahmed (1974).

[152]"Pakistan's economy experienced exceptional and spectacular growth rates in all sectors of the economy, which were the outcome of the 'functional inequality' growth strategy, highly protective industrial policy and US experts' direct involvement in the planning process. There was enviable growth, but it did not adequately trickle down to the poorer sections as well as regions". Afzal (2007), p. 725.

[153]Afzal (2007). See also Trickle Down Approach and its Efficacy. Dawn, 8 June 2009, www.dawn.com/news/838887/trickle-down-approach-and-its-efficacy (last accessed 3 May 2020).

[154]"The International Labour Organisation (ILO) review mission of 1986 found that as far as the Right of Association was concerned, Pakistani law excluded 75 per cent of the workforce from the Right of Association. And the remaining 25 per cent could not access this right without difficulties." See Sumbul and Ali, Labour Movement in Pakistan. Alternatives International, 1 June 2017, www.alterinter.org/?Labour-Movement-in-Pakistan (last accessed 12 May 2020).

[155]Examples include the West Pakistan Employees' Social Security Ordinance (1965), the Industrial Relations Ordinance (1969), the West Pakistan Industrial and Commercial Employment (Standing Orders) Ordinance (1968), the West Pakistan Shops and Establishments Ordinance (1969), the Workers' Welfare Fund Ordinance (1971), and the Employees' Old-Age Benefits Act (1976).

labour struggles.[156] In the more recent decades after the Cold War, workers movements in Pakistan have been completely destabilised due to intrusive policies adopted by institutions like the World Bank and the International Monetary Fund, and their Structural Adjustment Programs, as well as the EU's GSP+ programme.[157]

4.2 *Rising Trade Liberalisation and Falling Worker Safety: Pakistan Since the Cold War*

On the global front, when the Cold War ended, it appeared that capitalism had triumphed and newly independent or recently decolonised peripheral countries marched to legitimise themselves as liberal democracies.[158] Becoming a bona fide liberal democracy, that is truly open to aspirations of trade liberalisation and the accompanying baggage, became the undisputed ideal for all countries in the post-Cold War period. As a result, institutions that could facilitate the achievement of this ideal, such as the World Bank, IMF, World Trade Organization and relevant programmes of the European Union also gained more power.[159] The IMF and the World Bank extend large loans to peripheral countries purportedly to facilitate their development into robust liberal democracies. After these peripheral countries are deeply and inextricably indebted, the IMF and World Bank buy or forgive their debts in return for these countries make it "easier, cheaper and more profitable for foreign companies to invest."[160] Therefore, it is extremely important that the non-enforcement of labour laws described above should be viewed as part of a larger "imperial international economic policy" being implemented by the core countries through institutions like the IMF, World Bank and WTO.

Essentially, this policy is "concerned with (a) the regulation of trade and of the international monetary system; and (b) the monitoring of capital flows and 'foreign aid' between core and periphery."[161] Within this policy, the IMF has played a particularly key role in monitoring the economic policies of peripheral states, while the core countries have benefitted immensely. The global textile and garment

---

[156]Military dictatorships passed favourable laws, while mainstream political parties such as the Pakistan People's Party (PPP) also co-opted the rhetoric of the labour movement and ran election campaigns for the December 1971 election on the promise of land and labour reforms. See Pakistan Forum (1972).

[157]See Sumbul and Ali, Labour Movement in Pakistan. Alternatives International, 1 June 2017, www.alterinter.org/?Labour-Movement-in-Pakistan (last accessed 12 May 2020).

[158]Hobson (2009), p. 383.

[159]Sheth (1995), p. 35; Hobson (2009), p. 384.

[160]Orleck (2018), p. 125.

[161]Chossudovsky (1979), p. 64.

industry provides a prime example of this trend, as it "tripled in size and value between the years 2005 and 2015."[162]

Wielding this bolstered power, institutions like the IMF or World Bank etc. Have been able to ensure the aggressive theoretical deployment and practical abduction of occupational health and safety infrastructures[163] coupled with the liberalisation of economies to make them more amenable to foreign investment.[164] As this post-Cold War trade liberalisation gained a foothold in Pakistan, the state also began to suspend worker safety that was ostensibly guaranteed by law (at least in factories). As Mohammad Afzal describes it:

> Pakistan started liberalising the economy with the help of IMF and World Bank in 1982-83 [...] The process of liberalisation started during 6th Five-Year-Plan (1983-88) and was implemented with great force after 1988. The government pursued vigorous trade liberalisation in the beginning of 1990s to convert the economy from a relatively inward looking to an open and outward looking economy. Government has taken a number of measures during 1990s that includes: privatisation, liberalisation of trade and foreign exchange, and opening up its capital markets to foreign investors [...] to integrate its economy with rest of the world.[165]

In 1986, the IMF's Structural Adjustment Programs first came to Pakistan and obliged the country to engage in progressive privatisation (particularly) of public goods and open itself to liberalised international trade. At the same time, unannounced factory inspections were suspended in order to encourage trade (and discourage worker safety). According to PILER's Executive Director, Karamat Ali, General Zia-ul-Haq, who governed Pakistan from 1977 to 1988, even "formally announced that no inspection could take place without the concurrence of the employer. The 1986 ILO review mission on health and safety said that going by the current capacity of the inspectorate, a factory inspected in 1986 would only get its next turn for inspection after 30 years."[166] Then, in the early 2000s, there came a new wave of trade liberalisation under the regime of General Pervez Musharraf. Through new industrial policies that remain shrouded in mystery to this day, safety

---

[162]Orleck (2018), p. 126.

[163]Swaroop V, World Bank's Experience with Structural Reforms for Growth and Development. World Bank, May 2016, www.documents.worldbank.org/curated/en/826251468185377264/pdf/105822-NWP-ADD-SERIES-MFM-Discussion-Paper-11-PUBLIC.pdf, p. 2 (last accessed 6 August 2020); Pasha H, GSP Pus Status and Compliance of Labour Standards. Friedrich-Ebert-Stiftung, November 2014, www.library.fes.de/pdf-files/bueros/pakistan/11046.pdf (last accessed 4 August 2020).

[164]Trade liberalisation refers to the removal of tariffs and non-tariff barriers to trade so that economies can be integrated into the global economy. See IMF Staff, Global Trade Liberalization and Developing Countries. International Monetary Fund, November 2001, www.imf.org/external/np/exr/ib/2001/110801.htm (last accessed 23 May 2020).

[165]Afzal (2007), p. 726.

[166]See See Sumbul D and Ali K, Labour Movement in Pakistan. Alternatives International, 1 June 2017, www.alterinter.org/?Labour-Movement-in-Pakistan (last accessed 12 May 2020).

inspections were suspended.[167] Both General Zia-ul-Haq and General Musharraf's policies made it easier and cheaper for local manufacturers to set up or operate factories and to produce for foreign buyers. Meanwhile, workers suffered, poverty rose, and quality of life fell, particularly throughout the 1990s when access to education, health and housing decreased.[168] Local labour movements in many peripheral countries were further destabilised by the fact that workers could no longer raise their voices as a unified front because unionisation was heavily discouraged and penalized.[169] In Pakistan, workers' movements that were struggling for better and more equitable working conditions were suppressed, often brutally.[170] Workplaces became increasingly unsafe, terms of employment changed, and workers' jobs were contractualised *en masse*.[171]

4.3 Utopian Aspirations and Dystopian Actions

Based on the above discussion, I argue that peripheral countries are not considered part of the "human world," but essentially as savage peoples living on the margins of human civilisation.[172] Therefore, peripheral countries (are required to) maintain blind fidelity to formal structures, such as OSH laws that imitate and monkey liberal democracies of the core, but they are equally required to not have fidelity to the substantive content signified by these formal structures, that is, in this case to worker safety. In order to be considered civilised and to participate global politics, peripheral states must regurgitate the ideals and formal structures of the core. Yet, in order to survive global economics, they must abandon these purportedly universal norms and principles to get their hands dirty. The *form* of OSH infrastructure developed by former colonial masters and powerful liberal democracies has become entrenched as the universal yardstick and aspirational blueprint blindly adopted or continued by countries like Pakistan.[173] When laws, standards or mechanisms that mirror core countries are adopted in Pakistan, they are considered laudable, *regardless* of whether it is institutionally possible to implement them or whether they sustainably and realistically address its needs. It appears that there is comfort in promising

[167] Ijaz S, No Room to Bargain. Human Rights Watch, 23 January 2019, www.hrw.org/report/2019/01/23/no-room-bargain/unfair-and-abusive-labor-practices-pakistan (last accessed 12 August 2020); Enquiry Report: Fire Incident at Ali Enterprises S.I.T.E Karachi on 11th September 2012. Federal Investigation Agency, Sindh Zone Karachi, 3 October 2012, Court File of Constitutional Petition No. 3318 of 2012, p. 1333.

[168] Afzal (2007), p. 726.

[169] Orleck (2018).

[170] Pakistan Forum (1972), pp. 13–16; Ali (2005), pp. 83–107.

[171] Orleck (2018).

[172] Mbembe (2003); Deleuze and Guattari (1980), p. 445.

[173] Hobson (2009), p. 383.

everything. And because it is impossible to deliver that everything, the promise alone has to suffice. Nothing is delivered upon.[174] This is exemplified by the policies, to suspend inspections and contractualise workers, which were adopted by General Ayub Khan, General Zia-ul-Haq and General Parvez Musharraf on an ad hoc basis, and by provincial governments that created trade policies or issued orders that suspended factory inspections by their respective labour departments.[175] During his time in office, former Prime Minister Zulfiqar Ali Bhutto also had his share of stand-offs with the labour movement when they got in the way of his economic aspirations for the country, despite the fact that he ran for election on a pro-labour mandate.[176]

Slowly but surely, state suppression and direct and indirect violence wore down the labour movement in Pakistan.[177] At present, only one percent of the workforce is unionised. This makes workers' resistance to cruel and dehumanising labour practices more difficult, if not virtually impossible in practice. As a result, workplaces are increasingly unsafe and employers can get away with banning and sabotaging *bona fide* labour unions, and even setting up their own pocket unions to disrupt the work of *bona fide* unions.[178] Countries that once boasted strong labour movements now find themselves speeding towards a "global race to the bottom."[179] OSH is absent or

---

[174]For example, the Sindh Occupational Safety and Health Act 2017 promises inspections, trainings, curriculums, and coordination with the Sindh Building Control Authority (SBCA) and expands the scope of the OSH infrastructure all the way to self-employed persons. Yet, it is not based on any quantitative research and it provides no mechanism through which the Sindh Labour Department could actually achieve even half of these aspirations. For example, if the law had included an incremental implementation scheme where X, Y or Z had to be implemented within the next five years, then perhaps A, B and C could have been implemented in the next five years, and so forth. Alternatively, or additionally, the responsibility for implementing the Sindh Occupational Safety and Health Act could have been shared with the local governments' union councils, or inspectors from the SBCA and Sindh Labour Department could have been pooled to ensure quicker or more thorough inspections. However, this law was not designed to be enforced, only to imitate the ideal.

[175]"The policy for labor inspections changed in 2003 after a military coup by Gen. Pervez Musharraf [. . .] Punjab, the country's largest province, banned labor inspections through the Punjab Industry Policy in 2003 with the objective of 'developing an industry and business-friendly environment to attract fresh investment'." Ijaz S, No Room to Bargain. Human Rights Watch, 23 January 2019, www.hrw.org/report/2019/01/23/no-room-bargain/unfair-and-abusive-labor-practices-pakistan (last accessed 12 August 2020).

[176]Ali (2005).

[177]See Eleazar and Khan, White-lipped, Blue-collared and Invisible. Himal Magazine, 31 January 2018, www.himalmag.com/pakistan-privatisation-labour-unions-history/ (last accessed 12 May 2020).

[178]See Sumbul and Ali, Labour Movement in Pakistan. Alternatives International, 1 June 2017, www.alterinter.org/?Labour-Movement-in-Pakistan (last accessed 12 May 2020).

[179]Orleck (2018), p. 126; "Now, there are some 8,500 plus registered trade unions with a combined membership of not more than 500,000 workers. And these unions exist in not more than 1,500 enterprises. On an average, there are more than four or five unions in each plant." See Sumbul and Ali, Labour Movement in Pakistan. Alternatives International, 1 June 2017, www.alterinter.org/?Labour-Movement-in-Pakistan (last accessed 12 May 2020).

dysfunctional because vastly profitable foreign companies from core countries want cheap production and need or want peripheral countries to provide this at the cost of their labour and safety regimes. This is made possible by a combination of international pressure, enticement and directions from international financial institutions, such as the IMF, to open peripheral economies to international trade.

Interestingly, the core countries, just as colonisers did before them or as they did as colonisers, continue to peddle the narrative that these disruptions actually benefit peripheral countries. For example, in the mid-1990s, as part of its campaign titled the "girl effect," the biggest shoe company in the world, Nike, engaged the famous feminist historian Jill Ker Conway to tour college campuses and sell the idea that sweatshop work, in homes or in factories such as the Ali Enterprises factory, was liberating for women.[180]

5 Incarcerated on the Outside: The Contractual Worker—Legality Versus Reality

The workers at the Ali Enterprises factory worked for an average of 11 to 14 h a day, had no access to a healthcare plan, and, not even a single worker had an appointment letter that could establish a clear employment relationship with Ali Enterprises.[181] The majority of the Pakistani labour force, particularly in the garment and textile industry, is employed as contractual labour through third-party subcontractors.[182] As a matter of practice, relying on the indirect nature of the workers' employment, employers deny them basic rights and entitlements, such as proof of employment, safe workplaces, compensation in case of injury, fatality or disease, social security, healthcare, and even the timely payment of minimum wages.[183] Under the system of subcontracting, employers such as Ali Enterprises pay a lump sum to a subcontractor, who then hires and fires workers as it pleases them.[184] This is a dehumanising practice. Workers should be hired as formal or permanent employees who would have to be given their rights such as negotiating power and employment benefits.

[180]Orleck (2018), pp. 130–133.

[181]Farhat, Baldia Factory Fire Incident 4 years of successful campaign for justice. December 2016, www.piler.org.pk/wp-content/uploads/2017/02/Brief_Baldia_Factory_Fire-_Incident.pdf (last accessed 12 August 2020).

[182]Ijaz S, No Room to Bargain. Human Rights Watch, 23 January 2019, www.hrw.org/report/2019/01/23/no-room-bargain/unfair-and-abusive-labor-practices-pakistan (last accessed 12 August 2020).

[183]Ijaz S, No Room to Bargain. Human Rights Watch, 23 January 2019, www.hrw.org/report/2019/01/23/no-room-bargain/unfair-and-abusive-labor-practices-pakistan (last accessed 12 August 2020).

[184]Ijaz S, No Room to Bargain. Human Rights Watch, 23 January 2019, www.hrw.org/report/2019/01/23/no-room-bargain/unfair-and-abusive-labor-practices-pakistan (last accessed 12 August 2020).

Instead, the workers' labour is sieved from their humanity, and it is bought and sold from the subcontractor as if it were a textile sold by a retailer.

The trend towards hiring contractual labour is global, but it is particularly dominant in peripheral states. It is accompanied by trade liberalisation, absentee labour protections, and dishevelled labour movements.[185] This sterilised and zombified workforce is a manifestation of *homo sacer*. The workers whose employers "evade legal responsibility for meeting minimum wage, maximum hours, and safety standards by classifying them as 'temporary' or as 'contract' employees provided by third party labour suppliers" have no job security, seniority, or benefits.[186] I agree with Annelise Orleck; these workers are truly the "victims of what should be considered a vast criminal conspiracy."[187] Although there are nuances that differentiate contract workers from subcontracted workers and casual workers,[188] for the purposes of this discussion, I will collectively refer to those who are denied basic workplace safety and employment benefits, and thus reside in a limbo between worker and non-worker status, as the "precariat."[189]

It is a widely held belief that if a worker is a precariat, then they are not entitled to labour protections,[190] but, legally speaking, this is a mistake. In legal terms, there are various laws and a plethora of legal precedent from case law which confirm that the precariat must be as protected as any other worker in Pakistan, particularly in terms of workplace safety, and almost as protected with respect to their terms of employment. This is even obvious from the definitions of a "worker" provided in some of the key labour laws of Pakistan, as applicable to the province of Sindh. First, the Sindh Factories Act of 2015 stipulates that "no worker shall be employed through an agency or contractor or sub-contractor or middleman or agent, to perform production related work."[191] That is, first, the Sindh Factories Act 2015 forbids the hiring of workers through contractors or subcontractors. That is, it forbids the use of precariat labour.[192] The Sindh Workers' Welfare Fund Act of 2014 states that workers include anyone employed "either directly or through a contractor whether the terms of employment be expressed or implied."[193] The Sindh Employees Social Security Institution Act of 2016 states that an "employee" means any person "employed,

[185]Orleck (2018).

[186]Orleck (2018), p. 67.

[187]Orleck (2018), p. 100.

[188]Section 2 of the Sindh Terms of Employment (Standing Orders) Act, 2015 (Sindh Act No. XI of 2016).

[189]Orleck (2018), p. 100.

[190]Orleck (2018), p. 67; Ijaz S, No Room to Bargain. Human Rights Watch, 23 January 2019, www.hrw.org/report/2019/01/23/no-room-bargain/unfair-and-abusive-labor-practices-pakistan (last accessed 12 August 2020).

[191]Section 2(n) of the Sindh Factories Act 2015.

[192]Section 2(n) of the Sindh Factories Act 2015.

[193]Section 2(m) of the Sindh Workers Welfare Fund Act (2014).

whether directly or through any other person for wages or otherwise."[194] Even the 1923 Workmen's Compensation Act states that a "workman" is "other than a person whose employment is of a casual nature and who is employed otherwise than for the purposes of the employer's trade or business."[195] This thus includes contractual workers but omits casual employees from the ambit of workmen entitled to compensation, and has effectively read down with respect to this omission of casual workers[196] on the principle of consistency.[197]

According to the Sindh Terms of Employment (Standing Orders) Act 2015, a "'permanent worker'" is a worker who has been engaged on work of permanent nature likely to last more than nine months and who has satisfactorily completed a probationary period of three months"[198] and legal precedent clearly states that regardless of the garb under which workers have been hired, "it is essential to look to the nature of work against which he has been employed" in order to determine if they are to be deemed to have rights as permanent workers. That is, if the job is anticipated to last nine months, then the worker employed for it shall be deemed a permanent worker who cannot be arbitrarily removed from service.[199] The terms of employment of workers cannot legally be manipulated to deny the protections to which they would be entitled as permanent workers.[200] If the nature of a job is that of permanent work, then a worker is to be deemed a permanent employee.[201]

So, as the law strictly stands, the precariat is legally protected. Even generally, although previously the courts denied coverage of labour laws to contractual workers,[202] in recent years they have held that labour laws *do* apply to contract workers—on the principle of consistency.[203] Nevertheless, these developments in the ivory towers of law and law-making are distant from the lived reality of the precariat, who is in fact, not protected from even the worst form of abuse and

[194]Section 2(9) of the Sindh Employees Social Security Institution Act 2016.

[195]Section 2(n) of the Workmen's Compensation Act 1923.

[196]The doctrine of reading down provides judges with an interpretive tool for narrowing or widening the scope of a statute in order to make the statute accord with constitutional principles. See Hume (2014), p. 620.

[197]AIR 1946 All. 473; P L D 1964 Kar. 406; 1970 P L C 747; P L D 1971 Dacca 200: "In view of the above, it is apparent that a labourer who is paid his wages on a daily or weekly basis can also be termed as a workman within the meaning of clause (n) of section 2(1) of the P W. C. Act, 1923."

[198]Clause 1(b) of the Schedule to the Sindh Terms of Employment (Standing Orders) Act, 2015.

[199]2001 PLC Supreme Court 583 at Para 4.

[200]2002 PLC Supreme Court 67 at Para 8 & 11.

[201]2018 PLC Supreme Court 182 at Para 4; See also 2020 PLC Sindh High Court 19 at Para 4, 17 (Upheld decision of the lower court to reinstate workers not formally hired as permanent workers with back benefits) and 1989 SCMR 888 at Para 4 & 6(9) (regarding payment of social security being the responsibility of principal employer even if the subcontractor failed to make social security contributions).

[202]See 1993 S C M R 672; P L D 2000 Supreme Court 207.

[203]See 2011 PLD Supreme Court 37; 2012 PLC 232; 2018 PLC (CS) 228; 2016 P L C (C.S) 179; 2000 PLD Supreme Court 207.

endangerment, as has been exemplified by the AE factory fire. Since there is a large surplus of labour,[204] workers are replaceable and, as shown above, the law is unenforced as it is. Thus, the employers are neither threatened by a dearth of workers nor by punishment under the law. Using the fact that workers are hired through contractors, employers excuse themselves from responsibility by saying that the workers are not directly employed by them and thus manage to deny the workers their rights and entitlements. The precariat is confined on the outside of law.

Despite these legal protections, the precariat continues to be endangered. As Agamben asserts, the state of exception "is a hybrid of law and fact in which the two terms have become indistinguishable."[205] In case of injury, fatality or disease, the foreign companies whose product the precariat is making will not admit any liability and will hold the factory accountable, while the factory will hold the subcontractor accountable, from whom the precariat will often not even have proof of employment.[206] The precariat thus continues to be incarcerated in limbo, unprotected. The *homo sacer*—in this case, the incarcerated precariat—is "devoid of any representable identity" and "is absolutely irrelevant to the State."[207] Here, the precariat's factual existence, their work and their legal non-existence, without proof of employment or a clear employment relationship, are constantly interchangeable; "a continent may integrate on liberal-democratic agenda, still there would be no place for those who remain outside the law."[208]

5.1 Use and Abuse: Legal Protections Versus Contracts

Peripheral states are, of course, willing participants in the dehumanisation of their workers, who are forced into unsafe and cruel working conditions and suffer disasters like the Ali Enterprises factory fire. The peripheral state is haunted and animated by methods of the core.[209] The methodology of instrumentalisation of entire populations (workers in this case), as if they were a mere tool for statecraft, is perhaps equally rooted in colonial history and in the contemporary global political economy. Mass contractualisation of the workforce and the consequent denial of workers' rights and entitlements through the convoluted use of legal contracts, such as the one between the principal employer and the subcontractor, betrays an alarming truth—the law "only rules over what it is capable of interiorizing" and these internal

[204] Labour Force Survey (2017–18), Pakistan Bureau of Statistics.
[205] Agamben (1998), p. 170.
[206] As KiK initially did, for example.
[207] Agamben, Coming Community, pp. 86–87 quoted in Nashef (2017).
[208] Samaddar (2010), p. xxvi.
[209] Mbembe (2003), p. 25.

colonies of those confined on the outside of law are governed by the state of exception.[210] Here perhaps the postcolonial state is mirroring the character of its antecedent—the colony which "were 'frontiers' in which 'savages' resided."[211] Hence, the precariat is interiorised through oral or informal contracts and wages but exteriorised from the protections of labour law under which, for example, safe working conditions could be demanded. The precariat is banished to the state of exception where labour law practically does not apply.[212]

Labour law recognises the power differential between workers and employers. Accordingly, it grants concrete protections like guaranteed compensation in cases of workplace fatality, injury, or disease. On the other hand, contract law assumes the equality of contracting parties. Hence, the contractualisation of workers has pre-emptively thrown many workers outside the basic protections of labour law; the fact that contractual norms govern their day-to-day employment has meant that increasingly large numbers of workers are in muddy waters. Because workers are unprotected and the free supply of labour makes them readily replaceable, workers are more easily coerced into working in unsafe conditions. Contractualisation has thrown workers into uncertainties and made them excessively vulnerable to exploitation.[213]

---

[210] Mbembe (2003), p. 24.

[211] Deleuze and Guattari (1980), p. 445.

[212] Mbembe (2003), p. 24.

[213] The Ali Enterprises Factory was producing garments for the German company KiK. As it presently stands, hiring the services of a Pakistani worker is almost 24 times cheaper for a European company than hiring a European worker. For example, as of May 2020, the minimum wage payable to a Pakistani worker was approximately 17,500 Pakistani rupees per month. According to reports, the average textile worker works 10 h per day, six days per week. The German minimum wage for 2020 is 9.75 euros per hour, which is 1703 Pakistani rupees. If a worker in Germany works a 10-h day, even if they are not paid an overtime rate, they would be making 17,030 Rupees for 10 h of work. In one day, a worker in Germany is likely to make as much money as a worker in Pakistan makes in a month. Unlike the Pakistani worker, the German worker is also likely to have access to health insurance, workplace safety, adequate housing, sickness and unemployment benefits, free higher education, and (state run/price regulated) public transport. Moreover, the average household size in Pakistan is 6.8 persons, while the average household size in Germany is 2.1 persons. Therefore, the Pakistani worker has more dependents, including elderly family members (whom the state does not provide health or pension) and children (for whom the state does not provide healthcare or primary education and need to be educated on the worker's dime. So, it is even more important for the worker in Pakistan to have safe work and to stay healthy and alive even if just to sustain their dependents. However, do note that this comparison is not adjusted for the fact that the cost of living may be higher in Germany but it is believed that despite that, it is fairly straightforward to imagine that the workers in Pakistan are vastly disadvantaged compared to the ones in Germany. Additionally, production of goods for foreign markets also corrodes the limited pool of basic resources available to those in peripheral economies. For example, the production of one T-shirt takes approximately 2700 l of water while one pair of jeans consumes approximately 9982 l of water (Orleck 2018).

5.2 *The Bangladesh Accord on Fire and Building Safety*

In the face of apathetic government agencies, ineffective OSH infrastructure, and convoluted myths and realities regarding who is liable when workers suffer death, injury, or disease, workers have begun to seek means to hold foreign companies directly accountable. They are "no longer willing to let them hide behind their complex and fragmented global value chains."[214] Kalpona Akhter, the founder of the Bangladesh Centre for Worker Solidarity, puts it simply: "There is a worker and a clothing company. I don't want to know who is in between."[215]

In 2013, following in the wake of the Raza Plaza collapse, the Tazreen Fashions factory fire, and other disasters, the workers of Bangladesh, organising through trade unions and in cooperation with NGOs, international activists, and OSH experts drafted the Bangladesh Accord on Fire and Building Safety (Bangladesh Accord).[216] However, in mid-2018, the Bangladesh Accord was sued by a Bangladeshi factory owner, who had been removed from the list of approved suppliers due to safety breaches. In June 2018, the Bangladeshi Minister for Commerce stated that the government-led body, which in truth "reports a woefully low 29% completion rate for mandatory safety renovations at factories the government is ostensibly regulating,"[217] was somehow capable of overseeing workers' safety. As such, he announced that the Bangladesh Accord was no longer needed, saying "factories are now safe and worker-friendly."[218] Thus, the Bangladesh Accord now stands on precarious ground, much like the precariat, whose precarious employment and working conditions it aims to protect.

The key difference between labour law and most contractually governed frameworks is that the latter does not recognize power differential between workers and employers. Although the Bangladesh Accord is something like a traditional bargaining agreement between labour representatives and employers, its treatment by actors like the local manufacturers and the Bangladeshi government has resembled that of a (multi-stakeholder) contract. This is because there is no direct liability

---

[214]Orleck (2018), p. 139.

[215]Orleck (2018), p. 139.

[216]With the help of global partners, it was even able to take major international companies to the Permanent Court of Arbitration in Geneva and get large compensation settlements for workers. See: Bangladesh Accord arbitration cases – resulting in millions-of-dollars in settlements – officially closed, UNI Global, 18 July 2018, www.uniglobalunion.org/news/bangladesh-accord-arbitration-cases-resulting-millions-dollars-settlements-officially-closed (last accessed 24 May 2020); For a detailed discussion, see Ben Vanpeperstraete's chapter in this book.

[217]See Christie, Response to Today's High Court Hearing on Bangladesh Accord. Clean Clothes Campaign, 29 November 2018, www.cleanclothes.org/news/2018/11/29/response-to-todays-high-court-hearing-on-the-bangladesh-accord (last accessed 24 May 2020).

[218]See Davoise, On borrowed time: five years after the Rana Plaza disaster, the Bangladesh Accord faces Court ordered closure. INTLAWGRRLS, 28 November 2018, www.ilg2.org/2018/11/28/on-borrowed-time-five-years-after-the-rana-plaza-disaster-the-bangladesh-accord-faces-court-ordered-closure/ (last accessed 24 May 2020).

or legal obligation between the labour representatives, their allies and the foreign brands that (have been convinced to) make commitments under the Bangladesh Accord. Unfortunately, under the prevailing paradigm of "imperial international economic policy," and the resultantly fragmented global value chains and independent contracts, labour representatives and allies have had to creatively improvise but this has not protected them from attack. Because the Bangladesh Accord is essentially a contract between foreign companies and trade unions, NGOs, and INGOs, it is vulnerable to interventions from the local manufacturers, government and the courts of Bangladesh.[219]

Supply contracts of foreign companies for manufacturers in peripheral economies are often puffed up with requirements, such as the evidently hollow SA-8000 certification, which had been obtained by both the Ali Enterprises factory in Pakistan (approximately 20 days before the 2012 fire) and by Rana Plaza in Bangladesh (also less than a month before its 2013 collapse).[220] This ill-intentioned bid at seeking legitimacy without taking responsibility for safety lapses is somewhat similar to, although perhaps worse than, twentieth-century United States. In the early twentieth century, caught in the midst of a movement for workplace safety and facing increased costs for workplace injuries and fatalities, US businesses were also moved to self-regulate in what became known as the Voluntary Safety Movement. Under this movement, the Voluntary Safety Council was established in 1913 and it pushed for safety engineering and better working practices. However, this self-regulation reeked of the same self-interest that British textile interests had shown in British India. Most safety education imparted to workers was premised on the notion that the majority of workplace accidents were due to the workers' negligence. It promoted the notion of "their fault, their liability." The Voluntary Safety Movement also funded various propaganda. For example, in 1911, the year of the Triangle Shirtwaist Factory fire mentioned above (which took 146 lives mostly consisting of young immigrant women) the National Association of Manufacturers reigned in the support of progressive filmmaker James Oppenheim to produce the film *The Crime of Carelessness*, stressing that workers were the cause of workplace accidents.[221]

---

[219]See Christie, Response to Today's High Court Hearing on Bangladesh Accord. Clean Clothes Campaign, 29 November 2018, www.cleanclothes.org/news/2018/11/29/response-to-todays-high-court-hearing-on-the-bangladesh-accord (last accessed 24 May 2020).

[220]Theuws et al (2013).

[221]Occupational Health and Safety Administration, Can't take no more. 1980, www.youtube.com/watch?v=13gzGkQtVzg (last accessed 6 June 2020).

6 Conclusion

As we have seen above, the absence or presence of OSH depends on the needs of the global economy more than it does on actual workplace hazards. The history of OSH in Pakistan is one of regulation and dis-operationalisation, as per the needs of the powers that be. The OSH infrastructure in Pakistan is not meant to make the workplace safer, instead it is an empty signifier, an ornamental imitation of core countries' OSH infrastructures. These laws are utopian insofar as they do not reflect the economic or regulatory capacity of Pakistan, and dystopian in that completely disregarding them and endangering workers is allowed, if not encouraged, in practice. OSH infrastructures, whether deployed by peripheral states or at the behest of core countries, are a legal fiction at best—to be progressively realised at an unknown date in the unforeseeable future. A useful way to mitigate the existing problems, whilst recognizing the constraints of the global politico-economic order, may be to indigenise and democratise the OSH infrastructure through actual and substantive worker participation, legal liability for foreign companies (that outsource their production), and the activation of transnational solidarity among workers.[222]

On regulators' end, instead of blindly copying the OSH infrastructures of core countries, we would need to rethink OSH in terms of local context. As a first step towards worker safety, the OSH mandate needs to be stratified and staggered such that the higher priority safety requirements are separated in the interim and pursued with the full force of the existing institutional capacity, so that the most urgent needs of workplace safety can be addressed first and the rest can follow. The remaining aspects of workplace safety can be progressively mainstreamed as institutional capacities are improved and increased. Less expensive alternatives or community-based mechanisms of enforcement (such as Local Governments and Union Councils being made responsible for workplace inspections based on checklists prepared by technical experts) could also potentially be explored. Second, it is important for regulatory authorities to reject self-regulatory certifications that bolster supply contracts, such as the SA-8000. If worker safety is to be improved, labour law must be reinstated and the trend towards contractualization of labour law must be stopped. Third, regulator accountability mechanisms need to be established as well. Government regulators need to be capacitated, empowered, and held accountable. Fourth, this accountability would perhaps only be possible if the regulator was directly accountable to the workers, through participatory and democratic mechanisms. Eventually, the seats at the table need to be in proportion to the number of lives at stake, not only according to the profits at stake. To give each group one seat each would be to perpetuate the dehumanisation of the precariat by nakedly equating the value of money (of local and global companies), power (of regulators), and human life (of workers and families). Workers, foreign companies, local manufacturers and government agencies may need to sit on one representative table. The OSH council that is envisaged in the OSH Act of 2017, does have seats for workers'

[222] Orleck (2018).

representatives, and elected OSH representatives; this is a tiny step in the right direction. Much would have to follow for these carceral patterns and cruel work conditions to be disrupted—in Pakistan and across the globe.

References

Afzal M (2007) The impact of globalisation on economic growth of Pakistan. Pak Dev Rev 46 (4):723–734

Agamben G (1998) Homo sacer: sovereign power and bare life. Stanford University Press, Stanford

Ahmed F (1974) Pakistan forum: partners in underdevelopment: Pakistan and the US. MERIP Rep 26:23–27

Ali K (2005) The strength of the street meets the strength of the state: the 1972 labor struggle in Karachi. Int J Middle East Stud 37(1):83–107

Brown D, Brown C, Desposato S (2007) Promoting and preventing political change through internationally funded NGO activity. Latin Am Res Rev 42(1):126–138

Child FC, Kaneda H (1975) Links to the green revolution: a study of small-scale, agriculturally related industry in the Pakistan Punjab. Econ Dev Cult Chang 23(2):249–275

Chossudovsky M (1979) Human rights, health, and capital accumulation in the Third World. Int J Health Serv 9(1):61–75

Deleuze G, Guattari F (1980) A thousand plateaus: capitalism and schizophernia. Continuum, New York

Elshtain J (1991) Sovereign god, sovereign state, sovereign self. Notre Dame Law Rev 66:1355–1378

Feenstra R (1998) Integration of trade and disintegration of production in the global economy. J Econ Perspect 12(4):31–50

Gayer L (2019) Putting out the Baldia factory fire: how the trial of Karachi's industrial capitalism did not happen. In: Harriss-White B, Michelutti L (eds) The Wild East: criminal political economies in South Asia. UCL Press, London, pp 288–321

Gilbert M (1982) Lord Lansdowne and the Indian Factory Act of 1891: a study in Indian economic nationalism and proconsular power. J Dev Areas 16(3):357–372

Gramsci A (1971) Selections from the prison notebooks. In: Hoare Q, Nowell Smith G (eds) London

Hobson C (2009) The limits of liberal-democracy promotion. Altern: Global Local Polit 34 (4):383–405

Hume D (2014) The rule of law in reading down: good law for the 'bad man'. Melbourne Law Review, Melbourne

Kamat S (2004) The privatization of public interest: theorizing NGO discourse in a neoliberal era. Rev Int Polit Econ 11(1):155–176

Klimnik K (1988) German occupational safety and health regulation from an American perspective. Penn State Int Law Rev 6(2):143–235

Louai E (2012) Retracing the concept of the subaltern from Gramsci to Spivak: historical developments and new applications. Afr J Hist Cult 4(1):4–8

Manby B (2009) Struggles for citizenship in Africa. Zed Books, London

Mbembe A (2003) Necropolitics. Public Cult 1(15):11–40

Mende J (2020) Business authority in global governance: beyond public and private. WZB Berlin Social Science Center Discussion Paper 4:2020–2103

Meyer T (2018) Free trade, fair trade, and selective enforcement. Columbia Law Rev 118 (2):491–566

Nashef H (2017) Homo sacer dwells in Saramago's land of exception: blindness and the cave. Angelaki: J Theor Humanit 22(4):147

Orleck A (2018) We are all fast food workers now: the global uprising against poverty wages. Beacon Press, Boston
Otto D (1996) Subalternity and international law: the problems of global community and the incommensurability of difference. Soc Leg Stud 5(3):337
Powell B (2014) Meet the old sweatshops: same as the new. Indep Rev 19(1):109–122
Puplampu B, Quartey S (2012) Key issues on occupational health and safety practices in Ghana: a review. Int J Bus Soc Sci 3(19):151–156
Samaddar R (2010) Emergence of political subject. SAGE, London
Sheth D (1995) Democracy and globalization in India: Post-Cold War discourse. Ann Am Acad Polit Soc Sci 540:24–39
Spindler M (2013) World-systems analysis. In: International relations: a self-study guide to theory. Verlag Barbara Budrich, Toronto, p 177
Spivak G (2010) Can the subaltern speak?: Reflections on the history of an idea. In: Morris R (ed)
Theuws M et al (2013) Analysis of recent factory fires in Pakistan and Bangladesh: a call to protect and respect garment workers' lives. In: Stichting Onderzoek Multinationale Onderneminge (eds) Clean clothes campaign. Amsterdam

Palvasha Shahab was the joint executive director of the Rasheed Razvi Centre for Constitutional and Human Rights, and the Legal Aid Foundation for Victims of Rape and Sexual Assault through September 2020. She now works a consultant for RCCHR, LAFRSA, the Legal Aid Society and the Pakistan Institute for Labour Education and Research. She is on the Law Committee of the Sindh Commission of the Status on Women and advises on upcoming legislation. She is also an advisor to a transnational collaborative project on oral histories and social interventions titled "Karachi Beach Radio." She has also taught undergraduate courses on peace movements and international human rights law at SZABIST, Karachi. Shahab further curates and moderates important public discussions on national platforms such as the Adab Fest and The Second Floor. She holds a Master of Laws from Columbia Law School, New York, US, where she was also a Human Rights Fellow at the Human Rights Institute in 2017–18.

The KiK Case: A Critical Perspective from the South

Muhammad Azeem

Abstract Labour in Global South countries often has meagre social security protections and almost no representation in domestic legislatures. To address this deficit, labour law's clear orientation towards "distributive justice" and emphasis on constitutionally protected freedom of association and collective bargaining rights have been core values for workers and labour movements in the South. Over the course of the last century, labour law has increasingly sought to assure "distributive justice" by departing from the confines of "corrective justice" and the slippery "ethical" basis of private law in both civil and common law systems. This chapter asks how both multinational corporations' (MNCs) recent turn toward the use of codes of conduct in regards to labour and working conditions (labour codes) and, correspondingly, activists' increasing reliance on the private law doctrines of tort and damages to resolve labour disputes, dilutes labour law's focus on "distributive justice." What problems and challenges do these shifts cause for labour law practice and theory? Taking the KiK case as an example, this chapter applies a critical legal perspective to address these questions.

Keywords Labor law · Private law · Labor codes of MNCs · Distributive justice · Labor litigation · Critical lawyering

M. Azeem (✉)
Shaikh Ahmad Hassan School of Law, D.H.A, Lahore, Pakistan
e-mail: muhammad.azeem@lums.edu.pk

M. Saage-Maaß et al. (eds.), *Transnational Legal Activism in Global Value Chains*, Interdisciplinary Studies in Human Rights 6,
https://doi.org/10.1007/978-3-030-73835-8_14

1 Introduction

In the context of global value and supply chains,[1] workers in the Global South often struggle against the labour practices of both foreign investors and local manufacturers, where the latter are frequently dependent on the former for their foreign investment and capital. At times, labour unions in the Global North offer concrete transnational solidarity and unionisation support for workers and labour struggles in the South. Hence, both capital's overall structural logic (based on Northern investment and Southern dependency) and workers' collective struggles (based on international labour standards and transnational labour solidarity) dialectically shape labour conditions and labour law in the Global South.

Historically, both common and civil law systems considered the formation of labour associations and strikes to be modes of conspiring against business and property, and a violation of the "freedom of contract."[2] Yet, at the same time, private law's strictly moral and ethical basis, oriented toward "corrective justice," proved insufficient to adequately address the fundamental inequality between employers and employees. In response, labour law, with a strong orientation towards "distributive justice," emerged as an exception to and source of immunity and privilege for workers and organised labour from private law. At the national level, labour law took on a welfare orientation through social welfare legislation and state policy. At the international level, it developed through the International Labour Organization into a convention-based system of core standards tied to ratification, government responsibility, sanctions and enforcement mechanisms. Against this original labour law regime, the 1990s and the proliferation of neoliberal globalisation and rights-approaches to address human suffering saw the International Monetary Fund, the World Bank and the Organisation for Economic Co-operation and Development push the ILO into the role of a social mediator through an evolving rights-based approach to labour law.[3]

[1]I use the terms global supply chains (GSCs), global value chains (GVCs) and transnational supply chains (TSCs) interchangeably to refer to MNCs' complex global production networks and chains, understood as a new form of global economic organisation, production and management. The ILO uses the term "GSC." See ILO, Follow-Up to the Resolution Concerning Decent Work in Global Supply Chains (General Discussion), (GB.328/INS/5/1 Geneva: ILO, 2016), whereas IGLP Law and Global Production Working Group uses the term GVC. See IGLP Law and Global Production Working Group, The Role of Law in Global Value Chains: A Research Manifesto, London Review of International Law (2016), for "TSCs" see United Nations Conference on Trade and Development (UNCTAD), Global Value Chains: Investment and Trade for Development, World Investment Report (New York and Geneva, 2013).

[2]Wedderburn (1987), p. 6.

[3]This understanding is based on debate between Phillip Alston and Brian Langille and its more theoretical explanation by Judy Fudge; see Alston (2004), p. 458; Langille (2005), pp. 409–437; Fudge (2007), pp. 29–66.

This above shift in approach appeared in the ILO's Social Declaration of 1998 and, with some differences, in the EU's Charter of Fundamental Rights of 2000.[4] Declaration-based rather than entailing treaty ratification, a rights-based approach to labour regulation is promotional, meaning it aims to motivate stakeholders without binding sanctions, and shifts the regulatory burden away from governments onto corporations and consumers. Above all, it comprises "soft law"[5] mechanisms as opposed to "hard," binding statutory labour law. One of its newest forms includes MNC's labour codes, corporate social responsibility policies, and the use of private tort law to seek damages for corporate violations of the standards they outline.[6] As opposed to labour law's orientation towards "distributive justice," this rights-based approach to labour regulation is rooted in private law's emphasis on "corrective justice."

With this historical shift in mind, this chapter examines the KiK case as an example of the complex interactions and often diverging practices between international labour law standards and MNC's labour codes for manufacturers and/or contractors.[7] It also explores how the KiK case exemplifies labour resistance and mobilisation through domestic and international labour litigation. In an attempt to unpack the challenging questions the resulting dynamics pose for labour law practice and theory, it uses the KiK case to test a theoretical proposition from the perspective of the South, namely that: International labour law must be assessed in regards to its (original) core objectives of redistribution, representation and power for labour in the South. Labour struggles and labour law must enhance Southern workers' power, representation and ensure redistribution. When discussing the litigation in the aftermath of the 2012 Ali Enterprises factory fire tragedy, I divide it into two cases: litigation in local courts in Pakistan, which I refer to as the Ali Enterprises case, and litigation by the victims of the factory fire against KiK in Germany, which I call the KiK case.

In the first part of the chapter, I offer a brief history of labour law's departure from private law in the early twentieth century, and its drift back in the 1990s under neoliberalism. In the second part, I discuss the nature and inclusion of labour law in MNCs' labour codes, demonstrating how these codes avoid questions of redistribution and representation and, hence, disempower both labour struggles and states in the Global South. In this phase of production and manufacturing in global supply chains, conventional national labour law no longer seems to offer adequate redress for labour, leading NGOs to increasingly resort to private tort and contract law to achieve "corrective justice" against the violation of these codes. But these

[4]Fudge (2007), pp. 29–66.

[5]Alston (2004), p. 457.

[6]I use the term "MNC labour codes" to refer to sets of labour standards adopted by MNCs in their global value chains (GVCs), including private compliance initiatives (PCIs) like voluntary codes of conduct as well as multi-stakeholder initiatives (MSIs) like social auditing and certificate initiatives.

[7]I use the term "contractors" for textile and garment manufacturers in the Global South, and the term "suppliers" for MNCs that place manufacturing orders from the Global North.

approaches sidestep "redistributive justice," which has traditionally been at labour law's core. In the final section, I argue that a critical legal perspective is best suited to advance workers' interests in this situation.

2 Labour Law as a Departure from Private Law

In Western labour law debates, the "radical democratic tradition" emphasises the importance of statutory trade union recognition and rights to freedom of association, collective bargaining, and worker participation in corporate governance through a constitutional or public law lens.[8] Since the 1990s, however, labour law has been gradually turning away from such a public or constitutional law lens towards private (civil and common) law. This has also included a shift from binding convention-based labour law to voluntary and promotional rights-based soft law for labour regulation. This relatively recent shift represents a reversal of labour law's emergence and trajectory since the early twentieth century, which was characterised by its departure from private law's emphasis on "corrective justice" towards and an explicit focus on "redistributive justice."

2.1 Labour Law as a Departure from State and Courts

With the emergence of capitalism in the West, classical liberal thought came to hold that political freedom brings economic freedom. Accordingly, private law (in both civil and common law systems) and state regulation were first limited to property and contracts. Despite political freedoms in Europe, workers were still subordinate to the market and capital, that is, political freedom did not lead to economic freedom (for workers).[9]

This was the context that compelled labour law's founding father Hugo Sinzheimer to constitutionalise labour—the economic sphere of life—as separate from the political sphere. With the creation of an "Economic Constitution" in the German Weimar Republic, he envisioned autonomously-created labour relations and norms between employers and trade unions, without the involvement of the state and courts. This process, he hoped, would give various sections of society like trade unions and employers' associations the power to spontaneously create law.[10] Otto Kahn-Freund in England, like Sinzheimer, coined the idea of "collective laissez-faire," which entails employers bargaining with trade unions in spontaneous and non-institutionalised (i.e. non-legal) ways, and regulating conflict through statute. It

[8] For this debate, see Bogg (2017), pp. 7–37.

[9] Duke (2008), p. 346.

[10] Duke (2008), p. 346.

was primarily a governmental policy that let trade unions and employers collectively bargain with each other—for instance, to overcome the parties' inequality in labour contracts and resolve the perpetual conflicts between employers and employees—with limited oversight or regulation. With this concept, the law retreated from industrial relations and industrial relations retreated from the law.[11] While Sinzheimer and Kahn-Freund were both against the state and law's interference in industrial relations, they differed on the question of the state's role.[12]

It is pertinent to mention here that basis of private law is "ethical" and "moral" and it is based on corrective justice, whereas one of the core values of labour law is distributive justice. Kahn-Freund believed that private law could not control collective action, but considered it capable of regulating organisations' conduct.[13] Both, Sinzheimer and Kahn-Freund, believed, however, that civil law's freedom of contract—the idea that contracts are based on mutual agreement and free choice—was "pure fiction." On this basis, they argued that the market economy had no "natural law" of freedom of contract.[14] In that sense labour law is constitutionally protected, but remains a matter of policy, depending on employer and employee negotiations.

2.2 *Labour Law as a Matter of Policy and Not "Ethics" and "Morality" of Private Law*

As we have discussed so far, labour law was a large departure from private law, as it moved workers' economic concerns away from the state. Do today's MNCs' labour codes and rights-based approaches signify labour law's return to private law, its ethical grounds, and their slippery interpretation by the courts?[15] Here we must recall academics like Bill McCarthy, who were hesitant to bring ethics and rights into labour law.[16] In the KiK case, the German retailer KiK claimed that it paid some compensation to victims on "ethical" grounds, but later refused to pay "legal" compensation.[17] KiK also made clear that it understood labour codes to be an ethical steering instrument rather than a "contract for the benefit of a third party" or a

[11]Dukes (2009), pp. 222–223. For a good summary of the development of collective bargaining in the UK before Kahn-Freund, see Lewis (1979), p. 613.

[12]Kahn-Freund wanted the government to intervene, Dukes (2009), p. 244.

[13]Kahn-Freund (1970), pp. 241–267.

[14]Coutu (2013), pp. 607–608.

[15]For recent discussion among Clare Mumme, William Kalre Roberts, and Mathew Dimick, see Mumme (2019).

[16]McCarthy (1964), pp. 1–6.

[17]Letter and correspondence between KiK and the Pakistan Institute of Labour Education and Research (PILER), on file with the author.

"contract with protective effect to the benefit of a third party."[18] The Dortmund Regional Court that heard the case sided with the company, holding that "the code of conduct was addressed exclusively to the contractual partner of the defendant – in this case KiK – and that it urged the latter to maintain certain minimum ethical, social, and labour standards."[19] The court clearly said: "It cannot be inferred from the document that the employees of the defendant should be entitled to direct claims against the defendant as a result of the defendant's code of conduct."[20]

We can only comprehend this emphasis on labour codes as having an ethical bearing within the overall contemporary theoretical environment of labour law ideology. A relatively short time after labour law departed from private law, voices began circulating in the West warning of the "death of labour law" and the "crisis of labour law" in the late 1980s.[21] Under neoliberalism, following the IMF and World Bank's lead in advocating for "flexibility of labour" and avoiding rigid social welfare legislation, the ILO came to act as "a social mediator in the process of globalization,"[22] prompting the Declaration on Fundamental Principles and Rights at Work (1998), later known as the Social Declaration.[23] This transformed a legal matter of substantive distribution into a moral one, including words like "human dignity" and placing it on a new symbolic ideological plane.[24]

In the past, nationally, labour law with a public and constitutional law lens viewed unfair labour practices as an administrative wrong. Internationally, labour law was convention-based and binding upon ratification by the ILO member countries. In the years following the rise of neoliberalism, labour law has slowly been moving towards a rights-based approach, with private law remedies based on corrective justice. Most labour law scholars agree that a public or constitutional labour law lens can better assure labour interests. However, few favour the rights-based approach. Allan Bogg, for instance, wants private law and labour law to work together. For him, treating unfair labour practices as administrative wrongs is limited, and should be reshaped by developing remedial principles within private law and by developing substantive doctrines.[25] Similarly, Hugh Collins is fully convinced that labour law cases based on fundamental rights, not welfare or social justice, are weak.[26] He argues that labour rights are less compelling than human rights because they cannot

---

[18] *Jabir and Others v. KiK Textilien und Non-Food GmbH*, Case No. 7 O 95/15 (hereinafter KiK case) at 5.

[19] KiK case at 10.

[20] KiK case at 10.

[21] Ewing (1988), p. 293. See also Bercusson and Estlund (2006), pp. 1–6. For redefining the discipline of labour law from a gender perspective, see Conaghan (2005).

[22] Fudge (2007), p. 39.

[23] ILO Declaration on Fundamental Principles and Rights at Work, www.ilo.org/declaration/lang%2D%2Den/index.htm (last accessed 10 December 2019).

[24] Santos (2002), p. 483.

[25] Bogg (2017), pp. 7–37.

[26] Collins (2011), p. 140.

be categorised as universal. While fundamental rights are timeless, labour rights are not, as they change and evolve according to the system of production. Therefore, labour rights are time-bound, less absolute, less morally compelling and, hence, not *human* rights. He still insists, however, on using a rights-based approach to labour litigation.[27]

3 The Nature of International Labour Law in Labour Codes of MNCs

By promulgating labour codes, MNCs have effectively made themselves the global legislators of labour law.[28] The codes represent the "private governance" of labour in the Global South, in stark contrast to and in competition with "public governance" by national labour law regimes.[29] MNCs' most evident focus in their labour codes is workplace safety, primarily to avoid disasters and embarrassments such as the 2013 Rana Plaza factory collapse in Dhaka and the 2012 Ali Enterprises fire in Karachi, both of which shook Western consumers' consciousness. While it is true that safety conditions in Southern factories are often abysmal, MNCs' attempts to improve them frequently bypass national labour law regimes with "private auditing" or "hybrid governance" approaches to labour law like the Bangladesh Accord and the proposed Pakistan Accord.[30] More than 200 foreign brands initiated two factory safety programmes under the Bangladesh Accord for Fire and Building Safety and the Alliance for Bangladesh Worker Safety. Demonstrating the limited scope of good intentions, however, they encompass only 27 percent of the factories in Bangladesh.[31] National labour law regimes, in contrast, theoretically cover the entire country. Today, in Bangladesh, these labour codes bypass an already weak national labour law regime and cannot be said to strengthen it.[32]

Even after tragedies like Rana Plaza and Ali Enterprises, the ongoing, everyday structural exploitation of workers tends to remain hidden. Enforcing a minimum wage and providing social security are not directly linked to disasters, after all, and MNC labour codes usually only address structural exploitation issues with a check-list whose compliance is solely "assured" by social auditing firms. As revealed by the audit of the Ali Enterprises factory conducted by the social certifier RINA shortly before the 2012 fire, this type of auditing is easily corrupted or intercepted. Indeed, such social auditing processes are only cursory and partial by design. In the Rana Plaza tragedy, for example, the audit company Veritas asked the Canadian

[27]Collins (2011), p. 141.

[28]For the role of law in GVCs, see Santos (2016), pp. 36–39. See also Selwyn (2016), pp. 60–61.

[29]Milberg and Winkler (2013), p. 115.

[30]Becker (2015); Evans (2015), p. 597.

[31]Labowitz and Baumann-Pauly (2015), pp. 4–5.

[32]See Anner (2020), pp. 320–347.

retailer Loblaws to pay an extra 2000 US dollars for the audit to cover the construction and structural integrity of the Rana Plaza building. Loblaws refused and, instead, requested that the manufacturer pay only 1200 US dollars for the basic social audit. Had the full audit been carried out, the evaluation of Rana Plaza's construction and structural integrity may have prevented the tragedy altogether.[33] It must also be pointed out that only mega-corporations can afford this form of self-auditing. Finally, even if companies take auditing seriously, like Nike, which invests 10 million US dollars in auditing processes annually and hires almost 100 employees to monitor the implementation of labour standards in labour codes across its global value chain, I argue that labour justice cannot be achieved by bypassing the state and workers.[34]

3.1 Avoiding Distributive Justice in Labour Codes

Workers' safety and social security cannot be secured without assuring process rights, namely freedom of association and collective bargaining. According to Barbara J Fick, in a 1998 ILO study of 215 MNC labour codes, only 15 percent of them mentioned freedom of association and collective bargaining. Moreover, when the OECD published 246 MNC labour codes in 2001, only 60 percent mentioned core labour standards, and only 30 percent mentioned freedom of association. Similarly, out of 600 publicly-traded corporations' 2012 labour codes, only 43 percent mentioned freedom of association.[35] Instead of being based on democratically-elected, representative trades unions, the overall approach of labour codes authorised organising in "works councils," which are neither democratically elected nor designed for a power fight.[36]

Most of the "value added" is in "innovation" at the pre-production and post-production stages of the GVCs.[37] Manufacturing contractors of the South are assumed to add very little value despite the labourers' hard work at this stage of the production phase. At the same time, MNC labour codes transfer all labour responsibility and risk to manufacturing contractors in the Global South. In addition, the first-tier supplier gives third party contractors strict deadlines, which are passed down to labourers, often making them work overtime, in some cases even forcibly. Another dilemma is that profit redistribution is not recognised as a core value within MNC labour codes' "ethical" and "moral" intent. In interpreting these MNC codes in relation to the Rana Plaza disaster, courts in both Delaware in the United States and

[33]Doorey (2018), p. 12.

[34]As pointed out by Posthuma (2010), pp. 57–80.

[35]Fick (2014), p. 3.

[36]Engels-Zanden and Merk (2014), p. 466.

[37]"Value added" here is the difference between production cost and the price of a product, which MNCs add at their discretion, see ILO (2016), p. 30.

Ontario in Canada clearly concluded that they are mere moral and ethical statements, reaffirming that the codes have more cosmetic than preventive or corrective value.[38] Redistribution (distributive justice), according to Guy Davidov, is one of labour law's main goals, but is usually neglected in labour law literature. In this chapter, I use the term, borrowing from Davidov, in the broader sense of theories of distributive justice. Based on the theories of John Rawls and Ronald Dworkin, distributive justice can be understood as the distribution of resources through labour law. In Amartya Sen's approach, according to Davidov, distribution is based on equality of capabilities rather than labour law's fight against oppression, caste and hierarchies in the workplace, based on the distribution of power and risk.[39] With these understandings in mind, why do Southern workers and states not effectively resist the current turn away from labour law towards MNC labour codes? Dependent, investment-starved countries tend to not only avoid all confrontation with MNCs, but they also act within MNCs' corporate hegemonic agenda of global capitalism. Critics, meanwhile, call out states' "outsourcing of governance" to MNCs and lament how they have effectively turned "labour law" into "labour self-regulation."[40] "Self-regulation" means state interference in labour matters is reduced although MNCs can and often do ask investment-starved states to curb acts of labour dissent. In this context, workers are treated only as passive objects to be regulated by codes.[41]

Starting from the observation that few countries in the Global South currently have functional labour law regimes, some labour activists and analysts see MNC labour codes—especially contractually binding ones like the Bangladesh Accord—as helpful in preventing already "bad" labour conditions from getting "worse." For example, Pakistan has only one percent unionisation. If MNC labour codes protect say 10 percent of workers or workplaces, these activists and analysts reason, that this is still 10 times more than before. This argument aligns with the "context" approach in international law literature, which sees violence as internal to countries in the Global South due to their lack of democracy and "good" governance. A critical approach to international law, however, takes colonial, neo-colonial and current neoliberal factors into account to explain local problems and challenges.[42]

---

[38]KiK's claim was that "codes of conduct" are only an ethical steering instrument. The court accepted that they are used to "maintain a certain minimum ethical, social, and labour standard," see KiK case at pp. 5, 10.

[39]For usefulness and relevance of all these theories, see Davidov (2018).

[40]Mayer and Phillips (2017), pp. 134–152; Arup et al. (2006).

[41]Engels-Zanden and Merk (2014), p. 465.

[42]Anghie and Chimni (2003), pp. 77–103.

3.2 Diluting "Labour Representation" in Labour Codes

Critical labour law scholars like Karl Klare see redistribution as possible only through workplace democracy and participatory decision-making.[43] Historically, this has paved the way for worker representation in the legislature, which, in turn, has enabled the creation of welfare states.[44] In its simplest form, labour politics must involve worker representation at three progressive levels: in the workplace in the form of trade unions; in democratic state institutions and structures, such as parliament; and in international institutions. In this progression, labour representation at the workplace is a decisive indicator of representation at the national level, while both are prerequisites for active worker participation in institutions at the international level. If individual workers have low workplace representation and a negligible presence in the legislature, they can easily be ignored at the international level, whereas MNCs have a far easier time getting their voices heard. Claire Cutler points out, although the state is the subject of international law, MNCs have the power to influence transnational institutions like the EU, thus making them de facto members of such institutions.[45]

In many countries of the Global South, workers possess negligible representation in legislatures. Hence, when the US tried to add the topic of labour to the WTO agenda in the early 1990s, most member countries from the Global South strongly rejected attaching labour conditions to trade agreements. This was the main bone of contention in the two WTO ministerial conferences in Singapore (1996) and Seattle (1999). The EU and US have continuously pushed to include labour conditions in international trade agreements like the General Agreement on Tariffs and Trade (GATT) and, later, the WTO. Countries of the Global South have not only sought to avoid this, but have actively insisted that the ILO, not the WTO, be the chief forum for labour regulation.[46] Historically, however, the US has ratified very few ILO labour conventions, not wanting itself to be bound by them. Instead, it has tried to push soft law labour standards through trade and investment treaties. In this regard, I see the rights-based approach to labour law currently accepted and promoted by the ILO as an indicator of the US approach's success.

Although Global South countries wanted the ILO to be the sole forum for labour regulation and sought to prevent arbitrary labour conditions from being used against them,[47] we should not fool ourselves into believing that countries of the Global South were, therefore, in favour of strict labour law and distributive justice. A "global capitalist elite" has emerged in countries of the Global South that is not interested in the redistribution of wealth or worker safety. Instead, they aim to ensure global value chains and seek to keep the market running smoothly in order to

---

[43] Klare (1988), pp. 8–9.

[44] Klare (1988), p. 40.

[45] Cutler (2001), pp. 133–150.

[46] For details of this controversy, see Stern and Terrell (2003); See also Howse (1999), p. 131.

[47] See Alston (2004), p. 457.

safeguard their interests. According to BS Chimni, fractions of national capitalist classes have entered into coalitions with global production processes and emerged as the transnational capitalist class of the Third World. They are not junior to imperialist powers, but are independent players.[48]

3.3 *Labour Codes as a Question of Power and Ideology*

Borrowing from John Ruggie, international institutions' approval of MNC labour codes is an indication of MNCs' significant structural power.[49] Indeed, MNCs regularly exercise undue influence on international institutions. Global corporate spending on lobbying is 30 times that of unions and public interest litigation groups. In Brussels, where the EU is headquartered, businesses occupy 75 percent of all offices, while unions have less than five percent.[50] Given this power imbalance, workers often have no real choice but to accept MNC labour codes. While this is clearly a form of economic coercion, ideology also plays an important role in the process. In this vein, academics are presenting MNCs' global value chains as a very complex form of economic organisation, with particularly complicated governance and management structures capable of defying human understanding. The fact that businesses work transnationally, whereas regulation only extends nationally is an argument often cited in this regard. Meanwhile, a great deal of academic literature examines the complexity of labour in global value chains with various contractors and subcontractors,[51] where gender, ethnic and regional aspects add even more complexity.[52]

This emphasis on complexity represents a process of global value chain reification.[53] To elaborate this concept, Karl Marx gave the example of why the exchange value of diamonds is more than that of water, although water has far more use value than diamonds. According to Marx, the market determines the exchange value of commodities like diamonds, which completely abstracts it from their use value. Because this abstraction completely separates a commodity's exchange value from

[48]Chimni (2017), p. 37. For more on the Third World global capitalist class, see Harris (2009). For the transnational capitalist class, see Sklair (2000); see also Carrol (2010).

[49]Ruggie (2017), p. 7.

[50]Ruggie (2017), pp. 5–7.

[51]Chan (2013).

[52]Barrientos (2014), p. 791. Mezzadri and Lula (2018), pp. 1034–1036. Mezzadri (2016), pp. 1877–1900. Werner and Bair (2011), p. 988. Carr and Chen (2004), p. 129.

[53]Reification is the transforming of social relations/properties/actions into relations/properties/actions of human-made things. Through this process, human-being starts looking thing-like and the laws of human ways become the laws of things. In short, we start talking about social relations of producers as relations of products of labour. That is, I am a labourer and he is an intellectual and we are not human beings. Once this process is completed, commodity relations start looking like normal social relations. See Brosnan (1986–87), p. 279.

its material properties, only its supra-natural properties can explain its value.[54] Hence, the supra-natural presentation of global value chains as complex and MNC labour codes as benevolent for workers both contribute to this process of reification. In this sense, the very idea of CSR also has a role to play in that it presents corporations as good citizens.

MNC labour codes are given tremendous legitimacy by international institutions like the ILO and OECD, as well as other stakeholders like labour NGOs that participate in stakeholder initiatives and negotiations.[55] These legitimacy processes and discursive practices allow very mild responses to MNC labour code violations, such as merely asking for them to be binding contracts.

4 Private Law in Labour Litigation

Legal scholars and practitioners are divided on the use of private law doctrines in labour law violation cases. Since MNC labour codes tend to have a strong moral and ethical grounding, many suggest using tort and contract law to combat violations in global value chains.[56] However, the results of this type of litigation show the limits of this approach, and many writers increasingly suggest the need to go beyond the use of private law and labour codes.[57]

In the US, legal practitioners have often used the 1789 Alien Tort Claims Act (ATCA) against MNCs. Under this act, non-state actors can bring tort claims against US companies for violating the "law of nations."[58] Despite the somewhat encouraging case of *Sosa v. Alverez-Machin*,[59] however, this approach's utility for labour struggles has been limited in that US circuit courts have rarely entertained cases about sweatshop conditions. To date, they have only taken on sensational labour-related cases, such as those involving union leaders' murder, torture and rape, or those involving the slave trade. Apart from a successful 2004 case against Nike,[60] US courts have generally failed to address cases involving structurally poor labour

[54]Marx (1976), pp. 128, 149 as cited by McNally (2015), pp. 131–146.

[55]These are called "labour movement-oriented NGOs," which are different from "social service-oriented NGOs" or "legal rights-oriented NGOs." See Chan (2018), pp. 1–18. Chan (2012), pp. 308–327.

[56]For the overall return to private law, see Goldberg (2012); see also Smith (2017).

[57]Revak (2012), p. 1645.

[58]See for example, *Aldana v. Del Monte Fresh Produce N. A.*, Inc., 416 F. 3r 1242 (11th Cir, 2005), see also *Jane Does I v. Wal-Mart Stores Inc.*, No.CV05-7307 AG (MANx, 2007) WL 5975664 (C. D. Cal. Mar. 30, 2007), also *Does I v. Gap. Inc.* No. CV-01-0031, 2002 WL 1000068 (D. N. Mar. J May 10, 2002).

[59]542 US 692, 2004.

[60]See CCC (2004); Bas (2004).

conditions.[61] A 2007 case against Wal-Mart[62] was particularly disappointing for proponents of using private law for labour cases. In this case, lawyers invoked a third-party beneficiary breach of contract against the company for standard violations, unjust enrichment and profiting from factory sweatshop labour in China, Bangladesh, Indonesia and other countries. However, the US Court of Appeals for the Ninth Circuit rejected the claim on the grounds that the contractor's obligation to comply with labour codes was split between the contractor and Wal-Mart, not between Wal-Mart and factory workers.[63]

The attempt to provide workers with redress by expanding private law's scope is laudable. But according to statistics compiled by John Ruggie, out of 150 cases that have used the US Foreign Corrupt Practices Act and ATCA since 1997, only one case reached a jury, and the corporation won that case.[64] In two cases, the aggrieved party received modest settlements, while the remaining cases were all dismissed on various procedural grounds.[65] Today, conventional labour law seems to offer no remedy for labour violations in global production contexts, requiring activists to use private law to address labour grievances.

5 A Critical Reflection on the KiK and Ali Enterprises Cases

For workers in Global South countries with low social security protection and weak organised labour, the core values of labour law are redistribution and worker representation. This final section explores how labour activists and lawyers tried to use these values in litigating the KiK case in Dortmund, Germany, and the Ali Enterprises case in Pakistan. It concludes with some lessons for future litigation.

In the KiK case, lawyers and activists were very conscious about the limits of law and litigation. They were also clear that acts of solidarity and labour organising have the ability to be far more effective than resorting to the courts for justice. The KiK case was not (only) about winning a legal claim.[66] Instead, the general position of the lawyers and activists involved in the case was that "legal interventions like the lawsuit against KiK in Germany open a small space to imagine and to eventually claim a different economic, social and legal world order."[67] This is also evident in

---

[61] Maryanov (2010), p. 401.

[62] *Jane Does I v. Wal-Mart Stores, Inc.* No. CV 05-7307 AG (MANx), 2007 WL5975664; see *also Does v. Wal-Mart Stores*, US Court of Appeals 9th Circuit, 572 F. 3d 677 (2009).

[63] *Jane Does I v. Wal-Mart Stores, Inc.* No. CV 05-7307 AG (MANx), 2007 WL5975664; see also *Does v. Wal-Mart Stores*, US Court of Appeals 9th Circuit, 572 F. 3d 677 (2009).

[64] Ruggie (2017), p. 4.

[65] Ruggie (2017), p. 4.

[66] Bader et al. (2019), p. 167.

[67] Bader et al. (2019), p. 169.

their overall appraisal of the litigation's obstacles, strategies and achievements.[68] Yet, what is this "small space" that we can imagine? It is a space that lies beyond the current problematic dominance of the market economy and neoliberalism's theoretical underpinnings in international institutions' hegemonic agenda.

If we look at the redistributional aspect of labour law in the KiK case, workers received compensation, which was neither meant to be a substitute for human life nor about redistributing corporate profits. As Faisal Siddiqi, the main lawyer representing workers in the Ali Enterprises case, assessed the situation, using local labour courts would have led to very meagre compensation (see also chapter "Paradoxes of Strategic Labour Rights Litigation: Insights from the Baldia Factory Fire Litigation"). While this assessment was perhaps accurate, Siddiqi himself later came to regret the strong legal emphasis on compensation in the strategy devised by his legal team and collaborating activists, because it led them to overlook the potential benefits of long-term statutory and constitutional interventions, such as amending worker compensation and safety laws, among others.[69] In the end, however, the KiK case litigation and the overall pressure it helped generate from the EU around Pakistan's GSP+ status, did result in certain legislative advances for worker safety and domestic and home-based workers, even bringing agricultural labour within the ambit of formal labour law.[70]

Did the KiK case help in the enhancement of workers' representation? To expect that it could have occurred from mere legal strategy is certainly wrong, particularly due to the restrictive nature of civil law and civil procedure for advancing broader community concerns. Part of the strategy adopted in the KiK case was that four of those affected (workers, survivors, family members) would challenge the company in a foreign court, since the company is untouchable in Pakistan, and use the opportunity to speak out on behalf of the whole group of victims. This strategy sought to use the law's paradoxes for limited aims in the absence of (functional/ effective) transnational labour law.

Let us critically analyse the Ali Enterprises and KiK cases whilst presupposing that *labour law is a tool for gaining labour power*. In the Ali Enterprises case, activists diligently used power gaps in elite institutional structures. Rejecting the old Marxist position of law as an instrument of the local elite, Faisal Siddiqui and several labour activists used the "anarchy of law" in local courts to seek relief for workers by co-opting (the instrumentality of) law from the local elite.[71] This position sides with theories about law's relative autonomy, which hold that law is neutral and autonomous from social classes. Notably, law's instrumentality and relative autonomy are

---

[68] See for example Wesche and Saage-Maaß (2016), pp. 370–385; see also Terwindt et al. (2017).

[69] See chapter "Paradoxes of Strategic Labour Rights Litigation: Insights from the Baldia Factory Fire Litigation" by Siddiqi in this book.

[70] For example Sindh Occupational Safety and Health Act, 2017 and Punjab Occupational Health and Safety Act, 2019; see also chapter "Paradoxes of Strategic Labour Rights Litigation: Insights from the Baldia Factory Fire Litigation" by Siddiqi in this book.

[71] See chapter "Paradoxes of Strategic Labour Rights Litigation: Insights from the Baldia Factory Fire Litigation" by Siddiqi in this book.

not inherent characteristics of law. They come from the organised power of the working class or the community, be it the momentary consolidation of forces of a dominated class (leading to seemingly random and anarchic gains), as happened in the Ali Enterprises case, or durable and balanced power-sharing between classes (leading to social democratic legislation and its implementation through the courts). This shows that political struggles have primacy over legal struggles.

According to the critical approach of Peter Gabel and Paul Harris in the US context, US lower courts should be used as a real powerbase for alternatives and higher courts, especially the supreme court, should be used to shake up and challenge ideology.[72] Using this corollary to evaluate transnational litigation against MNCs, from the analysis so far, it seems that the case against KiK was more ideologically oriented. It explored the possibility of emancipation for labour through the labour codes of MNCs and the use of private law for labour litigation. The Ali Enterprises case on the other hand had a legal-power orientation as it used local power gaps and organised labour. Yet, we cannot separate the concrete expression of power (organised labour) from the power of ideology or the rights-based approach to labour law and its use of private law. Borrowing from Gabel and Harris and other critical scholars, outcomes of a case are not the only important factor. Rather it is further the very categories in which a dispute is defined.[73] According to Gabel and Harris, the law convinces us to accept hierarchy and pacifies conflict. Law channels social and economic conflicts into heavily-laden rituals and authoritarian symbolism. The law imagines a community with rights and under the "rule of law," whereas the real community seems to have neither. In this way, law receives "democratic consent" for an inhuman social order, which runs counter to real democratic participation.[74] A non-alienated consciousness and the empowerment of labour cannot be assured through a rights-based approach. Unless we engage in litigation critically, law disempowers workers rather than lifting them up.

Furthermore, a rights-based approach in litigation assumes that power resides with the state and corporations. However, power is an interdependent concept that can also be attributed to people who are organised. For example, critical legal scholars argue that strengthening tenant rights does little to challenge existing landlordism and actually accepts the inequality of land distribution. Similarly, collective bargaining accepts the hierarchy of prevailing labour relations, as well as the basic division of people into labour and capital.[75] Meanwhile, race and gender sensitive activists who have at times successfully used the courts and liberal rights to challenge racial and gender discrimination and subjugation,[76] strongly critique some of the more nihilistic strands in critical legal studies.

---

[72]See Gabel and Harris (1982).

[73]Gabel and Harris (1982), pp. 375–376.

[74]Gabel and Harris (1982), p. 372.

[75]Gabel and Harris (1982), p. 373.

[76]For a strong rebuttal by gender and race activists, see Williams (1987), pp. 401–434; Crenshaw (1988), pp. 1331–1387; Scales-Trent (1989), pp. 9–44; Schneider (1986), pp. 589–652.

Apart from this debate on rights in the critical legal tradition[77] and its rebuttal, we cannot escape courts and the law. We therefore need to build our critical practices on practical and theoretical insights into "critical lawyering," "collaborative lawyering" and "third-dimension lawyering."[78] The focus of this type of lawyering is on empowering communities and changing client-lawyer relationships by asking lawyers to be humble and reflective.[79] It is pertinent to mention here that NGO rhetoric including terms like "community," "empowerment," "social change," "grassroots" and "self-initiative" can be slippery and disempowering.[80] Therefore, it is important that critical lawyers and NGOs have a critical consciousness; they must see the poor as a historical class, not as atomised individuals; they must perceive class as an active human relationship in everyday life connected to a culture of domination and liberation. This consciousness should be the core of service litigation for individual clients, reform litigation to change institutional policies and practices, and even in remedial litigation in the field of the welfare state.[81]

The rights-based approach to labour law is channelled to Pakistan through labour NGOs, social movements and, now, through the "hybrid governance" of labour codes in global value chains like the Pakistan Accord.[82] "Rights" in social democracies with welfare states, where the working class has acquired reasonable political representation, mean a very different thing than "rights" in a dismantled environment like Pakistan. When Karl Klare critiqued the liberal market logic of collective bargaining in the US, he had the European welfare state in mind.[83] But labour in countries of the Global South is generally not allowed to organise and there are deliberate attempts under neoliberalism to roll back unions' meagre achievements. In this scenario, the rights-based approach, with its discursive power and inherent hegemonic liberal underpinnings, dilutes the institutional power arrangements that facilitate freedom of association and collective bargaining. The labour demand for workplace representation is not only important for redistribution, but also to address the dire lack of political representation in most Global South democracies.

To conclude, the values of redistribution and representation must remain central to labour struggles and labour law. MNCs' labour codes, rights-based approaches, and private law should not be and cannot be a substitute for the radical democratic tradition of labour law with its emphasis on guaranteeing workers' freedom of association and collective bargaining. Above all, legal strategies and labour law should be seen as questions of labour politics and labour power.

[77]For rights related to labour issues, see: Klare (1981), p. 157; for a general critique of the rights-based approach, see Chase (1984), p. 1541; Gable and Harris (1982), p. 1563.

[78]See for example Alfieri (1991), p. 2107; Alfieri (1988), p. 659; Lopez (2005), p. 2041; White (1994), p. 157.

[79]White (1995), p. 158.

[80]White (1995), pp. 169–170.

[81]Alfieri (1988), pp. 663–665.

[82]Mayer and Phillips (2017), pp. 134–152.

[83]Klare (1988), pp. 8–9.

References

Alfieri AV (1988) The antinomies of poverty law and a theory of dialogic empowerment. N Y Univ Rev Law Soc Change 16:663–665
Alfieri AV (1991) Reconstructive poverty law practice: learning lessons of client narrative. Yale Law J 100:2107
Alston P (2004) Core labour rights: the story. EJIL 15:457
Anghie A, Chimni BS (2003) Third World approaches to international law and individual responsibility in internal conflicts. Chin J Int Law 2:77–103
Anner M (2020) Squeezing workers' rights in global supply chains: purchasing practices in the Bangladesh garment export sector in comparative perspective. Rev Int Polit Econ 27 (2):320–347
Arup C, Gaham P, Howe J, Johnstone R, Mitchell R, O'Donnel A (2006) Labour law and labour market regulation: essays on the construction, constitution and regulation of labour markets and work relationships. Federation Press, Sydney
Bader M, Saage-Maaß M, Terwindt C (2019) Strategic litigation against the misconduct of multinational enterprises: an anatomy of *Jabir and Others v Kik*. Verfassung und Recht in Übersee 52:156–171
Barrientos S (2014) Gendered global production networks: analysis of cocoa-chocolate sourcing. Reg Stud 48:791
Bas FN, Benjamin M, Chang CJ (2004) Saipan sweatshop lawsuit ends with important gains for workers and lessons for activists. Business and Human Rights Resource Centre
Becker L (2015) Are supply chains transnational legal order? What we can learn from the Rana Plaza factory building collapse. UC Irvine J Int Transnatl Comp Law 11
Bercusson B, Estlund C (2006) Regulating labour in the wake of globalisation, 1st edn. Hart Publishing
Bogg A (2017) Labour, love and futility: philosophical perspective on labour law. Int J Comp Labour Law Ind Relat 3:7–37
Brosnan FD (1986–87) Serious but not critical. South Calif Law Rev 60:279
Carrol WK (2010) The making of transnational capitalist class: corporate power. In: The 21st century. Zed Books
Carr M, Chen M (2004) Globalization, social exclusion and gender. Int Labour Rev 143:129
Chan CK-C (2012) China class or citizenship? debating workplace conflict in China. J Contemp Asia 42:308
Chan MK (2013) Contract labor in global garment supply chains: key characteristics and recent trends. Women in informal employment: globalizing and organizing. WIEGO, Manchester
Chan A (2018) The Relationship between labor ngos and chinese workers in an authoritarian regime. Global L J 9:1
Chase A (1984) A challenge to workers rights. Nova Law Rev 8:671
Chimni BS (2017) Anti-imperialism: then and now. In: Nesiah V et al (eds) Bandung, global history and international law: critical pasts and pending futures. Cambridge University Press, Cambridge
Collins H (2011) Theories of rights as justifications for human rights. In: Davidov G, Langille B (eds) The idea of labour law. Oxford University Press, Oxford, p 140
Conaghan J (2005) Work, family, and the discipline of labour law. In: Conaghan J, Rittich K (eds) Labour law, work and family. OUP
Coutu M (2013) With Hugo Sinzheimer and Max Weber in mind: the current crisis and future of labour law. Comp Labor Law Policy J 34:607–608
Crenshaw KW (1988) Race, reform, and retrenchment: transformation and legitimation in antidiscrimination law. Harv Law Rev 101(7):1331–1387

Cutler A (2001) Critical reflections on the Westphalian assumptions of international law and organization: a crisis of legitimacy. Rev Int Stud 27(2):133–150
Davidov G (2018) Distributive Justice and Labour Law. In: Collins H, Lester G, Mantouvalou V (eds) Philosophical foundations of labour law, OUP
Doorey DJ (2018) Lost in translation: Rana Plaza, Loblaws, and the disconnect between legal formality and corporate social responsibility
Duke R (2008) Constitutionalizing employment relations: Sinzheimer, Kahn-Freund, and the role of labour law. J Law Soc 35(3):341–363
Dukes R (2009) Otto Kahn-Freund and collective laissez-faire: an edifice without a keystone? Mod Law Rev 72(2):219–246
Engels-Zanden N, Merk J (2014) Private regulation and trade union rights: why codes of conduct have limited impact on trade union rights. J Bus Ethics 123(3):123–466
Evans BA (2015) Accord on Fire and Building Safety in Bangladesh: an international response to Bangladesh labour conditions. N C J Int Law 40(2):597
Ewing K (1988) The death of labour law? Oxford J Leg Stud 8:293
Fick B (2014) Corporate social responsibility for enforcement of labour rights: are there more effective alternatives?
Fudge J (2007) The new discourse of labour rights: from social to fundamental rights. Comp Labour Law Policy J 29(1):29–66
Gabel P, Harris P (1982) Building power and breaking images: critical legal theory and the practice of law. N Y U Rev L & Soc Change 11:372
Goldberg JCP (2012) Introduction: pragmatism and private law. Harv Law Rev 125:1640
Harris J (2009) Statist globalization in China, Russia and the Gulf States. Science & Society 73:6
Howse R (1999) The world trade organization and the protection of workers rights. J Small Emerg Bus Law 3:131
ILO (2016) Report IV, Decent work in global supply chains
Kahn-Freund O (1970) Trade unions, the law and society. Mod Law Rev 33(3):241–267
Klare KE (1981) Labor law as ideology: toward a new historiography of collective bargaining law. Indus Rel L J 4:450
Klare K (1988) Workplace democracy and market reconstruction: an agenda for legal reform. Cathol Univ Law Rev 38(1):1–68
Labowitz S, Baumann-Pauly D (2015) Beyond the tip of the iceberg: Bangladesh's forgotten apparel workers. NYU Stern Centre for Business and Human Rights, New York, pp 4–5
Langille B (2005) Core labour rights – the true story. Eur J Int Law 16(3):409–437
Lewis R (1979) Collective agreements: the Kahn-Freund legacy. Mod Law Rev 42:613–622
Lopez GP (2005) Living and lawyering rebelliously. Fordham L Rev 73:2041
Maryanov DC (2010) Sweatshop liability: corporate codes of conduct and the governance of labour standards in the international supply chains. Lewis Clark Law Rev 14:401
Mayer FW, Phillips N (2017) Outsourcing governance: states and the politics of a "global value chain world". New Polit Econ 22(2):134–152
McCarthy B (1964) The closed shops in Britain as cited by Undy R. An overview of Bill McCarthy's academic and political engagement with industrial relations. Ind Relat J 46:1–6
McNally D (2015) The dialectics of unity and difference in the constitution of wage-labor: on internal relations and working-class formation. Cap Class 39(1):131–146
Mezzadri A (2016) Class, gender, and the sweatshop: on the nexus between labour commodification and exploitation. Third World Q 10:1877
Mezzadri A, Lula F (2018) "Classes of labor" at the margins of global commodity chains in India and China. The Institute of Social Studies, pp 1034–1036
Milberg W, Winkler D (2013) Outsourcing economics: global value chains in capitalist development. Cambridge University Press, New York, p 115

Mumme C (2019) Rights, freedoms, law, labour and industrial voluntarism: some comments
Posthuma A (2010) Beyond 'Regulatory enclaves': challenges and opportunities to promote decent work in global production networks. In: Posthuma A, Nathan D (eds) Labour in global production networks in India. OUP
Revak H (2012) Corporate codes of conduct: binding contract or ideal publicity? Hastings Law J 63:1645–1670
Ruggie JG (2017) Multinationals as global institutions: power, authority and relative autonomy. Regul Gov:1–17
Santos BD (2002) Towards a new common sense: law, science, and politics in the paradigmatic transition, p 483
Santos A (2016) The role of law in global value chains: a research manifesto. Lond Rev Int Law 4 (1):36–39
Scales-Trent J (1989) Black women and the constitution: finding our place, asserting our rights. Harv Civ Rights-Civ Liberties Law Rev 9:9–44
Schneider EM (1986) The dialectic of rights and politics: perspectives from the women's movement. N Y Univ Law Rev 61:589–652
Selwyn B (2016) The role of law in global value chains: a research manifesto. Lond Rev Int Law 4 (1):60–61
Sklair L (2000) The transnational capitalist class. Camb Rev Int Aff 14:67
Smith JM (2017) Enforcing corporate social responsibility codes under private law: on the disciplining power of legal doctrine. Ind J Global Legal Stud 24:99
Stern RM, Terrell K (2003) Labor standards and the world trade organization. Research seminar in international economics, Ann Arbor
Terwindt C, Leader S, Yilmaz-Vastardis A, Wright J (2017) Supply chain liability: pushing the boundaries of the common law. J Eur Tort Law 8:261
Wedderburn L (1987) Labour law: from here to autonomy. Indus Law J 16(1):1–29
Werner M, Bair J (2011) Commodity chains and the uneven geographies of global capitalism: a disarticulations perspective. Environ Plan 43:988
Wesche P, Saage-Maaß M (2016) Holding companies liable for human rights abuses related to foreign subsidiaries and suppliers before German civil courts: lessons from jabir and others v kik. Hum Rights Law Rev 16:370
White LE (1994) Collaborative lawyering in the field - on mapping the paths from rhetoric to practice. Clinical L Rev 1:157
White LE (1995) Collaborative lawyering in the field – on mapping the paths from rhetoric to practice. Clin Law Rev 1:158–170
Williams JP (1987) Alchemical notes: reconstructing ideals from deconstructed rights. Harv Civ Rights-Civ Liberties Law Rev 22:401–434

Muhammad Azeem is assistant professor at Shaikh Ahmad Hassan School of Law at Lahore University of Management Sciences in Lahore, Pakistan, where he teaches labour law, critical legal theory, as well as international law from a Southern, decolonialist perspective. He has published widely in Urdu and English, most recently on labour conditions in global value chains and the China-Pakistan Economic Corridor. After practicing law and pursuing public interest litigation around issues concerning workers and peasants in Pakistan's lower and high courts for several years, he obtained a Master of Laws and Doctor of Philosophy from Osgoode Hall Law School in Toronto, Canada. Azeem is a labour organiser and an active member of the Progressive Writers Association of Lahore. He also writes poetry and criticism in Urdu and Punjabi.

From Strategic Litigation to Juridical Action

Andreas Fischer-Lescano

Abstract With strategic litigation, lawyers and public interest NGOs have sought to bring socio-structural problems before courts around the world for many years. In doing so, they (a) initiate legally substantiated lawsuits that (b) pursue goals beyond a legal process' "success" and (c) address considerable political issues. Litigation strategists often strive to realise the judicial enforcement of human rights, environmental rights, trade union rights, migrant and refugee rights, and so on, in these proceedings. In other words, they seek to make the law "better." It is precisely here that legal mobilisation's structural limitations—also present in the day-to-day business of law—come to light in the context of strategic litigation.

Keywords Deconstruction · Collective rights · Critical theory · Juridical action · Legal subjects · Paradoxes of law · Poststructuralism · Representation · Strategic litigation · Violence

1 Critique of Strategic Litigation

The concept of strategic litigation[1] comprises a strangely narrow approach. The term "litigation" reflects that the law is part of the social crisis to be addressed. However, focusing on litigation as an answer to the crisis and using courts as forums for protest[2] entails the danger of underestimating non-legal forums' importance for the legal process and, at the same time, overestimating state institutions and courts' role in legal battles. In relation to the concept of property, Katharina Pistor asserts that "[a]sset holders do not need to capture the state directly, much less win class

[1]For an overview see: Baxi (1985); Duffy (2018); see further the definition by Graser (2019a), p. 4.
[2]Lobel (2003).

A. Fischer-Lescano (✉)
Universität Bremen, Bremen, Germany
e-mail: sekretariat-voelkerrecht@uni-bremen.de

M. Saage-Maaß et al. (eds.), *Transnational Legal Activism in Global Value Chains*, Interdisciplinary Studies in Human Rights 6,
https://doi.org/10.1007/978-3-030-73835-8_15

struggles or revolutions; all they need is the right lawyers on their side who code their assets in law."[3] This criticism of state institutions equally applies to strategic litigation, which often begins too late, addresses ineffective forums and reduces critical legal policy disputes to court battles.[4] Counterforces are too seldom positioned where needed[5]—in legislation, economic and trade circles, or universities and schools. At the same time, litigation strategists risk losing sight of potential allies outside of state forums, who also articulate very clear criticisms of the law and even imitate the law's procedural forms, such as social courts in the tradition of the Russell Tribunals and Milo Rau's Congo Tribunal.[6]

The adjective "strategic" with which litigation activists describe their practice is regularly used either in a trivial sense—all litigation could be classified as "strategic" after all, as nearly all decisions about legal proceedings are made with clear goals, based on rational reasoning regarding how to achieve them—or the protagonists overestimate strategic litigation's foreseeability, underestimating the fact that its unpredictability is a central element of the legal process. As Adam Weiss rightly observes, a process' strategic consequences often cannot be anticipated, only evaluated retrospectively,[7] which of course raises the question of what criteria should be used for this evaluation. Answering this question often abruptly leads into a circle of self-righteousness. Litigation strategists measure their "success" against their strategy concept, which they adjust over the course of the process. This way, of course, even the most brutal judicial defeats can be glossed over as successfully implemented strategies to expose a class of law or force moments of public awareness of legal loopholes. Regardless of a court case's outcome, these "legal miracles" confirm all parties' legal opinions. This is possible due to vaguely formulated strategies.

If, however, strategic litigation is discontent with formulating short-term public relations and fundraising strategies and instead wants to initiate social transformation, it will have to develop sustainable goal-setting connected to other social spheres and movements. Today, the field lacks critically-reflected strategy formation. Empirical studies about strategic litigators' strategic behaviour have only just begun, but their mission statements, content and introductory remarks on strategic litigation[8]

---

[3]Pistor (2019), p. 22.

[4]Roberto M. Unger's demand that the legally-supported democratisation of society should also apply to the economy and civil society is also critical of this. See Unger (1996), p. 164.

[5]If they are, they are often side-lined by strategic litigation, in which lynchpin social contact points are usually the concrete processes and legal relationships—whether in law clinic trainings, litigation-related NGO alliances, fundraising with interested members of the public, or by cooperating with the press in reporting on trials.

[6]Klinghoffer and Klinghoffer (2002) and Rau (2017).

[7]Weiss (2019), p. 30: "Anyone who tells you he is litigating a strategic case right now is wrong: it is impossible to know in advance if a case will prove to have been strategic or not, because unpredictability is a key element."

[8]See Fuchs (2019).

make it more than clear that conceptual strategy development problems arise that reduce strategic litigation's effectiveness in fighting injustice.

1.1 Lack of Ambition

Strategic litigation is rarely ambitious enough. It seldom questions the system in which it participates, frequently abstains from partisanship in favour of those affected, and often fails to articulate the injustice of the social order. As a result, it has a stabilising effect on the prevailing political and juridical system. As Christian Helmrich puts it: "Behind strategic litigation is belief in the existing system. There is nothing subversive about strategic litigation."[9] Strategic lawsuits against public participation (SLAPPs)[10] are thus not a hostile hijacking of a form of protest. Instead, they represent the flip side of an ambivalent practice that is not primarily concerned with changing the system, but with stabilising it. The mission statement of the Berlin-based NGO Gesellschaft für Freiheitsrechte (GFF) is "Our strategy: Better law through better lawsuits."[11] "Freedom" (Freiheit) in the NGO's name becomes a "signifier of (practical, political, but also theoretical) disorientation" for such litigation strategists.[12]

Anyone who limits themselves to making "better" law in order "to protect human and civil rights in Germany and Europe"[13] runs the risk that the defence of civil liberties "produces, reproduces and sediments the exact opposite of freedom, namely a lack of freedom."[14] A strategic concentration on civil rights in constitutional law in Germany and Europe inevitably leads to Eurocentric narrow-mindedness. Consequently, case selection is oriented towards European interests or handled in such a way that transnational issues of exploitation, environmental pollution and threats to peace can be addressed in European courts. The cross-border character of structural societal problems, the transnationality of social questions, and the hybrid public-private quality of surveillance measures all fall through the cracks.[15] In the defence

[9]Helmrich (2019a), p. 34.—Translation by the author.

[10]Pring and Canan (1996).

[11]Gesellschaft für Freiheitsrechte, Mission Statement 2019, www.freiheitsrechte.org/strategische-klagen (last accessed 17 July 2019).—Translation by the author.

[12]Ruda (2018), p. 8.—Translation by the author.

[13]See the self-description of the Gesellschaft für Freiheitsrechte, Mission Statement 2019, www.freiheitsrechte.org (last accessed 17 July 2019).

[14]Ruda (2018), p. 8.—Translation by the author.

[15]See, for example, GFF's reasoning for an amicus curiae brief in the *Microsoft v. United States*, 2nd US Circuit Court of Appeals, No. 14-2985, which it supported, leaving completely unmentioned that Microsoft itself is a data wholesaler and thus a human rights abuser: "GFF is submitting the amicus curiae brief in order to demonstrate how the forthcoming decision could have an unacceptable indirect impact on federal and European law guarantees. In principle, it therefore supports the arguments presented by Microsoft in the proceedings." (GFF, Amicus Curiae Brief

of liberty's pathos—GFF claims to "strengthen civil and human rights against state intrusion"[16]—it is lost that there is no existing freedom in society to be defended, as freedom can only be *established* in the fight against existing unfreedom.

Strategic litigation demands strategy formation through analysing the social situation at hand. It must not follow legal education's apolitical stagnant structure.[17] In order to bring about lasting change, procedural strategies and targets must be strategically reflected upon, especially in order to incorporate legal procedures' limitations. In this sense, Gayatri Spivak criticises juridical action's inadequate strategies as being potentially effective in the short term but, at best, only capable of accompanying rather than causing long-term change: "My principal argument continues to be that a combination of fear and pressure, today supported by these powerful paradisciplinary formations proliferating crude theories of cultural difference, cannot bring about either lasting or real epistemic change although, accompanied by public interest litigation, they may be effective short-term weapons."[18]

1.2 Depoliticisation

At the same time, strategic litigation often has a depoliticising tendency, despite legal processes' scandalising potential. This is due to proceedings' respective constellation. "Subjective rights," the core of Christoph Menke's apt criticism,[19] privatise the public sphere, which, in turn, forces litigation strategists to enforce rights with private means when it is actually socio-structural questions that need negotiation.[20] This can certainly be a suitable transformation strategy, as long as one reflects on how poorly the legal form mirrors the underlying socio-structural conditions and

---

U.S. Supreme Court, 19 January 2018, www.freiheitsrechte.org (last accessed 17 July 2019)). And GFF's dutiful thanks to the business law firm White & Case: "The amicus curiae brief was prepared by GFF with the support of the international law firm White & Case. They did this work pro bono, for which GFF would like to express its sincere thanks."—Translations by the author. This deliberately leaves unmentioned that White & Case's portfolio includes the representation of the high-tech giants Facebook, Google, PayPal, Avast Software etc. In view of the conflicting interests of this large law firm, which works closely with companies that endanger human rights themselves, from which GFF claims to protect them (and us), the "pro bono" seal is probably awarded somewhat lightly (for the White & Case portfolio, see www.whitecase.com/law/industries/technology#experience (last accessed 17 July 2019).

[16]GFF, Mission Statement 2019, www.freiheitsrechte.org (last accessed 17 July 2019).—Translation by the author.

[17]On the desiderata of socially responsible legal education and the failure of educational reforms, see Wiethölter (1981).

[18]Spivak (2004), p. 540.

[19]Menke (2015), p. 173.

[20]Ingeborg Maus criticises an "infantilism of faith in justice," over the course of which political activity is replaced by legalistic strategies to implement social justice and environmental protection "in the hope that these goods will be allocated by the highest court." See Maus (2018), p. 27.

conflicts, and how little the real social conflict (*différend*) is reformulated in the legal process (*litige*). As Jean-François Lyotard puts it, the *différend* does justice to the *litige*; however, the *litige* can never do justice to the *différend*.[21] Participants often lack necessary awareness of the obstacles and alienation effects of "the individualistically conceived planks into which (procedural) law usually forces strategic litigation."[22]

In the worst-case scenario, protagonists *negate* legal practice's political content, for example, when, in concession to the establishment, they appease others' demands:[23] "In our understanding, the objection that we politicised the legal system through our legal interventions is therefore also mistaken."[24] Instead of emphasising all law and jurisprudence's political momentum, one withdraws to technocratic legalism. The politicisation argument is rejected with reference to a purely legal approach, because one is only trying to "draw the judges' attention towards questions that are decisive from a fundamental and human rights perspective."[25] As if there were a right life in the wrong (Theodor Adorno), this makes the lie of apolitical law its own. Litigation strategists swim in "circles, empty phrases, alibis and taboos."[26] Hence, it is necessary to make clear the political aspect of law and its most significant expression: the prevailing view.[27] Without a political theory of law for the presence of a political society that "understands" how we are entangled in an outdated "legal culture," we will not reach the height of our time, but will freeze in the depths of prehistoric times.

1.3 Advocatory Violence

In the context of strategic litigation, there is often insufficient awareness of the danger of advocatory violence, particularly the danger that lawyers come to control

---

[21]Lyotard (1989), p. 9; see also Lyotard (2004), p. 43, on the contradiction (*différend*) as a sentence that cannot be articulated, but as an "affect sentence," always irreconcilably opposed to the legal dispute (*litige*). As a discourse sentence, it is never identical to the legal reformulation: "[The] articulated sentence and [the] affect sentence can only 'meet' each other by missing each other."

[22]Helmrich (2019b), p. 140.—Translation by author.

[23]The latter, for example, opposes strategic climate litigation with the argument that it ultimately weakens the judiciary itself, because social problems' juridification through court decisions "will meet with considerable political and social resistance." The "real political un-achievability of the reduction targets of the IPCC [Intergovernmental Panel on Climate Change] and other climate protection bodies" is asserted, and a concept of legitimacy that would do justice to the problem's transnational character is not developed at all (quotes by Wegener (2019), p. 12; critical of such objections: Graser (2019b), p. 271).

[24]Burghardt and Thönnes (2019), p. 68.—Translation by the author.

[25]Burghardt and Thönnes (2019), p. 68.—Translation by the author.

[26]Wiethölter (1986), p. 10.—Translation by the author.

[27]For classic arguments on this topic, see Wesel (1979), p. 88.

the narrative instead of their clients. Especially in transnational advocacy constellations, individual and collective interests rarely coincide.[28] The interests of the victims of the 2012 Ali Enterprises factory fire in Pakistan[29] are not necessarily identical with that of European NGOs wanting to create awareness of ongoing colonialism and illegalities in transnational supply chains.[30] And even if one has to give credit to the European Center for Constitutional and Human Rights (ECCHR) for the fact that in the Ali Enterprises and Rana Plaza cases it has in fact formed alliances "of workers, affectees associations and local unions along with international relief, campaign and human rights organizations,"[31] which is unprecedented in German legal practice and transnational in the best sense of the word, representation of the unrepresented always remains precarious.

When litigation strategists call for goal-setting with "all stakeholders involved,"[32] exclusion mechanisms are surely at work. In strategic corporate management it may be positive to extend the focus to all *stakeholders* rather than the usual concentration on *shareholders*.[33] However, the division of the legal-political world into "stakes" and "holders" inevitably leads to exclusionary situations for diffuse interests[34] and those who have no voice.[35] Various problems derive from this, including: (a) the fixation on legitimate interests, their owners and the legally enforceable (subjective) law as an instrument to solve social problems, which is a deeply European idea; (b) the fact that other models of social organisation and conflict resolution regularly fall out of sight due to this fixation; and (c) in the relationship between the helping NGOs and those affected, the danger of a colonial power dynamic (white saviour complex) is often immanent.[36] Litigation, if practised nevertheless, must reflect on these dangers and enact effective safeguards so that power asymmetries are not reproduced and deepened.

---

[28]A rule of doubt can only be a first move in dissolution. See Kessler and Borkamp (2019).

[29]See 7 O 95/15 Landgericht Dortmund judgment on 10 January 2019.

[30]Saage-Maaß and Terwindt (2020).

[31]ECCHR, Week of Justice, 4 November 2018, www.ecchr.eu/en/event/one-week-of-justice (last accessed 17 July 2019).

[32]Lindner (2019), p. 99.

[33]See Freeman (2010).

[34]On the difficulty of translating these into law: Kommer (2012).

[35]This is where Boaventura de Sousa Santos (2012), p. 52, comes in when he calls for a "Sociology of Absences:" "By sociology of absences I mean research that aims to show that what does not exist is actually actively produced as non-existent, that is to say, as an unbelievable alternative to what exists. Its empirical object is impossible from the point of view of conventional social sciences. Impossible objects must be turned into possible objects, absent objects into present objects."

[36]Do Mar Castro Varela and Dhawan (2015), p. 87.

1.4 Victimological Defensiveness

Finally, litigation strategies are quite often characterised by what we might call "victimological defensiveness," for example, when strategic litigation's main goal is "to limit interventions, especially on the part of the state, and to support affected social actors in mobilizing the law."[37] The fact that the aim should be to empower those affected from passive "victims" to become agents of transformation and enable social change in legal processes, which must lead to transformed economic power relations, in particular, is not given enough consideration in a merely defensively oriented legal position against "interventions." This is especially so if one takes a liberalist approach in the traditional sense and wants to counter "interventions, especially on the part of the state." Such approaches only reproduce the liberal misunderstanding of separation of state and society, of public and private. They insufficiently address the equally threatening dangers emanating from non-state spheres, while their destructive and self-rationality-maximising expansions into political and social processes (keyword: "market-conforming democracy") threaten the autonomy of political and social processes.[38] In other words, primarily state-directed legal strategies will not go far in addressing responsibility for inhumane and ecologically devastating global supply chains, the deaths of migrants and asylum-seekers in the Mediterranean, big data's effects, or the damage caused by a globalised financial market.

2 Juridical Action

In response to deconstructive legal criticism in the US, numerous parties have repeatedly emphasised that it is necessary to practice individual legal defence, rupture defence and strategic litigation "nonetheless."[39] This is not wrong, because legal struggles are dependent on established forms, but it should not be used as a pretext to consider strategic litigation in its existing form as immutable. A sustainable transformation of the legal form and the social structures that underpin it can only be achieved by a transformative legal policy of reflected anticipation: "It anticipates the other law counterfactually in the existing one. It is political fiction (or of the imagination)."[40]

In this view, strategic litigation's practices are rarely imaginative enough. They must therefore be transformed, for example, based on the 1923 legal mobilisation strategy developed by Karl Korsch, co-founder of the German Institute for Social Research, in the context of labour law. His concept of "juridical action" (*juristische*

[37]Burghardt and Thönnes (2019), p. 66.—Translation by the author.

[38]Fischer-Lescano (2016b).

[39]For a prominent example, see Williams (1987).

[40]Menke (2018), p. 30.—Translation by the author.

Aktion) does not dispense with strategic considerations, but seeks to take into account the unplannable, spontaneous, contingent and irrational in order to ultimately bring "chaos into order."[41] Korsch opposes "business as usual" (*das Weiter-so*) and distinguishes between two concrete steps in juridical action. First and foremost, he suggests that the points should be determined at which a conflict has already flared up or is currently in the process of flaring up between civil law and social law conceptions of the employment relationship. Second, an attempt must then be made at each of these individual points to deduce the consequences of the social-law viewpoint in a way that corresponds, as explicitly as possible, to the present historical situation.[42] This double movement of juridical action need not necessarily lead to litigation. What is central, however, is that (1) the analytical dimension involving the description of the conflict or paradox and (2) the activist conclusion of deducing consequences in a way that explicitly corresponds to the specific historical situation, are coordinated.[43] These two concrete steps constitute juridical action.

2.1 First Step

Juridical action's first step is to identify hidden, veiled and invisible paradoxes. One must name the social abyss, not cover it up. That the law is permeated by contradictions, ruptures and paradoxes is not a new idea, but has been central to (legal) philosophy since Heraclitus. This is expressed in Gustav Radbruch's "antinomies of the idea of law" just as much as in Jean-François Lyotard's concept of "contradiction," Jacques Rancière's "incomprehension," Jacques Derrida's "aporia," Ernesto Laclau and Chantal Mouffe's "dialectic," Amy Allen, Wendy Brown and Christoph Menke's reference to the "paradoxons" and Rudolf Wiethölter's famous "Factor X."[44]

Karl Marx's critique of Georg Wilhelm Friedrich Hegel's theory of the state also focuses on real contradictions and distinguishes true from vulgar critique, precisely by whether the former is able to do what the latter does not: grasp the necessity of the contradiction.

> Vulgar critique falls into [...] dogmatic error. For example, it criticizes the constitution. It draws attention to contradiction of powers, etc. It finds inconsistencies everywhere. This is still dogmatic critique that struggles with its subject matter, just as, for example, the dogma of the Holy Trinity was once eliminated by the contradiction of one and three. True critique, on the other hand, shows the Holy Trinity's inner genius in the human brain. It describes its birth. Thus, the true philosophical critique of the present state constitution does not only

[41] With reference to Adorno: Wiethölter (1994), p. 107.

[42] Korsch (1980), p. 392.

[43] Seifert (2013).

[44] Wiethölter (1988).

> show contradictions exist, it explains them, and understands their genesis, their necessity. It grasps their unique meaning.[45]

Such true legal critique, which opens up the possibility for contingency and transcendence, is "not simply a political or legal critique,"[46] but is embedded in social theory. It reconstructs the "distinctions of the natives"[47] and captures these structures' essential contradictions to explain the failure of traditional distinctions as well as create space for contingencies. A systemic critique in the name of the paradox of right and wrong can never reach a conclusion. Critique in the name of Factor X, in the name of justice, or in the name of deconstruction is a thorn in the flesh, a formula for searching instead of a yardstick.

2.2 *Second Step*

Juridical action, however, must not be exhausted in the theoretical posture of radical criticality; it must also take a second step, that of turning the identified contradiction into a contradiction against reality. It must actively work to tear up systemic contradictions[48] and use social forms against their own formal logics. Juridical action is a theoretical-practical form of action that "transfers" systemic forms into new, more just forms. It is a practice of form transcendence.

2.2.1 Legal Action Against the Far Right

The most important task of our time is to name all forms of soft and hard authoritarianism,[49] to reject right-wing legal nihilism[50] and right-wing nihilistic extremism, and to fight "rightlessness in an age of rights"[51] with radical juridical action.[52] This would include radical juridical action on issues like the totalitarian synchronization (*Gleichschaltung*) of the judiciary in Hungary, Poland and Turkey; institutional racism; the criminalisation in France of critical analysis of the political bias of judges

---

[45]Marx (2006), p. 296.—Translation by the author.

[46]See Michel Foucault's critique of juridicism in: Foucault (2018), p. 341.

[47]Luhmann (1993), p. 256.

[48]See objective formulation: Christodoulidis (2009), p. 25: "Forcing [the legal system] to confront a contradiction."

[49]For different forms of authoritarianism, see: Randeria (2019).

[50]Of frightening topicality, see Adorno's 1967 lecture in Adorno (2019); for more on right-wing strategies to abolish the rule of law with the means of the rule of law, see Kleinschmidt (2016), p. 169.

[51]Gündogdu (2015).

[52]Baer (2019).

in asylum cases (Platform Supra Legem);[53] the proclamation of "Get-out" (*Hau-Ab*) laws in Germany; and the declaration of states of emergency and armed assaults in response to terrorist attacks.

2.2.2 Decentralisation

Further, it is necessary to reflect on postcolonial critiques in order to overcome the law's Eurocentrism and imperial life's externalisation of costs: to "act as if another globalization were possible."[54] For this, Wiethölter suggests that not only Europe, but also the "subject of reason" must be decentralised and removed from its essential position in law. Instead of allowing the legal status relationship to merge into state-citizen relations, social rights must be formulated that do not conceive of interventions in merely statist logic. In other words, what is needed are new, non-rational legal entities (like animals, cyborgs and body fragments), new forms of organisation for social dissidence (from labour law to science law, tenancy law, environmental law and financial market law),[55] and new patterns of obligation (like human rights obligations of private individuals).

2.2.3 "Manufacturing" Law

In addition, one needs to fundamentally question the "distribution" of rights and prosperity through the development of novel patterns of allocation. As Wiethölter puts it, "right/freedom as freedom/right (*right-fabrication*!)"[56] is needed to radically address the question of property that is posed daily in the face of global inequality. This would seek not only to increase social ties and limit abuse, but would start with the use of property itself: to limit the concept of property itself, to oppose other rights,[57] and to legally address the postmodern class question as a question of "distribution of distribution"[58] in different functional contexts by developing new counter-rights that break up the traditional patterns of distributional allocation.[59] Derrida formulates it as "inventing new rights. Even if these new rights always remain inappropriate to what I call justice. A justice that is not law, even if it is to determine its history and progress."[60]

---

[53]Langford and Rask Madsen, France Criminalises Research on Judges, VerfBlog, 22 June 2019, www.verfassungsblog.de (last accessed 17 July 2019).

[54]Rau (2019), p. 26.

[55]Hensel (2019).

[56]Wiethölter (1986), p. 61, author's emphasis.

[57]See plea, still topical today, in: Ridder (1977).

[58]Luhmann (1985), p. 119.

[59]Loick (2018).

[60]Derrida (1998).

2.2.4 Culture of Dispute

Finally, it is central to end the *complicity* of human and civil rights movements as well as litigation strategists in the liberal human rights discourse. In Wiethölter's words, successor organisations need to be developed "for the – now permanently sussed out – loss of 'law' as a neutral (impartial) third party, which originally as God or nature, and later as order, market and freedom, promised a world of just 'allocations' and 'distributions,' but was not able to keep that promise."[61] While we certainly need to safeguard social spheres of freedom from state intervention, we do not need more enforcement of alleged achievements of European constitutionalism in liberalistic excesses in the forms of World Bank development programmes and US-American interventionism.[62] Our focus should lie on legal safeguards for the process of social democratisation. Here the challenge lies, as Spivak has rightly pointed out, in suturing "the habits of democracy onto the earlier cultural formation [. . .] the real effort should be to access and activate the tribals' indigenous 'democratic' structures to parliamentary democracy by patient and sustained efforts to learn to learn from below."[63] The task of law as a culture of dispute is then to enable this kind of subaltern appropriation of law, the legal organisation of democratic processes not only within the framework of parliamentary representation, but also within the framework of social forms of democracy. Law as a "culture of dispute" enables democratic debate in the respective social contexts.[64]

3 Conclusion: Juridical Action as a Strategy of Dissidence

Juridical action worthy of the name takes into account litigation's inadequacies and clarifies strategy before initiating any "strategic litigation." Juridical action de-centres the legal process by taking it seriously as a crystallisation point of social disputes, but is aware of the falseness of the *litige*. In this knowledge and despite all reservations, it uses the legal process as a forum for conflict staging, articulation and transformation,[65] but only to immediately transcend the legal process' limitations. Thus, juridical action transcends the legal system to incorporate politics, the arts, science, literature, theatre and economics. It eludes categorical functional differentiations. Like Franz Kafka's legal criticism, Peter Weiss's theatrical interpretation of the Auschwitz trial and Karl Kraus' cursing of procedure,[66] juridical action seeks to

[61] Wiethölter (1986), p. 62.—Translation by the author.

[62] So do Slaughter and Jackson (2019).

[63] Spivak (2004), p. 548.

[64] In this sense, also Kaleck (2019).

[65] See also Trüstedt (2012).

[66] Weiss (1991); on Kraus, see Trüstedt (2016); on Kafka's legal criticism, see Fischer-Lescano (2016a).

disrupt and to confront injustice. As an action critical of order (*contre-conduite*),[67] it is important for juridical action to increase the "rejection points" in the political fabric and expand the area of possible dissent.

References

Adorno T (2019) Aspekte des neuen Rechtsradikalismus. Suhrkamp, Berlin

Baer S (2019) Democracy in peril: a call for amici and amicae curiae and critical lawyering. Transnatl Leg Theory 10(2):140–162

Baxi U (1985) Taking suffering seriously: social action litigation in the Supreme Court of India. Third World Leg Stud 4:107–132

Burghardt B, Thönnes C (2019) Die Gesellschaft für Freiheitsrechte. In: Graser A, Helmrich C (eds) Strategic Litigation. Begriff und Praxis. Nomos, Baden-Baden, pp 65–72

Christodoulidis E (2009) Strategies of rupture. Law Crit 20(1):3–26

De Sousa Santos B (2012) Public sphere and epistemologies of the south. Afr Dev 37(1):43–67

Derrida J (1998) I distrust utopia, I want the impossible. DIE ZEIT, 5 March 1998

Do Mar Castro Varela M, Dhawan N (2015) Postkoloniale Theorie. Transscript, Bielefeld

Duffy H (2018) Strategic human rights litigation: understanding and maximising impact. Hart, London

Fischer-Lescano A (2016a) Franz Kafka's critique of legal violence. Revista Brasileira de Sociologia do Direito 3:9–51

Fischer-Lescano A (2016b) Struggles for a global internet constitution. Protecting global communication structures against surveillance measures. Global Constitutionalism 5(2):145–172

Foucault M (2017) Sicherheit, Territorium, Bevölkerung. Geschichte der Gouvernementalität. Suhrkamp, Berlin

Foucault M (2018) Die Geburt der Biopolitik. Suhrkamp, Berlin

Freeman E (2010) Strategic management: a stakeholder approach. Cambridge University Press, Cambridge

Fuchs G (2019) Rechtsmobilisierung. In: Boulanger et al (eds) Interdisziplinäre Rechtsforschung. Springer, Wiesbaden, pp 243–256

Graser A (2019a) Was es über Strategic Litigation zu schreiben gälte. In: Graser A, Helmrich C (eds) Strategic Litigation. Begriff und Praxis. Nomos, Baden-Baden, pp 9–19

Graser A (2019b) Vermeintliche Fesseln der Demokratie: Warum die Klimaklagen ein vielversprechender Weg sind. Zeitschrift für Umweltrecht 2019(5):271–278

Gündogdu A (2015) Rightlessness in an age of rights: Hannah Arendt and the contemporary struggles of migrants. Oxford University Press, Oxford

Helmrich C (2019a) Wir wissen eigentlich gar nicht, was strategische Prozessführung ist. In: Graser A, Helmrich C (eds) Strategic Litigation. Begriff und Praxis. Nomos, Baden-Baden, pp 31–35

Helmrich C (2019b) Strategic Litigation rund um die Welt. In: Graser A, Helmrich C (eds) Strategic Litigation. Begriff und Praxis. Nomos, Baden-Baden, pp 115–140

Hensel I (2019) Wissenschaftskampfrecht. Kritische Justiz 52(4):449–478

Kaleck W (2019) Mit Recht gegen die Macht. In: Graser A, Helmrich C (eds) Strategic Litigation. Begriff und Praxis. Nomos, Baden-Baden, pp 21–26

Kessler A, Borkamp U (2019) JUMEN e.V. In: Graser A, Helmrich C (eds) Strategic Litigation. Begriff und Praxis. Nomos, Baden-Baden, pp 73–80

[67] Foucault (2017), p. 292.

Kleinschmidt R (2016) Fallstudie: Die Rechte und das Recht. In: Braun et al (eds) Strategien der extremen Rechten. Springer, Wiesbaden, pp 167–195
Klinghoffer AJ, Klinghoffer JA (2002) International citizens' tribunals: mobilizing public opinion to advance human rights. Palgrave, Basingstoke
Kommer S (2012) Diffuse Umweltrechte in Brasilien. Zeitschrift für Umweltrecht 23(9):459–468
Korsch K (1980) Arbeitsrecht für Betriebsräte (1922). In: Buckmiller M (ed) Karl Korsch Gesamtausgabe. Europäische Verlagsanstalt, Frankfurt am Main, pp 279–492
Lindner C (2019) Strategic Litigation zwischen Wissenschaft, Lehre und anwaltlicher Praxis. In: Graser A, Helmrich C (eds) Strategic Litigation. Begriff und Praxis. Nomos, Baden-Baden, pp 91–102
Lobel J (2003) Success without victory: lost legal battles and the long road to justice in America. New York University Press, New York
Loick D (2018) Der Missbrauch des Eigentums. August Verlag, Berlin
Luhmann N (1985) Zum Begriff der sozialen Klasse. In: Luhmann N (ed) Soziale Differenzierung. Zur Geschichte einer Idee. Westdeutscher Verlag, Opladen, pp 119–162
Luhmann N (1993) "Was ist der Fall?" und "Was steckt dahinter?". Zeitschrift für Soziologie 22 (4):245–260
Lyotard JF (1989) Der Widerstreit. Wilhelm Fink, Munich
Lyotard JF (2004) Der Affekt-Satz. In: Lyotard JF (ed) Das Elend in der Philosophie. Passagen, Vienna, pp 41–49
Marx K (2006) Kritik des Hegelschen Staatsrechts. In: Marx Engels Werke. Dietz, Berlin, pp 203–333
Maus I (2018) Justiz als gesellschaftliches Über-Ich. Suhrkamp, Berlin
Menke C (2015) Kritik der Rechte. Suhrkamp, Berlin
Menke C (2018) Genealogie, Paradoxie, Transformation. In: Franzki et al (eds) Gegenrechte. Recht jenseits des Subjekts. Mohr-Siebeck, Tübingen, pp 13–31
Pistor K (2019) The code of capital. Princeton University Press, Princeton
Pring G, Canan P (1996) SLAPPs. Getting sued for speaking out. Temple University Press, Philadelphia
Randeria S (2019) Varieties of voice: ballot box, courts and streets. In: Meldolesi L, ĵaStame N (eds) A bias for hope. Italic Digital Editions, Rome, pp 226–240
Rau M (2017) Das Kongo Tribunal. Verbrecher Verlag, Berlin
Rau M (2019) Orestes in Mosul. Golden Book. Verbrecher Verlag, Berlin
Ridder H (1977) Der Grundrechtsschutz des Eigentums, seine Grenzen und Beschränkungen im Öffentlichen Interesse. In: Österreichische Juristenkommission (ed) Der Grundrechtsschutz des Eigentums. C.F. Müller, Heidelberg, pp 39–58
Ruda F (2018) Gegen-Freiheit. Komik und Fatalismus. Konstanz University Press, Konstanz
Saage-Maaß M, Terwindt C (2020) Recht der imperialen Lebensweise. In: Buckel et al (eds) Neue Theorien des Rechts. Mohr-Siebeck, Tübingen, pp 341–358
Seifert J (2013) Zum Stellenwert der juristischen Aktion bei Karl Korsch. In: Kritidis G (ed) Zur Aktualität von Karl Korsch und seine Bedeutung für die Entwicklung der sozialistischen Linken. Loccumer Initiative kritischer Wissenschaftler und Wissenschaftlerinnen, Loccum, pp 3–8
Slaughter AM, Jackson A (2019) Afghanistans vergessene Frauen. Blätter für deutsche und internationale Politik 29(4):49–50
Spivak G (2004) Righting wrongs. South Atl Q 103(2–3):523–581
Trüstedt K (2012) Nomos and Narrative: Zu den Verfahren der Orestie. In: Ladeur et al (eds) Die Innenwelt der Außenwelt der Innenwelt des Rechts. Fink, Munich, pp 59–77
Trüstedt K (2016) Der Fluch des Verfahrens: Karl Kraus und die Akten zum Fall Kerr. Mod Lang Notes 131(3):701–723
Unger RM (1996) What should legal analysis become? Verso, London
Wegener B (2019) Urgenda. Weltrettung per Gerichtsbeschluss? Zeitschrift für Umweltrecht 30 (1):3–13

Weiss P (1991) Die Ermittlung: Oratorium in 11 Gesängen. Suhrkamp, Frankfurt am Main
Weiss A (2019) The essence of strategic litigation. In: Graser A, Helmrich C (eds) Strategic Litigation. Begriff und Praxis. Nomos, Baden-Baden, pp 27–30
Wesel U (1979) Herrschende Meinung. Kursbuch 56:88–109
Wiethölter R (1981) Reformatio in peius. Zur Geschichte der Ausbildungsreform. Ein Gespräch. Kritische Justiz 14(1):1–17
Wiethölter R (1986) Rechtswissenschaft. Helbing und Lichterhahn, Basel
Wiethölter R (1988) Zum Fortbildungsrecht der (richterlichen) Rechtsfortbildung. Fragen eines lesenden Recht-Fertigungslehrers. Kritische Vierteljahresschrift für Gesetzgebung und Rechtswissenschaft 3(1):1–28
Wiethölter R (1994) Zur Argumentation im Recht: Entscheidungsfolgen als Rechtsgründe? In: Teubner (ed) Entscheidungenfolgen als Rechtsgründe: Folgenorientiertes Argumentieren in rechtsvergleichender Sicht. Nomos, Baden-Baden, pp 89–120
Williams PJ (1987) Alchemical notes: reconstructing ideals from deconstructed rights. Harv Civ Rights-Civ Liberties Law Rev 22(2):401–433

Andreas Fischer-Lescano is professor of public law, European law, international law and legal theory at the University of Bremen, Germany. He is director of the Center of European Law and Politics (ZERP) at the University of Bremen and co-editor of the journal *Kritische Justiz*. His research focuses on international law, human rights, European external relations and legal theory. He edited the book *Neue Theorien des Rechts* (third edition 2020, with Sonja Buckel and Ralph Christensen) and *Contested Regime Collisions. Interdisciplinary Inquiries into Norm Fragmentation in World Society* (Cambridge 2016, with Kerstin Blome et al.), and *Recht gegen rechts. Report 2020* (Fischer-Taschenbuch 2020, with Nele Austermann et al.).

Toward a Strategic Engagement with the Question of the Corporation

Critical Remarks on Business and Human Rights

Michael Bader

Abstract Corporations, in their quest for the highest profit margin, have violated human rights, labour rights and environmental standards for decades, with little to no accountability. In recent years, the fight for corporate accountability under the banner of "Business and Human Rights" has come to dominate civil society's engagement with the "question of the corporation." This chapter aims to critically examine the political objectives underpinning the broad-church project of Business and Human Rights in its world-making aspirations, taking the Legally Binding Instrument currently under discussion at the UN Human Rights Council as a case study. Using a historical narrative approach, this article first situates the evolution of Business and Human Rights within neoliberal globalisation and, against this backdrop, attempts to think through the "dark side" of this particular strand of human rights activism. By bringing critical legal scholarship on the corporation and human rights into closer conversation with Business and Human Rights, the article aims to excavate the latter's structural flaws, namely that it leaves the asymmetries in the global economy and the imperial corporate form unchallenged. By problematising Business and Human Rights' presupposition of business as fact and its uncritical embrace of rights as positive change-makers, the article presents an invitation to rethink strategic political objectives vis-à-vis corporate rights abuses.

Keywords Business and Human Rights · Corporations · Corporate power · Neoliberalism · Globalisation · Critical legal theory · Global governance · United Nations · OEIGWG

I would like to thank ECCHR's Business and Human Rights team, particularly Cannelle Lavite, Miriam Saage-Maaß, Christian Schliemann and Ben Vanpeperstraete, for valuable insights and fruitful discussions. Further I am grateful to Nicolas Bueno, Andreas Fischer-Lescano, Christopher Patz and Julia Sachseder for their valuable critique of and opinion on earlier drafts as well as Allison West and Arite Keller for their indispensable work on the text. All errors are mine.

M. Bader (✉)
European Center for Constitutional and Human Rights (ECCHR), Berlin, Germany
e-mail: bader@ecchr.eu

M. Saage-Maaß et al. (eds.), *Transnational Legal Activism in Global Value Chains*, Interdisciplinary Studies in Human Rights 6,
https://doi.org/10.1007/978-3-030-73835-8_16

1 Introduction

For decades, survivors, activists and an array of civil society organisations (CSOs) have worked to hold corporations to account for their abusive practices around the globe and to make them legally liable for the harm they cause. The grotesque structural set-up of corporate legality, pointedly termed "a structure of irresponsibility" by legal scholar Harry Glasbeek,[1] has, however, made achieving corporate accountability a difficult task, requiring much creativity from lawyers as they attempt to forge cases against the decision-making bodies of complex corporate networks, often headquartered in the Global North.[2] The legal struggle against the German retail company KiK, part of the broader accountability campaign related to the 2012 Ali Enterprises factory fire in Pakistan, is certainly one such case.[3] Due to the hardship faced by those affected by and survivors of corporate human rights violations, it seems almost a natural course of action for the bulk of CSOs, lawyers and policy-makers concerned with these violations to focus on establishing a legal pathway for remedy and (imagined) justice. From this viewpoint, one concerned with ensuring legal opportunity and access to remedy, the existing accountability vacuum with regard to corporations' transnational operations must be closed and related governance gaps filled.[4]

The project of "Business and Human Rights" in general, and the negotiation of the Legally Binding Instrument[5] in particular, have contributed to directing much public attention to "the question of the corporation" in the international realm, and brought together an array of activists, scholars and practitioners committed to fighting corporate abuse of people and the planet. While I share a central desire with Business and Human Rights and the proponents of the Legally Binding Instrument—namely to end corporate harm in the name of profit—I am highly sceptical of the draft treaty's prospects in attaining this goal. Although I have doubts about the legal design of the current Legally Binding Instrument, this is not the main focus of the present inquiry.[6] Rather, I am interested here in engaging with the

---

[1] Glasbeek (2010).

[2] A well-known example of such creative lawyering practice is Peter Weiss' excavation of a US Federal law, the Alien Tort Claims Act of 1789, for the purpose of making an extraterritorial legal claim in *Filártiga v. Peña-Irala*, which eventually, and for a few decades, led to significant corporate accountability practice in the United States.

[3] See chapter by Miriam Saage-Maaß in this volume; Bader et al. (2019).

[4] Bernaz (2016); Ramasastry (2015), p. 237; De Jonge (2011), p. 69.

[5] Legally Binding Instrument to regulate, in International Human Rights Law, the Activities of Transnational Corporations and Other Business Enterprises, currently in its Revised Draft version, see: OEIGWG Chairmanship Revised Draft 16 July 2019; www.ohchr.org/Documents/HRBodies/HRCouncil/WGTransCorp/OEIGWG_RevisedDraft_LBI.pdf (last accessed 1 August 2020).

[6] The major realist doubt is the idea that the Legally Binding Instrument will streamline, on a global scale, the efforts of Business and Human Rights. The human rights system, as it stands, is highly fragmented (see for example Payandeh 2015, p. 302). Therefore, the question arises as to how the dynamic linkage to "all human rights" in Article 3(3) of the Legally Binding Instrument will be

political objectives formulated by civil society and scholarly activists in the name of Business and Human Rights, in order to excavate the structural flaws underpinning this approach. By bringing Grietje Baars' monograph *The Corporation, Law and Capitalism* and other critical interrogations of rights and corporate power under neoliberalism into conversation with Business and Human Rights, I aim to provide a different perspective on the occurrence of corporate rights abuses in order to spur a reorientation of strategic engagement with the "question of the corporation."[7]

Taking the scholarly work of Robert Knox as a starting point for my train of thought, I understand strategic interventions as "revolutionary, inasmuch as they address critiquing or abolishing the basic logic of the system."[8] Importantly in Knox's account, strategic interventions are not less pragmatic than tactical ones, as both aim at finding the best possible engagement. Rather, the difference lies in the goal of the former to overcome or radically transform a structure or system, while the latter is concerned with "conjunctural moments" or "transitory conflicts."[9] Crucially, strategic objectives determine the overall frame for our actions, while tactics in service of a strategy must take care to evade capitulation to the logics of the very system the strategy seeks to overturn.

My main argument is that the political objectives of Business and Human Rights are not strategic and aimed at transformation or emancipation, but—at first glance, somewhat counter-intuitively as pointed out by Baars—run a high risk of legitimising and stabilising the status quo by not centring the composition of the global economy as well as the corporation's profit mandate in their quest for change. Importantly, however, this article does not in any way aim to denounce all scholarship produced under the auspices of Business and Human Rights, nor does it lament that more rights-based NGOs have started to attend to the topic of corporate exploitation and abuse. Crucially, too, it is not the usage of corporate accountability litigation as a tactical means of resistance that is problematised here, but rather the

dealt with, as it stipulates no new substantive provisions. It takes quite the imagination to envision states protecting against corporate abuse when they themselves are not bound by the human rights provisions they are supposed to oversee. This is especially so as, contrary to hopes of some civil society stakeholders and the unsuccessful aspirations of the UN Norms of 2003 (UN Doc.E/CN.4/Sub.2/2003/12/Rev.2 (26 August 2003); Weissbrodt and Kruger 2003; Miretski and Bachmann 2012), there is no set of rules binding corporations directly. The Revised Draft is more a repetition of already established duties of states, primarily, as De Schutter (2015), p. 67, argues, because it would not be politically feasible for corporations to be made direct subjects of international law. Equally unfeasible politically, but a provision that could have had a profound impact on the international legal sphere, was Article 13(6) of the Zero Draft, which proclaimed the primacy of human rights over trade and investment agreements. Much debated at the fourth session, as it is not a principle of international law *de lege lata*, such a primacy-of-human-rights clause, certainly possible *de lege ferenda*, would have represented a useful tool to mitigate state-corporate complicity and corporate coercion of states by ensuring that human rights provisions trump investment treaty clauses (Krajewski 2017; Amnesty International 2014, p. 173).

[7] Baars (2019) and Knox (2010).

[8] Knox (2010), p. 199.

[9] Knox (2010), p. 199.

turn from case-based struggles to world-making within a legal frame that takes the lack of remedy and redress as its starting point. My aim here is to question Business and Human Rights' presupposition of "business" as a natural phenomenon, its mobilisation of (human) rights as an unquestionable force for good, and its employment of (human) rights to save the world from bad corporate decision-making and corporate greed. Both the posture of leaving business structures unquestioned and the uncritical embrace of rights have, in my reading, implications for the prospect of ending corporate abuse.[10]

To elaborate on this, I first trace a historical narrative that situates the evolution of Business and Human Rights within the context of neoliberal globalisation. Against this backdrop, I aim to think through the "dark side" of this particular strand of human rights activism with a focus on its costs rather than benefits.[11] Finally, I offer an invitation to those equally concerned with Business and Human Rights' prospects for bringing about the change so direly needed, to consider more profound solutions to the question of the corporation that are attentive to both the corporate form and the global economic order in the quest for transformative change.

2 The Corporation, Neoliberal Globalisation and the Emergence of Business and Human Rights

As Baars has outlined, the evolution of Business and Human Rights and its focus on corporate accountability—from the voluntary UN Global Compact to the "soft law" UN Guiding Principles on Business and Human Rights (UNGPs) and now the Legally Binding Instrument—represents more an inevitable and logical continuation than a strategic roadmap for structural change. While over the last decades the corporation and the atrocities committed in the name of profit have both accelerated and become increasingly exposed, Business and Human Rights and the drafting of the Legally Binding Instrument neither radically question the system that produces corporate abuse, nor do they formulate strategic objectives. Rather, as Baars explains, Business and Human Rights and its focus on corporate accountability "shows how capitalist law generates seemingly emancipatory discourses and practices that, on closer inspection, turn out to follow the logic of capitalism itself."[12] Importantly, this capitulation to the logics of the system makes it so that corporate accountability becomes not a restraint on corporate value extraction activities, but rather a facilitator and stabiliser of corporate profit-making and corporate capitalism on the whole.[13]

[10]See also Baars (2019), p. 3.

[11]Kennedy (2004), p. 3.

[12]Baars (2016), p. 132.

[13]Baars (2016), p. 132.

By way of briefly touching upon the main regulatory attempts to tame the corporation after the Second World War, this section aims to situate the post-war evolution of the corporation and its rise to unprecedented influence and power under neoliberalism. Importantly, this narrative must start in the 1970s with the aspirations for a New International Economic Order (NIEO).[14] Rarely mentioned in Business and Human Rights scholarship, this third-way counter-proposal by the Group of 77 of the Non-Aligned Movement had the regulation of the corporation on its agenda, but was not narrowly focused on corporate (mis)conduct alone.[15] Instead, it comprised a broader struggle "for structural changes in the world economy that the new nations desired, in the interests of justice, world peace, and development."[16] While the newly independent states' proposal was met with strong resistance by the (mostly) former colonial empires,[17] neoliberal capitalism rose to dominance and spread across the globe by way of a universalised development paradigm.[18] It is here that the corporation (re)emerged as the dominant transnational economic actor. The following decades saw the behavioural patterns of corporate activity evolve to its current modus operandi through complex global value chains.[19] Although the corporation is not a new phenomenon, the current power and influence of transnationally operating businesses within today's globalised economy is unprecedented,[20] with

[14]See further Bockman (2015) and Volume 6 of Humanity (2015), wholly dedicated to an exploration of the NIEO.

[15]The NIEO's vision is mirrored in the two most notable international legal documents produced under its auspices, the Declaration of the Establishment of a NIEO of 1 May 1974 and the Charter of Economic Rights and Duties of States. See UNGA Res. 29/3281 (XXIX); UN Doc A/RES/S-6/3201 (1 May 1974); UNGA 3201 (S-VI); and UN Doc A/RES/29/3281 (12 December 1974). Article 2 No. 2(a) of the Charter provoked controversy as it holds that every state has the right to "regulate and exercise authority over foreign investment within its national jurisdiction [. . .]," while Article 2 No. 2(b) awards the host state the power to "regulate and supervise the activities of [the corporation]" (UNGA Res. 29/3281 (XXIX), (12 December 1974), Article 1). Further, it was in the wake of the NIEO that the UN Commission on Transnational Corporations and UN Centre for Transnational Corporations (UNCTC) were established. See ECOSOC Res. 1908 (LVII) (2 August 1974) and ECOSOC Res. 1913 (LVII) (5 December 1974). For further reading, see Hippolyte (2019), Sauvant (2015), Bair (2015) and Weber and Winanti (2016).

[16]Rajagopal (2003), p. 73.

[17]At first glance, it already becomes clear that the divide was among the "underdeveloped" Third World and its "developed" counterpart which, with the exception of Australia, opposed the charter (Belgium, Denmark, Germany, Luxembourg, the United Kingdom and the United States) or abstained (Austria, Canada, France, Ireland, Israel, Italy, Japan, the Netherlands, Norway and Spain). See Chatterjee (1991), p. 672.

[18]Pahuja (2011) and Slobodian (2018).

[19]Muchlinski (2007), p. 21; IGLP Harvard Law and Production Working Group (2016).

[20]De Jonge (2011), p. 66. For the historical roots of the corporation and its relationship with the state, see further: Baars (2015), Stern (2011) and Taylor (2006).

over 80 percent of global trade being attributed to corporations' global value chain networks.[21]

With the ascent of neoliberal globalisation came the rise of rights as the main language to bring human suffering into the realm of global governance,[22] notwithstanding, of course, that the current form of globalisation is somewhat "inimical to human rights protection."[23] As Mary Nolan contends, at the same time that the neoliberal project was first minted into concrete policy "the dominant understanding of human rights in the long 1970s encouraged governments, NGOs, and international institutions to focus on the individual, the legal and the political, and to ignore how neoliberal structural adjustment violated the economic and social human rights of so many."[24]

While the turn to neoliberalism was conventionally described as one of state retraction in order for the market to be "freed" from state interference through liberalisation, privatisation and deregulation measures,[25] historian Quinn Slobodian describes the role of the state in neoliberalism not as an outside force to the market, but a rather important component of the neoliberal project itself. According to its Geneva School architects, this neoliberal economic world order "depends on the protection of dominium (the rule of property) against the overreach of imperium (the rule of states)."[26] Slobodian therefore proposes the metaphor of "encasement" as best capturing the role of the state in the neoliberal project.[27] Rather than states with insulated economies that relate at the international level, he suggests it is the neoliberal international economic order that encases the state, its democratic rule and its national economies.[28] "What neoliberals seek," he contends, "is not a partial but a complete protection of private capital rights, and the ability of supranational judiciary bodies [. . .] to override national legislation that might disrupt the global rights of capital."[29]

As stories of corporate abuse increased and earlier attempts to regulate corporations' transnational activity failed,[30] the 2000 UN Global Compact, a global, principles-based but voluntary "corporate social responsibility" (CSR) initiative,

---

[21] United Nations Conference on Trade and Development (2013) World Investment Report, Global Value Chains: Investment and Trade for Development, p. iii., www.unctad.org/en/PublicationsLibrary/wir2013_en.pdf (last accessed 20 July 2020).

[22] Whyte (2019) and Moyn (2015, 2018).

[23] O'Connell (2007).

[24] Nolan (2013), p. 172.

[25] Muchlinski (2001) and Lang (2011).

[26] Slobodian (2018), p. 279.

[27] Slobodian (2018), p. 13.

[28] See further: Harvey (2005), pp. 64ff. An understanding of neoliberalism as not only an economic and political project, but a distinctly legal one, is also the point of departure for the detailed empirical case studies in the contributions to Brabazon (2018).

[29] Slobodian (2018), p. 12.

[30] Post-NIEO, and echoing the same, namely the UN Code of Conduct on Transnational Corporations of 1983.

was launched. Resting on a 10-principle approach across four pillars—human rights, labour, environment and anti-corruption—the UN Global Compact is the largest voluntary CSR group in the world, with a vast geographical reach.[31] Early on, however, many civil society groups raised concerns over corporations' exploitation of UN legitimacy by signing on to the compact, while continuing their problematic business practices.[32] This criticism and the non-adoption of the 2003 treaty-like set of Norms on the Responsibilities of Transnational Corporations and Other Business Enterprises with Regard to Human Rights (UN Norms),[33] led to the appointment of John Ruggie as the UN Special Representative of the Secretary-General, his drafting of the UN Guiding Principles (UNGPs) on Business and Human Rights, and the subsequent unanimous adoption thereof by the UN Human Rights Council in 2011.[34] Although the UNGPs' detailed three-pillar approach sets out a comprehensive international framework reiterating the state duty to *protect* against corporate human rights abuses, the corporate responsibility to *respect* human rights, as well as the need to achieve effective *remedy* for corporate violations, it does not provide a clear solution for closing the accountability gap.[35] The UNGPs were designed as a governance tool aimed at slow self-transformation through polycentric governance rather than as an international framework for legal accountability.[36]

As the UNGPs had not been satisfactory in providing legal tools to hold corporations to account, in June 2014, the UN Human Rights Council established the Open-Ended Intergovernmental Working Group on Transnational Corporations and Other Business Enterprises with Respect to Human Rights (OEIGWG).[37] The OEIGWG's first and second sessions focused on "the content, scope, nature and form of the future international instrument [. . .],"[38] while the third dealt with preparing "elements for the draft legally binding instrument."[39] In October 2018, the OEIGWG's fourth session involved heavy debate of the "Zero Draft" of a Legally Binding Instrument to Regulate in International Human Rights Law, the Activities of Transnational Corporations and Other Business Enterprises,[40] which included 15 articles and an optional protocol. With subsequent revision, the

[31]Rasche et al. (2012), p. 7; UN Global Compact, The Ten Principles of the UN Global Compact, www.unglobalcompact.org/what-is-gc/mission/principles (last accessed 1 August 2020).

[32]Rasche et al. (2012), p. 7.

[33]Weissbrodt and Kruger (2003) and Miretski and Bachmann (2012).

[34]UNHRC Res. 17/4, UN Doc A/HRC/RES/17/4 (6 July 2011).

[35]United Nations, Guiding Principles on Business and Human Rights – Implementing the United Nations "Protect, Respect and Remedy" Framework, 2011, www.ohchr.org/documents/publications/GuidingprinciplesBusinesshr_eN.pdf (last accessed 1 August 2020); Omoteso and Yusuf (2017).

[36]Ruggie (2018), p. 317; Taylor (2011), p. 9; see further: Ramasastry (2015).

[37]UN Doc A/HRC/RES/26/9, p. 2.

[38]UN Doc A/HRC/RES/26/9, p. 2.

[39]UN Doc A/HRC/RES/26/9.

[40]Zero Draft Treaty, Legally Binding Instrument to Regulate in international human rights law, the activities of transnational corporations and other business enterprises, Article 10, 16 July 2018,

OEIGWG's fifth session in 2019 again discussed the Legally Binding Instrument, which then contained 22 articles outlining the OEIGWG's vision for the future governance of the corporation with regards to its vast social and environmental impact.

The story typically advanced by the growing number of Business and Human Rights activists and scholars suggests that the UNGPs were a first step in the right direction, but are not enough. Instead, the UNGPs' "soft law" norms and obligations must now be "hardened" into a binding legal document.[41] Notably, however, both the UNGPs, underpinned by Ruggie's vision of embedded liberalism,[42] as well an eventual "hard law" international treaty in the form of the Legally Binding Instrument, rely on the state to tame the corporation's social impact. Considering that the state under neoliberalism is encased by an international order that protects the rights of capital over the rights of the vast majority of people, we must ask how this very same state will ensure that the rights of those within its jurisdiction are not violated.[43]

3 The Dark Side of Business and Human Rights

I now turn to the political objectives of activists, CSOs, policy-makers, scholars and other experts who imagine achieving the end of corporate abuse via the international Legally Binding Instrument and the mandatory national-level human rights due diligence framework it envisions. For most proponents of Business and Human Rights and the Legally Binding Instrument, "it is high time that [corporations] were recognized as having responsibilities as global actors under international law," because "rules imposing responsibilities and standards of behaviour on [corporations] have not kept up with the expanding reach of their actions."[44] The aim is to "[prevent] and [address] human rights violations by the business sector"[45] by "design[ing] legal solutions" to the problem of corporate misconduct.[46] The overarching objective is to "humanize business by effectively regulating the human rights violative activities of corporations."[47]

www.ohchr.org/documents/hrbodies/hrcouncil/wgtranscorp/session3/draftlbi.pdf (last accessed 1 August 2020).

[41]Macchi and Bright (2020).

[42]Ruggie (1982). For a critical interrogation of this Polanyian regulation of the economic, see Baars (2011).

[43]See further: Bueno (2019), p. 437.

[44]De Jonge (2011), p. 66.

[45]Bernaz (2016), p. 296.

[46]Bilchitz (2017), p. 4.

[47]Deva (2012).

While the vast array of cases brought against corporations (most of which have been and are still lost)[48] points to the continuous urgency for change, it seems that the lack of legal redress and the rise of rights under neoliberalism has shaped the engagement and apparent unity among the proponents of the Legally Binding Instrument regarding how to challenge corporations' systemic misconduct. At first glance, one could indeed be inclined to conclude that the drafting of the Legally Binding Instrument is a "step in the right direction." In a critical reading, however, it is somewhat revelatory that the names of both the emerging academic sub-discipline found in law and business schools alike, as well as the evolving subsections of rights-NGOs is Business and Human Rights.[49] This terminology semantically encapsulates what the activism in its name presupposes when political objectives are formulated: it suggests that business in its current form is an unchangeable, almost natural, occurrence and, borrowing from Nicholas Connolly and Manette Kaisershot, "that human rights represent the only meaningful attempt at a universally applicable a-religious 'moral' code – a blueprint to define reasonable regulation of human life [. . .]."[50] This leads to structural flaws and shortcomings in the approach of the Legally Binding Instrument, by attempting to mobilise rights as an external frame to ensure corporate accountability. Neither does doing so properly tackle corporate logic and decision-making, nor does it take into account the structural set-up of the global economy and its encasement of states, or the inevitable shortcomings of rights as "powerless companions" within this very structure.[51]

3.1 Corporate Logic and Decision-Making in the Global Economy

After tracing the evolution of the corporate form or "personality" and evaluating its organisational psycho-social structure, Joel Bakan concludes that corporations are "institutional psychopaths" necessarily "wont to remove obstacles that get into their way"[52] and "programmed to exploit others for profit."[53] Oriented toward profit maximisation for their shareholders, it is unremarkable that in the current global market economy corporations often strategically choose locations with cheap labour, lax regulation and implementation, and weak judicial infrastructure. These locations

[48]The most comprehensive database of human, environmental and labour rights violations by transnational business is found at the Business and Human Rights Resource Centre, www.business-humanrights.org/ (last accessed 1 August 2020).

[49]See for example Amnesty International, www.amnesty.org/en/what-we-do/corporate-accountability/ (last accessed 1 August 2020).

[50]Connolly and Kaisershot (2015), p. 665.

[51]Moyn (2015).

[52]Bakan (2004), p. 85.

[53]Bakan (2004), p. 85.

are frequently found in the Global South or Eastern Europe, where corporations can "seek greater profit margins and greater shareholder returns by participating in a 'race-to-the-bottom' which undermines human rights protection and provision to varying degrees in all states."[54] South Asia's garment industry, where major European and North American fashion brands flock to have their textiles and garments produced, is an emblematic example of such a race-to-the-bottom. In this context, the Ali Enterprises factory fire in Pakistan as well as the Tazreen factory fire and Rana Plaza collapse in Bangladesh, represent only the tips of icebergs of inequality.

Significant local and transnational activism occurred following these prominent garment industry disasters in Pakistan and Bangladesh, including efforts to secure corporate accountability on behalf of families and survivors, and to reform occupational health and safety (OHS) standards in factories.[55] Almost a decade later, however, most of the legal struggles have been unsuccessful in strictly legal terms, while the conditions in South Asia's garment factories remain largely unchanged.[56] Notably, the Business and Human Rights approach animating many of these efforts failed to address the underlying fact that global inequality neither starts with the lack of OHS standards in factories—which these events so brutally shined a light upon—nor with the lack of corporate accountability in the wake of their evident non-implementation.

Rather, global inequality is rooted in and produced through the global economy by a "power asymmetry" that Mark Anner suggests we can understand for the garment industry as working "through two mechanisms: a price squeeze and a sourcing squeeze."[57] Where the incentive of corporate entities is profit, lead firms or "brands" under "conditions of supply chain oligopsony (lead firm power concentration)," will "squeeze supplier firms on how, where and when they source their fabric and at what cost," and "this 'price squeeze' impacts workers."[58] A further layer of problems in the garment and textile industry is certainly added by the fact that global value chains can be diverted relatively easily to expedient jurisdictions—locations where profit is higher and corporate risks are lower. Because many "underdeveloped" states are starved for investment, large corporations can often pick and choose the best location to conduct their business and can also exert tremendous influence over how they operate in these jurisdictions. As both the lead firms of corporate networks as well as their local suppliers aim to maximise their profit for the sake of (shareholder) returns, both externalise their costs and risks onto workers in order to attain the highest profit margin possible. This frequently results in (*inter alia*) minimum wages too low to live, unpaid over-time work,

[54] Connolly (2012); Choi and Park (2014), p. 61. See further the chapter by Palvasha Shabab in this volume for an elaborate discription of the location of Pakistan in the global political economy.

[55] See chapter by Ben Vanpeperstraete in this volume.

[56] See chapter by Palvasha Shahab in this volume.

[57] Anner (2019), p. 22.

[58] Anner (2019), p. 2.

outsourced production to booming informal economies in order to avoid existing regulatory mechanisms, and the absence of social protections, strong labour unions,[59] and diligently implemented OHS standards, the latter of which represent just another cost factor for corporations to minimise. The problem of corporate violations should not, therefore, be understood as one of bad individual decision-making and greedy "bad-apple" corporate managers, but as one of a double-structure: the corporate form with its imperial profit mandate and the global economy structured along the "developed" and the "developing."[60]

3.2 *The Rights Lens: Masking Root Causes?*

Business and Human Rights aims to remedy the excesses of corporate risk externalisation by institutionalising a legal framework for corrective justice but leaves unchallenged the overall structure in which this externalisation occurs. This sparks the question of whether and how a human rights framework for business can change or, indeed, even mitigate, corporations' behavioural patterns structured along the lines of capital accumulation and their mantra of maximising profit and minimising risk for a small group of shareholders. In this context, relying on individual remedy, to which human rights language is confined, seems akin to putting a plaster on a gaping wound.

Susan Marks explains that the human rights movement and its earlier activism has tended to neglect root causes, "understood as the basis on which a given circumstance rests."[61] The "basis" on which the "circumstance" of corporate rights violations rests is not the absence of an international legal regime of human rights protections, as proponents of the Legally Binding Instrument seem to suggest. As far as international human rights law is concerned, states already have the duty to protect against rights violations by third parties in their territory and, thus, the duty to prevent corporate abuse.[62] Rather, the basis—or root cause—of corporate violations

---

[59]As Hansen-Miller (2017), p. 480, argues, this is because "[g]lobal production networks are primarily an instrument designed to avoid the power of organized labour."

[60]Harvey (2018); Pahuja (2011); Bueno (2019), p. 437.

[61]Marks (2011), p. 60.

[62]For instance, the Committee on Economic, Social and Cultural Rights highlights the state's duty to protect in regards to the right to water: "The obligation to protect requires State parties to prevent third parties from interfering in any way with the enjoyment of the right to water. Third parties include [. . .] corporations and other entities [. . .]" (UN Doc E/C.12/2002/11 (20 January 2003), para 23). The Committee on the Rights of the Child asserts that "States should require businesses to undertake child-rights due diligence. This will ensure that business enterprises identify, prevent and mitigate their impact on children's rights including across their business relationships and within global operations" (General Comment No. 16, UN Doc CRC/C/GC/16 (17 April 2013)). Similarly, the Inter-American Court of Human Rights asserts: "The State has a legal duty to take reasonable steps to prevent human rights violations and to use the means at its disposal to carry out a serious investigation of violations committed within its jurisdiction [. . .]. This duty to prevent includes all

is global capitalism and the prevailing neoliberal free market ideology and policy that treats workers and the environment as mere commodities, and prioritises privatisation and deregulation measures at the expense of the welfare state.[63] As the "main engine of capitalism"[64] in this context, the corporation comes to life through and is facilitated by the internal and external double-structure mentioned above. Internally, the structure of the corporate form itself, with its shareholder model and the director's mandate to maximise returns for a small group, transforms all obstacles to this objective into risks to be managed and impediments to be removed. Externally, the corporation finds fruitful ground for its transnational operations at the bottom of a global economic structure that facilitates transboundary exploitation and extraction.

While Marks contends that the human rights movement's neglect of root causes has significantly changed since the 1970s, she attests to three persistent shortcomings in the rights approach's framing and addressing of root causes: "In the first place, the investigation of causes is halted too soon. Secondly, effects are treated as though they were causes. And thirdly, causes are identified, only to be set aside."[65] Thus, while some root causes may indeed be detected by a human rights approach to address and remedy individual human suffering, others are concealed.[66] If one applies Marks' analysis or, indeed, warning, to the Legally Binding Instrument, which aims to institutionalise a human rights framework for business activity in order to ensure remedy and accountability for corporate harm, must we not ask if such an approach eventually conceals the underlying factors that make corporate cross-border operations exploitative and often deadly? Does the anatomising remedy of human rights—even if the Legally Binding Instrument was implemented in the way imagined by Business and Human Rights activists and scholars—not narrow our sight to the individual and thus hinder rather than further collective struggle to overturn the system that produces corporate violations?[67]

---

those means of a legal, political, administrative and cultural nature that promote the protection of human rights" (*Velásquez Rodríguez v. Honduras* (29 July 1988, para. 174–175)). Contrary to the hopes of some civil society stakeholders and the aspirations of the UN Norms of 2003, there is no set of rules that directly binds corporations (see Weissbrodt and Kruger 2003; Miretski and Bachmann 2012). The Revised Draft is a mediatory instrument at best (see Peters et al. 2020, p. 5).

[63]Harvey (2005).

[64]Baars (2019).

[65]Marks (2011), p. 70.

[66]Marks (2011), p. 77.

[67]Baxi (2006).

3.3 *Mandatory Human Rights Due Diligence: For the Rights-Holder or the Corporation?*

Rather than remaining in an abstract mode of criticism, I believe it is beneficial to zoom in briefly on the regulatory mechanism proposed by the Legally Binding Instrument for reducing and eventually eradicating corporate misconduct. Article 5 (2) of the Legally Binding Instrument foresees that: "State Parties shall adopt measures necessary to ensure that all persons conducting business activities, including those of transnational character, to undertake human rights due diligence [. . .]." Predating the implementation of the Legally Binding Instrument itself, national-level mandatory human rights due diligence (mHRDD) frameworks of the type envisioned by the instrument already exist and continue to evolve in many European jurisdictions as well as at the EU level.

Without aiming to change internal corporate or external economic structures, states parties to the Legally Binding Instrument will be obliged to advance compliance-model legislation that translates UNGP 15,[68] in one form or another, into concrete policy in order to "harden" this "soft law" principle.[69] Despite mHRDD taking centre-stage in campaigns and policy-drafting on how to eventually eradicate corporate abuse, it remains rather unclear what legal obligations such mHRDD would entail.[70] Much will depend on the way national policy frameworks are formulated and how they are interpreted by courts.[71]

Importantly, as Jonathan Bonnitcha and Robert McCorquodale explain, due diligence originates as a genuine business term and denotes "any set of processes undertaken by a business to identify and manage risks to the business."[72] They contend that "the basic understanding of due diligence in a business context is 'a procedural practice to assess risk in a company's own interest.'"[73] They, like most engaged with Business and Human Rights, seem to suggest, however, that the

---

[68]UNGP 15 reads: "In order to meet their responsibility to respect human rights, business enterprises should have in place policies and processes appropriate to their size and circumstances, including (a) a policy commitment to meet their responsibility to respect human rights; (b) a human rights due diligence process to identify, prevent, mitigate and account for how they address their impacts on human rights; (c) processes to enable the remediation of any adverse human rights impacts they cause or to which they contribute." See www.ohchr.org/documents/publications/guidingprinciplesbusinesshr_en.pdf (last accessed 1 August 2020).

[69]Bonnitcha and McCorquodale (2017a), p. 908, point out an example of what could well be the result of such policy, by taking the example of the UK Modern Slavery Act, where "the concept of due diligence, understood as a standard of conduct, plays no role [. . .]."

[70]See debate in the European Journal of International Law: Bonnitcha and McCorquodale (2017a); Ruggie and Sherman III (2017); Bonnitcha and McCorquodale (2017b).

[71]On the different forms of newly evolving due diligence policies, see Bueno (2019), p. 430ff. For a detailed evaluation of the relationship of mHRDD and corporate liability, see Bueno and Bright (forthcoming).

[72]Bonnitcha and McCorquodale (2017a), p. 902.

[73]Bonnitcha and McCorquodale (2017a), p. 902.

human rights risk in the mHRDD framework is not like other corporate risks because it is located "outside" of or external to the corporation in that it pertains to negative or adverse corporate impacts on third-party stakeholders, such as workers, communities, and the environment. Yet, because mHRDD frameworks leave the corporate form unchanged, a human rights risk as envisaged in such a framework will, from the perspective of a corporation, form just another corporate risk among many: a risk for the corporation to manage and minimise, if not remove entirely, in its quest to maximise profit.[74] Hence, we can understand why corporations that have been sued for their violative practices, such as the German discounter KiK in relation to the Ali Enterprises factory fire in Pakistan, have themselves become proponents of mHRDD legislation. As KiK put it: "Companies need legal certainty. For this reason, we have argued for a legal regulation of corporate due diligence."[75] KiK's reconsideration here is not despite corporate accountability but because of it:[76] like all corporations, KiK accounts for risks in its (transnational) operations. From a corporate perspective, the risk posed by a thoroughly formulated and fully implemented national mHRDD policy[77] amounts to the legal risk of being sued for non-compliance, which poses both financial and reputational risks.

But while a mHRDD frame will likely turn the current reputational risk posed by "soft-law" yardstick mechanisms like the UNGPs into a more straightforward financial risk for corporations when assessing their transnational business activity, it cannot be presumed "that the widespread institutionalisation of the [mHRDD] will necessarily translate into significant improvements in corporate respect for human

[74]For instance, Fasterling (2017) contends that human rights due diligence is conceptually incompatible with the management of social risk (defined as the actual and potential leverage that people or groups of people with a negative perception of corporate activity have on the business enterprise's value), because social risk management and human rights due diligence vary at each step of the risk management process (risk identification, risk measurement and assessment, and risk reduction measures). To resolve this incompatibility, he argues, respect for human rights would have to be elevated to a corporate goal that determines corporate strategy.

[75]Translation by the author of the original German: "Unternehmen benötigen Rechtssicherheit. Aus diesem Grund haben wir uns für eine gesetzliche Regelung unternehmerischer Sorgfaltspflichten ausgesprochen." See: Reiner Burger "Saeeda Kathoon gegen KiK – Ich will Gerechtigkeit" Frankfurter Allgemeine Zeitung, 29 November 2018, www.faz.net/aktuell/gesellschaft/ungluecke/der-kampf-der-saeeda-khatoon-15916387.html, (last accessed 1 August 2020).

[76]Baars (2015).

[77]Such desired full realisation seems unlikely given the politico-economic dynamics of and the corporate leverage in such legislative processes surrounding the corporation. While the German Initiative Lieferkettengesetz (a civil society group campaigning for a supply chain law) has published a detailed account of what a German mHRDD law must entail in order to function, the German government's "*Eckpunkte*" (Basic Points) for a such a law already gravely diminish hope for the possibility of making a legal claim, let alone the aim of "humanizing business." For instance, there is no reversal of the burden of proof and they introduce the concept of a "safe harbour" which would enable corporations to sign up to an industry standard in order to exclude their liability for ordinary negligence. See www.ecchr.eu/nc/pressemitteilung/eckpunkte-zum-lieferkettengesetz-ein-guter-beginn-aber-noch-lange-nicht-ausreichend/ (last accessed 1 August 2020).

rights."[78] Ingrid Landau, drawing on regulatory studies and Kimberly Krawiec's concept of cosmetic compliance,[79] asserts that there is "a significant risk that these regulatory interventions will result in companies adopting policies and implementing internal compliance structures that exhibit some or all of the formal elements of HRDD – and have the purpose of conveying the appearance of taking action – but ultimately fail to achieve the public goal they are designed to achieve: that is, the reduction or elimination of adverse human rights impacts."[80] By using empirical data on existing due diligence policies, she argues that there is mounting evidence that mHRDD will turn into a box-ticking exercise for corporations.[81] This, she contends, is not so much due to the business sector's misunderstanding or unfamiliarity with mHRDD, but inherent to the concept itself.[82] While its ambiguity, the proliferation of guidance, and the lack of transparency all increase the risk of cosmetic compliance, she posits a primary danger exists in mHRDD's very design, which is focused on procedures rather than outcomes.[83]

Problematically, mHRDD and its compliance framework will likely not entail a clear-cut corporate obligation to guarantee the non-violation of rights or the positive realisation thereof. While the Legally Binding Instrument in its Revised Draft version is ambitious in formulating measures states must take to ensure effective regulation and prevention, such as identifying and assessing risks, taking appropriate action to prevent them, monitoring them during the business activity, and communicating their efforts to stakeholders (Article 5), it remains a procedural compliance obligation. Crucially, the corporate obligation here is not to refrain from violating rights, but to have *a process in place* that aims to ensure rights are not violated. From a legal standpoint, if the corporation can show it has fulfilled its procedural compliance obligations, it will not matter if rights end up being violated and suffering is inflicted on other "stakeholders" or "rights-holders." Rather, gaining it further legitimacy, the corporation can legally exculpate itself in the legal process by showing it complied with its legal obligations, despite any harm that may have

[78]Landau (2019), p. 222.

[79]Krawiec (2003).

[80]Landau (2019), p. 222.

[81]Landau (2019), p. 235, draws on empirical findings from the UK Modern Slavery Act, the California Transparency in Supply Chains Act and the US Dodd-Frank Act. See also Baars (2020) The limits of law: Why "corporate accountability" will not change the corporation, www.tni.org/en/publication/the-limits-of-law (last accessed 1 August 2020): They argue that the set-up of compliance frameworks serves the corporation as yet another shield against (criminal) legal liability "by adopting programmes that provide compliance in technical terms while not actually reducing the incidence of 'violation.' If a company is charged with failure to exercise due diligence, a so-called 'due diligence defence' can be invoked, which allows the company to argue that managers had followed protocol."

[82]Landau (2019), p. 235.

[83]Landau (2019), pp. 235–239. See also Baars (2020) and Bueno (2019).

actually occurred in the course of its (transnational) operations.[84] Thus, while the instalment of a process to assess and prevent human rights risks might indeed generate impulses to secure non-violation, mHRDD nonetheless runs the risk of serving the corporation rather than the rights-holder. With its focus on process (due diligence compliance) instead of outcomes (human rights violation or non-realisation), mHRDD policy "runs the risk of becoming a substanceless sham, to the delight of corporate power-mongers who can bend it to their interests."[85] While the creation of legal certainty through mHRDD frameworks allows a corporation like KiK to more accurately refine its risk calculus, it does not necessarily deter its risky operations, should the corporation deem the potential human rights harm to be worth the profit.

This suggests the likelihood that the mHRDD mechanism envisioned by the Legally Binding Instrument will further legitimise the status quo without eradicating corporate abuse. The risk here is that on its current course, Business and Human Rights activism is drafting yet another smokescreen and a deterrence away from challenging the root causes of corporate harm by seeking refuge in an already established human rights doctrine.

4 Conclusion: Toward Strategic Objectives

What is the cost or "dark side" of pursuing and advocating for reforms in the name of Business and Human Rights in general and the Legally Binding Instrument in particular? I have tried to give a cursory answer to this question for civil society organisations and activists, for whom consideration of this cost is not least a question of resource allocation. Further, I have sought to bring critical legal scholarship on the corporation and human rights into closer conversation with Business and Human Rights in order to excavate the project's structural flaws, namely that too often it leaves the asymmetries in the global economy and the imperial corporate form

[84] At first glance, an exceptional formulation in the Revised Draft version of the Legally Binding Instrument gives hope in this regard. As Bueno and Bright (forthcoming) point out, Article 6(6) of the first Revised Draft ambitiously foresees liability for a corporation's "failure to prevent" a third party with whom it has a business relationship from violating rights. This would indeed disable a corporation's easy exculpation through cosmetic compliance. Of course, it remains to be seen whether this article of the Legally Binding Instrument's current version will remain, as the negotiation process is far from over. But even if it does remain, Bueno and Bright note that such a strong formulation for third-party wrongdoing may, in turn, create the problematic incentive for transnational business to withdraw from collaborating with or investing in partners deemed to be too risky. If anything, this exemplifies the problem of not tackling the prevailing structure of the global economy or the corporate form in Business and Human Rights' answer to the question of the corporation. It shows the impossibility of tackling corporate capitalism through rights-based compliance policy, pointing all the more to the need for more radical solutions to eventually eradicate corporate-inflicted suffering.

[85] Parker (2007), p. 209.

unchallenged. I have argued that this presupposition of business (encapsulating both the corporate form and the global economy) as a natural occurrence legitimises the status quo more than it presents a challenge to its logic, making Business and Human Rights interventions stabilising rather than challenging to systemic logics, if the strategic objective is radical ("root cause"), transformative change.[86] The uncritical embrace of rights as positive change-makers is problematic because their institutionalisation and formalisation runs the risk of masking the underlying factors that produce corporate violations. What is more, the approach of employing rights while leaving corporate logic and prevailing global economic structures unchallenged will continue to lead corporations to translate human suffering articulated through rights into corporate risk factors to be managed, accounted for and minimised in their pursuit of profit. By defining and clarifying what legal risks Business and Human Rights policy poses to the corporate entity, mHRDD, the main regulatory mechanism envisioned by the Legally Binding Instrument, will likely facilitate corporations' risk management process rather than rights-holders' quest for justice, bestowing increased morality and legitimacy upon corporations in the process. This is not only because mHRDD compliance mechanisms are likely to turn into a mere box-ticking exercise for companies, but also, and crucially, because mHRDD frameworks will rarely entail an opportunity for survivors or advocates to bring claims against corporations for the suffering they have inflicted, only for the compliance obligations they have failed to meet.

The political objectives as formulated by Business and Human Rights have been shaped and formed not only by the neoliberal proliferation of rights as the main remedy for human suffering over the last decades, but also by a well-intentioned and somewhat pragmatic translation of case-based struggles—lawsuits lost against corporate abuse—into world-making. But it is not the lack of remedy, formalisation and institutionalisation of rights that leads corporations to inflict and produce harm. Rather, it is the structural set-up of the corporate form and the global economy, neither of which often feature in Business and Human Rights scholarship or activism. The Legally Binding Instrument's compliance-model legislative framework and focus on corporate accountability are unlikely to change the asymmetries emanating from this structural set-up. Rather, as Baars argues, Business and Human Rights codifies the corporation, the "apparatus that facilitates the surplus value-extracting function of global capitalism,"[87] legitimising its existence and, with it, the existence of neoliberal corporate capitalism—the very root causes of corporate abuse and exploitation.[88]

While I acknowledge that from a legal or, better, a lawyer's perspective, the main problem seems to be that corporations abuse rights and avoid legal responsibilities, this does not necessarily warrant a call for more (dysfunctional) law. Rather, to put a difficult task simply, it calls for dismantling or fundamentally altering the corporate

[86]Knox (2009, 2010).

[87]Baars (2016), p. 131.

[88]Baars (2016), p. 132.

form and a radically different organisation of the global economic system. Thus, I agree with Amelia Evans that instead of "endlessly responding to abuses," we must aim to "[address] the incentives and decision-making structures that cause them."[89] Likewise, I concur with human rights defender and activist Alejandra Ancheita's recent assessment that: "Addressing the vulnerabilities faced by [*inter alia*] women, workers, and indigenous peoples will require a radical change in the economic model that will require a political movement unequivocally committed to human rights which, in the best-case scenario, will take decades to build."[90] In sum, rather than asking how we can broaden opportunities for corrective justice when abuse has already occurred by establishing yet another regulatory framework likely to boost corporate legitimacy while masking ongoing misbehaviour, I argue that we need more scholarship on and activism geared towards strategically reorganising the corporate form and global economy in a way that works for all equally and equitably.

References

Amnesty International (2014) Injustice incorporated – corporate abuse and the human right to remedy, www.amnesty.org/download/Documents/8000/pol3000122014en.pdf (last accessed 1 Aug 2020)

Anner M (2019) Squeezing workers' rights in global supply chains: purchasing practices in the Bangladesh's garment export sector in comparative perspective. Rev Int Polit Econ 27 (2):320–347

Baars G (2011) "Reform or Revolt?" Polanyian v Marxian perspectives on the regulation of "the economic". North Ireland Leg Q 62(4):415–431

Baars G (2015) From the Dutch East India Company to the corporate bill of rights: corporations and international law. In: Mattei U, Haskell J (eds) Research handbook on political economy and law. Edward Elgar, Cheltenham, pp 260–279

Baars G (2016) "It's not me, it's the corporation:" the value of corporate accountability in the global political economy. Lond Rev Int Law 4(1):127–163

Baars G (2019) The corporation, law and capitalism: a radical perspective on the role of law in the global political economy. Brill, Leiden

Bader M, Saage-Maaß M, Terwindt C (2019) Strategic litigation against the misconduct of multinational enterprises: an anatomy of *Jabir and Others v KiK*. Verfassung und Recht in Übersee 52(2):156–171

Bair J (2015) Corporations at the United Nations: echoes of the new international economic order? Humanity: Int J Human Rights Humanitarianism Dev 6(1):159–171

Bakan J (2004) The corporation – the pathological pursuit of profit and power. Constable, London

Baxi U (2006) The future of human rights. Oxford University Press, Oxford

Bernaz N (2016) Business and human rights: history, law and policy – bridging the accountability gap. Routledge, Abingdon

[89]Evans (2020) How to eradicate human rights abuses? Change the corporate model. Rethinking Corporate Governance, Business and Human Rights Resource Centre, www.business-humanrights.org/en/how-to-eradicate-human-rights-abuses-change-the-corporate-model (last accessed 1 August 2020).

[90]Ancheita A (2020) Inequality is the real pandemic, www.gi-escr.org/blog/inequality-is-the-real-pandemic (last accessed 1 August 2020).

Bilchitz D (2017) Introduction: putting flesh on the bone: what should a business and human rights treaty look like? In: Deva S, Bilchitz D (eds) Building a treaty on business and human rights. Cambridge University Press, Cambridge

Bockman J (2015) Socialist globalization against capitalist neocolonialism: the economic ideas behind the New International Economic Order. Humanity: Int J Human Rights Humanitarianism Dev 6(1):109–128

Bonnitcha J, McCorquodale R (2017a) The concept of "due diligence" in the UN Guiding Principles on Business and Human Rights. Eur J Int Law 28(3):899–919

Bonnitcha J, McCorquodale R (2017b) The concept of "due diligence" in the UN Guiding Principles on Business and Human Rights: a rejoinder to John Gerard Ruggie and John F. Sherman III. Eur J Int Law 28(3):929–933

Brabazon H (2018) Neoliberal legality: understanding the role of law in the neoliberal project. Routledge, Abingdon

Bueno N (2019) Multinational enterprises and labour rights: concepts and implementation. In: Bellace JR, ter Haar B (eds) Research handbook on labour, business and human rights law. Edward Elgar, Cheltenham, pp 421–438

Chatterjee SK (1991) The Charter of Economic Rights and Duties of States: an evaluation after 15 years. Int Comp Law Q 40(3):669–684

Choi J, Park BI (2014) Environmentally responsible management of MNE subsidiaries: stakeholder perspective. Multinatl Bus Rev 22(1):59–77

Connolly N (2012) Corporate social responsibility: a duplicitous distraction? Int J Human Rights 16 (8):1228–1249

Connolly N, Kaisershot M (2015) Corporate power and human rights. Int J Human Rights 19 (6):663–672

De Jonge A (2011) Transnational corporations and international law: bringing TNCs out of the accountability vacuum. Crit Perspect Int Bus 7(1):66–89

De Schutter O (2015) Towards a new treaty on business and human rights. Bus Human Rights J 1:41–67

Deva S (2012) Regulating corporate human rights violations: humanizing business. Routledge, Abingdon

Fasterling B (2017) Human rights due diligence as risk management: social risk versus human rights risk. Bus Human Rights J 2(2):225–247

Glasbeek H (2010) The corporation as legally constructed site of irresponsibility. In: Pontell H, Geis G (eds) The international handbook on white-collar and corporate crime. Heidelberg, pp 248–278

Hansen-Miller D (2017) Organizing in the nervous system: global trade unions and global production networks. In: Baars G, Spicer A (eds) The corporation: a critical, multi-disciplinary handbook. Cambridge University Press, Cambridge, pp 480–487

Harvey D (2005) A brief history of neoliberalism. Oxford University Press, Oxford

Harvey D (2018) Marx, capital, and the madness of economic reason. Oxford University Press, New York

Hippolyte A (2019) Foreign investment law and developing countries. In: Krajewski M, Hoffmann RT (eds) Research handbook on foreign direct investment. Edward Elgar Publishing, Cheltenham, pp 72–125

Kennedy D (2004) The dark side of virtue: reassessing international humanitarianism. Princeton University Press, Princeton

Knox R (2009) Marxism, international law, and political strategy. Leiden J Int Law 22(3):413–436

Knox R (2010) Strategy and tactics. Finnish Yearb Int Law 21:193–229

Krajewski M (2017) Ensuring the primacy of human rights in trade and investment policies: model clauses for a UN treaty on transnational corporations, other businesses and human rights. CIDSE, Brussels

Krawiec KD (2003) Cosmetic compliance and the failure of negotiated governance. Wash Univ Law Q 81(2):487–544

Landau I (2019) Human rights due diligence and the risk of cosmetic compliance. Melb J Int Law 20(1):221–247
Lang A (2011) World trade law after neoliberalism: reimagining the global economic order. Oxford University Press, Oxford
Macchi C, Bright C (2020) Hardening soft law: the implementation of human rights due diligence requirements in domestic legislation. In: Buscemi M, Lazzerini N, Magi L (eds) Legal sources in business and human rights – evolving dynamics in international and European law. Brill, Leiden
Marks S (2011) Human rights and root causes. Mod Law Rev 74(1):57–78
Miretski PP, Bachmann SD (2012) The UN Norms on the responsibility of transnational corporations and other business enterprises with regard to human rights: a requiem. Deakin Law Rev 17 (1):5–41
Moyn S (2015) A powerless companion: human rights in the age of neoliberalism. Law Contemp Probl 77(4):147–169
Moyn S (2018) Not enough human rights in an unequal world. Harvard University Press, Cambridge
Muchlinski P (2001) Human rights and multinationals: is there a problem? Int Aff 77(1):31–48
Muchlinski P (2007) Multinational enterprises and the law. Oxford University Press, Oxford
Nolan M (2013) Human rights and market fundamentalism in the long 1970s. In: Frei N, Weinke A (eds) Toward a new moral world order? Menschenrechtspolitik und Völkerrecht seit 1945. Wallstein Verlag, Göttingen
O'Connell P (2007) On reconciling irreconcilables: neo-liberal globalisation and human rights. Human Rights Law Rev 7(3):483–509
Omoteso K, Yusuf H (2017) Accountability of transnational corporations in the developing world: the case for an enforceable international mechanism. Crit Perspect Int Bus 13(1):54–71
Pahuja S (2011) Decolonising international law: development, economic growth and the politics of universality. Cambridge University Press, Cambridge
Parker C (2007) Meta-regulation: legal accountability for corporate social responsibility. In: McBarnet D, Voiculescu A, Campbell T (eds) The new corporate accountability: corporate social responsibility and the law. Cambridge University Press, Cambridge, pp 207–237
Payandeh M (2015) Fragmentation within international human rights law. In: Andenas M, Bjorge E (eds) A farewell to fragmentation: reassertion and convergence in international law. Cambridge University Press, Cambridge
Peters A, Gless S, Thomale C, Weller MC (2020) Business and human rights: making the Legally Binding Instrument work in public, private and criminal law. MPIL Research Paper 2020(6)
Rajagopal B (2003) International law from below: development, social movements and third world resistance. Cambridge University Press, Cambridge
Ramasastry A (2015) Corporate social responsibility versus business and human rights: bridging the gap between responsibility and accountability. J Human Rights 14(2):237–259
Rasche A, Waddock S, McIntosh M (2012) The United Nations Global Compact: retrospect and prospect. Bus Soc 52(1):6–30
Rodriguez-Garavito C (2017) Introduction: a dialogue across divides in the business and human rights field. In: Rodriguez-Garavito C (ed) Business and human rights: beyond the end of the beginning. Cambridge University Press, Cambridge
Ruggie JG (1982) International regimes, transactions, and change: embedded liberalism in the postwar economic order. Int Organ 36(2):379–415
Ruggie JG (2018) Multinationals as global institution: power, authority and relative autonomy. Regul Gov 12(3):317–333
Ruggie JG, Shermann JF III (2017) The concept of "due diligence" in the UN guiding principles on business and human rights: a reply to Jonathan Bonnitcha and Robert McCorquodale. Eur J Int Law 28(3):921–928
Sauvant K (2015) The negotiations of the United Nations Code of Conduct on Transnational Corporations: experience and lessons learned. J World Invest Trade 16:11–87

Slobodian Q (2018) Globalists: the end of empire and the birth of neoliberalism. Harvard University Press, Cambridge

Stern PJ (2011) The company-state: corporate sovereignty and the early modern foundations of the British empire in India. Oxford University Press, Oxford

Taylor J (2006) Creating capitalism: joint-stock enterprise in British politics and culture, 1800-1870. Boydell & Brewer, Woodbridge

Taylor MB (2011) The Ruggie framework: polycentric regulation and the implications for corporate social responsibility. Etikk i praksis, Nordic J Appl Ethics 5(1):9–30

The IGLP Law and Global Production Working Group (2016) The role of law in global value chains: a research manifesto. Lond Rev Int Law 4(1):57–79

Weber H, Winanti P (2016) The "Bandung spirit" and solidarist internationalism. Aust J Int Aff 70 (4):391–406

Weissbrodt D, Kruger M (2003) Norms on the responsibilities of transnational corporations and other business enterprises with regard to human rights. Am J Int Law 97:901–922

Whyte J (2019) The morals of the market: human rights and the rise of neoliberalism. Verso Books, London

Michael Bader studied law at Humboldt University in Berlin, Germany, and holds a Master of Laws (LLM) in Law, Development and Globalisation from SOAS, University of London. Bader joined the European Center for Constitutional and Human Rights in September 2019 as a Research Fellow in the Business and Human Rights programme with a focus on corporate exploitation in global supply chains. Since September 2020, he has been supporting ECCHR's Institute for Legal Intervention as a Bertha Justice Fellow.

The manufacturer's authorised representative in the EU is Springer Nature Customer Service Centre GmbH, Europaplatz 3, 69115 Heidelberg, Germany. If you have any concerns regarding our products, please contact ProductSafety@springernature.com

Printed and bound by CPI Group (UK) Ltd, Croydon, CR0 4YY
30/09/2026
02225696-0017